THE EMERGENCE OF EARLY YIDDISH LITERATURE

GERMAN JEWISH CULTURES

Sponsored by the Leo Baeck Institute London

The EMERGENCE *of* EARLY YIDDISH LITERATURE

Cultural Translation in Ashkenaz

JEROLD C. FRAKES

INDIANA UNIVERSITY PRESS

This book is a publication of

Indiana University Press
Office of Scholarly Publishing
Herman B Wells Library 350
1320 East 10th Street
Bloomington, Indiana 47405 USA

iupress.indiana.edu

The paper used in this publication meets the minimum requirements of the American National Standard for Information Sciences—Permanence of Paper for Printed Library Materials, ANSI Z39.48–1992.

Manufactured in the United States of America

Cataloging information is available from the Library of Congress.

ISBN 978-0-253-02551-7 (cloth)
ISBN 978-0-253-02568-5 (ebook)

1 2 3 4 5 22 21 20 19 18 17

Contents

Preface

THE SUB-CULTURAL FOCUS of this book is primarily on those literary borderlands that lie between the primarily Hebrew-Aramaic core of the traditional Ashkenazic textual culture and the vast realm of Gentile literary culture beyond the pale, especially in the textual worlds of Middle High German, Renaissance Italian, and Humanist Latin. The analytical focus of the book is on the period during which Yiddish emerged as a literary language in the interstitial cultural context of those Jewish and Gentile textual worlds. As Benjamin Harshav has astutely remarked, "Hebrew poetry in the past three millennia and Yiddish poetry in the past seven hundred years were situated in the midst of languages not necessarily related, making them 'comparative' literatures par excellence."[1] This book is thus at all times a work of comparative studies, perhaps even in two senses of the slippery but often useful designation "comparative literature": it "relates" texts of two or more cultural traditions (i.e., the more-or-less conventional pre-Derridean definition of the field) at the same time as it also articulates those texts with discourses of gender, cultural identity, resistance to cultural Otherizing, and pre-postcolonialism (i.e., several of the post-Derridean concerns of the field). It is thus not at all—or at least not simply—a book in the field of Yiddish studies, and those expecting such a book are likely to find themselves on unfamiliar, not to say uncomfortable, ground. It is not—to use Robert Bonfil's tactically employed terminology (in a very different context)—centripetal, inward-facing, exclusionary, but vigorously centrifugal, outward-facing, inclusionary.

The book has had a long gestation period, dating back to 1997. Preliminary versions of parts of several chapters have been presented publicly at a number of conferences and university fora: the Twelfth World Congress of Jewish Studies, the Association for Jewish Studies, the American Comparative Literature Association, the Renaissance Society of America, the Sixteenth Century Studies Conference, the Modern Language Association, the Oxford Centre for Hebrew and

Jewish Studies, Fordham University, Columbia University, Harvard University, the University of California (Berkeley), McGill University, Boston University, Boğaziçi Üniversitesi (Istanbul), the Humboldt Universität (Berlin), the University of Toronto, and the Università degli Studi di Palermo. In addition to the attendees at those public presentations, many of whom offered insightful questions and comments that led me to further thinking and rethinking, I would also like to thank the fellows of the seminar of the National Endowment for the Humanities ("Shaping Civic Space in Renaissance Venice," Venice, Summer 2006, directors: Dennis Romano and Gary Radke) who offered trenchant critiques of chapter 3. I am especially grateful to the Radcliffe Institute for Advanced Study at Harvard University (2013–2014) and the John Simon Guggenheim Memorial Foundation (2014–2015) for research fellowships specifically in support of this project.

Non-Roman alphabetic texts will be treated as follows: text citations are presented in the original orthography (with English translation where appropriate; unless otherwise noted, translations are my own); pre-nineteenth-century titles are initially presented in the original orthography, along with an English translation that is then generally used thereafter; titles from periods since the nineteenth century are transcribed according to standard academic Roman-alphabet transcription systems. This distinction is maintained in order not to involve the reader on every page in thorny, often (here not *specifically* relevant) insoluble issues of grapho-phonemics of the *earlier* period of the languages.

Note

1. Benjamin Harshav, *Three Thousand Years of Hebrew Versification: Essays in Comparative Prosody* (New Haven, CT: Yale University Press, 2013), xiv.

Acknowledgments

The author gratefully acknowledges the kind permission granted by the following libraries to quote from the identified documents in their collections.

The Master and Fellows of Trinity College Cambridge

Trinity College Library, F.12.44

Trinity College Library, F.12.45 [*olim* MS Addl. 136]

The Syndics of Cambridge University Library

Cambridge University Library T.-S. 10K22

Leipzig, Universitätsbibliothek B.H. 18 [*olim* Leipzig, Stadtbibliothek 35]

Oxford, Bodleian Library, MS Can. Or. 12

Munich, Bayerische Staatsbibliothek, Cod. hebr. 100

Milan, Biblioteca Ambrosiana, C. 282 inf.

Abbreviations

Arab.	Arabic
BT	Babylonian Talmud
Dan	Daniel
Dt	Deuteronomy
DWB	*Deutsches Wörterbuch*, ed. Jacob and Wilhelm Grimm, 2nd ed. (Leipzig: Hirzel, 1854–1971; repr., Hildesheim: Olms, 2003–); http://germazope.uni-trier.de/Projects/DWB.
Est	Esther
Ex	Exodus
EYT	*Early Yiddish Texts, 1100–1750, With Introduction and Commentary*, ed. Jerold C. Frakes (Oxford: Oxford University Press, 2004; rev. ed. 2008).
Gen	Genesis
Hebr.	Hebrew
Kid	*Kiddushin*
Ket	*Kethuboth*
Lam	Lamentations
Lev	Leviticus
Meg	*Megillah*
MER	*Midrash Esther Rabbah*
MHG	Middle High German
NHG	New High German
Prov	Proverbs
Ps	Psalm
RSV	Revised Standard Version
Sam	Samuel
Sanh	*Sanhedrin*
2TargEst	*Targum Sheni* of Esther

THE EMERGENCE OF EARLY YIDDISH LITERATURE

Chapter One

Introduction

WHY WOULD A DEEPLY devout religious community suddenly adopt a foreign *and* secular literary genre for which there is no precedent in the entirety of that culture's history? What conditions would, for instance, enable traditional fourteenth-century Ashkenazic Jews suddenly to begin producing swashbuckling epics with knights in shining armor and damsels more or less in distress—in Yiddish? What mechanisms of adaptation enabled the cultural translation (in terms of aesthetics, politics, narratology, and gender) of such texts such that they had a function and found an audience in this culture? What was going on some six hundred years ago when Ashkenazic Jews suddenly began writing epic poetry about King Arthur and his ilk, some five hundred years ago when they began writing love poems in the style of Petrarch, and some four hundred years ago when they began writing farcical plays about ancient Persia that quickly grew into grand opera? And why did they write them *in Yiddish*?!

Already in this initial evocation of the central issue of the study, it would be useful to pause for a moment to problematize the expression "cultural translation," which appeared in the previous paragraph and indeed also in the volume's title, since it constitutes one of the fundamental nodes of analysis in the study. Translation in its most basic sense comprises the transfer of linguistic content from one language to another; for instance, the English "prayer" might generally be translated into Yiddish as *tfile*. There are, however, various kinds of prayer in both Anglophone and Yiddish-speaking Jewish cultures, such that the proper translation of any given instantiation of "prayer" will likely involve far more than a mere word-to-word equivalent. With other such complex issues, such as, for instance, "meat," "piety," "marriage," "heroism," and so on, it quickly becomes clear that translation can in fact rarely be so simple as "prayer" = *tfile*. Here, one already approaches the sphere of cultural translation.

In the present volume, the issues involved are further complicated by their embedding in distant historical periods of European Christian and Ashkenazic Jewish cultures, which interacted in complex, nuanced, and ever-shifting patterns in various places and over the course of centuries. Intellectual transfer across those concrete linguistic and more complex cultural boundaries often involved cultural translation, the selective borrowing, revision, adaptation, and integration of ideas, practices, literary modes, actual texts, and the cultural practices and vocabulary associated with those texts across those boundaries. Rarely does such a transfer involve nothing more than a substitution of the semantic quasi-equivalents of the borrowing culture for that of the lending culture. When, for instance, Ashkenazic Jewish culture borrowed not simply the word "knight," not simply the conception of a knight, but the literary genre in which a sword-wielding, swashbuckling, aristocratic knight in shining armor is the focal hero of a long poetic narrative, a massive exercise in cultural translation was required, since for medieval European Jews, knights—that is, Christian knights—had historically been anything but heroes and could hardly be conceived as the credibly legitimate protagonists of moral tales of heroism. Thus the terminology necessary to depict such a character and his exploits did not traverse the linguistic barrier onto the Jewish page without being transformed and transforming both the book in which such a narrative was contained and the reader who read those adventures (or the listener who heard them read aloud). Moreover, the translation of the terminology itself would not have sufficed to make such a narrative interesting or engaging for a Jewish reader. Even to make sense to such a reader, to be interpretable by that reader, to be articulated with the reader's known cultural expectations and practices, somehow to be integrated into that reader's cultural conception, something more had to happen. The cultural formation of the reader had to be slightly or not so slightly altered to accommodate that new material.

Once it was possible to imagine the legitimacy of such a poem in which the quasi-secular exploits of a knight who fought for his own glory *and* as a moral agent for good and against evil, the conception of poetry in Ashkenazic culture had changed, its literary canon and its stock of conventional literary expression had been altered. A process of cultural translation had occurred. Such change did not happen all at once, nor did the consequent cultural transformation overturn Jewish literature or bring about a cultural revolution, whether in the short or long term. Nonetheless, over the course of centuries, its effects were indeed profound. The study of such processes necessarily involves complex theorizing of modes of translation, transfer, cultural contacts, and the complex differentiation of period, location, and points of access. It is messy work that rarely yields simple solutions. Indeed its conclusions often can do little more than identify somewhat more precisely than had earlier been the case what it is that we still do not know. Even such modest returns may nonetheless be of value. In any case, such is the protean task of the present study.

Yiddish literature as such emerged in the late Middle Ages and by the fourteenth century began producing lengthy manuscript texts that have survived to the present, and almost from the beginning that literature achieved an aesthetic maturity that approached that of the vernacular literatures of the majority European Christian cultures within which most Ashkenazic Jews then lived. While much, indeed most early Yiddish literature belonged to pious genres, quasi-secular literary genres also developed quite early, and it is on the early Ashkenazic versions of what we might delicately and tactically shoehorn into the genre categories of lyric, drama, and epic that the present study focuses. While these literary genres as such date back at least to the ancient Greeks, they are in the early modern period again the most important literary genres in Christian literature (e.g., Spenser, Ariosto, Shakespeare, Petrarch). In Jewish culture, on the other hand, epic and drama had never before existed. The same cannot be said of lyric, of course, which—however, one might wish to define that genre—had existed in Hebrew literature from the earliest extant documents in that language. There would furthermore be no legitimacy in attempting to claim that it was first in Yiddish that quasi-secular lyric appeared, since in fact there were non-religious erotic Hebrew lyrics from Iberia that preceded Yiddish lyric, and quasi-historical Hebrew event poems from Central Europe either before or contemporary with parallel quasi-secular Yiddish event poems.

From one perspective, it would have been significant if it were the case that before these genres appeared in Yiddish there had been no lyric, no epic, and no drama of any kind in any period of Jewish culture. But in fact nothing in the design of the present study depends on that kind of priority, and as will become clear again and again in the course of the study, the simple paradigm, the incontrovertible item of evidence, and the ultimately conclusive argument toward which scholarship often seems compelled to strive here remain generally elusive. In the end, the significance of the present case does not depend on a chronological precedence of these Yiddish genres in Jewish culture, for it is rather a matter of the predominant *focus* of these new modes of literary expression in Yiddish (which had then already been the spoken language of Ashkenazic Jews for several hundred years) and not in Hebrew (which had then already been the language of Jewish high culture for two millennia). It is in these genres that Yiddish created its most accomplished literary works of the period and established a permanent basis for the second burst of Yiddish literary creativity in the late nineteenth and early twentieth centuries.

Lest the impression arise that the study proceeds from a basis in genre analysis, however—since the genre designators epic, lyric, and drama have already appeared more than once—let it be acknowledged even here that these genres are by no means essential to a conception of early Yiddish literature, nor may they be so defined, nor are they constituted in precisely the same way as in the co-temporal Gentile literary traditions in the midst of which Yiddish-language culture arose (the genres as such undergo cultural translation). The terms "genre," "lyric," "epic," and "drama" are no more than terms of convenience in the pages that follow, and the reader will notice that after these introductory remarks they are seldom used and nowhere conceptually essential to the analysis.

The historical context of Yiddish literature's emergence may not be imagined simply as "background" but rather must be acknowledged as an essential factor in understanding all aspects of that cultural phenomenon. As Jean Baumgarten brilliantly articulates the complexly woven skeins of social upheaval and as David Ruderman's general survey has recently corroborated, even as the Renaissance reorganized the landscape of Christian intellectual and artistic culture, Jewish life was all but defined by massive, continent-wide expulsions, massacres, and discriminatory legislation that profoundly altered the cartography of European Judaism and shook the very foundations of traditional Jewish society.[1] In this context, Yiddish literature—as was also the case with other contemporary European *vernaculars*—became the sounding board of social, economic, and religious conflicts, tensions, and major upheavals while simultaneously attempting to offer solutions. In here attempting to articulate the connections between that socio-historical context and the literary texts, my interest is never in source study (who borrowed what from whom at what time, in which lines of which texts), but rather in the larger questions of how, in this world defined by cultural upheaval, such literary innovation was manifested in texts, and in particular what the implications of this kind of cultural translation were. My attempt at least to contextualize if not to answer these questions leads to an examination of Jewish and Christian literary and cultural relations over the course of three and a half centuries by means of a series of concrete, tactical analyses of a selected range of texts types.

Since two of the three text types involved are *not* traditionally Jewish but rather from the outset foreign imports, their appearance in Yiddish required a kind of intercultural exchange within the interstices of majority Christian and Ashkenazic Jewish culture. The focus of the book is on how this necessarily intercultural origin shaped the texts and the literature by combining elements from both sides of the cultural divide, causing a kind of hybrid literary identity through slippage or displacement of cultural identity.[2] The book's post-philological interests are in—among other things—issues of politics, gender, narratology, and cultural liminality and hybridity.

If such issues are as significant as I would like to claim—and it was through these newly imported modes of literary expression that quasi-secular Yiddish literature essentially sprang into existence all but fully formed in order to answer deep cultural needs in Ashkenazic society—one might wonder why a book such as this one has not already been written. Indeed one might well ask why there are in general so few studies of *early* Yiddish literature, for it is a scholarly field rather sparsely planted. The reasons are complex but easily outlined: in the absence of a "Yiddishland" in the world, there has never been a "national" school system or network of Yiddish-language universities and thus no comprehensive instructional programs of Yiddish literary history that would both require and train secondary-school teachers and university faculty and research scholars. Furthermore, if we for a moment focus our attention on only a tiny corner of the incomprehensible human catastrophe of the Holocaust, then we must note that while all fields of Jewish scholarship suffered—Jewish scholars and professionals in all fields were murdered by the Nazis without discrimination—Yiddish studies is a special case. For while there were academic scholars of, for instance, the Bible, the Talmud, medieval Jewish philosophy, Sephardic poetry, and the Haskalah living on six continents, Yiddish scholarship—and in particular scholarship focusing on early Yiddish—was concentrated in Eastern Europe (in Kiev, Warsaw, Vienna, Minsk, and Vilnius), where in the two decades before the beginning of the Second World War it flourished at an academic and even institutional level. As a result of the Holocaust, however, Old Yiddish studies were all but exterminated, and the field has not yet recovered from that devastation. Only in recent decades has the field begun to be reestablished and return to the basic scholarly tasks interrupted by the Holocaust.

To say that "everything" still needs to be done in the field would, however, be gross overstatement, although frustrated students and researchers may sometimes almost imagine that to be the case; there exists, for instance, no dictionary or even introductory primer of the Old Yiddish language, and only a single history of early Yiddish literature has been published in the last half century. The pioneering studies in the field (as in its sister medieval disciplines in French, German, etc.) were not surprisingly staunchly philological in nature, whether before the Holocaust (in the socialist philology of Max Erik,[3] the nationalist philology of Israel Zinberg,[4] the sociological philology of Max Weinreich[5]) or in the postwar re-inauguration of the field in the continued work of Weinreich, or those who began work after the war and attempted to salvage the fragments and carry on the foundational work so brutally cut off, such as Chone Shmeruk, Chava Turniansky, Erika Timm, and Jean Baumgarten.[6] Even up to the present only a bare handful of studies of early Yiddish have ever ventured beyond a strict philological methodology (e.g., Baumgarten, Armin Schulz, and Jeremy Dauber).[7]

While he was professor of Anglo-Saxon at Pembroke College at Oxford University, J. R. R. Tolkien famously remarked in his now classic essay "*Beowulf*: The Monsters and the Critics," "I have read enough, I think, to venture the opinion that *Beowulfiana* is, while rich in many departments, especially poor in one. It is poor in criticism, criticism that is directed to the understanding of a poem as a poem."[8] Similarly, Tomás Ó Cathasaigh more recently commented on the state of early Irish studies that scholars in that field "all too seldom have shown sufficient interest in the historical or literary content of what they so skilfully edit."[9] I think that three-quarters of a century after Tolkien's statement and two decades after Ó Cathasaigh's, essentially the same can be said for the study of early Yiddish literature: while there is of course still much foundational work to be done, it nonetheless seems time to move beyond the strictures of conventional philology, indeed to move the study of early Yiddish literature into the context of twenty-first century "criticism," that is, literary and cultural study, in order to address the issues identified above that have thus far generally remained beyond the scope of scholarship in the field.

It would be useful at the outset to try and articulate how such an analysis might proceed, especially since the field of cultural studies in early Yiddish is, as noted, still in its developmental stages. In attempting to come to terms with late medieval and early modern Yiddish literature as a cultural phenomenon, there are several possible theoretical models that might guide the inquiry into this large, polymorphic corpus that extends over a period of a half-millennium—up to the generally agreed-upon onset of literature in Modern Literary Yiddish in the late eighteenth century.[10] Early Yiddish literature originated in Ashkenazic Jewish communities in southern Germany, northern Italy, Amsterdam, and the Polish-Lithuanian commonwealth, and in each of these sites, those Jewish communities were surrounded by a majority Christian culture that was at best indifferent, often hostile, rarely if ever overtly benevolent.[11] It was, however, precisely the relations across these boundaries between Christian and Jew that were so often economically, politically, and indeed culturally productive, including in the sphere of literature. While the dictum that Jews of the period lived *in* but were not *of* the majority culture also obtains in the corpus of early Yiddish literature, there is a great deal that began as an *external* impulse, motif, text, or genre that traversed the cultural boundary only to be radically transformed into a cultural product suitable for an *internal* audience.

The negotiation of the cultural interstices between Ashkenazic and Christian cultures of the period is then the interpretive and the theoretical problem at issue in the present study. A number of useful conceptions of how one might understand this cultural divide that is simultaneously a space of potential connection have been proposed in recent decades, some more generally, others having specifically to do with Jewish-Christian relations in the early modern period. A brief interrogation of these methods will make possible an articulation of a mode of working for the present project.

This cultural divide between inside and outside, the majority Christian and the minority Ashkenazic cultures, might initially put one in mind of the concept of a *littérature mineure*, as outlined by Gilles Deleuze and Félix Guattari, which, in addressing the question "Qu'est-ce qu'une littérature mineure?" (What is a minor literature?), attempts to come to terms with the cultural, political, and literary implications of the use of standard German as a literary language by Franz Kafka, a Jewish resident of Prague in what is now the Czech Republic but was during his lifetime part of the Austro-Hungarian Empire.[12] Their conception of *littérature mineure* has three components: "la déterritorialisation de la langue, le branchement de l'individuel sur l'immédiat-politique, l'agencement collectif d'énonciation," "the deterritorialization of language, the connection of the individual to the immediate political environment, and the collective organization of speech," which on the surface at least seem to resonate with issues already outlined for the present project.[13]

Since, however, the conception of *littérature mineure* by Deleuze and Guattari is fundamentally based on the fact that the minor literature is written in the *standard* majority language (not a dialect or related language; e.g., Kafka in German, Toni Morrison or Salman Rushdie in English), it cannot apply to Yiddish literature, since Yiddish and German have been distinct languages for centuries, just as their literary traditions are quite distinct even back to the period of the Old and Middle Yiddish literature on which the present study focuses.[14]

If one were tactically and only momentarily to set aside that particular criterion of Deleuze and Guattari's conception of *littérature mineure,* their other criteria would seem quite relevant to the conception of Yiddish as a cultural phenomenon: deterritorialized, politicized, and with collective import for Ashkenazic Jews (at least prior to the "post-vernacular" period[15]). For even if one eschews the "lacrymose conception" of Jewish history, the historical record indicates that since the Assyrian conquest of the (Northern) Kingdom of Israel by Shalmaneser V in 722 BCE (and the consequent exile of much of the Israelite populace), the history of Hebrew > Israelite > Jewish communities has been one punctuated if not defined by recurring conquest, large-scale expropriation, expulsion, and exile or threat thereof.[16] The textual record of Ashkenaz during the period of early Yiddish literature does nothing if not corroborate this pattern, for Ashkenazic communities of Europe were rarely granted the legal right to own real property and were all but constantly faced with the possibility of expulsion and expropriation, as widely documented also in the broad range of Yiddish historical poems of the period, that is, concerning the Chmielnicki massacres in the Ukraine, the Fettmilch insurrection in Frankfurt, and the Swedish siege of Prague, among others.[17] In a significant sense, Ashkenazic culture itself existed until very recently in a state of definitive and permanent deterritorialization.

The issues of overt politicization and the expression of a collective sensibility seem initially also directly relevant, since the aforementioned texts chronicling the suffering of Jewish communities from war and anti-Semitic oppression give very clear expression to both a politicized critique of contemporary events and a collective conception of community experience—which is (as will be explored in the relevant chapters below) of *primary* importance in the tradition of early Yiddish Purim plays. Other genres of early Yiddish textuality (such as the broad range of prayers, guides for Jewish women's purity, biblical glossaries, biblical translation and paraphrase, midrashic epic, and guides to ethics and morality) clearly function in the sphere of a collective expression of community needs. At the same time, however, there are many other early Yiddish texts that are neither overtly politicized nor collective but rather function as modes of individualized and ostensibly apolitical expression, such as the oldest extant love song in Yiddish (fourteenth to fifteenth century; *EYT* 14), the fourteenth-century charm against labor pains (*EYT* 13), Elia Levita's biting Venetian satire (*EYT* 35), or even his post-courtly epic *Bovo d'Antona* (*EYT* 33). It is to be noted that while there is indeed a great deal of political content in most of these texts, the political context in which they operate is rarely concerned even obliquely with contemporaneous Jewish-Christian relations but rather most often with political concerns *internal* to the Jewish community. They are thus not expressions of a politicized agenda of Jews as a collective in opposition to majority culture.

In the larger context, however, it is precisely from a fundamental and productive engagement between the already long Jewish textual tradition and the contemporary literature of the surrounding Christian culture that quasi-secular Yiddish literature emerged during the late Middle Ages. That is, the components of that literary tradition comprised a *historical* culture on the one hand (as its cultural foundation) and a strictly contemporary culture on the other: the long tradition of Jewish culture (textual and otherwise) provided whatever *historical* grounding was necessary, for Ashkenazic culture did not look to the *past* ages of the majority culture of its environment (e.g., German or Italian culture) for legitimization or even, to put a fine point on the issue, for tales to adapt into Yiddish. There are thus no Yiddish (or even Hebrew) adaptations of, for instance, Homer, Aeschylus, Vergil, or Statius from this period.[18] The two literary traditions that melded *in some genres* of early Yiddish literature were then complementary, fulfilling quite different functions in the society: the "native" historical Jewish traditions provided the fundamental *cultural* grounding, perspective, and moral purpose in Yiddish literature (and Gentile traditions did not), while contemporary Gentile *literary* repertoires provided selective source materials for some particular modes of belles-lettres (and Hebrew-Aramaic traditions did not do so for *those* modes).[19] A concrete example will illustrate the connecting node of these multifarious strands: if there was to be epic poetry in late medieval and early modern Ashkenaz, then it was to be in Yiddish (not Hebrew-Aramaic); and if there was to be such poetry, then it would consist of adaptation either of Jewish traditions (e.g., midrashic traditions of biblical heroes) or *de-ideologized* contemporary Christian epic—the imported "knights in shining armor" of Yiddish epic do not, for instance, go on Crusade, or quest for the Holy Grail, or (with one significant and glaring exception) operate in a Christian-conceived world in which Muslims are construed as the quintessential enemy to be exterminated (on which, see chapter 8).

While historical research of recent decades has gone far to debunk the scholarly and popular myth that Jews were hermetically sealed off from productive reciprocal contact with Christians throughout the Middle Ages and early modern period, in the present context a specific restriction obtains: as long as the issue is a written text and not oral communication, then with few and ultimately insignificant exceptions, non-Yiddish speakers have never read Yiddish literature (until the very recent mediated access granted by translation).[20] As a result there is no evidence that during the medieval or early modern period there was ever any Yiddish influence on non-Jewish literature. Even with Purim plays—insofar as those texts had an oral performative aspect, which thus made them at least partially comprehensible to at least some Christian auditors in those historically few performance spaces to which they were admitted (especially in Amsterdam)—it is clear from the extant texts that comprehension by non-Yiddish-speaking German- or Dutch-speakers would have been fragmentary and sporadic. Beyond these exceptions, however, early Yiddish literature was otherwise quite literally a closed book, in important respects hermetically sealed to the outside: it absorbed selectively from majority culture but gave nothing back.[21] This situation raises another distinction between early Yiddish literature and Deleuze and Guattari's conception of *littératures mineures:* Yiddish did not and could not "represent" the minority culture to the majority culture. While it could and sometimes did politicize and give expression to collective Ashkenazic concerns, its audience was never imagined as including anyone other than Yiddish-speaking Ashkenazic Jews.

At issue then is the circumscribed permeability of the cultural borderlands between Ashkenaz and the culture of its surrounding Christian majority that enables this productive mode of literary engagement and creativity. As Victor Turner argued over the course of his long career in anthropology, "'Meaning' in culture tends to be *generated* at the interfaces between established cultural subsystems."[22] Such border sites are necessarily unstable and do not comprise dividing lines but rather interstitial spaces that *join* adjacent territories. According to the more recent work by Homi Bhabha, such interstitial spaces are zones of creativity where new concepts and forms of existence are tested: "These 'in-between' spaces provide the terrain for elaborating strategies of selfhood—singular or communal—that initiate new signs of identity, and innovative sites of collaboration, and contestation, in the act of defining the idea of society itself."[23] While Turner merely hints at the possibility, Bhabha identifies this space as *necessarily* creative and having directly to do with the formation of political identities:

> It is in the emergence of the interstices—the overlap and displacement of domains of difference—that the intersubjective and collective experiences of *nationness,* community interest, or cultural value are negotiated. How are subjects formed "in-between," or in excess of, the sum of the "parts" of difference (usually intoned as race/class/gender, etc.)? How do strategies of representation or empowerment come to be formulated in the competing claims of communities where, despite shared histories of deprivation and discrimination, the exchange of values, meanings and priorities may not always be collaborative and dialogical, but may be profoundly antagonistic, conflictual and even incommensurable?[24]

Such interstitial boundary zones then function as sites of cultural engagement that often result in transformative creativity. For Bhabha, it is precisely in such zones that it is possible for the cultural Other to clear space for him-/herself to "write back" against the crushing weight of the hegemonic discourse of the Other, that is, to transform oneself from the object of Euro-Christian representation into a subject of one's own mode of creativity.[25] David Myers articulates this node of creativity as it functioned in the Jewish-Christian confrontation: "What the experience in sixteenth-century Venice or Rome offers is a window into a complex dynamic by which a minority group, armed with its own competing desires, encounters a surrounding society simultaneously open and hostile to it. . . . The currents of cultural exchange in early modern Italy were multidirectional, moving back and forth between Jewish and Christian communities. One result was undeniably an expansion of the Jewish cultural appetite."[26] The relationship between Ashkenaz and majority culture has conventionally in fact reversed the center-margin model: in refusing the mere possibility of integration or assimilation as a long-term trajectory of cultural aspiration, Ashkenazic culture *centered itself* as an enclave in the surrounding majority culture, turning that "alienized" culture into its own quasi-periphery.[27]

In coming to terms with Yiddish as a literature of an ethnic minority in the larger context of dominant Christian culture, one might be tempted to engage with recent interrogations of the predominantly economic model of center-margin or core-periphery,[28] to which reference was just made, but despite some conceptual value in the model, it corresponds rather poorly to the facts of this particular case: since Jewish communities existed as enclaves within the larger majority community, the spatial dimensions of the core-periphery model do not correspond to the historical situation. While diasporic Jewish societies have historically been dominated politically and economically by the co-territorial majority culture, it has not conventionally been the case that the majority culture has progressively encroached on Jewish society (a basic tenet of core-periphery relations), especially at the level of culture. That is, Jewish culture itself (religion, literature, customs) has with few and only partial exceptions not *historically* succumbed to a progressively increasing dominance by the co-territorial culture: until the twentieth century, Jewish communities had historically never experienced cultural integration to such an extent that that "internal" ethnic identification became secondary or subordinate to "external" political (national or quasi-national) identity.

The problem at issue is the extent to which Ashkenaz was open to outside cultural influence and the mechanisms of that influence. The ramifications of this seemingly innocent issue are many, far-reaching, and of profound significance in the history of Jewish culture, for it is perceived by many to have directly to do with the maintenance of the cultural integrity of Jewish society. Let us therefore proceed with some care. According to Ivan Marcus, while Jewish culture "actively and inwardly acculturates," that does not bring about a secularization of the culture.[29] Arthur Lesley concurs that "to assume that a minority culture that has long survived, such as that of the Jews, automatically imitates whatever it encounters in the surrounding society both ignores the internal dynamics of Jewish life and reduces intercultural relations to simplistic alternatives of borrowing or complete originality."[30] Bell remarks on the period and specific social engagement at issue in the present study: "Jews in Renaissance Italy did not resist or ignore humanism; they chose what interested them and disregarded the rest."[31] David Ruderman views the issue as one that still requires more attention: "The history of Jewish society and culture in early modern Europe is more than a mirror of the Christian world and needs to be described more accurately and more comprehensively. . . . It also needs to be viewed simultaneously from both external and internal perspectives."[32] He poses the very provocative question in a subchapter title "Did Jewish Mobility Engender Cultural Productivity?" to which his answer is a complex and nuanced affirmation: "Jewish intellectual life and cultural production were shaped to a great extent by Jewish intellectuals who moved from place to place."[33] He acknowledges that the hypothesis is difficult to prove and guards against overstating the case by focusing on concrete examples of Jewish intellectuals on the move: "The sheer number of these examples and the prominence of the intellectuals mentioned herein might at least suggest the possibility of some causal relationship between mobility and cultural production."[34]

Thus in the context of the participation of individual Jewish intellectuals along the margins of Renaissance and Humanist culture, Robert Bonfil's redeployment of these terms usefully designates the tension between centripetal (systemic or system-preserving) and centrifugal (anti-systemic) forces that has often been employed not just in physics but more recently in political science. In the present context, Bonfil employs the terms to indicate forces that act on individual Jews and Jewish culture in general to strengthen or weaken traditional Jewish culture. Bonfil has been especially concerned to counter what he perceived as a tendency among scholars—especially Cecil Roth and his scholarly progeny—to overemphasize both the idyllic conditions of life for Jews in Renaissance Italy and the assimilationist tendency in Jewish culture of the period.[35] On the basis of detailed examination of a broad range of evidence, he rejects the claim that a high level of Jewish cultural exchange and even cultural integration demonstrates assimilation as such. He thus favors a centripetal interpretation.[36]

There is nonetheless very concrete evidence of multiple modes of cultural rapprochement between Jews and Gentiles, and not just at the level of elite, individual scholars. Bonfil neither ignores nor downplays that evidence, but rather attempts to put it into the context of continued Jewish cultural integrity. His complexly argued point is that Jews in Italy whose relations with Christians included shared interests in poetry, music, and theater did not conceive of that association as compromising their own Jewish identity, nor did those who fostered such associations tend to convert to Christianity. Those who did convert at that time and place were concerned "for the salvation of their souls," not for cultural assimilation for the sake of enjoying the benefits of the majority culture: "Culture no more led the Jews out of Judaism than it led the Christians out of Christianity. There is nothing to prove that the choice of those who converted was imposed by their choice of the pleasures of the middle class lifestyle—poetry, music, theatre, sports, society games, and all the other phenomena customarily cited when describing the alleged tendency of the Italian Jews to limit the significance and definition of their own identity in terms of its Otherness with respect to Christian identity."[37]

Bonfil further attempts to problematize the conventional scholarly notion that the situation is to be viewed as a conflict between a centrifugal Jewish interest in Gentile culture versus the centripetal anti-rationalistic bent of the rabbinate, which allegedly desired to insulate the Jewish community from all contact with Gentile culture. He counters that even the definitional terms of contrast in this stark dichotomy between "Jewish" culture and "Italian" culture of the period in northern Italy lack rigor, since the borders between the two terms and the two practices are not as distinct as has often been assumed. He then makes very fruitful use of—selective—inventories of books owned by individual Jews and Jewish communities in the sixteenth century (especially the Mantuan censor's list of 1595), pointing out that very few of those books were in Italian (0.6 percent), and only 11.2 percent of Jewish collections included any Italian books at all, while most books owned were liturgical works, biblical exegesis, ritual custumals, and Talmud.[38]

Bonfil then makes the less compelling claim—unsupported by the evidence that he had just presented—that "throughout the entire period under examination, the books that Jews kept in their libraries, and the works that they read and studied, were almost all in Hebrew. The language of cultural communication of Italian Jewish society was Hebrew and Hebrew alone."[39] This claim is erroneous in as many ways as one might care to enumerate. First, as scholars know, the language of the books in a scholar's library need not definitively identify the "language of cultural communication"; while Italian Jewish scholars of the period certainly read and wrote in Hebrew, they did not *speak* Hebrew as their "language of cultural communication." Second, Bonfil acknowledges the presence of Italian books in the libraries and, further, of the ubiquitous presence of the Talmud, of which the majority (the Gemara) is of course written in Aramaic, so his claim of "Hebrew alone" simply collapses through imprecision. Unmentioned by Bonfil in his Hebraist exclusionism is also the fact that even in the Mantuan censor's list there is clear documentation of the significant presence of Yiddish books in the private collections of northern Italian Jews of the sixteenth century. As Shifrah Baruchson documents and comments: בתחום הספרות היפה בולטת תפוצת ספרי היידיש יותר מבכל תחום אחר. הם היו כ־25% מכלל ספרי הסיפרות והשירה שהיו בידי תושבי הקהילה "In the domain of belles lettres the distribution of Yiddish literature is more conspicuous than in any other domain. They [sc., Yiddish books] constitute some 25 percent of the general books of literature and poetry/songs possessed by members of the community."[40] Likewise unacknowledged by Bonfil is the fact that among Ashkenazim of this period—whether in Poland, the German territories, or Ashkenazic communities of northern Italy—Yiddish would have been the primary language of daily communication and even the de facto (non-liturgical) spoken language of the study house (in the sense that it has remained such in Yiddish-speaking Orthodox and Hasidic communities up to the present). Hebrew was thus in *no* functional sense the exclusive "language of cultural communication" in northern Italian Jewish communities.

The mode of Jewish-Christian relations at issue in the present study—especially as it addresses those relations in northern Italy—is one that has often been treated by scholarship since at least the mid-twentieth century as a prompt to address the vexed issue of whether some Jewish intellectuals were authentic participants in the Renaissance and thus whether it makes sense to categorize them as "Renaissance men" or even "Jewish Humanists." Hava Tirosh-Rothschild conveniently (and provocatively) lists the relevant questions:

> Although modern Jewish historians have paid considerable attention to Renaissance Italian Jewry, there is no consensus about the meaning of the Renaissance in Jewish history. Scholars debate such questions as: What was the status of Jews in Italian society? Does the Renaissance constitute a meaningful

> category in Jewish history? Did Jews undergo a Renaissance parallel to and coterminous with the Italian Renaissance? Did the culture of Italian Jewry during the Renaissance differ from other Jewish subcultures? Did the Renaissance account for the distinct features of Judeo-Italian culture? If the Renaissance did exert some impact on Jewish culture, what was the nature and scope of this impact? What was the relevant cultural context of Italian Jewry?[41]

And as she further suggests, the answers to such questions ultimately depend less on empirical data than on the questioner's "conception of the Renaissance and on one's understanding of Jewish history."[42] Her own answer, for instance, is couched in a terminological context that immediately reveals its assumptions: "While Renaissance humanists accorded an unprecedented respect to Judaism and collaborated with a few Jewish scholars, Renaissance humanism was a thoroughly Christian phenomenon. Jewish scholars could not partake in it *qua* Jews; they were expected to convert. Humanism continued to assert the spiritual superiority of Christianity over Judaism, so that the relationship between the two religions remained unchanged: hostility and rivalry."[43] The arguments possible on multiple sides of the focal issues have in general been adequately articulated in recent decades, especially by Tirosh-Rothschild, Robert Bonfil, and Arthur Lesley, among others, and there is nothing substantive to be added here to the issues for the larger field.[44] To the extent that it is tactically of essential relevance to the present study, however, the issue is problematized in chapter 3 concerning Elia Levita.

Within the sphere of Ashkenazic literature, Yiddish literature occupies a restricted range. The general twenty-first-century layperson's assumption about early Yiddish literature is that if it existed at all then it must have consisted of nothing but pious texts for Hebrew-illiterate women (and men) and "folklore," however that term might be defined.[45] And indeed pious texts do constitute the majority of early Yiddish texts, of which some—but by no means most—were indeed written specifically for the use of Jewish women. But there is also a broader range of other types of texts. Indeed one finds essentially the same genres in early Yiddish as in the literary traditions of the majority cultures among whom Ashkenazim lived: custumals, debate poems, Arthurian epic, religious epic, ethical and moral treatises, letters, fables, glossaries, historical poems, historical treatises, legal texts, liturgical texts, lyric, lamentations, medical texts, magical practice, proto-journalism, satirical poems and diatribes, prose narrative and tales, travel guides, mathematical treatises, technological treatises, biblical translation/paraphrase, among others (in addition to a range of specifically Jewish genres). One of the great pioneers of post-Holocaust Yiddish studies, Chone Shmeruk, acknowledged the undeniable fact that during the late medieval and early modern periods the textual realm of *loshn-koydesh*, "the holy language," that is, Hebrew-Aramaic, was the dominant textual force in Ashkenazic society, leaving no more cultural space for Yiddish literature than a mere niche. Nonetheless, whether for lack of a Hebrew-language audience or absence of a canonical paradigm, such literature of the interstices is written in Yiddish. David Neal Miller clarifies Shmeruk's "subversive maximalism" and its fundamental significance: "Yiddish literature only fills the gap in the Jewish intralinguistic polysystem; that gap is Literature in any modern sense of the word."[46]

Despite this seeming breadth of Yiddish literature (within its niche) and the general resemblance of this part of its canon to that of the surrounding majority culture, however, one must not err in the other direction by imagining that early Yiddish literature—beyond the pale of Hebrew-Aramaic—is simply a slightly Judaized canon of medieval and Renaissance Christian genres. Very strictly traditional Jewish texts such as Old Yiddish *tkhines* (prayers of supplication), collections of women's commandments, liturgical and para-liturgical hymns, biblical translations/paraphrases, biblical and Talmudic glossaries, and above all *musar* (ethical-moral treatises) in fact form the core of the early Yiddish canon and are of essential importance in understanding the textual culture of Ashkenaz. That basic fact must be borne in mind by the reader of the present volume at all times, because otherwise, since its focus lies absolutely elsewhere, it might mistakenly be imagined that the volume presupposes or argues for a secularization of Ashkenazic culture by means of early Yiddish literature. Nothing could be farther from the truth—for this volume and for early Yiddish literature.

The specific focus here enables an essential question to be posed in a precise but broadly significant formulation: how is one to comprehend the sudden explosion of Ashkenazic interest in and cultural integration and prolific production of a *range* of textual genres that had not been approximated in Jewish culture since the closure of the biblical canon a millennium and a half earlier? The question is especially important because in this period (as also for Israelites in the period of biblical canon formation) the permeable boundaries of Jewish-Gentile literary culture enabled the integration of "foreign" genres and sensibilities that utterly transformed the literary landscape of Ashkenaz as had never happened before, or—arguably—since, for the second productive period of Yiddish literature (in the nineteenth and early twentieth centuries) in a sense simply continued the exploration of the formerly alien but by then already internalized modes of literary production and the cultural porosity already utilized by earlier Yiddish literature.[47]

Despite this specific focus, however, I do not here propose that early Yiddish literature is legitimated by or derives its constitutive identity from any dependence on the appearance of epic, drama, and its specific modes of lyric as if Christian genres or quasi-Aristotelian genres. One must guard against the "Naipaul fallacy," a term coined by Anthony Appiah to designate the assumption that non-mainstream (minority) literature gains legitimacy only if, when, and insofar as it attains some measure of identity with European literary genres, content, and style.[48] As already noted, Yiddish literature—of both the earlier and the more recent period—comprises a broader range of genres than here treated, because it expresses the entirety of Jewish culture (within its niche), which then necessarily includes *as essential components* a broad range of overtly religious texts, as well as texts related to community practices (e.g., women's commandments, custumals). One must keep in mind at all times that while the range of literary text types addressed in the present study may (to some) seem to comprise Literature as such, they do so only in the peculiar (and tactically legitimate) sense proposed by Shmeruk and Miller, as noted earlier, but with the further restriction that among specifically Yiddish-language genres the subset of quasi-secular genres constituted a relatively small minority of *both* genres and statistically reckoned numbers of actually existing books in sixteenth-century Yiddish literature.[49] There is no pretense here that Yiddish literature had somehow "arrived" in the sixteenth century because it produced so many epics, for instance. Instead it is precisely the cross-border intellectual negotiations and cultural translation that are of interest, for it is through them that this—for all intents and purposes—aberrant intrusion into centripetal Jewish culture became so significant for Ashkenazic culture of that and subsequent periods.

Another issue directly arising from potential anachronistic preconceptions of the means through which that intrusion took place needs to be unpacked here: unlike the second wave of Yiddish literature in the nineteenth and early twentieth centuries, which came from the pens of Jewish authors who made their ways into a secular Jewish or even wholly Gentile cultural sphere (the vast majority of whom, one should keep in mind, had nonetheless had very traditionally pious origins, upbringing, and educations), this earlier wave in Yiddish literature most definitely did not produce a literature written by or for "former" Jews, "lapsed" Jews, converts to Christianity, freethinkers, merely "cultural" Jews, "secular" Jews, or however else one might wish to imagine them. This earlier wave comprised both authors and audience who were simply "ordinary" fourteenth- through eighteenth-century Jews; that is, in the period before Hasidism and any and all more recent reform movements, they were simply what we might somewhat tactically (and anachronistically) call "lowercase" orthodox Jews. This is not to deny that there were converts to Christianity during the period—although there were in fact relatively few Ashkenazim among them—or that there were *apikorsim* (renegades from strict observance) who did not convert—although there were in fact very few of them—but rather simply to observe that the vast majority of the audience and the authors of the quasi-secular genres of early Yiddish literature, as of the more pious genres, were simply ייִדן פֿון אַ גאַנץ יאָר, that is, ordinary, everyday Ashkenazic Jews, the men among whom prayed three times a day and did their best to observe the 613 commandments imposed on them by tradition, and the women among whom did their best to adhere to the three explicit injunctions on women and the hundreds of traditional customary directives.[50]

The emergence of such alien literary impulses that broadened to permeate the entire culture perhaps constituted in some restricted sense a literary revolution but by no means signaled a concomitant religious or theological revolution, despite the fact that at precisely this same period in the dominant Christian cultures surrounding the Ashkenazim, multivalent cultural revolutions, integrating literary, philosophico-theological, scientific, and social components, raged. The emergence of Yiddish literature is dialectically related to the social turmoil of the period—within Jewish culture and beyond its confines; in fact it grew out of that chaos, fed back into it, and attempted to offer solutions to concrete problems. But when, as it were, the dust settled, this first explosion of quasi-secular Yiddish literature had had few if any specifically theological repercussions, unlike, for instance, the catastrophe of the messianic Shabbatai Ẓevi episode in the mid-seventeenth century or, for obvious reasons, the rise of Hasidism and the importation of the Enlightenment-based Haskalah a century thereafter.

Baumgarten's analysis of the socio-historical context in which Yiddish literature was established is significant: "Without going to the extreme of considering that literature no more than an unmediated 'reflection' of the crisis that shook Jewish society at the beginning of the modern period, it is nonetheless clear that the general European atmosphere beginning in the sixteenth century weighed heavily on the emergence of Yiddish literature."[51] This is a social context, he notes,

> marked by a series of expulsions, by discriminatory legislation, even by massacres that both profoundly altered the cartography of European Judaism and shook the very foundations of traditional Jewish society. Secondly, this period, which coincides with the Renaissance in Europe, is characterized by a reorganization of the intellectual landscape, a spiritual revival, and a desire on the part of the authorities to strengthen the foundations of community life, in order better to control the endemic crises which were menacing Jewish existence. Nonetheless, it is inappropriate to reduce this era to no more than its most distressing and tragic aspects. First, because such extreme and coincident situations are characterized by obvious paradoxes: on the one hand, the violence against the Jews, whose roots were already old in Europe, continued and intensified, exacerbated by social antagonisms, resentment based on economic factors, and religious squabbles. The various social groups and strata which comprised feudal society at the time—the clergy, the aristocratic authorities, the guilds formed by the urban middle classes, and the general populace—participated, to diverse degrees and with local variation, in this wave of hatred for the Jews. It served to stigmatize the Jewish presence within Christian Europe and to reduce its participation in economic, religious, and social life. Sudden anti-Jewish eruptions could take numerous forms, such as theological

> polemic, pogrom, extortion, expulsion, or discriminatory measures that decimated and weakened the Jewish population. . . . While one may not, of course, directly link the emergence of Yiddish literature with these external factors, it was nonetheless by means of such changes that Yiddish was able progressively to penetrate and permeate the cultural space of Jewish society. Literature in the vernacular became a sounding board of multiple developments which characterized this period; it reflected the conflicts, tensions, and the major upheavals, at the same time that it helped to provide solutions—limited but original—to specific problems presented to Jewish society.[52]

Through war, some entire regions were essentially emptied of their Jewish populations, while the Black Plague (1347–1350) quickly resulted in the degrading of the juridical status of Jews, initiated a deep economic recession, and in the end reduced the Jewish population of Europe by half. Finally, in hundreds of communities in German-speaking lands, there were massacres and expulsions. Baumgarten comments that "one of the dominant characteristics of this troubled period was the sense of anxiety that affected every stratum of the Jewish populace."[53] As Jews were banished to the villages and hamlets that formed the periphery of cities, where many Jews managed to survive as merchants, tradesmen, and artisans, there were direct negative consequences for the transmission of Judaism. It was, not surprisingly, in such social circles that a focused interest in issues of exile, messianic hope, and popular themes in Kabbalah developed and there also that the readership of Yiddish books developed. As Baumgarten argues, "The works of Elia (Baḥur/Bokher) Levita, Azariah de' Rossi, Joseph Solomon Delmedigo, and Leone (Judah Arye) of Modena (Mutinensis) clearly express this 'breaking of the vessels,' that is: the tremors internal to the Ashkenazic world and the appearance of a 'secular' component in Jewish culture."[54] Thus it was not simply that Yiddish literature echoed the widespread crisis in (western) Ashkenazic culture of the period, but indeed that the texts engaged directly in the tensions of that crisis, attempting to propose creative solutions to the problems. This literature was by no means simply a vernacularization of the learned culture of Hebrew-Aramaic, but indeed itself a vernacular culture not altogether independent of the intellectual culture of Ashkenaz and by no means merely a sop for the ignorant. The growing cultural abyss between the educated elite in society and those marginalized from intellectual culture as the professionalization of knowledge progressed among a tiny minority of scholars (who then controlled access to that tradition) spawned further tensions and further vernacular attempts to compensate for such divisions and to minimize the "cultural disparities that had developed between the *litterati* and *illitterati*."[55]

It was precisely in this conflictual social morass that Yiddish literature, especially quasi-secular Yiddish literature, appeared and developed into a mode of expression for an entire segment of the culture's creative impulses. In its "vernacularization of the tradition's canonical texts," as Baumgarten expresses it, Yiddish literature "seemed to be the beginnings of a gradual emancipation of knowledge from the exclusive guardianship of the scholars, the *talmidei khakhomim,* who exercised a monopoly on the writing, the interpretation and the reading of the texts."[56] There is in this emancipatory impulse of early Yiddish literature something quasi-revolutionary—again, in a cultural, not a theological or political sense—for, as Jeremy Dauber points out, Yiddish literature has "twin roles . . . subordinate and subversive, internal and other, adaptive and creative."[57]

This phenomenon is the "invention" of what has here thus far been hesitantly designated "quasi-secular" Yiddish literature, and might better have been designated "~~secular~~" in its crossed-out or *sous rature* font mode, conceived in the Heideggerian/Derridean sense of a definitionally inadequate but tactically necessary term.[58] For one must take great care to guard against assuming that contemporary dichotomies are applicable to other periods and/or cultures. While contemporary intellectual culture may legitimately distinguish between religious and secular culture for some segments of some contemporary societies, that distinction often makes little sense outside those defined contexts, and certainly not in early modern Ashkenaz, where the category in opposition to the religious would not be the secular, but rather the blasphemous or heretical. There was no possibility of a strictly secular culture as such in early Ashkenaz. In such a traditional culture, all things were related in an all-exclusive totality of a life defined by the inherited culture of the community of believers (whether a given individual was actually pious or not), such that no act or thing existed outside relation to that system.[59] From a twenty-first-century perspective, there may be perceived some occasional indicators of forays out of the strict confines of traditional sixteenth-century religious culture, but that modern perception was almost certainly not shared by those responsible for such indicators, and those who took responsibility for policing community behavior either would have classified such forays as benign or in any case would have neither praised nor condemned their secularism, but rather if deemed antinomial would have been concerned for the souls of the perpetrators as heretics.

The emergence of what may be perceived as quasi-secular Yiddish literature is thus not simply a questioning of the cultural hegemony of Hebrew-Aramaic in Ashkenazic culture via the composition of pious works in Yiddish, but also a co-optation of the right to select and adapt from the literature of dominant (Christian) culture into Yiddish, which put such innovators on the liminal borders of legitimate cultural activity, without, as already noted, providing reciprocal access to its own versions of these texts to outsiders (except in the single form of drama that existed in early Ashkenaz, i.e., Purim plays, to which some Christians had limited aural access). This co-opting of alien genres transforms the canon of

Jewish literature, however, making space for new modes of cultural expression never before possible in Jewish culture.

Having now defined the function of the term “quasi-secular/~~secular~~” in the present study, another term, often already used in relation and sometimes even almost in opposition to that term, requires further definition: midrashic. The two terms are especially useful in the analysis of early Yiddish epic,[60] but not just there. The term “midrashic epic” was introduced by Wulf-Otto Dreeßen to designate epic narrative in early Yiddish that was based as much on post-biblical Jewish cultural traditions of biblical narrative (e.g., Talmud, biblical commentary, midrash, homiletic traditions) as on the Bible itself.[61] With respect to Yiddish epic, *midrash* (< Hebr. מדרש *midrash,* “study” < Hebr. דרש *darash,* “inquire/seek,” designating one of the four particular methods of exegesis traditional in Judaism, characterized by a comparative homiletic, often metaphorical mode) makes possible more precision in identifying the subjects and sources of the epic narratives than does any other term. While Christian literary adaptations of biblical stories of, for instance, Abraham, Joseph, David, or Esther most often essentially recapitulate the biblical narrative, almost nowhere in Jewish literature does the Bible function in this way as a primary literary source.[62] Jewish adaptations rarely recapitulate the biblical narrative, routinely including—or often consisting wholly of—episodes that are strictly extra-biblical, deriving from the post-biblical Jewish commentary or homiletic tradition.

A prime example would be the earliest of Yiddish midrashic epics (or, perhaps better: heroic lay), the late fourteenth-century אברהם אבינו “Our Father Abraham,” which relates various (comic) stories from Abraham’s early youth as the traveling sales representative of his father’s Mesopotamian idol-manufacturing firm. Obviously none of these stories is biblical, but they are nonetheless all such widely known components in the Jewish cultural tradition that their “originality” in this early Yiddish text—which might seem indisputable from a Gentile perspective—could well be denied from a Jewish perspective. Their cultural significance in establishing the individual responsibility for Abraham’s commitment to Hebrew monotheism is fundamental and thus directly relevant to the biblical narrative that enacts the foundation of both the nationhood of Abraham and his descendants and their intimate and necessary connection with the Hebrew God.

In addition, Yiddish midrashic epic incorporates much from the epic traditions of the dominant culture in which Jews lived—for example, the broad traditions of Middle High German epic, such that, for instance, in the Middle Yiddish ספֿר שמואל *Book of Samuel,* a midrashic epic based on traditions associated with the biblical books of Samuel, Sir David and his knights (!) often seem to fight for honor and glory in a manner characteristic not of the Bible but instead of Arthurian epic of the High Middle Ages. Midrashic epic is thus very clearly a hybridized tradition, including, frequently and rather surprisingly, clearly non-Jewish components, even in metrics, rhyme scheme, and stanzaic structures.

The biblical and extra-biblical traditions may be quite distinct in terms of their textual histories, but their cultural histories are entangled such that they have in the Jewish intellectual and folk traditions become inextricably united. It is from this hybridized textual tradition that midrashic epic arises. For a post-Talmudic Jewish thinker to write anything about a biblical text without reference to the midrashic tradition would have been unusual (Rabbi Samuel ben Me'ir and Abraham ibn Ezra would have been exceptions), and in many traditions all but unthinkable (at least until very recently); it would in most instances seem almost tantamount to a repudiation of Judaism (or at least a very deliberately provocative political statement). Early Yiddish midrashic epic is thus—from a non-Jewish perspective—distinctly "extra-biblical" even while based on biblical characters and biblical narratives. From a Jewish perspective, of course, the sharp distinction between the biblical and the extra-biblical that seems so clear to the non-Jewish reader is anything but sharply distinct, for the culturally defined border between the written and the oral Torah (i.e., the biblical text and the textual traditions of Mishnah, Gemara, canonical commentaries, and supercommentaries) is fluid, to say the least, and—narratively, at least—not necessarily definitive. The use of the term "midrashic epic" is thus quite compelling, and the category itself has proven quite useful in literary analysis.

The reader will have by now noticed that, *mutatis mutandis,* the sense of cultural translation developed earlier with respect to quasi-secular literature in early Yiddish may also be applied to midrashic literature in early Yiddish, in that it results from the hybridization of the sacred textual traditions of Hebrew-Aramaic with the literary traditions of the non-Jewish majority culture (e.g., the midrashic traditions of the biblical books of Samuel with the literary traditions of Middle High German epic). Even so, this latter mode of hybridization makes only sporadic appearance in the present study, since the primary focus here is predominantly on quasi-secular literature in early Yiddish (although, especially in the chapters on Purim plays, due attention is given to the Bible, as well as to both Talmud and midrash).

Despite the radically innovative tendencies in early Yiddish literature, its immediate function seems to have been less to undermine and subvert than to supplement, but through its supplementation, it ultimately did subvert and undermine by broadening the scope of literature, enlarging the palette, and increasing the vocabulary of literary and cultural expression. Moreover, once that had been accomplished, it could not effectively be undone, and those originally supplementary, now integrated texts and genres continued to be part of the culture's passive repertoire even in periods (such as, in general, the later eighteenth century) when new works in those initially innovative genres were no longer being composed.[63] Thus they continued to be read and could be reactivated by individual writers and communities of writers at appropriate moments—as the centuries-long popularity of Elia Levita's *Bovo d'Antona* and its successors demonstrates (even in periods when there were no epic poets). It might be useful to unpack this notion of supplementarity somewhat more fully, for from the perspective of traditional Ashkenazic culture, these genres were in fact extra, supplementary, intrusive, foreign, alien.[64] But in the absence of what post-Derrideans might deem a (fictive) center that would purport to anchor and provide interpretive stability for the system, in this case of (quasi-secular) literature, substitution and supplementarity eternally undermine whatever system one might imagine: the supplement is only possible because it was already prefigured by an absence, a lack, a quasi-deficiency in the canon. A "complete" canon of Jewish literature, even in terms of genres recognized, is not possible.

As indicated earlier in this introduction, the study proceeds through an analysis of three literary modes: short poetic texts ("lyric"; two chapters), Purim play ("drama"; three chapters), long poetic narrative ("epic"; two chapters). As has already been intimated and as will become clearer in the course of the book, these three modes are constituted rather differently in Yiddish than in other co-temporal literary traditions. Early Yiddish "lyric," for instance, is rather unlike lyric traditions in late medieval and early modern French, English, German, Italian, Latin, and Hebrew. For the general response to the idea of medieval European lyric poetry is to expect as a significant component of the corpus a range of love poems in the style of the Provençal *trobador,* the northern French *trouvère,* the Italian *dolce stil novo,* or the Middle High German *Minnesänger.* There is, however, no Yiddish Guillaume de Machaut, Walther von der Vogelweide, François Villon, Petrarch, nor indeed even a Solomon ibn Gabirol. There is nonetheless a relatively broad range of short metrical poetry in a variety of sub-genres, and it might be useful here to sketch that range, in order to contextualize the issues and poems chosen for analysis here.

The earliest extant sentence in Yiddish is indeed a single rhymed couplet of exhortation inserted into the *Worms Maḥzor* (holiday prayer book) (1272–1273; *EYT* 2). Pious songs are in general well represented in the canon, as in Jacob ben Elijah Halevi Teplitz's געטליך ליד "A Pious Song" (1650; *EYT* 103) and גאר איין שון נויאן תורה ליד "A Very Fine, New Torah-Song" (1605–1615; *EYT* 92); Rebecca bas Meir Tiktiner's איין שמחת תורה ליד "A Simḥes-Torah Song" (1650; *EYT* 104); and איין שין ליד נייא גימאכֿט בלשון תחינה "A Fine, New Song in the Style of *Tkhinous*" by Taube (wife of Jacob Pan, b. Leyb Pitsker) (ca. 1700; *EYT* 127). An unorthodox mode of piety is also apparent in Benjamin Tousk's איין שוין נייא ליד פון משיח "A Fine, New Poem on the Messiah" (1666; *EYT* 108) by a devout believer in Shabbatai Ẓevi as the messiah.

There are also early Yiddish lyrics that resemble those found in other co-temporal traditions, such as Eizik Wallich's self-reflective, quasi-philosophical ווייל איך איצונדרט אן מיר ואר שטיא "Because I Now Understand about Myself" (often designated "Memento Mori" by previous scholars; ca. 1600; *EYT* 87) and the anonymous קלאג ליד אויף דען יונגין מלך זיין טוט "Lamentation on the Death of the Young King" (on the death of Ferdinand IV, son of the Holy Roman emperor; 1654; *EYT* 106). As conventional in the early modern period, most prefaces to early Yiddish books, whether prose or verse, are themselves in verse, such as, on the one hand, prefaces to pious works like the one by Löb Brześć / Leyb Bresh of Cremona to the Yiddish translation of the Pentateuch (1560; *EYT* 58), or the preface by Royzl bas Joseph Levi (Fishl), מיט דער הילף גוטש יתֿ "With the Help of God, Blessed Be He," to Moses Shtendl's translation of the Psalms (1586; *EYT* 68), and, on the other hand, prefaces to more mundane works, such as that by Shvarts Kalman to his ווש מן בידרף צו דער לגן *Handbook on Laundry* (sixteenth century; *EYT* 81). As in other co-temporal lyric traditions, debate poems were popular in Yiddish, which generally pose questions not necessarily of burning political relevance but rather of often amusing cultural confrontation, such as מחלוקת יין והמים "Debate between Wine and Water" (1516; *EYT* 36) or זמר נאה של ריב וקטט חנוכה עם המועדים "Debate between Hanukkah and the Other Holidays" (1574; *EYT* 61), by Zalmen the Scribe, and דז מענש גיגליכן "On the Ages of Life" (1554; *EYT* 53), which is not quite a debate poem, but one in which the alternating Yiddish and Judeo-Italian stanzas nonetheless seem to respond to each other as the progressive ages of a human life are characterized. A primary mode of early Yiddish lyric is cultural critique or satire, such as Anshel Levi's "The Conceited King," inserted into his translation of the Mishnah tractate, מדרש לפרקי אבות *Midrash on Pirkei Avot* (1579; *EYT* 64), and Elia Levita's הַמַבְדִיל בֵין קוֹדֶש לְחוֹל "Ha-Mavdil Song" (1514; *EYT* 35; see chapter 3 below). There are lyrics integral to community life, such as איין כלה ליד "A Bride's Song," by Jacob ben Eliezer (Ulma) (1593; *EYT* 73), and those that the community might prefer to suppress, such as drinking songs like the anonymous פומייא איר ליבן גיזעלין "Pumay, You Dear Companions" (ca. 1600; *EYT* 86) and איין שין נייא ליד פון דריי ווייבר "A Fine, New Song of Three Wives" (ca. 1650; *EYT* 102).

One of the primary modes of early Yiddish poetry is the so-called *khidushim*-poems that commemorate a historical event or incident, especially as that event impacts the Jewish community.[65] Among the significant Yiddish poems of this sub-genre are Joseph ben Eleazar Lipman Ashkenazi's קינה על גזירות הקהילות דק"ק אקרייני "Lamentation on the Ukrainian Massacre" (concerning the Chmielnicki massacres; 1648; *EYT* 99), Elḥanan ben Abraham Hellen's דברי השירה הזאת [מגילתווינץ] "The Song of Vints Hans [Megilas Vints]" (on the Fettmilch insurrection in Frankfurt; 1648; *EYT* 100), and the anonymous שווידש ליד "Swedish Song" (on the siege of Prague near the end of the Thirty Years War; 1649; *EYT* 101).

From this range of lyric modes in early Yiddish, three instantiations are analyzed here in two successive chapters: first, the oldest love poem in Yiddish, וואו זאל איך הין "Whither Am I to Go?" (*EYT* 14), and then the two brief Yiddish poems by Elia Levita—his *khidushim*-poem די שריפה בון וונידיג "The Great Fire of Venice/*Sreyfe*-Song" (*EYT* 34) on the burning of the Rialto Bridge in Venice in 1514, and, more extensively, his biting satirical pasquinade הַמַבְדִיל בֵין קוֹדֶש לְחוֹל "Ha-Mavdil Song" (*EYT* 35) of the same year. As much as any other lyric poems in the early Yiddish tradition, these three force a critical confrontation with that interstitial borderland between Jewish and co-territorial Gentile culture that is a primary concern of the present study. In the case of each poem, that dividing-connecting cultural suture is between Ashkenazic and Gentile culture in Italy, especially in Venice and the Veneto, a cultural hotbed during the sixteenth century for both Jews and Christians, and especially for Yiddish literature. Consideration of this brief love poem and especially Levita's pasquinade immediately plunges the analysis into a confrontation with cultural issues of the High Renaissance and Humanism in Germany, Rome, and Venice as they impinge upon and are selectively integrated into the Ashkenazic intellectual sphere.

Historically, the genre of drama was not merely alien to Jewish culture, but indeed anathema, essentially prohibited by rabbinical antagonism over the course of the millennia since the first contact between ancient Judaism and the Hellenistic traditions of drama that spread through the vast territories conquered by Alexander the Great, including ancient Israel. By the seventeenth century, however (and probably a century earlier), a fledgling dramatic tradition had become established in Ashkenaz, again a hybrid genre that borrowed the literary-cultural form from co-territorial Gentile culture, while imbuing that form with strictly traditional Jewish content that itself had nonetheless also been adapted to its new cultural context. The corpus of early *Yiddish* drama in large part comprises the corpus of early *Jewish* drama and consists exclusively of Purim plays. Thus any analysis of the earliest dramatic traditions in Ashkenaz is necessarily a study of the tradition of the holiday of Purim and of Purim plays. The stable core of that particular dramatic tradition has remained—even up to the present in pious Jewish communities—the Esther narrative from the Bible, supplemented with later midrashic traditions.[66] Thus, here, too, in the analyses of the earliest period of Yiddish drama, the focus is on the earliest "Ahasuerus plays" from the late seventeenth and early eighteenth centuries in terms of three salient issues: (1) the inevitability that these plays about the ancient Jewish avoidance of genocide via political integration and triumph also function as vehicles of political expression in the period of their performance, (2) the plays' problematization of Queen Vashti in what to twenty-first-century eyes would seem the politics of gender, and (3) the political and cultural implications of the semiotics of space at the court of the king, especially with respect to Mordecai as cultural mediator between inside and outside.

Since a tradition of epic was essentially absent from Jewish cultural history until the late Middle Ages,[67] its sudden appearance at that time in Yiddish is somewhat shocking even from the present distance. It is difficult to decide which of the two primary sub-genres is most surprising. One might imagine that quasi-secular epic, derived directly from co-territorial Gentile models, would be culturally most accessible in terms of producing actual narratives in Yiddish, but—with their fantastical world of knights and ladies, giants and dragons, monstrous Muslims and saintly heroes—that they would at the same time seem just about the least likely candidates for finding an Ashkenazic audience. Even so, some epics of the Gentile tradition—of strictly controlled content—apparently interested a large segment of the Ashkenazic population immediately and over the course of centuries. On the other hand, the genesis of midrashic epic was in terms of cultural translation still more complex, since its existence presupposes the integration of the (secular) epic model of Gentile literature into quasi-secular Yiddish epic, which only then can be reconceived and transformed to become an expression of midrashic tales of traditional Jewish heroes, such as Abraham, Joshua, Joseph, David, and so on. The broad-ranging genre of early Yiddish epic is a testament to the appeal of this twin genre, including both midrashic epics and heroic lays, אברהם אבינו "Our Father Abraham" (1382; *EYT* 5), יוסף הצדיק "Joseph the Righteous" (1382; *EYT* 6), [מלכים-בוך] ספר מלכים *Book of Kings* (1543; *EYT* 45), Moses Esrim Vearba's [שמואל-בוך] ספֿר שמואל *Book of Samuel* [*Shmuel-bukh*] (1544; *EYT* 47), ספֿר דניאל *Book of Daniel* (1557; *EYT* 57), עקידת יצחק "The Binding of Isaac" (1570; *EYT* 60), and the quasi-secular epics, דוכוס הורנט *Duke Horant* (1382; *EYT* 9),ווידווילט *Vidvilt* (fifteenth to sixteenth century; *EYT* 80), Elia Levita's בבֿא דאנטונא *Bovo d'Antona* (1507; *EYT* 33), the anonymous פאריז אונ' וויענה *Pariz and Viene* (1594; *EYT* 74), and הער דיטרייך *Sir Ditraykh* (1597; *EYT* 78). As indicated, this entire genre in early Yiddish exists always as a product of mediated cultural negotiation between Ashkenazic and co-territorial Gentile culture. Essentially any substantive cultural issue present on one side of the cultural suture is potentially significant interpretively as it appears on the other side. Two such issues (primarily) in the sub-genre of quasi-secular epic have been chosen here not as illustrative of any imagined whole, but rather as indicators of modes of the practice of cultural translation: first, the issue of bridal quest or wiving—which functioned as one of the primary plot motivators of medieval and early modern Christian aristocratic epic—as it is translated into a Jewish culture in which essentially all conditions and practices of marriage arrangement were radically different; and second, the Ashkenazic representational strategies employed to deal with another of the primary plot motivators of co-temporal Christian epic: the demonization of Islam as the essential enemy of Christendom and thus also of the Christian epic hero.

The present study comprises seven discrete moments of analysis of early Yiddish literature as it emerges from the cultural interstices between Ashkenazic and

Christian society. Some might thus object that it does not constitute a full-scale, comprehensive survey or history of early Yiddish literature. It is not intended to do so. There is no pretense or aspiration in this volume toward "coverage," that is, I do not intend or imagine that my tactical interventions on Yiddish lyric in the Veneto, the politics and semiotics of the earliest Yiddish Purim plays, and issues of ethnic identity, gender, and pre-postcolonialism in early Yiddish quasi-secular epic somehow might constitute a history of Old Yiddish literature. The purpose is instead to extract and distill an essence from several significant moments of early Yiddish literature, in order to suggest some interpretive strategies for coming to terms with the suddenly intrusive phenomenon of quasi-secular Yiddish literature as a hybrid cultural formation in its particular place and time. But, one might object, the title of the project, *The Emergence of Early Yiddish Literature: Cultural Translation in Early Ashkenaz,* seems even broader and more ambitious. Perhaps so, but that broader topic will be explored by means of tactical interventions that in the end, one might hope, point toward a clearer conception of its scope. Where to begin? With something small, seemingly insignificant, and "supplemental," an afterthought, a brief scrap of a love song scrawled irreverently on the protective outer page of a religious text.

Notes

1. Jean Baumgarten, *Introduction à la littérature yiddish ancienne* (Paris: Cerf, 1993), ed. and trans. Jerold C. Frakes, *Introduction to Old Yiddish Literature* (Oxford: Oxford University Press, 2005), chap. 2; David B. Ruderman, *Early Modern Jewry: A New Cultural History* (Princeton, NJ: Princeton University Press, 2010).

2. As Edward Said has remarked, "One of the great advances in modern cultural theory is the realization, almost universally acknowledged, that cultures are hybrid and heterogeneous and . . . that cultures and civilizations are so interrelated and interdependent as to beggar any unitary or simply delineated description of their individuality"; Edward Said, *Orientalism* (New York: Random House, 1978), 347.

3. Max Erik, *Di geshikhte fun der yidisher literatur: fun di eltste tsaytn biz der haskole-tkufe, fertsnter-akhtsnter yorhundert, mit bilder un melodyes* (Warsaw: Kultur lige, 1928; repr., New York: Congress for Jewish Culture, 1979) and *Vegn altyidishn roman* (Warsaw: M. Rayz, 1926).

4. Israel Zinberg, *Altyidishe literatur fun di eltste tsaytn biz der haskole-tkufe* (Vilnius: Tomor, 1935), vol. 6 of *Di geshikhte fun der literatur bay yidn*, 9 vols. (Vilnius: Tomor, 1929–1937; repr., Buenos Aires: Alveltlekher yidisher kultur-kongres, 1964–1970); English trans.: *Old Yiddish Literature from Its Origins to the Haskalah Period*, vol. 7 of *A History of Jewish Literature*, trans. Bernard Martin (Cincinnati: Hebrew Union College Press, 1975).

5. Max Weinreich, *Shtaplen: fir etyudn tsu der yidisher shprakh-visnshaft un literatur-geshikhte* (Berlin: Vostok, 1923) and *Bilder fun der yidisher literatur-geshikhte* (Vilnius: Tomor, 1928).

6. Chone Shmeruk, ed., *Pariz un Viene: mahadura biqqortit be-ẓeruf mavo, he'arot ve-nispaḥim* (Jerusalem: Israel Academy of Sciences and Humanities, 1996); Shmeruk, *Sifrut yidish: perakim le-toldoteah* (Tel Aviv: Porter Institute for Poetics and Semiotics, 1978), revised

Yiddish translation: *Prokim fun der yidisher literatur-geshikhte* (Tel Aviv: I. L. Peretz, 1988); Shmeruk, ed., *Meḥazot mikrayim be-yidish (1697–1750)* (Jerusalem: Israel Academy of Sciences and Humanities, 1979); Erika Timm, "'Beria und Simra': Eine jiddische Erzählung des 16. Jahrhunderts," *Literaturwissenschaftliches Jahrbuch*, n.s., 14 (1973): 1–94; Timm, "Wie Elia Levita sein *Bovobuch* für den Druck überarbeitete: Ein Kapitel aus der italo-jiddischen Literatur der Renaissancezeit," *Germanisch-romanische Monatsschrift* 41 (1991): 61–81; Timm, *Historische jiddische Semantik* (Tübingen: Niemeyer, 2005); Timm and Gustav Adolf Beckmann, eds., *Paris un Wiene: Ein jiddischer Stanzenroman des 16. Jahrhunderts von (oder aus dem Umkreis von) Elia Levita* (Tübingen: Niemeyer, 1996); Chava Turniansky, "Pariz un Viene—mi-sifrut yidish be-italyah shel ha-meah ha-16," *Chulyot* 4 (1997): 29–37; Turniansky and Erika Timm, eds., *Yiddish in Italia: Manoscritti e libri a stampa dei secoli XV–XVII / Manuscripts and Printed Books from the 15th to the 17th Century / Yidish in Italya* (Milan: Associazione Italiana Amici dell'Università di Gerusalemme, 2003); Baumgarten, *Introduction.*

7. Armin Schulz, *Die Zeichen des Körpers und der Liebe: "Paris und Vienna" in der jiddischen Fassung des Elia Levita* (Hamburg: Kovac, 2000); Jeremy Dauber, *In the Demon's Bedroom: Yiddish Literature and the Early Modern* (New Haven, CT: Yale University Press, 2010).

8. J. R. R. Tolkien, "*Beowulf*: The Monsters and the Critics," *Proceedings of the British Academy* 22 (1936): 245–295; often reprinted, including in *An Anthology of Beowulf Criticism*, ed. Lewis E. Nicholson (Notre Dame: University of Notre Dame Press, 1963), 51–103, here 52.

9. Tomás Ó Cathasaigh, "Early Irish Narrative Literature," in *Progress in Medieval Irish Studies*, ed. Kim McCone and Katherine Simms (Maynooth: National University of Ireland, 1996), 55.

10. See Dov-Ber Kerler, *The Origins of Modern Literary Yiddish* (Oxford: Oxford University Press, 1999).

11. Robert Bonfil remarks on one specific situation: "The history of the Jews of Italy in the Renaissance is the history of the encounter between a minority determined to perpetuate its own Otherness and a majority equally bent on its assimilation"; *Jewish Life in Renaissance Italy*, trans. Anthony Oldcorn (Berkeley: University of California Press, 1991), 3.

12. Gilles Deleuze and Félix Guattari, *Kafka: Pour une littérature mineure* (Paris: Éditions de Minuit, 1975), 29–50. Deleuze and Guattari inadvertently seem almost to have founded a theoretical school that in recent decades has swept through the academy, even recently reaching the field of Yiddish studies, in the insightful study by Marc Caplan, *How Strange the Change: Language, Temporality, and Narrative Form in Peripheral Modernisms* (Stanford, CA: Stanford University Press, 2011). On the early stages of the "minor literature" phenomenon, see, for instance, Brian Massumi, *A User's Guide to Capitalism and Schizophrenia: Deviations from Deleuze and Guattari* (Cambridge, MA: MIT Press, 1992).

13. Deleuze and Guattari, *Kafka*, 33.

14. In quite a different context, Shlomo Berger concurs that Yiddish cannot function as a minor literature in the sense of Deleuze and Guattari; see Shlomo Berger, "Functioning within a Diasporic Third Space: The Case of Early Modern Yiddish," *Jewish Studies Quarterly* 15 (2008): 74.

15. On the concept of "post-vernacular Yiddish," see Jeffrey Shandler, *Adventures in Yiddishland: Postvernacular Language and Culture* (Berkeley: University of California Press, 2006).

16. The phrase "lacrymose conception" is a coinage of Salo Wittmayer Baron; see his *A Social and Religious History of the Jews*, 18 vols., 2nd ed. (New York: Columbia University Press, 1993).

17. Well illustrated in Middle Yiddish literature, as well: Joseph ben Eleazar Lipman Ashkenazi, קינה על גזירות הקהילות דק"ק אקרייני *Lamentation on the Ukrainian Massacre* (1648), *EYT* 99; Elḥanan ben Abraham Hellen, [מגילת ווינץ] דברי השירה הזאת *The Song of Vints Hans* [*Megilas*

Vints] (1648), *EYT* 100; the שווידש ליד *The Swedish Siege of Prague* (1649), *EYT* 101; the book of Glikl bat Leyb Pinkerle [Glückel von Hameln] (1691–1719), an excerpt in *EYT* 131.

18. The one interesting exception might in this respect be the Hebrew adaptation of the ancient narrative traditions of Alexander the Great, although the particular version adapted into Hebrew in the fourteenth century by Immanuel ben Jacob Bonfils was the later, *medieval* prose summary in Leo Presbyter's *Historia de proeliis*: Immanuel ben Jacob Bonfils, ספר תולדות אלסנדרוס המקדוני *The Book of the Gests of Alexander of Macedon*, ed. Israel J. Kazis (Cambridge, MA: Mediaeval Academy of America, 1962); Wout Jac. Van Bekkum, ed., *A Hebrew Alexander Romance According to Ms Héb. 671.5 Paris, Bibliotheque Nationale* (Leiden: Brill, 1994); *A Hebrew Alexander Romance according to MS London, Jews' College no. 145*, ed. and trans. Wout Jac. van Bekkum (Leuven: Peeters, 1992). One should also note that Alexander had entered the Jewish narrative tradition early on and was thereafter not in the least alien to it.

19. In this sense the two traditions mirror—in a severely restricted and focused sense—the divided functionality of Hebrew-Aramaic and Yiddish in late medieval and early modern Ashkenazic culture: Hebrew-Aramaic was the language of liturgy and study and Yiddish was not (with some important exceptions), while Yiddish was the language of *belles-lettres* and Hebrew-Aramaic was not (with some important exceptions).

20. For a collection and translation of the relevant early texts (with brief commentary), see Jerold C. Frakes, ed., *The Cultural Study of Yiddish in Early Modern Europe* (New York: Palgrave, 2007); based on my translations of the original texts, Aya Elyada provides further commentary: *A Goy Who Speaks Yiddish: Christians and the Jewish Language in Early Modern Germany* (Stanford, CA: Stanford University Press, 2012).

21. Robert Bonfil makes essentially the same general point about Hebrew literature during the period: "This entire literary production was essentially conceived and experienced as the creation of Jewish culture for Jews. In other words, the affinity between Jewish and non-Jewish literary production manifested itself at the center, not at the edges, of the Jewish cultural space" (*Jewish Life*, 151).

22. The stimulus for Turner's theorization was Arnold van Gennep, *Les rites de passage* (Paris: É. Nourry, 1909); English trans.: *The Rites of Passage*, trans. Monika B. Vizedon and Gabrielle L. Caffee (Chicago: University of Chicago Press, 1960), 10–24, 65–68. Turner's subsequent work over the course of several decades is documented in a wealth of publications; see below, chapter 6 on liminality.

23. Homi K. Bhabha, *The Location of Culture* (London: Routledge, 1994), 1–2; see also Homi K. Bhabha, "Frontlines/ Borderposts," in *Displacements: Cultural Identities in Questions*, ed. Angelika Bammer (Bloomington: University of Indiana Press, 1994), 271.

24. Bhabha, *Location*, 1.

25. One of the most influential early explorations of this cluster of issues in contemporary cultural studies was Gayatri Spivak's "Can the Subaltern Speak?" in *Marxism and the Interpretation of Culture*, ed. Cary Nelson and Lawrence Grossberg (Urbana: University of Illinois Press, 1988), 271–313.

26. David N. Myers, introduction to *Acculturation and Its Discontents: The Italian Jewish Experience between Exclusion and Inclusion*, ed. David N. Myers et al. (Toronto: University of Toronto Press, 2008), 5.

27. In this respect—albeit without the subversive political implications—the insistent cultural autonomy of historical Ashkenaz resembles the focus of the conference organized by Abdul R. JanMohamed and David Lloyd, i.e., "as a means of marginalizing the center—of permitting a theoretical and potentially practical work among minorities that did not require passage through hegemonic culture, a passage that is always ultimately assimilative and tends to

restore the canonical forms of majority domination"; see Abdul R. JanMohamed and David Lloyd, eds., *The Nature and Context of Minority Discourse* (Oxford: Oxford University Press, 1990), ix.

28. The model has been especially widespread in the field of anthropology; for an early formulation see Sherry B. Ortner, "Theory in Anthropology since the Sixties," *Comparative Studies in Society and History* 26 (1984): 126–166, and the reappraisal by Arjun Appaduraia, "Theory in Anthropology: Center and Periphery," *Comparative Studies in Society and History* 28 (1986): 356–374. In economics, see Paul Krugman, *The Self-Organizing Economy* (Oxford: Blackwell, 1996).

29. Ivan G. Marcus, *The Jewish Life Cycle: Rites of Passage from Biblical to Modern Times* (Seattle: University of Washington Press, 2004), 5–6; the quotation is the comment by Dean Phillip Bell, *Jews in the Early Modern World* (Lanham, MD: Rowman and Littlefield, 2008), 196. David Myers has reminded scholars working on this issue of the extreme implications of the term "*acculturation*," which " was most definitively introduced into the American sociological lexicon . . . to describe a form of absorption of mainstream cultural norms by a minority group"; Myers, *Acculturation*, 7; Myers here cites Milton Gordon, *Assimilation in American Life: The Role of Race, Religion, and National Origins* (New York: Oxford University Press, 1964).

30. Arthur M. Lesley, "Jewish Adaptations of Humanist Concepts in Fifteenth- and Sixteenth-Century Italy," in David B. Ruderman, ed., *Essential Papers* on Jewish Culture in Renaissance and Baroque Italy (New York: New York University Press, 1992), 46.

31. Bell, *Jews in the Early Modern World*, 198.

32. Ruderman, *Early Modern Jewry*, 9.

33. Ruderman, *Early Modern Jewry*, 41.

34. Ruderman, *Early Modern Jewry*, 43.

35. See especially Bonfil, *Jewish Life*, 1–15; Cecil Roth, *The Jews in the Renaissance* (Philadelphia: Jewish Publication Society, 1959); see also the attempt to contextualize Bonfil's position by David N. Myers, *Acculturation*, 5–6.

36. Bonfil, *Jewish Life*, 102.

37. Bonfil, *Jewish Life*, 118–119. The rapprochement school of scholarship of Roth and Heinrich Graetz had ample precedent, however, even among the Christian contemporaries of the early modern Jews, who imagined a stark dichotomy between Jews and the Renaissance and thus imagined any Jew who somehow participated in the Gentile cultural practices of the Renaissance as ripe for conversion (*Jewish Life*, 167–168). In case after case, however, such Christian expectations were disappointed (e.g., Azariah de' Rossi, Elia Levita, Sarra Copia Sulam).

38. Bonfil, *Jewish Life*, 146–148. One should acknowledge, however, that since the focus of the censor's inventory was of course on specifically Jewish books, the listing of non-Jewish (Italian and other) books could best be described as less than comprehensive.

39. Bonfil, *Jewish Life*, 148.

40. Shifrah Baruchson, *Sefarim ṿe-ḳor'im: tarbut ha-ḳeri'ah shel yehude iṭalyah be-shilhe ha-renesans* (Ramat Gan: Bar-Ilan University Press, 1993), 158; the section on belles lettres comprises 155–160. Chone Shmeruk reckons the number of Yiddish titles printed in Italy between 1545 and 1609 as thirty-three; in "Yiddish Printing in Italy," in Turniansky and Timm, *Yiddish in Italia*, 171. That listing includes ninety-nine individual items among Yiddish manuscripts and printed books from Italy of this period (seventeen of which are no longer extant). Moreover, as other library inventories (albeit mostly of Sephardim) cited by Bell indicate, there were many Jews of the period in northern Italy whose book collections included a far larger percentage of non-Hebrew books: among the various Finzi family libraries, one included 226 Hebrew manuscripts, of which 18 were prayer books, 21 had philosophical content, and 31 were medical;

other Finzi collections included "large numbers of Italian literature, such as Petrarch" as well as classical literature, such as Ovid's *Metamorphoses.* In Amsterdam, Isaac Aboab da Fonseca had 373 Hebrew books and 179 books in languages other than Hebrew, including Latin and Greek (Bell, *Jews in the Early Modern World,* 197).

41. Hava Tirosh-Rothschild, *Between Worlds: The Life and Thought of Rabbi David ben Judah Messer Leon* (Albany: State University of New York Press, 1991), 1–2.

42. Tirosh-Rothschild, *Between Worlds,* 2.

43. Tirosh-Rothschild, *Between Worlds,* 3–4.

44. Robert Bonfil, "Bittuyim le-yihud ʿam Israel be-Italia be-tekufat ha-renesans," *Sinai* 76 (1975): 36–46; *Bonfil, Jewish Life*; *Bonfil,* "How Golden Was the Age of the Renaissance in Jewish Historiography?" *History and Theory: Studies in the Philosophy of History; Essays in Jewish Historiography,* ed. Ada Albert-Rapaport, *Beiheft* 27 (1988): 78–102, repr. in Ruderman, *Essential Papers,* 219–251; *Bonfil,* "The Historian's Perception of the Jews in the Italian Renaissance: Toward a Reappraisal," *Revue des Études Juives* 143 (1984): 59–82; Tirosh-Rothschild, *Between Worlds;* Tirosh-Rothschild, "In Defense of Jewish Humanism," *Jewish History* 3, no. 2 (1988), 32–57; Tirosh-Rothschild, "Jewish Culture in Renaissance Italy: A Metholodological Survey," *Italia, Studi e ricerche sulla storia, la cultura e la letteratura degli ebrei d'Italia* 9 (1990); 63–96; Arthur M. Lesley, "Hebrew Humanism in Italy: The Case of Biography," *Prooftexts* 2 (1982): 163–177; Lesley, "Jewish Adaptations," 45–62.

45. It often seems that the same assumption is held by non-Yiddishist scholars of Jewish studies and even by Yiddishists who work solely in nineteenth- and twentieth-century Yiddish culture.

46. Shmeruk, *Sifrut yidish,* 22–23; Shmeruk, *Prokim,* 28–29; David Neal Miller, "Transgressing the Bounds: On the Origins of Yiddish Literature," in *Origins of the Yiddish Language,* ed. Dovid Katz, Winter Studies in Yiddish 1 (Oxford: Pergamon, 1987), 101. Miller's conception of "polysystem" is rooted in the term's use in Yiddish studies and is only tangentially related to the sense developed by Itamar Even-Zohar in a series of articles in the 1970s and then elaborated further in the 1990s, especially *Polysystem Studies,* a special issue of *Poetics Today* 11 (1990): 1–268; see the thorough discussion of Evan-Zohar's conception by Philippe Codde, "Polysystem Revisited: A New Comparative Introduction," *Poetics Today* 24 (2003): 91–126. Shlomo Berger attempts to incorporate early Yiddish into the conception of Even-Zohar's polysystem: Shlomo Berger [translated by Gregor Pelger], "Jiddisch und die Formierung der aschkenasischen Diaspora," *Aschkenas* 18–19 (2008–2009): 519.

47. One should also note that between the sixteenth and nineteenth centuries, epic as the genre of long narrative of course developed into its more modern successor: the novel.

48. See Anthony Appiah, "Strictures on Structures: The Prospects for a Structuralist Poetics of African Fiction," in *Black Literature and Literary Theory,* ed. H. L. Gates, Jr. (New York: Methuen, 1984), 145–146.

49. The sense of capitalized "Literature" derives from Terry Eagleton's more than slightly ironic sense; see Terry Eagleton, "What Is Literature?" in *Literary Theory: An Introduction,* 2nd ed. (Minneapolis: University of Minnesota Press, 1996), 1–14.

50. See Bonfil: "The cultural identity of the Christians could be constructed along the lines of gradual detachment from the field of religion in the proper sense of the word, without necessarily endangering their Christian identity. Things were quite different in the case of the Jews. Jewish Otherness was essentially a matter of religious belief, so that any cultural deviation from a religiously based culture would have immediately put their Jewish identity in crisis. To have allowed secular cultural tendencies to develop toward an ever increasing detachment from religion would have meant anticipating problems that have become typical

of the modern period: how a nonbeliever is supposed to set about defining his/her Jewish identity, or the problem of the believer's greater or lesser cultural alienation. The result would have been a crisis of Jewish identity similar to that prevailing in the modern era. This did not occur" (*Jewish Life*, 157).

51. Baumgarten, *Introduction*, 26.

52. Baumgarten, *Introduction*, 26–28.

53. Baumgarten, *Introduction*, 29.

54. Baumgarten, *Introduction*, 31–32.

55. Baumgarten, *Introduction*, 33.

56. Baumgarten, *Introduction*, 36.

57. Dauber, *Demon's Bedroom*, 6.

58. See Gayatri Chakravorty Spivak, "Translator's Preface," in Jacques Derrida, *Of Grammatology* (Baltimore: Johns Hopkins University Press, 1967), xiv–xvii.

59. Cf. also Bonfil: "Once Jewishness had been identified with the sacred space, the coherence of that space with every aspect of cultural expression was a logical consequence. It was somewhat as if the Jew had declared, *Nihil humanum alienum a me puto* ('I think nothing human alien to me')—but from inside the synagogue! Whereas the Christians marched on toward modernity *separating* secular thought from the strictly religious sphere, the Jews continued to follow the opposite course: that of an ever closer link between secularization and religious expression" (*Jewish Life*, 159).

60. Chone Shmeruk has claimed that there is in fact no genre of secular epic *in Yiddish*, since he views the texts conventionally so identified simply as German epics that have been *transcribed*, not translated into Yiddish and adapted for an Ashkenazic audience; see "Tsi ken der kembridzsher manuskript shtitsn di shpilman-teorye in der yidisher literatur?" *Di goldene keyt* 100 (1979): 251–271. The mode and extent of adaptation in these texts have, however, prevented his view from finding favor with scholars; see my *The Politics of Interpretation: Alterity and Ideology in Old Yiddish Studies* (Albany: State University of New York Press, 1989).

61. Wulf-Otto Dreeßen, "Midraschepik und Bibelepik: Biblische Stoffe in der volkssprachlichen Literatur der Juden und Christen des Mittelalters im deutschen Sprachgebiet," *Zeitschrift für deutsche Philologie* 100 [Sonderheft] (1981): 78–97.

62. Christian biblical narrative is generally also imbued with Christological imagery and interpretive additions, which, naturally, are absent from Jewish midrashic narrative.

63. In rather a different context, David Ruderman also remarks on the cultural decline of the late eighteenth century: "From the perspective of the dynamic intellectual universe of the sixteenth and seventeenth centuries, the eighteenth century in Jewish thought seems rather unspectacular in the novelty of its formulations and in the intensity of its contacts with the outside world" (*Early Modern Jewry*, 195).

64. Cf. Robert Bonfil's pertinent comment: "It should be stressed at this point that for the Jews the only 'true' knowledge was the knowledge linked to their traditional culture. Other cultural fields were considered at best a sort of supplementary superstructure. This is a fact of major importance which must be borne in mind when approaching the question of Jewish participation in Renaissance culture" (*Jewish Life*, 139–140).

65. On the term "*khidushim*-poem," see Shmeruk, *Prokim*, 93 n. 59.

66. As will be detailed in chapter 4, there are also Purim plays on other biblical figures, such as King David.

67. See my *Early Yiddish Epic* (Syracuse: Syracuse University Press, 2014), xvii–xxii.

Chapter Two

"Whither Am I to Go?"

Old Yiddish Love Song in a European Context

Judah ben Samuel of Regensburg (1140–1217), also called Judah he-Ḥasid (Judah the Pious), the founder of the mystical movement of the Chassidei Ashkenaz, condemned the binding of Hebrew books with parchment pages on which vernacular romances had been written, and lest one imagine that he was thinking of a hypothetical case, he noted that a pious man had ripped the cover off a Pentateuch on which a vernacular romance concerning knights and tournaments had been copied.[1] Such outer parchment coverings of manuscripts did present a tempting open space for scribes to write various kinds of texts that generally had nothing to do with the primary text(s) of the book. Thus, on the outer leaf of a fourteenth-century manuscript of Rashi's commentaries on the Prophets and Hagiographa (*ketuvim*), now in the Biblioteca Ambrosiana in Milan, one finds some indiscriminate scribbling, a number of pen trials, a few brief Hebrew notes, and *not* a vernacular romance, such as Judah he-Ḥasid loathed, but a vernacular love song: a brief poetic text in Yiddish.[2] Several earlier scholars have printed the text, although it seems that among them only Abraham Berliner, Ber Borochov, and Karl Bernheimer (in that chronological order) actually saw the manuscript itself. Moyshe (Morris) Basin based his printing of the text on Borochov's edition; Yisroel Tsinberg in turn based his text on Basin's version of Borochov; Max Erik did not identify his source, but it seems likely that he, too, used Borochov's reading.[3]

Berliner includes only a quasi-German translation in his main text, "Wo soll ich hin, wo soll ich her? Wo soll ich mich hinkehren? Ich bin einzünt, mein Herz, das brennt, ich konn's nit losweren, da späht die Herz allerliebst mein, die ich hab auf dieser Erden," relegating the original Hebrew-alphabet text to a footnote (according to his transcription): וואו זאל איך הין ווא זאל איך הער וואו זאל איך מיך הין קירין

איך בין איין צינט מיין הערץ דאש ברענט איך קוינש ניט לאס ווערען דא שפיט דיא הערץ אליר ליבשט מיין דיא איך האב אויף דיזער ערדן.[4] In his Latin-language catalog of the Hebrew-alphabet texts of the Ambrosiana, Bernheimer designates this text "nota germanica lingua sed hebraicis litteris," "a note in the German language but in Hebrew letters," and thus after his rendering of the Hebrew-alphabet text, he also offers a quasi-German version: "Wo soll ich hin wo soll ich her wo soll ich mich hinkehren, ich bins ein Sünd' mein Herz das brennt, ich kunn's nit heilig wahren, da steht die (!) Herz aller liebst mein die ich hab auf dieser Erden."[5]

While such a constructed editorial thicket is not exceptional in medieval studies, this one does obscure what this text actually is, which ought to be stated plainly and directly: the oldest extant love song in the Yiddish language. It is important to insist on the word "extant," because, as in every language and culture, there were certainly love songs in existence in Yiddish before any given one of them—such as this one—was written down, even if, as noted earlier, scrawled irreverently on the outer page of a Rashi commentary. As far as the actual age of the song, one might only speculate. Even the age of the text itself—that is, the inscription on this manuscript—is not easy to determine. The date of the Rashi text of the manuscript—fourteenth century—might seem to offer a *terminus post quem,* since logically the Yiddish song could not have been written on this book before the book existed. But, on the other hand, it was certainly sung before it was written down and could well have been "composed" long before that moment.[6] Since, unlike with many scribal traditions (e.g., of Latin book hands and even other European vernacular scribal traditions), no comprehensively effective mode of dating Hebrew-alphabet scribal hands of the broad late medieval and early modern period has been devised, the dating of the inscription cannot be aided by such considerations. One seems then to be left only with the evidence of the language and orthography as hints at the age of the text. Here, too, specification is unfortunately not possible. One might simply opine that the very earliest period of Yiddish orthography—as witnessed in the glosses on Torah and Talmud by Rashi himself (d. 1105) and the *Worms Maḥzor* couplet (1272–1273)—might be ruled out, while the period of the anthology of Yiddish poetry from the Cairo genizah (ca. 1382)[7] might indeed stand near the beginning of the period in which the song might possibly have been inscribed. Let the careful reader note the succession of hesitant quasi-subjunctives of the previous sentence.

Before we proceed, it would be useful to provide an edition of the poem, which is unfortunately also not so simple: the ink of the text is now so faded that it is quite invisible in conventional photography, and the Biblioteca Ambrosiana was (in 2001) unable to supply ultraviolet photographs. Thus the manuscript was examined on-site at the Ambrosiana and the edition based on that examination. Some letters are more legible with incandescent, some with ultraviolet light.[8]

וואו זאל איך הין וואו זאל[9] איך הער
וואו זאל איך / מיכש הין קירן[10]:
איך[11] בינש איין צינט
מיין הערץ / דאש ברענט·
איך קוינש[12] ניט פֿרֵילך ווערן:
דא שפֿט[13] דיא הערץ אליר ליבשט מיין·
דיא איך האב אויף דיזר[14] עֵרדן[15]

While the text presents numerous philological difficulties—in decipherment, linguistic interpretation, and cultural affiliation—most can be resolved. With a couple of exceptions to be discussed below, I am reasonably confident in the accuracy of my reading of the text, especially when that reading differs from those of earlier editors. Technical as the initial notes here are, preliminary to the more interpretive discussion that follows, they may indicate the range of considerations in coming to an interpretation of the text.

The word following ניט in line 5 requires some attention. There are three interpretive possibilities. If the word is read as פֿר ולך, with the third letter construed as a consonant, as often in Old and Middle Yiddish, then one might understand the word as an interjection "cursed" and thus interpret the line as "I cannot, dammit, fend it off!" This seems to me the least likely possibility. The second possibility, Bernheimer's reading as היילך, is only slightly more likely: under incandescent light, the first letter appears to my eye a פ written with a single stroke (as modern cursive) with a faint superscripted horizontal line (i.e., *raphe*); but it may be that the single stroke of the letter is ever so slightly broken at the bottom left, which makes possible the construal of the continuation of that line as a smaller reverse *c* inside the larger reverse *C*, in which case it resembles the form of the "double reverse *C*" ה as that letter in fact appears elsewhere in this short text; it could nonetheless just as easily be a פ in the form of a reverse *C* with a short horizontal stroke (-) bisecting the open space, as is also common in scribal hands of this general period.[16] However, the second letter of the word, construed by Bernheimer as י, seems too long for a *yud* (although there are in fact other examples of *yud* in this text that are almost as long), and thus much more likely a *resh*. If the first letter were ה and the second י, then Bernheimer's reading of היילך would be possible, and the sense would then be "whole/healthy." Thus the only real problem with this word is in the first two letters, for the last three are (reasonably) clear: -ילך. In one view, those initial letters are פֿרֵ, while in the other they are הֵי. Thus in the former case, "happy"; in the latter, "whole/healthy." In either case, the resulting sense fits the context.

The only other serious problem arises in line 6, in which the first two words—דא שפֿט—make for interpretive difficulties. The all-but-invisible text is at precisely this point even less visibly distinct than elsewhere. Among the interpretations of the second word by previous scholars, Bernheimer's סתיט is simply a misreading. Berliner's *späht* / שפיט "peek/peer/peep" is remotely possible in terms of the manuscript reading, but at the same time seems irrelevant to both the specific context of the line and the larger cultural context of this mode of love poetry. The reading by Erik שפייט and Tsinberg שפָייט are paleographically far less likely, while their glossing of that reading as שפירט "feel/perceive,"[17] although by no means irrelevant, nonetheless seems less immediately pertinent to the sensibility of the late Renaissance courtly love context of the dominant culture that surrounds the Yiddish poem and provides its immediate secular interpretive context. It would also seem—strangely—that both Erik and Tsinberg construe the second *yud* of their reading in fact as a *resh* if they are to turn שפייט into שפירט.

If my reading of the manuscript as שפֿט is accurate (which, under ultraviolet light, does seem the most likely reading), however, then there seem several interpretive possibilities. First, the word might represent a finite verbal form of the modern Yiddish reflex שפעטן/שפּאָט "mock" (which would require one to discount the *raphe*) or a finite verbal form of the modern Yiddish reflex שאַפֿן "create/cause," either of which is orthographically possible, based on the manuscript form, and either of which would yield a relevant interpretation in context: "the most darling beloved that I have on earth *mocks / is the cause of* that (דאש) [i.e., my pain]" or "the most darling beloved that I have on earth then/there [דא] *mocks / is the cause* [implied: of what has just been expressed, i.e., my pain]." While the convention of courtly love poetry that styles the beloved as cruel in her rejection of the lover's attentions would be well represented here by the sense of "mock," the direct sense of the beloved's causality of the lover's pain may be more compelling.

Further problems arise, as the insertion of דא/דאש in the two interpretations offered in the previous paragraph indicate. The manuscript reads דא שפֿט, which one *might* construe as a degeminating spelling of דאש שפֿט—by means of which one of two like consonants across a word boundary may be deleted in (non-normative) speech.[18] Admittedly, however, *orthographic* degemination, that is, actually representing that pronunciation in writing, would be quite unusual. It would be a peculiar and speculative interpretation at best, but to my mind an improvement on the no less speculative interpretations of my predecessors: "the most darling beloved whom I have on this earth *causes* that." In the end, however, it seems most plausible to construe the verb שפֿן in the sense "command/order," commonly found in contemporaneous German (cf. Lexer and Grimm) and thus *potentially* also relevant in Old Yiddish, which would then eliminate the speculative degemination.[19]

The attentive reader will have noted that several types of "evidence" enable my reading: paleographical (i.e., a minute examination of what letters are on the page), linguistic (i.e., what grammatical and lexical forms might be represented by the paleographical evidence), semantic (i.e., what those forms might mean in Old Yiddish), and—generally least compelling—cultural (i.e., determining what the context of this mode of poetry in this particular time and place might make "relevant"). While I am convinced of the paleographical, linguistic, and cultural plausibility and relevance of my interpretation, I do not by any means imagine it as definitive. In any case, I would suggest the following tentative translation of the poem:

Whither am I to go?
Whence am I to come?
Where am I to turn?
I am inflamed.
My heart is ablaze.
I can find no peace.
Here rules the most darling beloved
Whom I have on this earth.

Such is then the text itself. Extracted as it has been here thus far from its cultural and historical context, it may seem of slight interest and value, conventional and banal. But context there is and must be, and in outlining some recoverable aspects of that context in the pages here to follow, it will become clear how these few poetic lines open onto a world of cultural contact and interchange, indeed of cultural translation. It might first be useful to consider what little can be determined concerning the history of the actual book on whose outer cover the poem is written: this commentary on the Prophets and Hagiography was of course written during Rashi's lifetime (d. 1105), and this particular copy of that text can be dated to the fourteenth century and was at one time in the library of Pietro Bembo (1470–1547), the Venetian-born friend of Ariosto (poet of the Renaissance romance-epic *Orlando furioso*) and himself author of a love dialogue, *Gli Asolani* (1505), a treatise on the composition of poetry in the vernacular, the *Prose della volgar lingua* (1525), and a history of Venice (*Historia Veneta*, 1551). Bembo studied at the university in Padua, was in Rome as Leo X's secretary (1513–1521), left Rome for the north in 1521 after Leo X's death, and was again in Venice 1529–1539. One might here also note that in this trajectory, Bembo was often in the same city at the same time as the famed Jewish grammarian, lexicographer, and poet Elia Levita, and, based on their mutual acquaintances and intellectual interests, they may well have met. Bembo was also notoriously the lover of the infamous Lucrezia Borgia (daughter of Pope Alexander VI and wife of Bembo's patron and employer, Alfonso d'Este), state-appointed historiographer of Venice, librarian of Cardinal Bessarion's collection at St. Mark's, and eventually cardinal (1539).

Pietro Bembo's father, Bernardo (1433–1519), had earlier amassed an impressive library in the course of his long life,[20] while Pietro, in the course of his likewise long life, assembled a still more extensive collection, indeed one of the largest libraries of the Humanistic period, spanning an astonishing range of fields of artistic, literary, and scholarly endeavor. In 1527, some years after his father's death, Pietro had the combined collection of father and son transferred to Padua from Ca' Bembo, one of the family palaces in Venice (on the Grand Canal near the Rialto). Immediately after Pietro's death in 1547, his illegitimate son Torquato began selling his father's library (in order to finance his own artistic collecting). While the library was dispersed over the course of decades to a variety of buyers, it was through one them, Giovanni Vincenzio Pinelli, that a cache of books was eventually bought by Cardinal Federico Borromeo in the early seventeenth century, which then passed into the collection of the Biblioteca Ambrosiana, which Borromeo himself founded. It is most likely that it was by this route that the Rashi manuscript came to Milan and the Ambrosiana (thus not suffering the fate of some of Borromeo's collection, which en route to Milan was captured by Turkish pirates and thrown overboard into the Bay of Naples).[21]

But that route of transfer of this particular volume can of course only be speculative, albeit based on some plausible circumstantial evidence. The biography of this book *before* it passed from the Bembo family to the Ambrosiana—that is, the period perhaps most pertinent to anyone interested, for instance, in the Yiddish poem—is probably irrecoverable. It does not seem possible to determine specifically when this particular book entered the Bembo collection—whether of Bernardo or Pietro—since both Bembi were lifelong collectors, and Pietro was already an avid bibliophile even in his youth. But one might speculate that it would have likely been no earlier than circa 1450, had Bernardo acquired it, or no earlier than circa 1490, had Pietro acquired it. Those dates would be important in attempting to narrow the time frame of the inscription of the Yiddish song, since it would seem improbable that anyone (i.e., a Yiddish-literate Jew) capable of so casually inscribing that text on the outer leaf of a holy text would have had both access to the book *after* it had entered the Bembo library (since it was from then on in the possession of Christians and/or Christian institutions) and the authority or audacity to "deface" such a Christian-owned book with a vernacular love song. Thus one might narrow the window for the Bembo acquisition of the book to the years circa 1450–1547 (or 1490–1547 if the book were acquired by Pietro), suggesting a possible *terminus ante quem* of 1547. While the probable north Italian provenance of the Rashi manuscript itself and the likewise probable Italian venue of the acquisition of the manuscript by one of the Bembi do not necessarily identify the locale where the poem was inscribed, they do indicate where the codex itself most likely was at its moment of origin and at its moment of withdrawal from the further probability of the poem's inscription. If nothing else, then, these considerations might suggest that the poem was inscribed on the outer cover of the manuscript no later than the mid-sixteenth century, probably in Italy.[22]

The Yiddish poem bears eloquent witness to a Petrarchan erotic sensibility characteristic of that time and place, which must be here explored more extensively, but one must first acknowledge—and not in merely perfunctory manner—that by the period in question literary-erotic passion had already had long precedent in Hebrew poetry, dating back even to the Psalms and the Song of Songs. Psalm 38:7–11 (RSV 38:6–10), for instance, engages similar themes and imagery:

נַעֲוֵיתִי שַׁחֹתִי עַד-מְאֹד; כָּל-הַיּוֹם, קֹדֵר הִלָּכְתִּי.
כִּי-כְסָלַי, מָלְאוּ נִקְלֶה; וְאֵין מְתֹם, בִּבְשָׂרִי.
נְפוּגוֹתִי וְנִדְכֵּיתִי עַד-מְאֹד; שָׁאַגְתִּי, מִנַּהֲמַת לִבִּי.
אֲדֹנָי, נֶגְדְּךָ כָל-תַּאֲוָתִי; וְאַנְחָתִי, מִמְּךָ לֹא-נִסְתָּרָה.
לִבִּי סְחַרְחַר, עֲזָבַנִי כֹחִי; וְאוֹר-עֵינַי גַּם-הֵם, אֵין אִתִּי.

> I am utterly bowed down and prostrate; all the day I go about mourning. For my loins are filled with burning, and there is no soundness in my flesh. I am utterly spent and crushed; I groan because of the tumult of my heart. Lord, all my longing is known to thee, my sighing is not hidden from thee. My heart throbs, my strength fails me; and the light of my eyes—it also has gone from me. (RSV)

The opening of the Yiddish poem also echoes some ideas of the opening verse of canticle 6 of the Song of Songs (albeit with a change of the persona's perspective): אָנָה הָלַךְ דּוֹדֵךְ, הַיָּפָה בַּנָּשִׁים; אָנָה פָּנָה דוֹדֵךְ, וּנְבַקְשֶׁנּוּ עִמָּךְ "Whither has your beloved gone, O fairest among women? Whither has your beloved turned, that we may seek him with you?" (RSV).

There are likewise echoes in Hebrew literature that are not so distant in time and space—in the erotic poetry of Andaluz and indeed Renaissance Italy—especially in displaying the general poetic and erotic sensibility and hints of the same specific phraseology, especially in sixteenth-century Hebrew verse, such as the sonnet קוֹלֵךְ צְבִיָּא by David Onkinerah, an Istanbul native, which in its first tercet displays images similar to those of the Yiddish song, while the poem יְשֵׁנָא אַתְּ by Joseph Tsarfati, a native of Rome who experienced the sack of Rome in 1527 (as did Elia Levita), includes the image of the flame of the lover's desire (בְּתוֹךְ אִשֵּׁךְ, line 8).[23] Nonetheless, as was the case in the broad range of European erotic lyric of the period, and as Raymond Scheindlin points out specifically concerning Hebrew lyric, "Hebrew love poetry is conventional in content and stylized in form. Its themes and rhetorical figures are drawn from the common fund of literary material that the Jewish literati first acquired through their education in Arabic poetry, then used and recycled."[24]

Borochov suggests an analogue outside the Jewish tradition but in some senses perhaps even more proximate to the Yiddish text: an Italian poem by Lucrezia Borgia, which returns the focus again to Pietro Bembo, who was her lover and owned the manuscript on which the Yiddish poem is written.[25] While one might momentarily imagine that the interpretive circle had therewith grown tighter, unfortunately Borochov does not identify what specific poem he has in mind, nor have I been able to identify any such poem. The task is made more difficult by the fact that while Lucrezia Borgia is known to have composed some poems, they have not been identified, collected, and edited. In her letter of 25 May 1503 to Pietro Bembo, however, she copied a poem by the Spanish poet Lope de Estuñiga, in which there are at best distant echoes of the Yiddish song:

> Yo pienso si me muriese
> y con mis males finase
> desear,
> tan grande amor fenesciese
> que todo el mundo quedase
> sin amar.
> Mas esto considerando,
> mi tarde morir es luego
> tanto bueno,
> que devo razon usando
> gloria sentir en el fuego
> donde peno.

> I think, if I were to die, and in my misery ceased to desire, such a great love would end and leave the whole world without love. Considering this more deeply, then to delay death is better, for, following reason, I am obliged to feel bliss in the fire where I suffer.[26]

Borochov's suggestion thus remains tantalizing, but quizzical. One might also note that the quasi-analogues of the Yiddish poems thus far cited, whether from the Psalms or from Lucrezia Borgia's letter, should not be imagined as concrete sources. In fact, the similarity in imagery simply indicates the poems' participation in the larger tradition of erotic poetry, both Jewish and especially the Gentile tradition in early modern Europe (whether Spain or Italy), partaking of the common styles and stock of images.

Even more so than in his correspondence with Lucrezia Borgia, however, the letters and poems that Bembo exchanged with an earlier lover, Maria Savorgnan in 1500–1501, seem particularly relevant, especially with respect to the Bembo-style Petrarchism of fire imagery.[27] She was the daughter of Matteo Griffoni de Sant' Angelo in the duchy of Urbino and the widow of Giacomo Savorgnan (d. 1498), whose daughter, Lucina, was the inspiration for Luigi da Porto's *Giulietta e Romeo* (a copy of which was sent by the author to Bembo, his mentor, upon its publication), which became the direct source of Shakespeare's dramatic reworking.[28] When Savorgnan and Bembo became acquainted, she was likely in her late twenties, while he was nearing thirty years of age. They each wrote seventy-seven letters to the other, many of them for the purpose of arranging and canceling assignations.[29] While those letters reveal some information about the affair and much about the participants' literary conception of it, as Elena Croce astutely comments in her general reflections on the character of this amatory correspondence: "L'illusione, o ambizione di ricostruire analiticamente la realtà delle storie d'amore è un miraggio che si è ormai smesso di persequire," "The illusion or drive to reconstruct analytically the reality of the love story is a mirage whose pursuit has by now been halted."[30] The letters were couriered back and forth by Savorgnan's maid and apparently also occasionally by a Jewish goldsmith (*medaglista*) named Moisè.[31] Intriguingly, in indeterminate connection with Moisè, on the reverse of Savorgnan's letter numbered 75 by Dionisotti (unnumbered in Bembo's own compilation), dated "xxiiij Aug. MDI," there is a brief Old Yiddish message of slightly more than six lines, written vertically along the right edge of the page.[32] Much of the first two lines has been lost through trimming of the edge of the page. Dionisotti does not include the Yiddish text in his edition, but it is now easily accessible on the open-access Vatican website. While Dionisotti opined that the "contenuto familiare e economico," "domestic and financial content," would seem to have no relation either to Savorgnan or to Moisè, Braden suggests that the letter might have been written on some of Moisè's scrap paper.[33] Neither opinion can be confirmed on the basis of the extant evidence.

It is in any case clear that there was at least one—at some level—*trusted* Yiddish-speaker (?) in Bembo's and Savorgnan's acquaintance and apparently in the occasional employ of one or both of them, who, perhaps as courier, seems to have had access to the love letters of Savorgnan and Bembo and who, one might further speculate—and one dare not lose sight of the fact that it is merely speculation—might have even had access to Bembo's study and library. Might Moisè have been the author (? scribe, adapter, or translator) of the Yiddish love song? If one were to entertain such a possibility, then it would be necessary to revise the conditions suggested above concerning the improbability that the poem was inscribed on the Rashi manuscript *after* it had come into the possession of the Bembi.

Among the poems in the Bembo-Savorgnan corpus, poem 132 (Savorgnan to Bembo) includes several images similar to those of the Yiddish poem: the same images of fire (*il foco*), flame (*la fiamma*), and torment (*il chiodo*) appear, but here they are deployed as the signals of the *end* of love, not its beginning or its tormented practice.[34] In Savorgnan's first sonnet, with which she opens her epistolary exchange with Bembo, the same metaphors appear: "io mi consumo in fiame ardente," "[so that] I am consumed in a burning flame" (line 5); "dolce foco," "sweet flame" (line 6); "l'ardor cocente," "seering ardor" (line 7).[35] Tantalizing similarities they may be, but again, without *concrete* connection with the Yiddish poem.

After this cursory glance at both the Hebrew tradition of love poetry and the Christian literary milieu of the manuscript's documentable biography, it is of course necessary to look to the Yiddish literary context of the Ashkenazic community in which the physical book almost certainly existed initially and sketch the literary context it might provide for the poem. In Elia Levita's adventure epic *Bovo d'Antona,* composed in Padua in 1507, when the eponymous hero Bovo laments the loss of his beloved Druzeyne, his twin sons, and his comrade Pelukan, all of whom he thinks have been killed by lions (while in fact only Pelukan has actually suffered that fate), his words echo those of the Yiddish poem of the Bembi's Rashi manuscript:

ווש זול איך אן היבן ווש זול איך טון·
או ווי דער גאר קלייני ווריידן·
איך מיינט איך ווער אויז אל מיינם אונגליק נון·
דא היבט זיך ערשט אן מין ליידן·
(st. 503,1–4)[36]

> What should I now begin? What should I do? Alas, what minuscule joy! I thought that I had now left behind all my misfortune. Now my grief is just beginning.

In the nearly contemporary, anonymous Ariostan epic *Pariz and Viene* (the earliest extant edition was published in 1594, although an earlier edition from 1556 is documented), which focuses to a far greater extent than does *Bovo* on erotic love in the sensibility common in Renaissance literature, there is a stanza spoken by Princess Viene to her nurse and confidante whose central lines seem almost to paraphrase the emotions expressed in the poem here at issue:

או ליבי או טרוייטי שוועשטר מיין
וואז זול איך טון וויא זול איכֿש האלטן·
בֿון שטונד צו שטונד מירט זיך מיין פיין
דש ווייזט דיר וואל מיין בויז גישטאלטן·
איין ולאם קאם אין מיין הערץ היניין
אונ' נוימר לוט זי מירש דרקאלטן·
איך הב דיר אופֿט גיזגט מיט מונד ביטר
וויא מיך אים הערצן ליבט איין אידלר ריטר:
(st. 151)[37]

> O, my dear and beloved sister! What am I to do? How am I to bear it? Hour-by-hour my pain increases. That is displayed to you by my poor appearance. A flame has entered my heart and never lets it cool. I have often said to you with bitter words how a noble knight loves me in his heart.

One finds oneself here in the conventional storehouse of imagery of sixteenth-century European love poetry.[38] While the similarity of some of the same images and sensibility—whether with these lines from *Bovo* or from *Pariz and Viene*, or in the poem by Lope de Estuñiga sent by Lucrezia Borgia to Pietro Bembo, or indeed in the biblical tradition or the sixteenth-century Hebrew traditions of love poetry—draws our attention, there is no similarity close enough to suggest that they have any clear connection except that they all partake in the vocabulary and sensibility of a particular poetic discourse of the erotic.

This oldest extant Yiddish love song would likely have sounded familiar to its fifteenth- and/or sixteenth-century Italo-Jewish auditors, who likely sometimes heard similar sentiments, imagery, and erotic sensibilities in popular vernacular love songs and perhaps even Renaissance Spanish and Italian love poetry of the dominant culture that surrounded them, and indeed it echoes the same discourse found in Hebrew love poems, whether ancient or early modern, as well as other examples of specifically Yiddish-language love complaint, embedded in the period's epic poetry. Interestingly, however, there seems to have been no full-scale *literary* tradition of such erotic lyric in early Yiddish, such as one does find, for instance, elsewhere in European literature. Thus this brief poem, written on the outer wrapping of a Rashi text, seems perhaps at first sight a literary orphan unconnected with the world around it. On examination, however, it becomes clear that it is a tell-tale sign of yet further very human and personal connections between members of the Ashkenazic and the dominant Italian cultures of the time, and thus in a larger sense between the cultural practices of Yiddish-speaking Jews in northern Italy and the aesthetic practitioners of the Italian Renaissance. Especially in the context of similar sentiments expressed in the epics *Bovo d'Antona* and *Pariz and Viene*, it bears witness to a clear moment of cultural translation, significantly (although perhaps not altogether defiantly) written on a holy book and thus complicating even here the fluid though no less perceptible boundaries between the pious and the quasi-secular. Brief as it is, the poem thus displays precisely that intense erotic affect characteristic of the Renaissance heritage of Petrarchan love lyric and of lyric outpourings in Ariostan epic. It is a sensibility informed by the already centuries-old and sublimated tradition of courtly love, with its lovers disoriented by their passion, their inflamed hearts and complexions pale unto death. While these various sixteenth-century Yiddish witnesses may or may not document the earliest appearance of this erotic sensibility in Yiddish literature, they do indicate that by this period it had entered the mainstream of Yiddish narrative and, demonstrably, of Yiddish lyric. In any case, whatever the charms of this brief love song, it seems *not* to have participated in a broad and deep *Yiddish* tradition of erotic poetry, such as is documented, for instance, in Latin, French, German, and Italian for centuries before this period. Even so, that sensibility is already at home in Yiddish in this song. There is nothing particularly innovative here in terms of the conventionality of the expression of that mode of erotic literary passion *except* that that expression is here couched in the Yiddish language, for the first time among Yiddish lyrics now known. And that is, in itself, not insignificant: a Petrarchan erotic sensibility in a Yiddish lyric of the (probably) mid-sixteenth century at the latest.

Notes

1. Leo Landau, ed., *Arthurian Legends: The Hebrew-German Rhymed Version of the Legend of King Arthur*, Teutonia 21 (Leipzig: Avenarius, 1912), 21; cf. also Curt Leviant, ed. and trans., *King Artus: A Hebrew Arthurian Romance of 1279*, Studia Semitica Neerlandica 11 (Assen: Van Gorcum, 1969), 56–57.

2. Milan, Biblioteca Ambrosiana, C. 282 inf., fol. 1r.

3. Abraham Berliner, *Ein Gang durch die Bibliotheken Italiens, Vortrag* (Berlin: Julius Benzian, 1877), 23, 33; repr. in *Gesammelte Schriften* (Frankfurt am Main: J. Kaufmann, 1913), 3–29. Ber Borochov, "Di geshikhte fun der yidisher literatur, 4) Venetsyaner geshefts- un libshaft-briv," in *Shprakh-forshung un literatur-geshikhte*, ed. Nakhman Meizl (Tel Aviv: Peretz, 1966), 192–194. Borochov added his own conjectural vowel points to his printing of the text. Carolus Bernheimer, *Fontes Ambrosiani in lucem editi cura et studio Bybliothecae Ambrosianae, V: Codices Hebraici Bybliothecae Ambrosianae* (Milan: Biblioteca Ambrosiana, 1933), 23–24, no. 23; M. Basin, *Antologye finf hundert yor yidishe poezye*, 2 vols. (New York: Literarisher farlag, 1917), 27. In printing his version of the text, Basin "corrects" the manuscript's spelling. Yisroel Tsinberg, *Altyidishe literatur fun di eltste tsaytn biz der haskole-tkufe* (Vilnius: Tomor, 1935), vol. 6 of *Di geshikhte fun der literatur bay yidn*, 9 vols. (Vilnius: Tomor, 1929–1937; repr., Buenos Aires: Alveltlekher yidisher kultur-kongres, 1964–1970), 53. Tsinberg notes that he "modernizes" the orthography; Max Erik, *Di geshikhte fun der yidisher literatur: fun di eltste tsaytn biz der haskole-tkufe, fertsnter-akhtsnter yorhundert, mit bilder un melodyes* (Warsaw: Kultur lige, 1928; repr., New York: Congress for Jewish Culture, 1979), 173.

4. Berliner, *Ein Gang*, 23, 33.

5. Bernheimer, *Fontes*, 23–24.

6. Theoretically, of course, the poem could have been written on the sheet of parchment before it was used as a book cover for this Rashi volume; but just as easily, the outer parchment could have been added to the volume some time after the volume was copied.

7. These texts are all edited in *EYT* 1, 2, 5–9.

8. I would like to thank the staff of the Ambrosiana for permitting me to make use of the ultraviolet lamp in facilities not designed for its use (a card catalog room) and under circumstances that were (thankfully only briefly) trying for all concerned. The text here printed reproduces my edition in *EYT* 14; in the following notes, the siglum M identifies readings from the Milan manuscript; the slash mark / indicates a line break in the manuscript; the raised dot and colon-like marks of punctuation are those found in the manuscript. Unless otherwise specified, the readings of previous editors provided here should not be construed as alternate possibilities, but simply as documentation of the editorial history of the text.

9. 1 זאל] M אל is ligature.

10. 2 קירן] Berliner קיריין M there is room for the second י, but no visible ink on the page.

11. 3 איך] Bernheimer היך.

12. 5 קוינש] M נש ligature פֿרילך] Bernheimer היילך Borochov פר(?)ך translates as פריי; the mark under ר is faint and perhaps connected with the ascender of the ל in ליבשט in the next manuscript line; the word's first letter is problematic, but under ultraviolet light it seems much more likely פֿ than ה; the horizontal mark above the letter then becomes a normal *raphe*; under ultraviolet light it seems remotely possible that the third letter might be ו rather than י.

13. 6 שפֿט] Bernheimer סתיט, Berliner שפיט, Erik שפייט, Tsinberg שפָייט; Borochov, Erik, and Tsinberg gloss as שפירט; Berliner translates as *späht*.

14. 7 דיזר] Erik omits Borochov דער.

15. 7 עֶרדן] M the vowel point is in darker ink, perhaps later than original text.

16. The only other פ in this text is in line 6 שפט, and there the letter has a different form: a reverse *C* with a bottom stroke extending diagonally down with a final up-hook and a short vertical stroke in the hollow space of the letter; the use of multiple letter forms by a single scribe in a single text is, however, rather common.

17. Borochov enigmatically reads שפת but also glosses שפירט (p. 193); see also the English translation of Tsinberg's book by Bernard Martin: Israel Zinberg, *A History of Jewish Literature*, vol. 7, *Old Yiddish Literature from Its Origins to the Haskalah Period* (Cincinnati: Hebrew Union College Press, 1975), 42: "that is felt. . . ."

18. See Neil G. Jacobs, *Yiddish: A Linguistic Introduction* (Cambridge: Cambridge University Press, 2005), 130–131 on Yiddish degemination.

19. This last interpretation was suggested to me by Leyzer (Alec) Burko.

20. According to Carol Kidwell, Bernardo began collecting in 1450: *Pietro Bembo: Lover, Linguist, Cardinal* (Montreal: McGill-Queen's University Press, 2004), 5.

21. In general on Bembo's library, see Cecil H. Clough, "Pietro Bembo's Library Represented in the British Museum," *British Museum Quarterly* 30 (1965): 3–5.

22. An interesting detail, likely of little direct relevance to the issue of the date of the Yiddish poem's inscription is the fact that on the final page of the manuscript (fol. 185v, the back covering folio), there is the Hebrew inscription חקרטי וזיקקתי הס' הזה ראוי אני דומיניקוֻ ירושלמי "I examined and expurgated this book properly, I, Domenico Yerushalmi." This inscription was written by the (in)famous, Jerusalem-born rabbi Samuel Vivas (1555–1621?), who converted to Christianity in 1593, took the name Domenico Gerusolimitano, and worked thereafter as a censor of Hebrew books in Mantua, Monferrato, Milan, and Rome. See Alfredo Mordechai Rabello, "Domenico Gerosolimitano," in *Encyclopaedia Judaica*, 2nd ed., ed. Michael Berenbaum and Fred Skolnik (Detroit: Macmillan Reference USA, 2007), 5:739. Such censoring would have been the result of an ecclesiastical order, *perhaps* when the codex passed from one owner to another, if for some reason as a result of the transaction the codex passed through Christian hands or to a Christian buyer.

23. T. Carmi, ed., *The Penguin Book of Hebrew Verse* (New York: Penguin, 1981), 462, 454.

24. Raymond Scheindlin, *Wine, Women, and Death: Medieval Hebrew Poems on the Good Life* (Philadelphia: Jewish Publication Society, 1986; repr., Oxford: Oxford University Press, 1999), 77.

25. Borochov, "Di geshikhte," 194.

26. Perhaps Lucrezia Borgia did not copy the Spaniard's poem but wrote it down from memory or deliberately revised it somewhat, for, while the text of the poem as found in the letter includes many of the same lines as Lope de Estuñiga's poem, one might argue that it is not (quite) the same poem, as a close comparison with that poem demonstrates: cf. *Cancionero general: que contiene muchas obras de diuersos autores antiguos* (Anvers: M. Nucio, 1557), lxxix. The Spanish text (from Borgia's letter) cited here is from Sarah Bradford, *Lucrezia Borgia: Life, Love and Death in Renaissance Italy* (London: Viking, 2004), lxxviii–lxxix; see also Gordon Braden, "Applied Petrarchism: The Loves of Pietro Bembo," *Modern Language Quarterly* 57, no. 3 (1996): 405–406, and Giulia Raboni, ed., *Pietro Bembo e Lucrezia Borgia. La grande fiamma. Lettere 1503–1517* (Milan: Rosellina Archinto, 1989).

27. I would like to acknowledge the interest in this aspect of the issues of the chapter and advice offered by Professor Paolo Pucci (private correspondence). On the Bembo-Savorgnan exchange, see also Braden, "Applied Petrarchism," 412–423.

28. Da Porto was apparently bewitched by the sixteen-year-old Lucina Savorgnan's sweet singing and musicianship on the clavichord in 1511 and later penned the novella, published in 1530, long after she had been married off to another. See Edward Muir, *Mad Blood Stirring: Vendetta and Factions in Friuli during the Renaissance* (Baltimore: Johns Hopkins University Press, 1993), 82–89, 158–159.

29. The correspondence was published by Carlo Dionisotti, ed., *Carteggio d'amore, 1500–1501: Maria Savorgnan—Pietro Bembo* (Florence: Felice le Monnier, 1950). Gildo Meneghetti provides an elaboration of Savorgnan's family history and a reconstructed narration of the Bembo-Savorgnan affair (based on a broad range of documentary evidence); Gildo Meneghetti, *La vita avventurosa di Pietro Bembo: Umanista, poeta, cortigiano* (Venice: Tipografia Commerciale, 1961), 20–39; Marina Zancan places Savorgnan in a more expansive intellectual context: Marina Zancan, "L'intellettualità femminile nel primo cinquecento: Maria Savorgnan e Gaspara Stampa," *Annali d'Italianistica* 7 (1989): 42–65.

30. Elene Croce, *Periplo italiano: Note sui narratori italiani dei primi secoli* (Milan: Mondadori, 1977), 91; her attention to the topic comprises 89–93.

31. Kidwell, *Pietro Bembo*, 63, 64, 66, 414 n. 58.

32. Dionisotti misreads the date as "XIIII Aug. MDI" (*Carteggio*, 42). The text is in the collection of letters and poems to Pietro Bembo: Vatican City, Vat.lat. 14189, fol. 75v (http://digi.vatlib.it/view/MSS_Vat.lat.14189/0154); cf. also Paul Oskar Kristeller, *Iter italicum: A Finding List of Uncatalogued or Incompletely Catalogued Humanistic Manuscripts of the Renaissance in Italian and Other Libraries*, 3rd ed. (Leiden: E. J. Brill, 1977), vol. 2 (*Italy: Orvieto to Volterra, Vatican City*), 349.

33. Dionisotti, *Carteggio*, 154; Braden, "Applied Petrarchism," 413. Kidwell identifies Moisè as "semi-literate" (*Pietro Bembo*, 66), but she is almost certainly speculating on his knowledge of Tuscan. In any case, the Yiddish text on the back of Savorgnan's letter—whether by Moisè or not—is both idiomatic and legible. The Yiddish text is unrelated to the Yiddish love song at issue in this chapter, but instead treats of someone named שמשון "Samson" and the payment of a debt.

34. Cf. Braden, "Applied Petrarchism," 422.

35. Marked: "Venetiis. Quarto Kal. Iun. MD. Primus" (= Venice, 29 May 1500); Dionisotti, *Carteggio d'Amore*, 3. See also Antonio Enzo Quaglio, "Intorno a Maria Savorgnan I: Per una riedizione delle lettere," *Quaderni Utinensi* 5–6 (1985): 103–118; and Antionio Enzo Quaglio, "Intorno a Maria Savorgnan II: Un 'sidio' d'amore," *Quaderni Utinensi* 7–8 (1986): 77–101.

36. The epic was composed in 1507 by Elia Levita, ultimately based on a Tuscan version (*Buouo di Antona*) of the early thirteenth-century Anglo-Norman original, *Boeuve de Haumtone*. The Anglo-Norman text was recently re-edited by Christopher Sanders, ed., *Bevers Saga, with the Text of the Anglo-Norman* Boeve de Haumtone, Stofnun Árna Magnússonar á Íslandi, Rit, 51 (Reykjavík: Stofnun Árna Magnússonar á Íslandi, 2001). The Yiddish epic has three text witnesses: the *editio princeps*, published in 650 ottava rima stanzas in Isny in 1541, not simply authorized by the author himself but indeed typeset by him, the quintessential example of a last-hand edition, (http://archive.org/details/nybc207004); one fragmentary manuscript that may predate the publication of that edition (Paris, Bibliothèque Nationale, MS. hébr. 750, fos. 123–157; fragmentary, st. 238–590); and a further almost complete manuscript that seems to postdate the *editio princeps* (Jerusalem, Jewish National and University Library, Heb. [2]8° 7565; almost complete: lacking the preface and breaking off at st. 633), (http://primo.nli.org.il/primo_library/libweb/action/dlDisplay.do?vid=NLI&docId=NNL_ALEPH000043972). The manuscript's signature is troubled: the library catalog identifies the manuscript as 8° 7565, while the manuscript itself is marked 28° 7565 (which is the signature that has most often been

cited by scholars). Dr. Ezra Chwat of the library's Department of Manuscripts enigmatically identifies both signatures as correct (personal communication). Thus my own hesitant use of (2)8° 7565 here. A facsimile edition of the 1541 *editio princeps* was published by Judah A. Joffe, ed., *Elye Bokher: poetishe shafungen in yidish* (New York: Judah A. Joffe, 1949); excerpt in Frakes, *EYT* 33; translated in Frakes, *Early Yiddish Epic*, 238–316; see also Shmeruk, *Prokim*, 97–120, 141–156; and Baumgarten, *Introduction*, 163–206. Claudia Rosenzweig's lavish but misguided recent edition of the text is marred by philological naïveté and a fanciful approach to both editorial practice and semantic interpretation: Claudia Rosenzweig, ed., *Bovo d'Antona by Elye Bokher: A Yiddish Romance* (Leiden: Brill, 2015). She seems indeed not quite to grasp the principles of a critical edition, i.e., the type of edition that she claims to have produced (she seems equally confused about what constitutes a facsimile edition; see chap. 8, n. 61, below). Under the conditions noted above, i.e., the presence of a last-hand edition of the author, a critical edition seems at best an ill-conceived project, for on what authority would a modern editor ever reject a reading chosen, approved, authorized, and printed by the author himself and instead print a reading from one of the manuscripts? Perhaps only if the reading of the *editio princeps* were obviously a misprint or somehow garbled. Rosenzweig seems blithely unaware of any such principle. Thus, while claiming almost incidentally that the 1541 edition is the base text of her edition, she generally treats the two manuscripts as evidence of equal weight and indeed seems almost to favor the Jerusalem manuscript when it differs from Levita's edition, and she very often simply prints the divergent readings from the manuscripts in her text without even noting the reading of her alleged base text. Sometimes this practice requires her to stand on her editorial head even to conjure some sense for the reading chosen. Let one example illustrate: Near the end of the narrative, Druzeyne plans to play music during the celebration attendant on Bovo's impending wedding to Margarete and, in Levita's edition of the text, identifies her potential audience as גישבֿייארן (st. 618,8); cf. MHG *geswîe*, "in-laws" (Matthias Lexer, *Mittelhochdeutsches Handwörterbuch* [Leipzig: Hirzel, 1872–1878; repr., Stuttgart: Hirzel, 1979], vol. 1, col. 940), NHG *Geschwei*, "relative / in-law" (*DWB*, vol. 5, col. 3985), which I translated in the particular narrative context as "wedding guests" (*Early Yiddish Epic*, 311). On the other hand, Rosenzweig tacitly ignores Levita's text and instead prints only the reading of Jerusalem (2)8° 7565, f. 61r גישנייארן (she seems also unaware that the נ of the manuscript is likely an example of the common scribal error for the ב of Levita's text), and then, obviously at a loss for what her reading might possibly mean, she inexplicably connects the word to modern German *Geheier*, which she glosses as "Engl. 'fucker'" (*A Yiddish Romance*, 460) and which she claims gains its intrusive "*-schn-*" by way of "euphemism" (*A Yiddish Romance*, 341). Even the most generous reader who has followed Rosenzweig this far will likely still be baffled by the inexplicably vulgar insult of the potential wedding audience that she attributes to Druzeyne. Rosenzweig on the other hand seems altogether unconcerned with the irrelevance of her interpretive concoction to the narrative context and passes blithely on. Her edition should be consulted with extreme caution. I cite the text from the *editio princeps* (with reference to the sixteenth-century manuscripts, when relevant).

37. This anonymous Yiddish epic comprises 717 ottava rima stanzas in ten cantos directly influenced by Ariosto's *Orlando furioso*. Up until the discovery of a complete copy of the Verona 1594 edition, whose preface mentions Levita apparently as the mentor of this text's translator/adapter, this hitherto fragmentary poem had often been attributed to Elia Levita, which now seems more than unlikely. The epic nonetheless clearly participates in that same north Italian Renaissance cultural milieu in which Levita worked. The conventional plot of the vassal's son who must prove himself before being granted the princess as bride is transformed from hackneyed cliché into a complexly layered and dramatically progressing, politically

serious, and delightfully humorous tour de force. See Shmeruk, *Prokim,* 97–120; Anna Maria Babbi, "In margine alla fortuna del Paris e Vienna," *Quaderni di Lingue e Letterature* (Verona), 11 (1986): 393–397. A facsimile edition of the 1594 text was published by Valerio Marchetti, Jean Baumgarten, and Antonella Salomoni, eds., *Elia Bahur Levita, Paris un Viene, Francesco Dalle Donne, Verona 1594* (Bologna: Università degli studi di Bologna, Dipartimento di discipline storiche; Arnaldo Forni Editore, 1988). The definitive text edition is Chone Shmeruk, ed., *Pariz un Vyenah: mahadura biqqortit be-ẓeruf mavo, he'arot ve-nispaḥim* (Jerusalem: Israel Academy of Sciences and Humanities, 1996); excerpt in Frakes, *EYT* 74; translated in Frakes, *Early Yiddish Epic,* 317–403. See also Armin Schulz, *Die Zeichen des Körpers und der Liebe: "Paris und Vienna" in der jiddischen Fassung des Elia Levita* (Hamburg: Kovač, 2000); Baumgarten, *Introduction,* 186–206.

38. One should, however, keep in mind, as Raymond Scheindlin reminds, that conventionality "does not argue against its sincerity" (*Wine,* 78).

Chapter Three

(Non-)Intersecting Parallel Lives

Pasquino in Rome and on the Rialto

ELIJAH BEN ASHER ha-Levi Ashkenazi / Elia(s) Levita / Elye Bokher / Elyahu Baḥur אליה בחור (1469–1549) long served as a cultural mediator between Christian and Jewish culture. He had a traditional Jewish education near Nuremberg before moving to Italy and living in Padua, Rome, and his beloved Venice, where he died at the age of eighty. He worked as a teacher, printer, translator, and author of scholarly texts in the fields of Hebrew grammatical study, Jewish lexicography, and Masoretic studies, in addition to his composition of a wealth of occasional poems. He corresponded and/or collaborated with Humanist scholars such as Erasmus, Paulus Fagius, Johannes de Kampen, Sebastian Münster, and, most notably, Cardinal Egidio da Viterbo, in whose Roman palace he was the resident Hebraicist cum kabbalist for a decade,[1] almost certainly learning some Latin and apparently also some Greek in the process.[2] He authored the most important grammar of Hebrew of his time and compiled lexica of Talmud and Targum that long served primarily Christian but also many Jewish scholars.[3] He translated the Psalms into Yiddish (Venice, 1545) and penned dozens of complex and erudite Hebrew poetic prefaces and afterwords to the books that he wrote or edited, and in Yiddish he also wrote an event poem and a poetic satire and adapted a Tuscan epic.[4] It is perhaps in Levita's bibliography that the key intellectual and sociological issues that complicate his relationship with Gentile culture are most clearly illustrated and given a subtle but important twist, especially because he, like many of his contemporaries, Christian and Jewish, also wrote occasional poems and popular literature, also in the vernacular, in his case Yiddish. That activity was not accidental, and it was in no sense trivial. It would seem in fact key to understanding his intellectual and social role as a *Jewish* participant in the intellectual life of sixteenth-century northern Italy, whether one might wish to designate him a Humanist (or perhaps better: humanist) or not. Specifically: how, in pre-ghetto Italy (when his extant Yiddish works were written), did Levita negotiate the already existing cultural, if not always enforceably spatial, barriers between Jewish and Christian, conservative religious and Renaissance conception? Levita was a typical inhabitant of intercultural borderlands, culturally liminal in a functional sense, even though it seems altogether unlikely that he ever imagined his own allegiance and identity as anything other than strictly Jewish. He thus embodied, quite concretely, the marginal and liminal, a creator and purveyor not of a *littérature mineure* in Yiddish, but of an interstitial, a hybrid literature.[5]

Levita thus, as a multilingual, internationally known and respected scholar and publisher, poet and teacher, may initially seem to demonstrate quite concretely an aesthetic sensibility appropriate to sixteenth-century Central Europe as a Humanist and to northern Italy as a classic "Renaissance man." In his biographical study of Levita, for instance, Weil styles him "un humaniste juif" (a Jewish humanist). He nonetheless clearly understands the historical and cultural problems involved in such a designation:

> Dans quelle mesure peut-on dire d'un Juif qu'il est devenu un humaniste? L'histoire a donné deux définitions de l'humaniste: c'est un savant versé dans la connaissance des langue et de la littérature des anciens; c'est un des érudits qui, au cours des XVe et XVIe siècles, par leurs leçons et leurs éditions, remirent en honneur les chefs-d'œuvre de l'antiquité classique.
>
> To what extent can one say that a Jew has become a Humanist? History provides two definitions of Humanist: it is a scholar versed in the knowledge of the languages and literatures of the ancients; it is one of the scholars who in the course of the fifteenth and sixteenth centuries, by means of their editions, restored the masterpieces of classical antiquity to favor.[6]

Thus Levita is strictly not a Humanist by either definition. Even so, Weil quizzically claims, Hebrew was practically his native language. Likewise quizzically, in this same passage, Weil grants him the status of Humanist on the basis of his poetic compositions. Similarly Moses Shulvass comments: "הצעיר מאשכנז נכנס במהירות לתוך החברה בת הריניסאנס ונעשה הומאניסט מובהק, אל כל מעלותיו וחסרונותיו" "The young immigrant from Germany quickly penetrated Renaissance society, acquiring all the virtues and faults of the Humanists."[7] In a qualified sense, Erika Timm concurs, when she comments on the sixteenth-century Yiddish epics *Pariz and Viene* (which she erroneously attributes to Levita) and *Bovo d'Antona*, "[Sie] sind jedoch um ein Vielfaches stärker als alle bisher genannten Texte durchtränkt von der Welt der italienischen Renaissance," "They are, however, a great deal more strongly than all texts mentioned thus far imbued with the world of the

Italian Renaissance."[8] N. B. Minkoff simply calls Levita "the Renaissance bard" in the English introductory note to his brief Yiddish book, although interestingly, in the Yiddish text, he does not use corresponding vocabulary,[9] nor does Judah Joffe do so in his introduction to the facsimile edition of the *Bovo.*[10] Jean Baumgarten also identifies Levita as the "humaniste juif italien."[11]

The scholarly goals of the Italian Renaissance were—if a momentary and tactically reductive summary be permitted—to renew those aspects of Greco-Roman antiquity that it defined as desirable. While there was a great deal of variation among exponents of what from the present vantage point might be defined as the Italian Renaissance, Petrarch may serve well here (as so often elsewhere) as a general guide. Among the components of his program was the regaining of the literary excellence characteristic of Augustan Rome (the age of Cicero, Virgil, Horace, and Ovid, among others) and the public virtue he perceived in that period, as opposed to the medieval barbarism that had—he thought—dominated Italian culture since the end of Roman antiquity. He called for a true *imitatio* of the ancients, via a consciously conceived and executed intellectual life in the service of the polity (which in northern Italy of the period generally and rather perversely turned out to be the city-states of the region with their autocratic rulers), unlike the idealized ancient Athens as democratic *polis* or the idealized ancient Rome as republic.

No matter how it might be conceived, it is clearly not possible to integrate Levita's intellectual work into such a cultural program. As Robert Bonfil has demonstrated in his study of Jews in sixteenth-century Italy, the Petrarchan program, no matter how it is qualified by other details and emphases, is simply incompatible with *any* Jewish conception, especially with respect to intellectual pursuits—if they can be even momentarily separated from a larger integrated conception of life. For sixteenth-century Jews did not view any period in the non-Jewish past as a Golden Age of intellectual or civic achievement that concretely needed to be renewed, revived, or reborn; and certainly there was no such Jewish conception of the age of Plato and Aristotle, or of Cicero and Augustus, for after all the post-Aristotelian Hellenistic culture ravaged Israel during the Maccabean period, while it was that same Rome that destroyed Jerusalem and the Second Temple.[12]

Furthermore, unlike the Humanist revolt against a medieval scholasticism perceived as sterile, there was no Jewish revolt against any Jewish intellectual establishment of any more recent past—such as that of the Talmud and the midrashic traditions—in favor of a more distant past, no rejection of a canon of later quasi-scholastic authorities that overlay and overshadowed the original Truth, as it were.[13] Whatever form Jewish messianic hopes took over the course of the millennia, it is clear that they never came very close to the program of Renaissance Humanists' notions of a renewal of the past.

Levita's biography and bibliography certainly give no hint that he might have shared the goals, purposes, or even practices of Christian Humanism. While his activities were intellectually quite varied, he nonetheless never tried his hand, for instance, at philosophy, and his works offer none of the typical evidence of the "Renaissance man" *outside the research library*; he did not, as far as is known, paint, compose love poems, music, or plays for the theater, nor sculpt, design architectural structures, or invent machines; nor was he an astronomer or astrologer, physicist or physician, geologist or geographer. Instead, he wrote about Tanakh (the Hebrew Bible), Targum, and Talmud, in Hebrew; he edited and published books about Tanakh, Targum, and Talmud, in Hebrew; he taught Tanakh, Targum, and Talmud (and Kabbalah on demand). His work had nothing to do with Cicero, Plato, or Aristotle, whom some of his fellow Jews during this period *did* in fact manage to work credibly into their own studies, as David Ruderman has demonstrated, for instance, for Abraham (ben Hananiah) Yagel,[14] and Herbert Davidson for Leone Ebreo and Judah Moscato [and Moses Isserles and Judah Loeb of Prague], who could and did achieve a kind of syncretism that allowed them to quote Plato and Augustine *and* the Talmud to address moral issues, or to make use of Greek mythology and philosophy as "naturally" as did Christian Humanists.[15] But such Jewish intellectuals of the period are rare, and there are practically no peers of a David ben Judah Messer Leon, who, in the words of Tirosh-Rothschild, "incorporat[ed] the *studia humanitatis* into the Jewish curriculum . . . admired Roman orators, poets, and historians, and regarded the classics worthy of emulation . . . shared his contemporaries' admiration for Petrarch and Boccaccio . . . [and] enlarged the scope of secular studies to encompass both humanist and scholastic curricula."[16] Even so, as both Bonfil and Tirosh-Rothschild argue in ample detail, a specifically "Jewish humanism," as it were, did develop to serve specifically Jewish needs. Alongside the (Christian) Renaissance *homo universalis* there developed the Jewish concept of the חָכָם כּוֹלֵל "general scholar," who knew the liberal arts, philosophy, and medicine, but also and always the rabbinical tradition.

As Arthur Lesley has demonstrated in a series of studies, Jews also began to develop a sense of looking back to a cultural period, or rather to a specific text *as* culture, which, while it was not the object of any comprehensive, broad-based *imitatio*, as was the case with Rome for Christian Humanists, did offer an antiquity comparable to the Humanists' Augustan Rome; that text was of course the Hebrew Bible, which simultaneously functioned as one of the ancient cultural objects, a direct knowledge of which was most desired by *Christian* Humanists as well. From this perspective Jews did not need to look, for instance, to a Cicero, for they already had a far more valuable (even from the Christian perspective) antiquity of their own. The textual study long integral to traditional Jewish education now moved gradually toward a specifically grammar-based program—at least temporarily, and in Italy—in many respects quite similar to the Humanistic program of Latin and Greek study, and one that was also easily appropriated by

Christians for their own study of the Hebrew Bible. Here, finally, appears something of direct relevance to Levita's life and work in teaching Jews and Christians alike the textual traditions of Tanakh, Targum, Talmud, and Kabbalah as a *philological* project. While Levita's access to the Jewish textual tradition was nothing new and certainly not a renewal—nothing needed to be *recovered* (in the sense that Renaissance Christians recovered access to a perceived ancient Greek Truth)—even so, his extensive grammatical studies, his various lexica of the sacred texts, even his detailed study of the Masoretic tradition (whatever its perceived purpose might have been) actually functioned—to apply (momentarily and tactically) an overtly Humanistic interpretative notion—to strip off the textual accretions of post-biblical, quasi-scholastic, rabbinical Jewish interpretive traditions of scholarship in order to uncover a more original text of the Bible, as it were, a task in which many would recognize some faint echo of the mode and manner of Humanistic textual criticism as it struggled through the supposed detritus of medieval Christian scholastic traditions back toward the perceived "Truth" of the sacred texts in their original languages. One thinks here, of course, of the quasi-parallel in the Christian sphere of Erasmus with his edition of the Greek New Testament. And, significantly, Levita, the German-born, Venetian-Ashkenazic scholar, wrote a most refined form of what one might designate a Hebrew more directly based on biblical rather than rabbinical usage. Dare one, along with Lesley and Roth, call it a classicized or Humanistic Hebrew?[17] If so, then Levita's Hebrew was "classical" in essentially the same way that Humanistic Latin was "classical" and by means of essentially the same, consciously constructed process of philological acquisition.[18] Indeed as Lesley argues, it "was not unreflective imitation of a foreign fashion that produced the admired Hebrew of Italian Jews. Instead, the Italian Jews were pursuing a resolutely independent religious and learned program, which they articulated by selectively adapting to their own intellectual heritage the literary, linguistic, and political arts that they could appropriate from humanism. It was in this way that the Jews in fifteenth- and sixteenth-century Italy, a marginal community, succeeded in opening themselves to the world without being assimilated by the world."[19] While Levita never really expresses it quite this way, the Bible comes to function as the model for this practice of what we might—momentarily, tactically, tentatively, and with some exaggeration—call a "Jewish humanism,"[20] as did the Greco-Roman models for Christian Humanists; it became the classical canon of "Jewish humanism," and that Jewish model is visible in the Hebrew style of *Italian* Jewish scholars of the time, which became the model of fine, elegant Hebrew style.

While outsiders—Christian Humanists—could and did occasionally make use of the scholarly results of this specifically "Jewish humanism," it was generally not intended explicitly *for* them and was certainly not *about* them. "Jewish humanism" was centripetal, focused inward and drawing inward those elements of external culture that might be deemed useful. While some Jewish intellectuals did indeed move out of the Jewish community, and some even converted to Christianity (including, for instance, Levita's grandsons, who typeset his *Bovo d'Antona* and added their own colophon), they constituted neither a significant number nor included many important Jewish scholars of the age.[21] Certainly the means and ends of Christian Humanism never functioned effectively as a centrifugal force on the Jewish community. Rather, it so functioned that "Jewish humanism" imported individually culled non-Jewish elements into a Jewish matrix, synthesizing within the *synagoga*, rather than seeking and achieving a rapprochement with the *ecclesia* or with non-Jewish culture and systems of thought, in general.

Levita was thus no full-fledged participant in the Italian Renaissance or Christian Humanism, not a Humanist at all, unless—or perhaps, even if—multiple, supplementary qualifying modifiers be added to the label. From the specifically *pragmatic* Christian perspective of Cardinal Egidio da Viterbo, for instance, in whose Roman palace Levita lived and worked, he was simply a hired hand, not unlike the scholarly and less-than-scholarly, but—to the Western Christians—always theologically and culturally suspect, Byzantine Christians who flooded the intellectual circles of Italy in the mid-fifteenth century after Mehmet II finally laid to rest the fiction of an independent and Christian empire ruled from Constantinople by battering down a part of its Theodosian walls and taking possession of the scattered orchards and urban ruins and cultural remains that had been left by the Venetians in the wake of *their* conquest of the city during (or *as*) the Fourth Crusade of 1204. Like those Byzantine refugees, Levita assisted Egidio and other such Humanists in one of the individual tasks of the overall program of a specifically Christian Humanism—the study of the original languages of the Bible, in his case Hebrew (and to a lesser extent, the study of Talmud and Kabbalah, and thus his importance to his Christian students for Aramaic study). Levita's scholarship is of course written not in a revived classicized Latin—the badge of the Humanist—but in Hebrew: his quasi-biblically classicized Hebrew. Thus his cultural production is clearly centripetal—he writes on traditional Jewish topics in a Jewish language (at least in large part) for Jews. This is certainly the case for his lexicographical work and grammatical treatises, and even his Masoretic analysis takes place within the context of Jewish culture and a Jewish tradition of scholarship, even if his scholarly conclusions concerning what constituted the ancient text of the Bible were not, and in most cases still are not, accepted by normative, orthodox Judaism. This was true even though he worked with and for Christians sporadically for most of his adult life and even though he specified in his מסורת המסורת, on the age of the Masoretic vocalization of the biblical text, that he expected that both Christians and Jews might benefit from his argument.[22]

Moreover, there are several items in Levita's bibliography that give it a valence radically different from the profiles of his contemporary "Jewish humanists" (the חָכָם כּוֹלֵל, as counterpart to the Renaissance *homo universalis*): an event poem, a biting satirical poem, and a lengthy romance epic, all composed in Yiddish. And it is precisely on those texts and their sixteenth-century Italian cultural context, that is, the cultural context of sixteenth-century Ashkenazic Jews in Christian Italy, that the analysis focuses in the present chapter. That non-scholarly poems were written in the vernacular was certainly not a rarity among Christian Humanists, while it was quite rare among Jewish intellectuals of the time, only relatively few of whom wrote in Italian.[23] With Levita, however, the vernacular in question is of course not Italian, but Yiddish, already long the primary spoken language of Ashkenazic Jewry, and thus also of a sizable percentage of northern Italian Jews up to the end of the sixteenth century—in many such communities indeed they would have constituted the majority of the Jewish populace[24]—most of whom were either immigrants or the descendants of immigrants from north of the Alps to northern Italy, where at this time still much, if not most early Yiddish literature was published and found its immediate audience.

After having lived for some time in Padua, Levita fled from there to Venice at the end of July 1509 as a result of the capture of the Jewish quarter of Padua by the forces of the League of Cambrai, and along with him came five thousand other Jews from all regions of the Venetian *terraferma*. By October 1510, official permission had been granted for Jewish congregational prayer, followed in 1513 by official permission for Jewish residency and for Jewish-owned shops in the Rialto quarter.[25] In October 1513, the Venetian forces lost the battle of Motta to the League of Cambrai;[26] three months later the Rialto quarter burned (16 Shevat 5274; 23 January 1514),[27] including the famous bridge over the Grand Canal, as well as the shops on and around the bridge,[28] the flames whipped up by a strong north wind that prevented its being extinguished, while the immediate source of water to extinguish the flames, the Venetian canals, had been frozen by a freak winter storm.

In the first of Levita's short vernacular poems, די שריפה בון וונידיג "The Great Fire of Venice," Levita topicalizes that catastrophe, thus engaging in one of the more important genres of Old and Middle Yiddish literature, what Chone Shmeruk called *khidushim-lider*, "account-, report-, or event-poems"—using a term contemporary with the texts—poems that memorialized specific historical events, necessarily from the perspective of the affected Jewish community, such as the 1614 Fettmilch insurrection in Frankfurt (*EYT* 100), the Swedish siege of Prague near the end of the Thirty Years War (1649, *EYT* 101), and here the burning of the central part of Venice and especially the aftermath when the shops on the Rialto were looted, which relates this catastrophic event to the Jewish community in whose physical midst it took place.[29] Often such Jewish event-poems corroborate non-Jewish reports of the event, frequently with substantial detail that differs from them, due to a distinctive cultural perspective on the events.

Although the famed Venetian diarist of the period, Marino Sanuto, demonstrates great concern with the widespread looting that occurred during and after the fire, he, unlike Levita, does not mention any Jewish looters. The fact that Levita also makes a point of dealing with the libelous accusations by a certain Hillel Cohen—that Levita himself participated in the looting or at least in the harboring of stolen goods after the fact[30]—concretizes on the level of both the personal and the ethnic subdivisions of the city what seems to be, from Sanuto's lengthy treatment of the events surrounding the fire and its aftermath, a catastrophe into which specific personal and ethnic identity hardly intruded. Individuals named by Sanuto function only as examples of the economic catastrophe on the civic scale and focalize specifically Christian-Venetian conceptions of political identity; he mentions identified socially defined groups only insofar as he repeatedly accuses *forestieri* (non-Venetians), *rebeli* (rebels), and *padoani* (Paduans) as the likely arsonists.[31] While a modern reader sensitive to the broad modal ranges of anti-Semitism might be tempted to construe the first two designators as coded references to Jews (and perhaps the last, as well, since essentially the entire Jewish community of Padua had by this point taken up residence in Venice), it seems unlikely that Sanuto would have disguised his anti-Semitism here, since he does not do so elsewhere: when he wishes to specify Jews as malefactors, he does so overtly through the use of the ethnic identifier *zudei*.[32]

Levita notes that while Christian merchants and gentlemen suffered, so, too, did Jews (st. 2). Both Sanuto (458–462) and Levita (st. 3) note that *some* were glad to see the disaster and thought to become rich quickly by doing further damage themselves through looting. Both Levita and Sanuto likewise situate the fire in a more comprehensive moralizing construct: Sanuto says that the fire crossed no canals but burned deliberately and by divine will (461), making reference to the particular hardship faced by Venice because of the war against the League of Cambrai; Levita specifies that the fire was a divine punishment that ought to exhort one to moral behavior, making specific reference to the lament of the poor in the face of ostentatious wealth, and then he curses all war and the one who invented it (st. 21–24).

Just as Levita's first vernacular poem obviously belongs to the specific genre of the *khidushim-lider* (of which there were, of course, analogues in co-temporal Christian literatures, as well), his second participates directly in the genre of pasquinade that seemed almost ubiquitous in the dominant Christian culture that surrounded him in both Rome and Venice.[33] The poem is entitled המבדיל or המבדיל בין קודש לחול "Ha-Mavdil Song," a scathing attack on Hillel Cohen, whose serial marriages, apparent sexual impotence, and routine use of dead fish and live birds in the wedding bed are interwoven into a quasi-narrative plot that provides an initially hilarious and ultimately horrifying portrait of this Jewish schoolmaster, constructed as a personal enemy of Levita's and a danger to the Jewish community.

"The Great Fire" as an event-poem and "Ha-Mavdil Song" as a libelous personal attack both also participate in the multivalent and multi-cultural milieu of the occasional poem, a particular variant of the *khidushim-lid.* "The Great Fire" concludes with a wish for all to have a blessed Purim (st. 25), which has sometimes been taken as proof that it is a Purim song, a Purim parody, and to be construed in the pre-history of Purim plays.[34] "Ha-Mavdil Song," on the other hand, is a focused character assassination of a single individual and seems to have been composed and posted on a public wall in Venice specifically as a pasquinade. As a scandalously humorous text, it would certainly have been in the spirit of Purim celebrations. But in fact, neither of the poems is a *parody* of anything or anyone, except insofar as they each make use of the well-known literary forms of specific traditional songs. Before making facile assumptions that any given song that mentions Purim or that any given character assassination in poetic form must be a "Purim song," one would do well to recall that for genre categories to have any analytical value, they must have some definition.

As a poem about a natural catastrophe that affects the economic life of the city of Venice, "The Great Fire" certainly shows a world turned on its head, as is generally the case in Purim poems. But that is about as far as such a connection can be taken in the case; this text has no optimistic or celebratory turn, as is characteristic of such poems, and more importantly lacks the essential point of the Purim celebration and Purim poems: catastrophe *avoided* (or transformed after the fact) by means of Jewish virtue and/or divine intervention (as in the holiday's founding myth in the biblical book of Esther and subsequent literary documentation of secondary Purim celebrations), especially as concretized via anti-Semitic depredation threatened but halted, or suffered but rectified. One should also note that the tradition of Purim songs had not, at least up to 1514, included libelous character assassination, nor indeed does it become a defining feature thereafter.

It seems that Levita's poem, based on the fire of January 1514, was indeed complete by Purim (22 March 1514), but if it is to be reckoned as a Purim song—as opposed simply to a song that was composed around the time of Purim and mentions the holiday—that is, if "Purim song" identifies a particular content, literary mode, even genre, then the definition of that genre would require a great deal of adaptation to accommodate this particular poem, and that adaptation would in turn require scholarly argument supported by evidence, not merely the offhand assignment of a label.

Be that as it may, both poems participate in that common confluence of piety, venom, intricate poetic form, and ribald humor that was so characteristic of Renaissance occasional poetry, but which in these examples remains, in construction, poetic aesthetic, and execution, essentially Jewish. The two poems are the most neglected of Levita's works and have drawn surprisingly little scholarly interest since the publication of the Yiddish texts in the early and mid-twentieth century, due in part to the difficulty of the language and the esoteric network of reference in the poems themselves, but also to long-standing scholarly anti-Yiddish prejudices and/or prudishness, such as the claims by Meir Medan that they "lack any literary value" and by Erika Timm that "[sie] sind viel zu früh und alles andere als 'reif,'" "they are much too early and anything but 'mature.'"[35] Quite to the contrary, these learned and consummately artistic poems operate within the great traditions of Hebrew, Humanistic, and Renaissance Italian occasional poetry and are in fact masterpieces of the genre, penned by one of the most important Jewish intellectuals of the period, and "Ha-Mavdil Song" is additionally a magnificent example of the period's penchant for bawdy and (often) hilarious poetic satire. Both of the poems demonstrate the principles of Jewish and in particular Yiddish cultural liminality and literary hybridity that have characterized Ashkenaz from its very origins. While it would be a slight exaggeration to claim that the poems are unimaginable in Jewish literature except in sixteenth-century Italy, the fact is that once they are sited in Venice of the *cinquecento*, there is an immediate sense that the fit is perfect. There is close attention to poetic form, ottava rima—a new form at the time, known otherwise still only in Italian and Hebrew poetry written in Italy—in one of the poems, as also in Levita's (pre-)Rabelaisian Yiddish epic *Bovo d'Antona*, where the typically picaresque plot, the not-so-subtle humor, eroticism, and corporeal earthiness are perfectly at home, particularly when one notes that they come from the pen of a well-known scholar.

These three Yiddish texts composed by Levita are, however, centripetal—Jewish literature for Jews—even though they are all three, as noted, quasi-secular. But since the texts are written in Yiddish, they could not function as Italian satire and/or Romance-language texts written by Christian Humanists for Italian Christian readers would have functioned. Levita's Yiddish works do not constitute a movement away from traditional Jewish culture or religion, but rather function clearly as a reaffirmation of the inner, centripetal identity of the Jewish community, and not just because they are linguistically inaccessible to outsiders.

This is most obviously the case with the short poems, particularly "Ha-Mavdil Song," which was apparently posted as a broadsheet on the walls of Venice (st. 69),[36] where it could only have been read by members of the Jewish community, who alone would have been able to understand the language, would have known the position of the object of the satire, the *melamed* (teacher) Hillel Cohen, and would have understood the complex references to traditional aspects of Jewish life used to characterize Cohen. Thus only Ashkenazic Jews would have been able to appreciate the savage humor of Levita's character assassination of Cohen.[37]

One of the as yet unsolved riddles concerns the issue of where "Ha-Mavdil Song," as a Yiddish-language pasquinade, could have been *effectively* posted in pre-ghetto Venice? Were the poem datable to the period after the establishment of the Ghetto nuovo in 1516, one would automatically be inclined to site the posting in the *campo* of the ghetto itself, where it could have been seen and read by several hundred Yiddish speakers within a few hours of its posting.[38] But the poem predates the establishment of the ghetto by two years, so that particular scenario is not a possibility, since the area of the ghetto was not yet inhabited by Jews.

The tradition of hanging satirical broadsheets on walls around Italian cities was, however, both long-standing and widespread during this period, and the specifically Venetian tradition thereof is still well represented. A fascinating collection of pasquinades confiscated by the Venetian state police in the course of the fifteenth through eighteenth centuries (and labeled by date and place found) is preserved in a separate document case (*busta*) in the Venetian Archivio di Stato and includes poems, songs, and satires in Tuscan, Venetian, Latin, French, and Greek—but not Yiddish or Hebrew—thus bearing witness to the fact that satires were in fact being pasted up all over town (some examples of which in this *busta* still retain remnants of their adhesive) and included character assassination and obviously also political denunciation as part of their function. But there is unfortunately nothing directly relevant to Jewish satire in the *busta*.

Likewise unfortunate for the present issue, there is no evidence for the direct relevance of the famous Venetian sites at which pasquinades were posted, for it was not until 1541 that satirical poems were routinely posted on the then newly sculpted and installed statue (that came to be called "Gobbo"[39]) across the *campo* from San Giacomo di Rialto, near the Rialto market; and not until a couple of decades after that did the statues by Antonio Rioba on the Campo dei Mori just northeast of the ghetto begin to function as a site of pasquinade postings. Moreover, the Gobbo and the Mori became famous as sites of Italian-language or specifically Venetian-dialect satirical postings, while there is no indication that they ever drew pasquinades in Yiddish—although, it should be noted, there is likewise no evidence that they did not do so. In any case, neither of these sites—insofar as they are defined by the statues involved—comes into question as pertinent in determining the site of Levita's posting simply because of chronology, and otherwise no sixteenth-century information about specifically Jewish posted satires in Venice has come to light. At the same time, however, there is no reason on principle to rule out the *sites* later associated with the posting of pasquinades as possible points at which broadsheets were posted, even before the erection of the statues; it is less likely that the erection of the statues themselves would suddenly have constituted those locales as posting sites for pasquinades than that once erected they simply became the objects on which the tradition of pasquinade posting at that site was continued.

In the absence of pertinent information about the location of potential posting sites for specifically Jewish pasquinades, it would be very useful to ascertain where Jews lived in Venice before the establishment of the ghetto, since Yiddish-language broadsides posted in those areas would have been most accessible to their target audience. Gérard Weil suggests that it was particularly in the three rather widely scattered parishes of San Canciano, Sant'Agostin, and San Geremia that Jews settled after their flight to Venice in 1509.[40] Thus a pasquinade posted even in one of those three *campi* would not necessarily have been seen by a majority of Ashkenazi Jews resident in Venice. Indeed both the Senate document that established the ghetto and Marino Sanuto, who says slightly more about that event, indicate that one of the motivating factors for the establishment of the ghetto was "che tutj li zudei che de presentj se attrovano habitar in diverse contrade de questa cità nostra," "that all the Jews are currently found to live in various districts of our city."[41] If that was in fact the case, and not simply an exaggeration intended to foment xenophobic sentiment (of which Sanuto was perfectly capable), then it would seem almost impossible to determine a particular *residential* parish in which Levita's Yiddish-language character assassinations would have most easily found their Yiddish-literate audience in the spring of 1514.[42] Sanuto does provide a bit more detail by naming the parishes that were, from his perspective, "contaminated" by Jews, and significantly, they are not the same as those suggested by Weil: San Cassiano, Sant'Agostin, Santa Maria Mater Domini, and San Polo, which, interestingly, form a concentrated rectangular area some 350 × 300 meters only a couple of minutes by foot west of the future site of the Gobbo statue in the Rialto market area, which is obviously the spatial focus of Levita's "The Great Fire."[43]

While, as already noted, there is no concrete evidence concerning the posting of Jewish satires or notices of any kind during the pre-ghetto years, the general area of the Rialto would be a likely place to suspect, particularly since it was also one of the two places in the city where all state regulations were proclaimed, even and very specifically those concerning Jews.[44] In other words, Jews were expected to be aware of what went on around the Rialto in both a general and a quite specific, legal sense. Thus Shakespeare's "What news on the Rialto?" (*The Merchant of Venice,* 1.3 and 3.1) was another of his acute cultural insights, for in Venice, if it was news—even or especially Jewish news—it came from or at least was known on the Rialto.

Intriguingly, Levita himself provides the most concrete evidence concerning Jewish pasquinades and their posting, although it is quite oblique and ultimately does not answer the most pressing questions, but it does at least, even in the absence of examples from the Archivio di Stato, suggest in compelling fashion that Jewish pasquinades did exist in Italy during the period. In the entry for כַּתַּב in his *Tishbi*, a Hebrew-language lexicographical work that defines 712 words found in the Talmud and midrash, Levita remarks: בימים קדמונים היו בעלי צחיות ומושלי משלים כותבים דבריהם על פתחי בתי הנדיבים או ברחובת הומיות בסתר כדי שלא יודע מי הוא הכותב. וכן מנהג עוד היום ברומי ואותן הדברים נקראים כתבות "In the past, eloquent people and *mesholim*-authors secretly wrote their things on the doors of rich houses or in noisy streets, so that no one would know who the writer was. This is still done nowadays in Rome, and these same things are called *katoves*."[45] While one should be cautious about discounting the literal interpretation of his words, it seems more likely that such texts were written on paper and then attached to the doors of the wealthy rather than actually being written directly on the doors. Again, precisely *where* these wealthy Jews lived or which "noisy streets" Levita might have had in mind is not clear, and those two sites would logically perhaps seem least likely as places to write satires on the doors or even to post them if one wished to remain undetected and anonymous, unless, obviously, executed in the dead of night when the street was not in fact so noisy and the wealthy Jew's or patrician Christian's doorkeeper might have been dozing.

Such information about the definition and posting of pasquinades by the author of the pasquinade here at issue is pertinent indeed. Unfortunately, however, while he does indicate that the practice persisted in Rome in 1541, he reveals no specifics of his own practice of twenty-seven years earlier in Venice, when he almost certainly composed "Ha-Mavdil Song" between January and the summer of 1514, when he left Venice for Rome. While it could theoretically have been written later, after he was living in Rome, before or after he became employed by Egidio da Viterbo, it seems far less likely, since the poem would, with the passage of time, quickly have lost its local Venetian currency, and it obviously would have been less relevant to a Judeo-Roman than a Judeo-Venetian audience.[46] Gérard Weil matter-of-factly notes that "Ha-Mavdil Song" was *also* hung up on the walls of the city, duplicating the pattern of pasquinade practice in Rome, indicating (in the immediate context of his argument) that he also imagined that "The Great Fire" had earlier been posted.[47] According to Weil, "Ha-Mavdil Song" "vibre d'une verve rabelaisienne," "resonates with a Rabelaisian wit."[48] Levita's satire is sharp-edged, indeed savage in the Juvenalian sense that, according to Roger Kimball, aims primarily at the catharsis of exposure, and only incidentally at justice and reform.[49]

The "Ha-Mavdil Song" participates in both the centripetal Jewish intellectual tradition and the developing Italian tradition of the pasquinade, while remaining hermetically sealed to outside view.[50] At the same time, through the poem's narrative, it adroitly sets up spatial relations that establish a Jewish presence in Venice and the Veneto by means of an implied movement back and forth between the urban center and the periphery at and beyond the boundaries of Venetian territory. This dynamic might not be immediately apparent on a first reading of the poem, since that is not ostensibly its focal subject. Nonetheless, the mode of Levita's construction of the poem demonstrates clearly how it functions centripetally—open to a Jewish audience, closed to a Gentile audience—and is even now sporadically almost banal in translation for a reader without a knowledge of that tradition, while still participating at least obliquely in the satirical traditions of the Italian Renaissance. The poem's complexities must thus be unpacked.

The poem's title is identical to the traditional Hebrew-language *zemer* (Sabbath song) recited after *havdole* (havdalah), the ceremony that marks the end of the Sabbath, which thus forms a division between the temporally sacred and the profane, followed by the post-Sabbath night, the Yiddish pasquinade's implication clearly being that the distinction between the sacred and the profane reflects that between Levita and Cohen. The traditional Hebrew hymn contains an acrostic of the name of the author, Isaac the Younger (probably Isaac ben Judah ibn Ghayyat, Spain, 1030–1089), and comprises ten couplets, in each of which the first three hemistichs rhyme, while the last always ends with the Hebrew word לילה *layla,* "night." Levita's pasquinade lacks the acrostic but retains the same stanzaic and rhyme structure, and each stanza also closes with the word לילה.[51]

Levita then further demonstrates his characteristic satirical wit by means of the traditional convention of compounding meaning via numerological parallel (*gematria*), that is, associating two or more words by means of the sum of the numerical value of their individual alpha-numerical letters. While this practice often seems contrived to those whose poetic or intellectual culture does not engage in such artifice, it is nonetheless an essential element in traditional Hebrew-language intellectual playfulness and thus occurs repeatedly in some modes of Jewish poetry, and its presence and significance were immediately recognized by those members of its target audience attuned to the practice. Thus, the numerical value of both the first and last names of the satire's object, Hillel Cohen (הילל כהן), equals 75, just as does the value of לילה "night," which is additionally an anagram of הילל "Hillel." With the closing word of each stanza the poet thus repeats and contorts Hillel's name and associates it with both darkness/obscurity ("night") and the profane realm following the Sabbath. The number 75 is then also identified as the year about to begin, ע"ה (i.e., רע"ה = [5]275 = 1514–1515 CE), and is also identified as the number of stanzas in the composition. To practiced eyes among the Venetian Ashkenazic audience, this mode of language play was immediately apparent.

In his lampooning of Cohen, Levita constructs Venetian Jewish life by positioning it in Jewish spaces that at the same time necessarily signify in relation to Venetian political space. Hillel is, Levita claims, known throughout the Veneto, wherever he has spent a single לילה (st. O3). His behavior in three specifically Jewish community sites in Venice characterize him—the synagogue, the הקדש "charity ward," and חדר "elementary school"—especially in the synagogue, where Hillel rarely appears, since his brother is a גלך "a Catholic priest/monk" (st. 5,3), and he is a גוי גומר (literally: a "total Gentile"; idiomatically: a Jew who is so impious/immoral that he might as well be a Gentile), who cannot pray even as far as ברוך שאמר, the *opening* blessing of the *beginning* of the morning prayer (st. 6). Even for the instruction of young children—his mode of employment—his ignorance is so profound that it is entertaining just to watch him *impersonate* a teacher (st. 13): he does not even know the בנין (ה)קל, the base form of the Hebrew conjugational system (st. 9); the simplest textual issue stumps him (st. 7); he cannot even account for the seemingly feminine termination of the masculine noun לילה "night"; and his incompetence is so well known that he earns very little even though he teaches twenty-*five* hours a day (st. 15). Within these communal spaces of Jewish Venice, Hillel is thus characterized as a charlatan.

Furthermore, Levita continues, Cohen is immoral. His sexual behavior is, to say the least, non-conforming; even before one reaches the lengthy section on Cohen's marriages, Levita already claims that Cohen's beloved came to him in Venice from across the lagoon in Marghera (מַרגֶער) and lay beneath him, but that the two of them did not "draw near" to each other all night long (st. 18). Cohen is a gambler who associates with Gentiles until late in the night (st. 19), and he participates in the extensive system of spies organized both formally and informally by the Venetian government in order to foment the anonymous and secret denunciation of one Venetian by another. Cohen himself spies on Jews and denounces them to governmental agencies; he has thus ruined the lives of Matis and Kalman Terviz (Treviso), for "he makes denunciations so that they stick to a person like glue," in order to be rewarded by gaining *their* property (i.e., his governmentally sanctioned share of the confiscated goods, st. 21); he is always ready to bear false witness (st. 24). But, the reader is consoled, he will eventually be caught and get his well-deserved reward (st. 23), for in fact he is himself pursued by several instances of the Venetian judiciary, which makes him not merely a scoundrel but a recognized criminal on the "most-wanted list" (st. 19–21).[52]

In the central stanzas of the poem, Cohen's "emasculating" sexual practices are construed as perversions and mocked in rather graphic detail. He is pointedly accused of a homosexual liaison with a Greek man (st. 25), as prelude to the narrator's enumeration of his failed serial marriages—"Now, because I wish to entertain you well, / Then I will sing to you of his three wives" (st. 26)—in which he apparently never fulfills his marital duties according to the norm of the culture. Significantly, this entire section of the poem seems to express Cohen's deficiencies also in terms of space: not communal/sacral space as in the earlier references to synagogue, school, or charity ward, but rather its obverse in the personal sphere (which may incidentally more appropriately be considered "private" than would be the case for the homes of Venetian patricians, although the Jewish home was in most senses a continuation of the sacral community space). In this instance, that focal space is the marriage bed and the demarcated territories and boundaries within it, movements back and forth across it, with lovers and/or spouses approaching each other (or not) and touching each other (or not). Between marriage partners, this space is the specifically designated and regulated site of the מצווה "sacred duty" of marital relations that is here *not* being performed (esp. st. 34), and its nonperformance is, significantly, here plotted spatially. Thus in one space after another in the constructed conception of Jewish life, Cohen fails miserably.

His first marriage had to be annulled because he could not consummate it (st. 27–28); significantly in this cultural-spatial context, that deficiency on Cohen's part is expressed as: he never "went even a single mile with her" (st. 27,2). Everything she ever got out of him, she later, with a different man, managed to equal in a single לילה. With his second wife, Cohen again lacked the "strength" to consummate the marriage; so he bought a carp, which he gutted during the wedding night in order to smear its blood on the sheets. Unfortunately for him, the women who came to inspect the sheets the following morning (to "certify" both the bride's virginity and the marriage's consummation) found some only momentarily enigmatic fish scales adhering to the sheets along with the blood, so that everyone even across the lagoon in Mestre (מיינשטרש), on the mainland, knew the tale before sunset and the onset of לילה (st. 30–32). About his poor wife, it is said: זיא האט אבר בייא אין איין ורײדא איין קלייני: / ניא קיין גוטאן יום נוך קיין גוטי לַיְלָה "Yet she had from him but little delight: / Never a good day, and never a good night" (st. 29,3–4). She herself comments:

34 וויא הון איך אזו גאר איין שלעכ֗ט מאן:
איין גאנצי נכ֗ט רֻיִרט ער מיך ניט אן:
רויק איך מיך שון צו אים: זוא רֻיִקט ער זיך הין דאן:
וְלֹא קָרַב זֶה אֶל זֶה כָּל הַלַּיְלָה:

> "O what a 'proper'[53] husband I have! He does not even touch me the whole night long. If I move over close to him, he then moves farther away." And the one did not draw near to the other the entire night.[54]

Cohen abandoned her and moved to Cividale del Friuli (שיבדעטלן), while she became a beggar (st. 35), moved back to her mother's house in Udine (ווײדן), since she had no money to move to Portogruaro (פורטיגוועער) (st. C36), and eventually moved in with her father in Ferrara (פארער) and died there (st. 36).

In his quest for a third wife, Cohen traveled the whole countryside, chasing marriage brokers until he finally found one in Mantua (מַאנְטוֹ), where no one knew him, and thus his reputation would not scare away potential brides (st. 38–39). He immediately drove this third wife out of his Venetian house to work as a servant in another house, so that he would not have to occupy the same bed with her every לילה (st. 40). With her, too, he tried the trick with the blood of a slaughtered animal on the wedding night, this time with a פוטה *puta,* "magpie" (st. 43,2),[55] while begging his wife to keep her silence and maintain his reputation: זאג אידרמן וויא איך בין גיוועזן איין מאן "Tell everyone how I was a man" (st. 45,1, again recalling the narrator's earlier accusation of homosexuality). He carried on some unspecified ווילדאן האנדיל "wild business" and משונה דינגאר "strange things," apparently with his fingers or by clawing or scratching (st. 41, 42, 46, 52–53), which made her weep by day and scream by night (st. 41–42). She thereafter maintained her distance by claiming to be menstruating—and thus ritually inaccessible sexually—whenever he indicated any interest: עֶרֶב וָבוֹקֶר יוֹם וָלַיְלָה "evening and morning, day and night" (st. 47,4), humorously echoing the recurring formulaic phrase from the creation myth of Genesis (and perhaps the *Shemoneh Esreh* prayer). She fled by ship (st. 49); he overtook her, boarded the ship, and asked why she wanted to leave him, the question wittily formulated as the initiating question of the Passover liturgy: מַה נִשְׁתַּנָּה הַלַּיְלָה "How is this night different [from any other night]?" (st. 50,4). He demanded that she return with him to Venice; they argued; he beat her; the case was brought before the rabbinical court (st. 52–56); they divorced; he was awarded all the property (st. 57).

Thereafter he found no other woman who would marry him, מִפַּחַד בַּלַּיְלָה "for terror of the night" (st. 58,4). His inability to find another bride is expressed in a significant manner: no ship will לֵיוֶוערַן *leveran,* "raise, lift, take on [a passenger]"; and no woman wants to אימפּאַצֶערן *impazirn,* "hinder, burden" herself with him (st. 58)—both common words in the language of Yiddish business, and both obviously derived directly from Venetian dialect.[56] Unlike other old men, he refused to treat his young wives well by day, and נוך ערגיר הוט זיא עש בייא דער לַיְלָה "she has it still worse by night" (st. 59,4).[57] In the end, his behavior tailed off into bestiality and the sexual abuse of children: in addition to his bizarre practices with fish and fowl (st. 64),[58] he slept in the same bed with and "tortured" (וואר ער . . . מְעַנֶּה; st. 60,3) cats and dogs, and in Volta dei Negri (וָאלְטַה דֵי נֶיגְרַה, in Padua), he sexually abused four- and five-year-old girls (st. 62–65). In addition to its other modes of libel, the poem then constitutes a broad and sustained attack on Cohen's sexuality, including allegations of homosexuality, bestiality, pedophilia, and abusive, non-normative (non-reproductive) heterosexual practices.

The poem ends by closing the frame that was opened already in the third stanza, where it is said that Cohen had *again* written (and posted) a poem about Levita, in response to Levita's first poem ("The Great Fire," 3–4). Now Levita refers to the present poem as "this ציטל [scrap of a] "page upon the wall" (st. 69) and claims that he will write another one that same evening, and before the month is over yet another in Hebrew (st. 70); he hopes that the poems go as far as a bat flies at night (st. 71); Cohen, it is claimed, would have been better off had he just stayed at home [and thus out of Levita's sights] (st. 67,2).

Levita's "Ha-Mavdil Song" concerns many things: obviously Cohen's alleged character flaws, immorality, and criminality, but especially, through his negative example, a behavioral norm in the Jewish community of Venice. In the course of this exposition, Levita also sets up spatial relations on at least three levels: within the home (especially in the marriage bed), in the public institutions of the community (חדר, הקדש, שול "elementary school, charity ward, and synagogue"), and then on a larger scale, the centripetal tension between the geographical center (Venice) and its immediate periphery on the mainland (Mestre and Marghera) and its further periphery in the Veneto and the territories just beyond its boundaries, for Ferrara, Mantua, Cividale, Udine, and the ship on the Adriatic constitute the periphery just beyond the south, west, north, and eastern borders of the Veneto, with Venice as the center.[59] There is a recurring push and pull, movement into and away from this center. Cohen's failures to negotiate the tensions of these spatial relations effectively signal his eventual isolation and ultimately even exclusion from the community and Jewish life. If in the beginning he is a גוי גומר, a Jew who seems more like a Gentile, then by the end of the poem he might as well be an actual גוי.

With its raucous, quasi-obscene attack on a disgraced and ostracized member of the Jewish community, the poem is quite striking in the context of traditional Askenazic society. But one must keep in mind that the poem is after all centripetal—Jewish for Jews—which effectively prevented this Jew-on-Jew (textual) violence from becoming visible to the non-Jewish majority culture and thus directly compromising or indeed endangering the community or any member of it (unlike, for instance, Cohen, whose denunciations to Venetian authorities functioned in precisely that way).[60] Levita's threat to write another pasquinade about Cohen in Hebrew would broaden that audience to include all (Hebrew-literate) Jews, whether Ashkenazim or not, in Venice, while still excluding Gentiles.[61]

More striking still, and more importantly in terms of the literary and cultural significance of the poem, Levita here reveals a literarily productive connection with popular culture beyond the bounds of the Jewish community that is rare if not unprecedented at the time. The specific mode of satire employed by Levita recalls non-Jewish literary traditions on both sides of the Alps, for while the Italian Renaissance certainly provided ample such models, Northern European Humanism did not lag behind. Chief among them is to be counted the *Epistolae obscurorum virorum* ("Letters of Obscure Men," 1515, enlarged editions 1516 and 1517), which participated in a larger ideological and theological debate on the eve of the Reformation.[62] This particular controversy eventually divided the whole of German Humanism into two camps, initially sparked by the extremist writings published under the name of Johannes Pfefferkorn, a convert from Judaism, although it may well have been the case that he was merely the front man for a rabid group of Dominican theologians from Cologne who had assumed the right to define and punish heresy in Germany, one of their customary objects—not surprisingly—being Jews (and former Jews), expressed particularly through the Dominicans' attack on the Talmud and pressure to have it confiscated and burned. In any case, Pfefferkorn advocated the customary anti-Jewish measures, such as forcing Jews to listen to sermons, forbidding usury, exiling the Jews from German states, and burning all their books with the exception of the Bible. In staunch opposition to this position stood Johannes Reuchlin, at the time one of the most respected Christian Humanists in Northern Europe, who should not, however, be imagined as an innocent champion of the Jews. He was after all a staunch advocate of the conversion of the Jews. He simply favored somewhat less violent methods to achieve that goal than did many of his contemporaries. He also defended the historical and cultural importance (for Christian culture and scholarship) of extra-biblical Jewish texts, such as the Talmud.

In any case, in 1509, Emperor Maximilian I ordered Jewish books confiscated. When the archbishop of Mainz objected, the emperor consulted with scholars, Reuchlin among them. The conflict escalated and led to quite personal and vicious verbal attacks by Reuchlin and Pfefferkorn and the Cologne Dominicans. Soon the controversy spread, polarizing scholars throughout the German lands (and beyond), with conservatives supporting the Dominicans, while Humanists took Reuchlin's more "enlightened" position. Pope Leo X, the son of Lorenzo di Medici, took up the case and appointed a commission to examine it. When all but one of the twenty-two commissioners decided in favor of Reuchlin, the pope rejected the majority opinion and in 1520 compelled Reuchlin to pay court costs, which, according to some accounts, reduced him to penury for the remainder of his life.[63] Interestingly, one of Reuchlin's staunchest champions in Rome was Levita's patron, Egidio da Viterbo.[64]

In the earlier stages of the controversy, many Humanists wrote to Reuchlin expressing their support. He published a selection of those letters in 1514 as *Clarorum virorum epistolae* ("Letters of Eminent Men"). The following year that collection's counterpart, as it were, the *Epistolae obscurorum virorum* ("Letters of Obscure Men"), appeared, purportedly a collection of letters addressed to and in support of Ortwin Gratius, one of the Cologne theologians who opposed Reuchlin. The letters and their outlandishly named authors were, however, the brilliantly fictive inventions of two Humanist supporters of Reuchlin, Crotus Rubeanus and Ulrich von Hutten. The letters are constructed as fawning fan mail, written in appallingly bad Latin by uneducated, immoral, and willfully stupid boors whose conception of intellectual life consisted at best in quibbling. Especially in the letters of Conradus de Zuiccavia (Conrad of Zwickau), there are attempts, for instance, to justify fornication by clerics through quasi-theological argumentation (see epistle IX, 26–29, among others). In epistle XL from Herbordus Mistladerius (German *Mistlader* = "manure-loader"), Rabelaisian "earthiness" comes to the fore—it details Ortwin Gratius's public, visible, and uncontrollable diarrhea, followed by a pseudo-learned suggestion for a remedy, which consists of complete quackery. The theological, linguistic, and general ignorance of the letter writers is manifest at every point: not only is their Latin execrable, they know no Greek whatsoever and even deny that it might be relevant for theological study (apparently unaware of, or indifferent to, the fact that it is the original language of the New Testament), and they deride a knowledge of Hebrew as tantamount to heresy. The overall tone of the collection is one of crudeness and stupidity; the effect, even now, is often hilarity. There is little wonder that the book is one of Europe's most famous satires.[65] In significant ways, the portraits of the boors there obviously resemble the tone and in part the content of Levita's lampoon of Hillel Cohen.

Even so, while this mode of satirical letters is pertinent to Levita's Venetian satire, a more directly relevant mode of satire is found in the poetic flytings from the world of William Dunbar and John Skelton in sixteenth-century England and Scotland.[66] As R.B. Gill points out, "Flytings are exchanges of invective in verse between two opponents," and "few sixteenth-century poetic forms are as full of the overflowing vigor of Renaissance life as flytings. . . . Flytings are important as early examples of Renaissance satire; their structures, strengths, and problems can be considered paradigms of other Renaissance satire."[67] Performed at court, Gill suggests that flytings may not have functioned as actual insult, but rather as a performance mode, much like the twentieth-century African-American practice of "the dozens," in which such insults as "Your mother eats dog food" never elicit denial ("No she doesn't"), which would imply that the statement was taken as one whose truth value was at issue, but rather are perceived as prompts for counter-insults that raise the stakes, such as "*Your* mother eats rat heads." The whole is then a matter of rhetorical display, performance discourse, not actual biographically based insult.[68] Flytings thus constitute art as a contest of poetic skill demonstrated here via skill in composing invective. One wonders what role such performance practice might have played in the supposed Levita-Cohen confrontation via broadsheet postings.

Yet a third tradition of satire must be taken into account here, because Levita's literary practice, his mode of distribution, and his mode of reception quite strictly parallel that of what seems a culturally far more relevant phenomenon: the originally Roman festival of Pasquino, which indeed provides the modern English (and Italian) name of the literary genre to which Levita's satires belong, and the term used to designate them thus far in this chapter. The tale of Pasquino is a long and circuitous one, but even in the brief form here presented demonstrates its relevance to Levita's satirical practice.

In Rome, probably during the 1430s, by the *torre de gl'Orsini* near the ruins of the stadium of Domitian (whose shape is still preserved in the unusual long oval of the Piazza Navona), a fragmentary Hellenistic statue (ca. second century BCE) in marble representing two partial torsos (variously identified as Menelaos, Herakles, or Patroklos) was excavated and soon set up on display nearby.[69] By 1500 there were explicit references to the statue, which Cardinal Oliviero Carafa, cardinal-protector of the Dominican Order and the power behind Pope Innocent VIII, had set up in front of the Palazzo Orsini (now Palazzo Braschi), where he lived (near its present site, on the Piazza del Pasquino, to which it moved in 1791), with the inscription (now gone) "Oliverii Carafae beneficio hic sum, anno salutis M.D.I.," "I am here through the good offices of Oliviero Carafa, in the year of the redemption 1501."[70] In the final years of the fifteenth century a tradition arose by which the statue was called Pasquino and students and other wags pasted *Latin* verse on the base of the statue and the palace wall behind it.[71] Exactly why it was named Pasquino is not known. Some sixteenth-century speculations suggest that a like-named tradesman, shoemaker, workman, innkeeper, or barber was the origin; or perhaps a tailor who openly criticized the papal curia, safe due to the range of his clients among internationally high-ranking aristocrats and ecclesiastics. In any case, already by 1501 satirical verse directed especially at the papacy constituted a substantial portion of the verse that was attached to the statue.

In 1509 Giacomo Mazzocchi began publishing an annual selection of the poems; his motivation seems in part at least to have been pedagogical: to improve the Latin of the writers and readers involved, urging them away from a medieval and toward a Humanistic Latin style. He claimed that the original Pasquino was a schoolteacher who lived across from the excavation site. The priests belonging to the faculty at the local school of San Lorenzo in Damaso covered the statue with verse, soon followed by students attaching their own verses, lampooning their pedantic priestly teachers. Mazzocchi also documented and explained the decoration of the statue on Saint Mark's feast (25 April) as various mythological figures. Verses relevant to that figure and to current events were attached, and then after that single day, the costume and poems were removed.[72] This event seems to have been under the control of powerful cardinals or perhaps even the papacy, with an attempt to direct the proceedings to support the pope, in what otherwise would apparently have become an anti-papal movement. As Barkan comments on the origins of the satirical usages surrounding the statue:

> In sum, the pasquinade—a mediated outlet for social dissatisfaction and exercise in philology and goliardic high spirits, an annual day of license sanctioned and manipulated by the Curia—is one of those overdetermined cultural events that has too many causes. What is probably most true about the origins of the festival is that they are collective and that several independent strands go into the creation: revived ancient festivals of misrule; activities of local churches and schools; the celebration of Easter—after all, neither the April date nor the verbal coincidence of *Pasqua* and *Pasquino* can be accidental; and the recently revived *Paliliae*, or birthday of Rome, which fell on 20 April.[73]

With the passage of years, the Roman Pasquino tradition became established, and as Barkan summarizes, the pasquinade spread far beyond its original city of origin: "The *Pasquino*, in countless modern languages, is the eponymous originator of a genre or mode of satire in which powerful figures in authority are attacked in some public way, often scurrilously or even obscenely, by individuals who operate under the cloak of anonymity."[74]

Enter Pietro Aretino (1492–1556), who was to become altogether identified with Pasquino. The son of a cobbler, Aretino probably had no formal education, knew no Latin, and could thus never fully participate in the intellectual life of the Renaissance and Humanism. He was nonetheless intellectually brilliant and attracted aristocratic patrons, first in Perugia (1510–1517), then in Rome, and later in Venice. His move to Rome is generally dated to 1516–1517, by which time the Pasquino poems had, according to Waddington, become increasingly "partisan and satiric" and developed a motif of sexual aggressiveness.[75] In Rome Aretino found patronage in the house of Agostino Chigi (likewise the patron of Raphael), where he also participated in the outer circle of Pope Leo X; in addition he frequented various aristocratic and ecclesiastical salons around the city. Aretino was thus privy to much gossip from inside the curia and soon had the opportunity to use that knowledge satirically. It was in fact during the papal conclave following Leo's death (1 December 1521) that savagely satirical poems concerning the culinary, gustatory, libidinal, and excretory excesses of prelates, cardinals, and popes were pasted up on Pasquino, penned by Aretino, who guided the Roman pasquinade to its defining turn, whereby this phenomenon took on long-term, pan-European cultural importance under his direction, as he emerged as the definitive Pasquino poet.[76] First, he changed the language of the tradition from Latin to the vernacular, which opened it to the entire Roman and Italian population as a potential (at least aural) audience; second, while Pasquino had until then been the anonymous voice of the Romans—or at least the Latin-literate among them—now Aretino openly avowed his authorship and even cultivated his popular identification as the embodiment of the vernacular Pasquino.[77]

Macabre as it may now seem to some, the lampooning of a dead pope, as Hösle points out, had at that time already had a long tradition.[78] Leo's death under mysterious circumstances and what then seemed the inordinate length of the ensuing conclave (27 December–9 January) provided even more incentive for rumor and invective. By this time Aretino had by means of his wit also acquired the patronage of Cardinal Giulio de' Medici, whose candidacy in the papal election he adamantly supported with his pen via savage pasquinades. For Romans, a conclave was by definition a Roman party; so the eventual election of the puritanical Hadrian VI of Utrecht (who had been the teacher of Charles V) was perceived as a betrayal and even as the *finis Italiae*, "end of Italy," which sentiment seemed indeed to be fulfilled five years later with Charles's sack of Rome (by which time Hadrian was, however, long dead). While Hadrian did not arrive in Rome until August 1522, his entourage did approach Rome in triumph, prompting Aretino, not surprisingly, to leave the city in something of a rush, in the company of Giulio de' Medici. Aretino arrived in Florence after having barely survived a knife wound sustained in an assassination attempt in July 1522 (satire sometimes does have very tangible, personal consequences!). Aretino was then in and out of Rome over the next few years, depending on whether he stood in the good graces of any given, newly elected pope (and/or patron) or had already offended him.[79] Hadrian even ordered Giulio to hand Aretino over to him, prompting Giulio merely to equivocate. Hadrian died in 1523 and was succeeded in fact by Giulio as Clement VII. Aretino's return to favor was short-lived, however, since he again was forced into exile after publishing his *Sonetti Lussuriosi* to accompany Giulio Romano's drawings of sixteen copulatory positions, engraved by Marcantonio Raimondi. His attacks on Bishop Giovanni Giberti led to yet another, nearly successful, assassination attempt in 1525. While his literary reputation is in part based on those works and on his letters, collected and published after he took up residence in Venice, it is his Roman pasquinades that are obviously of particular relevance in the present context.

Fifty-one of Aretino's pasquinades, in the augmented sonnet form (*sonnetta caudata*), from the period during and after the papal conclave of 1521–1522 are preserved.[80] The poems were popular not just in Rome or indeed Italy, but were eagerly awaited at aristocratic and royal courts and at the desks of Humanists throughout Europe. The first provides an irregular list of the candidates and does not spare in its mockery of them for nepotism, sodomy, bribery, and so on. The tenth pasquinade takes Cardinal Colonna as its target, listing his faults and comparing them to those of other cardinals. His pasquinades numbered XXXIII–LI were composed after Hadrian's election.

Aretino was, not so incidentally, also well known and generally admired among sixteenth-century English and Scottish Renaissance intellectuals and greatly influenced their own satires and bawdiness. Some of his works were republished in London (and occasionally used by Protestants to demonstrate Catholic immorality).[81]

It might be useful to pause for a moment and recontextualize: when Levita wrote his satires, he was no longer a small-town "innocent" from the Bavarian hinterland, but already a consummate literary artist, who had lived several years in northern Italy and written a radically adapted Yiddish version of post-courtly Tuscan epic. It is thus enigmatic that Weil claims that until Levita left Venice for Rome, he was still completely a small-minded *melamed*, and it was only in Rome that he discovered the world of Humanism.[82] While there is no doubt that in the palazzo of Egidio da Viterbo, the general of the Augustinian order, Levita encountered Humanism on an order that he had perhaps not witnessed before and himself became personally involved to an extent to which he had never before participated, his Venetian pasquinade demonstrates rather clearly that he was not without understanding of the intellectual atmosphere of high culture—both Jewish and Christian—of the period in general and of at least some aspects of the Humanist intellectual project in particular.

During Levita's residency in Rome (1514–1527), he lived in Egidio's palazzo in the Augustinian complex at the junction of Via della Scrofa and Via de Porthogesi (now Via dell'Orso), only a few hundred meters to the northeast of the Palazzo Orsini, where the statue of Pasquino stood. He could thus have easily kept abreast of Pasquino's literary adventures perhaps even during the pre-Aretinian period of the anonymous (Latin) pasquinades, but certainly after Aretino (who was sporadically in Rome from 1517 until 1527) assumed his mask as the vernacular Pasquino.

At this point it would be salutary to articulate and attempt to disentangle the various relevant cultural strands interwoven in the convoluted argument of this chapter. While the *Epistolae obscurorum virorum* and the tradition of Scottish flyting are precisely relevant to Levita's satirical practice, and moreover *almost* coincide chronologically, there is no practical possibility that Levita could have known the Scottish tradition, although through his connections in Egidio's Roman palace he could theoretically have known the satirical texts that responded to the Reuchlin controversy. But more importantly, one must acknowledge the chronology of the analogues adduced in the present chapter: Levita's residence in Rome took place immediately *after* the composition of his Venetian pasquinade, which he composed the year *before* the publication of the *Epistolae obscurorum virorum*.[83] Furthermore, unless the distribution of Latin-language Roman pasquinades reached Venetian Ashkenazim while Levita still lived in the north—which seems extremely unlikely—he would, again, have remained outside the range of direct contact with that particular Christian Humanist-Renaissance tradition of pasquinade that could otherwise have had a direct effect on his own poems. And finally, of course, Aretino's literary adventures as the vernacular Pasquino postdate Levita's satire by several years.

Thus what is at issue here is not an attempt to propose a specific model or source for the Venetian Yiddish poem, whether in the Scottish or German Humanist North or the Renaissance Roman South, but rather to identify a cross-cultural Christian-Jewish literary context and one of the period's most pervasive literary genres in the socio-historical mode of satire. Clearly Levita's 1514 poem could not have derived from the "obscure men's" 1515 poems or Aretino's 1521 poems (nor is there—as far as I can imagine—any possibility of Levita's having influenced their composition), but rather Levita's poem (pre-)existed as part of the same larger cultural and literary context, partaking of—in addition to the centripetal Jewish satirical traditions—the general intellectual culture of the Humanistic period and its *potentially* pervasive effect even among Jewish intellectuals.

In May 1527, just in advance of Charles V's Sack of Rome, most intellectuals in the city undertook a northward flight, marking the end of the Roman High Renaissance, which had of course already been in steep decline following the deaths of Bramante (1514), Leonardo (1519), and Raphael (1520). Significantly, the annual celebration of Pasquino—an expression of precisely that mode of Renaissance-inflected Humanism—ceased about that same time, for among those fleeing northward was Aretino, in addition to Levita, Titian, and Sansovino, all of whom made their (almost certainly separate) ways to the safe haven of Venice.[84] Levita's patron, Egidio da Viterbo, was not in Rome at the time of the Sack and thereafter dwelt first in Venice (as did Levita) and then in Padua.[85]

For Aretino and Levita, Venice was thereafter, despite a few brief sojourns elsewhere on the part of both, their home for the remainder of their lives. From this anti-papal, extra-imperial enclave, Aretino developed a new weapon, the *Avisi*, the horoscope or news broadsheet, into a vehicle of political and personal satire, holding all of Italy more or less in a *Belagerungszustand* "state of siege," as no less an authority than Jacob Burckhardt maintained, identifying Aretino as "der größte Lästerer der neuern Zeit," "the greatest blasphemer of modern times," who enjoyed a kind of political asylum during his final thirty years in Venice. Both Charles V and Francis I provided him with pensions, hoping for immunity from Aretino's pen while he skewered the other.[86] In the 1532 revision of *Orlando furioso*, Ariosto identified Aretino as the *flagello de' principi*, "scourge of princes" (canto 46, st. 14).[87] Baca acknowledges that Aretino "in fact often struck terror in the hearts of princes and prelates, not to mention Popes and kings."[88] While in Venice, Aretino penned—in addition to his *Avisi*—the *Ragionamenti* (first part, 1534), pseudo-philosophical dialogues carried on by prostitutes, which thus satirized—by its very existence—the genre of the philosophical dialogue, as well as several plays, including the anti-intellectual comedy *La cortigiana* (1525), and two religious works.

In Venice Aretino thus continued his post-pasquinade satirical work, while Levita merely returned to the scene of his earlier pasquinade and lived there for the remainder of his life, continuing his *scholarly* work for more than two decades, until his death in 1549, writing—as far as is known—no further vernacular satires or epics.[89] There is no evidence that the two men were acquainted or even knew of each other's existence, although it is unlikely that Levita would have broken his ties with Egidio and his broad intellectual circle (especially since Egidio lived just upriver in Padua), which was at least in part the same circle inhabited by Aretino in Rome, on the fringes of which Levita had also lived for at least a decade. Given the tiny world of Venetian geography and the even more intimate realm of Venetian intellectual life, it is intriguing to entertain the fantasy of these two brilliant satirists over the course of this twenty-year period, in the prime of their intellectual lives, occasionally sitting down together for an *ombra* on the Piazza San Marco, sipping a crisp, light, (and, at least for Levita, necessarily kosher) white wine from the Friulian hill country and poking fun at the already numerous mid-sixteenth-century tourists—but only because in point of fact they could share nothing more than an *ombra*—that is, a drink in the *afternoon* shade—because unlike in 1514, when Levita penned his satire and then left Venice for Rome, by 1527, when he returned there from Rome, he would have had to be locked into the Ghetto nuovo by an hour after sunset and the onset of לַיְלָה.

Notes

1. At least by 1517–1518, Levita and his family were living in Egidio's palace; see Gérard E. Weil, *Élie Lévita: Humaniste et Masorète (1469–1549)*, Studia Post-Biblica 7 (Leiden: E. J. Brill 1963), 90. David Werner Amram claims that Leo X was "without doubt well acquainted" with Levita, albeit without adducing specific evidence; *The Makers of Hebrew Books in Italy: Being Chapters in the History of the Hebrew Printing Press* (London: Holland Press, 1963), 237, 238.

2. On Levita and the teaching of Hebrew and Kabbalah to Christians, see Yitzhak Penkower, "Iyyun Meḥuddash be-Sefer Massoret ha-Massoret le-Eliyyahu Baḥur: Iḥur ha-Niqqud u-Biqqoret Sefer ha-Zohar," *Italia* 8 (1989): 36–50 and the references in n. 93 (37–38). Levita himself comments on his knowledge of Greek (in the introduction to his תשבי *Tishbi*, Isny 1541), acquired during the years that he lived in Egidio's house.

3. Among his publications relevant to this field: (1) מהלך (Padua 1504; printed Pesaro 1508, Venice 1546), a commentary on the Hebrew grammar of Moise Qimḥi; (2) ספר הבחור (Rome 1517; printed Rome 1518, Isny 1542), a grammar of Hebrew (later translated into Latin by Sebastian Münster); (3) תשבי (Venice-Isny 1540–1541; printed Isny 1541), a lexicon of the Hebrew in the Talmud and of medieval Hebrew; (4) מסורת המסורת (Venice 1538), a pioneering investigation of the origin of the technical terms and signs of Masorah, including the vowel points, concluding that only the consonantal text of the Bible is ancient; (5) זכרונות (written Rome 1516–1521 [mss. Munich und Lyon] and Venice 1536 [ms. Paris]), a concordance of the Bible, never published in toto; (6) מתורגמן (written Rome-Venice 1526–1531; printed Isny 1541), a dictionary of the Targumim; (7) שמות דברים (Isny 1542), the first known Yiddish-Hebrew dictionary, comprising 985 words.

4. See below, chapters 7 and 8 on the epic.

5. On this issue, one might compare Chone Shmeruk, "Ha-shir al ha-sreifah be-venetsyah le-Eliyahu Baḥur," *Kobez al yad*, n.s., 6 (16), part 2 (1966): 353; and the comment by Claudia Rosenzweig and Anna Linda Callow, trans., *Elye Bokher, due canti yiddish: rime di un poeta ashkenazita nella Venezia del cinquecento* (Siena: Bibliotheca Aretina, 2010), 57.

6. Weil, *Élie Lévita*, see especially 209–216, here 211–212.

7. Mose Shulvass, *Ḥaye ha-yehudim be-italyah bi-teḳufat ha-renesans* (New York: Ogen, 1955), 278 (cf. also 141); cf. the rather loose English translation by Elvin I. Kose (here slightly modified for the sake of accuracy): Moses A. Shulvass, *The Jews in the World of the Renaissance* (Leiden: Brill, 1973), 288 (cf. also 154).

8. Timm, "Wie Elia Levita," 63.

9. N. B. Minkoff, *Elye Bokher un zayn Bovo-bukh* (New York: M. Vakser, 1950).

10. Joffe, introduction to Elias Levita, *Elye Bokher: poetishe shafungen in yidish*, ed. Judah A. Joffe (New York: Judah A. Joffe Publication Committee, 1949).

11. Baumgarten, *Introduction*, 40; in the English translation: "the Italo-Jewish humanist," 49.

12. Cf. Lesley: "Rome, which was both the destroyer of the second Temple and the capital of western Christendom, was far from being the object of Jewish nostalgia" (in Ruderman, *Essential Papers*, 46). According to Lesley, "Jewish interest in humanist scholarship was anything but automatic. Indeed, Jews could well have been expected to disregard or resist Italian humanism." Since, outside of Iberia, they had little connection to the transmission and revival of knowledge of Aristotle, Plato, and Greek scientific writings via Arabic channels, and since few Jews knew Latin and fewer still knew Greek, there was little in Humanism to interest Jews. Even so, Lesley maintains, "Jews in Italy did not resist or ignore humanism" (46).

13. For that kind of revolution, one would have to wait until the Haskalah/Enlightenment still some two centuries in the future, from Levita's perspective.

14. David B. Ruderman, *Kabbalah, Magic and Science: The Cultural Universe of a Sixteenth-Century Jewish Physician* (Cambridge, MA: Harvard University Press, 1988).

15. Herbert Davidson, "Medieval Jewish Philosophy in the Sixteenth Century," in Bernard Dov Cooperman, ed., *Jewish Thought in the Sixteenth Century* (Cambridge, MA: Harvard University Press, 1983), 138–139.

16. Tirosh-Rothschild, *Between Worlds*, 232.

17. See Lesley, "Jewish Adaptations," 49–50, and Cecil Roth, *A History of the Jews in Italy* (Philadelphia: Jewish Publication Society, 1916), 216, on the development of a "classical" Hebrew style among Italian Jews of the period.

18. As Arthur Lesley notes, "Already forty years ago, Cecil Roth formulated the essential insight into the way that Hebrew writers appropriated elements of Italian humanism: 'The Italian Jews became famous in the Jewish world for their flawless style and composition, in striking contrast to the studied inelegance of their northern European contemporaries. . . . In the same way as the humanistic scholars modelled their prose style on Cicero and Livy, abandoning the barbarous traditions of medieval Church Latin, so their Jewish contemporaries went back to the Bible' "; Lesley, "Jewish Adaptation," 59, citing Roth, *A History*, 216.

19. Lesley, "Jewish Adaptation," 59.

20. I will retain the quotation marks to emphasize the provisional nature of the phrase.

21. Bonfil's claim that "in the period we are considering, conversion was a large-scale phenomenon" (*Jewish Life*, 117) lacks compelling evidence.

22. Christian D. Ginsburg, ed., *The Massoreth ha-Massoreth of Elias Levita* (London: Longmans, Green, Reader and Dyer, 1867), 95–96.

23. Of course one need not look far to find examples of Jewish intellectuals whose satires, bawdy poems, and poetic contacts with the Christian community provided precedents for Levita. Immanuel of Rome (ca. 1261–ca.1332), known among Christians as Manuello Giudeo, composed and exchanged Italian sonnets with his Christian colleagues. Don Vidal Benveniste (fl. early fifteenth century) wrote the bawdy *maqama* מליצת עפר ודינה. Moses da Rieti (1388–after 1460) adapted Dante's *Commedia* into Hebrew terza rima, מקדש מעט, in addition to writing a satirical poem directed against German Jews. Joseph Tsarfati (d. 1527, known among Christians as Giuseppe Gallo), a physician and Roman native, translated a play into Hebrew (of which only the prologue is extant) and introduced ottava rima into Hebrew. Sa'adiah Longo (sixteenth century) of Salonika wrote ribald poems and versified polemics. Selections from works by these authors are included in Carmi, *Hebrew Verse*. One should likewise note that Levita's satirical poems are not the only extant Yiddish satires of the period; cf. the poem by Moyshe Cohen of Talheim, Oxford, Bodleian Library, Can. Or. 12, fol. 207v–211r, and two poems in the sixteenth-century collection of Isaac ben Moyshe Wallich of Worms, edited by F. Rosenberg, "Über eine Sammlung deutscher Volks- und Gesellschaftslieder in hebräischen

Lettern," *Zeitschrift für die Geschichte der Juden in Deutschland* 2, no. 3 (1888): 232–296, here 257–258, and 3, no. 1 (1889): 14–28, here 24–25.

24. In addition to the long-standing communities of Italian Jews, in the course of the sixteenth century the numbers of Sephardic, Ottoman, and Ponentine refugees and immigrants grew substantially.

25. See Weil, *Élie Lévita*, 58; Cecil Roth, *History of the Jews in Venice* (Philadelphia: Jewish Publication Society, 1930; New York: Schocken, 1975), 40. The more recent articles by Zelda Kahan Newman, "Elye Levita: A Man and His Book on the Cusp of Modernity," *Shofar* 24 (2006): 90–109; Deena Aranoff, "Elijah Levita: A Jewish Hebraist," *Jewish History* 23 (2009): 17–40; and Edith Wenzel, "*Bovo d'Antona (Bovo-bukh)* und *Paris un Wiene*. Ein Beitrag zur jiddischen Literaturgeschichte des 16. Jahrhunderts," in *Integration und Ausgrenzung. Studien zur deutsch-jüdischen Literatur- und Kulturgeschichte von der frühen Neuzeit bis zur Gegenwart*, ed. Mark H. Gelber, Jakob Hessing, and Robert Jütte (Tübingen: Niemeyer, 2009), 19–34, provide summary information and basic bio-bibliographical data gleaned from the research of earlier scholars.

26. Robert Finlay presents a very effective summary of the events of the war against the League of Cambrai relevant to the period of the foundation of the ghetto; in "The Foundation of the Ghetto: Venice, the Jews and the War of the League of Cambrai," *Proceedings of the American Philosophical Society* 126 (1982): 140–147.

27. Weil, *Élie Lévita*, 58–61.

28. The Rialto bridge was at the time still constructed of wood, as is indeed depicted in Vittore Carpaccio's painting "Il miracolo della reliquia della Santa Croce" (1494; in the Accademia, Venice). On the history of the bridge in this period, see Donatella Calabi and Morachiello, *Rialto: le fabbriche e il Ponte. 1514–1591* (Turin: Einaudi, 1987).

29. "The Great Fire" is edited in Shmeruk, "Ha-shir al ha-sreifah," 343–368, and *EYT* 34; references in the present chapter are to the latter edition. The poem is extant in two manuscripts: Oxford, Bodleian Library, MS Can. Or. 12, fos. 258r–261v (1553), and Cambridge, Trinity College Library, F.12.45 [*olim* MS Addl. 136], fos. 2r–3v (sixteenth century). The "Ha-Mavdil-lid" was first edited by Nokhum Stif, "Elyohu ha-Levis lid 'ha-Mavdil,'" *Tsaytshrift* 1 (1926): 150–158; more recently: *EYT* 35; it is extant in two manuscripts: Oxford, Bodleian, MS Can. Or. 12, fos. 203r–207r (1553), and Cambridge, Trinity College Library, F.12.45 [*olim* MS Addl. 136], fos. 4r–9v (sixteenth century). Since the poems are not widely known, an English translation of them is provided below, in the appendix. One may consult the following with caution: Rosenzweig and Callow, *Due canti*, which includes a reasonably accurate summary of previous research (11–71) but an unreliable Italian translation of the poems (77–123); see Jerold C. Frakes, "Outliers of Yiddish Literature: Early and Late, Italy and Poland, Rhetorical and Peripheral," *Jewish Quarterly Review* 104 (2014): 289–306. Rosenzweig has also announced a new edition of the poems: Claudia Rosenzweig, "Parody, Infamy and History in a Yiddish Manuscript of the Italian Renaissance," 105–113, in *Report of the Oxford Centre for Hebrew and Jewish Studies, Academic Year 2011–2012* (Oxford: Oxford Centre for Hebrew and Jewish Studies, n.d.). Cf. also the descriptive summary by Arnaud Bikard, "Elia Levita's Yiddish Works: Echoes of the Italian Renaissance in the Poetical Creation of a Jewish Humanist," in *Jewish Migration: Voices of the Diaspora*, ed. Raniero Speelman, Monica Jansen, and Silvia Gaiga, Italianistica Ultraiectina 7 (Utrecht: Igitur Publishing, 2012), 32–39. Among other epics, Levita's epic *Bovo d'Antona* is analyzed in chapters 7 and 8, below. The term *khidushim-lid* is introduced by Shmeruk, *Prokim*, 93 n. 59; the term does not appear in the corresponding passage of *Sifrut yidish*, 69 n. 51.

30. Interestingly, Sanuto notes that those whose denunciation of the thieves led to the recovery of goods received some part of the goods as compensation; Marino Sanuto, *I Diarii*, ed. Federico Stefani et al., vol. 17 (Venice: A spese degli editori, 1886), 476.

31. Sanuto, *I Diarii*, vol. 17, esp. 458–474 on the Rialto fire and its aftermath.

32. Cf. *Senato Terra*, reg. 19, cc. 95r–96r, 29 March 1516.

33. Rosenzweig questions the classification of the poem as a pasquinade, since, she suggests, "*pasquinate* are usually brief compositions, for the most part sonnets, and as a rule they have a clearly political component, attacking the popes and clergymen"; "Rhymes to Sing and Rhymes to Hang Up: Some Remarks on a Lampoon in Yiddish by Elye Bokher (Venice 1514)," in *The Italia Judaica Jubilee Conference*, ed. Shlomo Simonsohn and Joseph Schatzmiller (Leiden: Brill, 2013), 160. While those characteristics are indeed relevant for sixteenth-century Rome, it would seem somewhat myopic to restrict the genre's definition to them, since that would exclude the remainder of the broad and deep corpus of pasquinades that have been recognized and studied by centuries of literary scholarship around the world.

34. Including Rosenzweig (*Due canti*, 51–52) who advances the peculiar claims that the burning of the Rialto functioned as a secondary Purim and that the poem was a "canto di *Purim*," albeit without offering any evidence for either claim. See Butzer, *Die Anfänge*, 137–145, for a summary of the research. See also my own earlier ambivalent characterization of the two poems in *EYT* 140–149.

35. Meir Medan, "Elijah Levita," in *Encyclopaedia Judaica*, 2nd ed., ed. Berenbaum and Skolnik, 12:732; Timm, "Wie Elia Levita," 64.

36. See also Weil, *Élie Lévita*, 40: "il savait aussi placarder sur les murs de la ville des pamphlets en judéo-allemand, destinés à servir sa vengeance," "he was also able to post Yiddish lampoons on the walls of the city, intended to be in the service of his vengeance."

37. In an earlier publication, I acknowledged the theoretical possibility that Levita's Cohen could have been a fictional character constructed for the sake of the literary text (*EYT* 149). If that were the case, however, there would be serious interpretive consequences, for if Cohen were simply a fiction, then the function of the poem as an actual pasquinade would be lost, and the poem would then need to be classified at a higher level of abstraction, since it would lose its obvious socio-literary function within the Jewish community of readers. Evi Butzer has gone far beyond my obvious suggestion that a literary character may be fictional: she suggests not only that Cohen *is* in fact fictive but that Levita constructed Cohen as a means of satirizing *himself* (*Die Anfänge*, 145). For there to be any practical interpretive value in such a suggestion, however, there would need to be some concrete evidence. Butzer offers none, and based on what is known of Levita's biography, in contrast with the "biography" of Cohen presented in the poem, it is hard to imagine how anyone could imagine the latter as related to the former. Rosenzweig seems unable to distinguish my suggestion from Butzer's very different claim and thus imagines them identical (*Due canti*, 60).

38. Marino Sanuto estimated that there were seven hundred Jewish men resident in Venice in 1516; *I Diarii*, ed. Rinaldo Fulin et al. (Venice 1879–1903), 12:110–111, 13:105–106. Most Jews resident in Venice at this period were Yiddish-speaking Ashkenazim, a situation that would steadily change as the sixteenth-century progressed (via the immigration of non-Ashkenazim and the linguistic assimilation of the Ashkenazim), until, by the turn of the seventeenth century, there were few Yiddish speakers in the city.

39. By that time there was a second ghetto for the Levantine Jews, generally Ottoman citizens who, unlike the Ashkenazim, were admitted to Venetian residence specifically for the purpose of international trade. *They* would have been in the Rialto on a daily basis—just as the Ashkenazim had been in the earlier period—but it is extremely unlikely that very many of the Ottoman Jews would have known Yiddish. On the Gobbo, see esp. Andrea Moschetti, *Il Gobbo di Rialto e le sue relazioni con Pasquino* (Venice: Frateli Visentini, 1893) (from *Nuovo Archivio Veneto*, vol. 5, part 17); and Andrea Moschetti, *Ancora il Gobbo di Rialto* (Venice:

Fratelli Visentini, 1896). Moschetti argues that the common claim that Gobbo is a mere epigone of the Roman Pasquino is inaccurate: "Le prime satire o *pasquinate*, comparse in Venezia, furono attaccate ad alcune colonne di Rialto qualche giorno prima del 29 novembre 1532," "The first satires or pasquinades to have appeared in Venice were attached to some columns of the Rialto, a few days before 29 November 1532" (9), as reported by Sanuto in *I Diarii*, who attempted to copy down the sonnets for his *nepoti*, *I Diarii*, ed. Guglielmo Berchet et al. (Venice: A spese dell'editore, 1902), 57: col. 288 (29 November 1532). Moschetti notes that the first mention of a satire that had been attached to the Gobbo dates from 1550 (18).

40. Weil, *Élie Lévita*, 57; more generally on the capture of Padua and the flight of the Jews, see Benjamin Ravid, *Studies on the Jews of Venice, 1382–1797* (Aldershot: Ashgate, 2003), 1:238.

41. *Senato Terra*, reg. 19, cc. 95r–96r, 29 March 1516; cited by Ravid, 248–250; cf. also Ravid, 217–218; Sanuto quotes the formulation of the Senate document: vol. 22 (1888), ed. Federico Stefani, col. 85–87, on the establishment of the ghetto in 1516, here col. 86. He provides here a thorough description of the initial conditions for use and regulation of the ghetto (conditions and rules repeated 390–392). Sanuto claims that the ghetto was justified "per obviara la perfidia hebraica," "in order to obviate Jewish perfidy" (85). Patricia Fortini Brown notes on the ghetto: "The area, called 'terren del Geto,' had already been developed with rental housing around the middle of the fifteenth century by two merchant brothers, Costantino and Bartolomeo da Brolo. They constructed a cistern beneath the large *campo*, installed three well-heads, and built a two-story row of modest housing around the perimeter. It was not much different from other island parishes except that it lacked a church. With the decree of 1516, the existing renters were moved out, the outside windows walled up, the Jews moved in, and rents raised by a third"; *Private Lives in Renaissance Venice: Art, Architecture, and the Family* (New Haven, CT: Yale University Press), 214.

42. So also Girolamo Priuli, who openly expresses his anti-Semitism and attributes it to Venetian Christians in general: "lo populo veneto cridava grandamente di questi Judei," "'the Venetians complain greatly about these Jews"; in *I Diarii di Girolamo Priuli*, vol. 4, ed. Roberto Cessi, *Rerum Italicarum Scriptores*, vol. 24, part 3 (Bologna, 1938), 96; he also repeated the common anti-Semitic lie that they—on the mainland—murdered Christian infants and drank the blood of innocents (vol. 4, 253).

43. *I Diarii, ad* 6 Apr 1515. Concrete data on pre-ghetto Jewish demographics in Venice are hard to determine; in general see Robert Finlay, "The Foundation of the Ghetto: Venice, the Jews and the War of the League of Cambrai," *Proceedings of the American Philosophical Society* 126 (1982): 140–54, especially Finlay's comment on San Polo: "one of the neighborhoods most heavily settled by Jews" (151); see also Benjamin Ravid, "The Religious, Economic, and Social Background and Context of the Establishment of the Ghetti of Venice," in *Gli ebrei e Venezi, secoli XIV–XVIII*, ed. Gaetano Cozzi (Milan: Edizioni Comunità, 1987), 214–215; David Jacoby, "Les juifs à Venise du XIVe au milieu du XVIe siècle," in Hans-Georg Beck et al., eds., *Venezia centro di mediazione tra Oriente e Occidente (secoli XV–XVI); aspetti e problemi*, 2 vols. (Florence, 1977), 1:163–216; Ennio Concina, "Parva Jerusalem," in Ennio Concina, Ugo Camerino, and Donatella Calabi, *La città degli ebrei: il ghetto di Venezia: architettura e urbanistica* (Venice, 1991), 11–24; Benjamin Ravid, "The Legal Status of the Jews of Venice to 1509," *Proceedings of the American Academy for Jewish Research* 54 (1987): 169–202.

44. As an incidental notice by Sanuto makes quite clear, proclamations and notices are made public on the Rialto, even for Jews (vol. 23 [1888], 59).

45. *Sefer ha-Tishbi* (Isny: Fagius, 1541), marked "12" at the top of the page and "ל" at the bottom (here ל, the twelfth letter of the Hebrew alphabet is reflected in the Arabic numeral at the top of the page and thus does not signify the number 30, as customary in the Hebrew alpha-

numeric system). Thus the markings indicate the recto of the first folio of the book's twelfth quire: לlr; facsimile in *Yiddish in Italia*, 116 (lacks quire marking); the 1557 edition is available online: http://books.google.com/books?id=M31b4Wj23rgC&printsec=frontcover&source=gbs_ge_summary_r&cad=0#v=onepage&q&f=false, Hebrew text, 179; in his facing-page Latin translation to that later edition, Paulus Fagius translates the term *katoves* as *facetiae*, "wit/drollery /humor" (180).

46. See also Weil, *Élie Lévita*, 64, who insists that the composition would have been impossible after Levita left Venice.

47. "Lui aussi affiché sur les murs de la ville," "it was also affixed to the walls of the city" (Weil, *Élie Lévita*, 63).

48. Weil, *Élie Lévita*, 65.

49. Roger Kimball, "Lessons from Juvenal," *New Criterion* 21, no. 8 (2003), http://ancienthistory.about.com/gi/dynamic/offsite.htm?zi=1/XJ&sdn=ancienthistory&zu=http%3A%2F%2Fwww.newcriterion.com%2Farchive%2F21%2Fapr03%2Fjuvenal.htm.

See also Anne Lake Prescott, who notes that the Renaissance distinguished two forms of wittiness in ancient humor: the urbane (Horace) and the vitriolic (Juvenal), the latter of which was to "destroy or cure vice with caustic ridicule." While many Renaissance wits mixed the two modes, there is a difference between [Sir Thomas] More's dismay at his own Utopia and [Pietro] Aretino's prostitute's conversations or Rabelais's humor; see Anne Lake Prescott, "Humour and Satire in the Renaissance," in *The Cambridge History of Literary Criticism*, vol. 3, *The Renaissance*, ed. Glyn Norton (Cambridge: Cambridge University Press, 1999), 285.

50. Weil matter of factly opines, "Tous ceux qui passaient dans les rues de Venise purent, lire, affichées sur les murs, les turpitudes de Hillel" (Weil, *Élie Lévita*, 63), "All those who passed through the streets of Venice could read, affixed to the walls, the turpitudes of Hillel," apparently losing sight of the fact that only Jews, and among them, only the Yiddish-literate (i.e., generally, Ashkenazim) could in fact read the posted Yiddish-language pasquinades. While it is not always possible to identify and define the literate populace in historical periods, literacy itself is in fact always a *very* specifically definable skill.

51. With the exception of stanza C36; see appendix.

52. The *Capi sestiere* (< *Cavi di Sestire*), "the [Venetian] district chief"; *l'Avogaria* (< *La Vorgaria*), "judiciary/judicial bench"; *Corte Forestiera* (< *Corte Forestire*), "court for foreigners"; *Pioveghi* (< *Piovige*), "commercial court" (dealing with usury and contracts); *Cattaveri* (< *Cataveri*), "office of tax collection and financial administration" (st. 20).

53. See the note in the appendix on this term.

54. Cf. st. 18,4.

55. See the note on this line in the translation (in the appendix).

56. See the note to this line in the translation.

57. Interestingly, a similar formulation recurs in Levita's Old Yiddish epic *Bovo d'Antona* (st. 6), again in relation to the malaise of a young bride with an aged husband.

58. It is said that in Padua he פלקט "pursues/persecutes" a chicken day and night; although it seems just as likely that the verb is to be understood with the common, tabu-conditioned metathesis of stop + liquid (here: *g/k + l*) as פקלט "screws/shags" (cf. MHG *vogelen*, NHG *vögeln*); perhaps the duality of the manuscript reading *and* its metathesized form is to be appreciated.

59. Cf. also the more general assessment by Shtif that the significance of the narrative is essentially embedded in and around Venice; "Naye Materyaln," *Shriftn* 1 (1928): 177.

60. Indeed even more restrictively in the multi-cultural Jewish community of Venice, the poem is not merely Jewish for Jews, but Yiddish for the Yiddish-speaking Ashkenazim only.

61. Perhaps one should also reckon among the potential audience any Christian Hebraists in Venice. Thus far no trace of the promised Hebrew-language poem has been found.

62. Francis Griffin Stokes, ed. and trans., *Epistolae obscurorum virorum* (London: Chatto and Windus, 1925).

63. On the entire affair, see most recently the analysis by David Price, *Johannes Reuchlin and the Campaign to Destroy Jewish Books* (Oxford: Oxford University Press, 2010).

64. See Weil, *Élie Lévita*, 204.

65. As noted by Prescott, the *Epistolae obscurorum virorum* are based on medieval, not classical, traditions of satire ("Humour and Satire," 287).

66. See especially R. B. Gill, "The Structures of Self-Assertion in Sixteenth-Century Flytings," *Renaissance Papers* (1983): 31–41.

67. Gill, "Structures," 31.

68. Gill, "Structures," 32, 36; he cites the now classic study by William Labov, "Rules for Ritual Insults," in *Language in the Inner City: Studies in the Black English Vernacular*, ed. William Labov (Philadelphia: University of Pennsylvania Press, 1973), 297–353. He also refers to Stanley Fish's study of Skelton, whose personal invective is there deemed "a display of rhetorical (or vituperative) virtuosity for its own sake"; *John Skelton's Poetry* (New Haven: Yale University Press, 1965), 208.

69. On the facts of the discovery and display, see Leonard Barkan, *Unearthing the Past: Archaeology and Aesthetics in the Making of Renaissance Culture* (New Haven, CT: Yale University Press, 1999), 208.

70. Barkan provides a photograph of the statue in its present location (*Unearthing the Past*, 208).

71. As illustrated in Antoine Lafréry's engraving in *Speculum Romanae magnificentiae* (Rome 1546), reproduced in Barkan, *Unearthing the Past*, 214.

72. The papal protonotary Johannes Goritz established a counter-tradition on the Feast of Saint Anne, holding poetic feasts with the resulting poems attached to Sansovino's statue of Anne in the basilica of Sant' Agostino; see Raymond B. Waddington, *Aretino's Satyr: Sexuality, Satire, and Self-Projection in Sixteenth-Century Literature and Art* (Toronto: University of Toronto Press, 2004), 19.

73. Barkan, *Unearthing the Past*, 218. As Anne Reynolds interestingly elucidates, the origin of the celebration of Pasquino was almost certainly more overdetermined still: as Roman Humanists often incorporated pagan Roman festivals into Christian feast days, the Pasquino celebration absorbed the Roman Robigalia (cf. Ovid, *Fasti* 4.901–42). The basic sense of *robigo* is mildew or rust on ripening grain, and the function of the ancient Roman rite was to prevent its occurrence. *Robigus* was the *numen* invoked, while the Robigalia itself was modeled on Cerealia and Floralia, all geared to what some imagine the original religion of Rome to have been, i.e., essentially an agricultural cult. The word *robigo*, however, also designated other kinds of ulcerations, including those from "excessive libidinousness" and from slander and satire, as noted by Seneca and Martial, among others. The Humanists' attempt to "perceive intellectual and cultural continuity principally within the history of Rome and to restore and revitalise contemporary religious practice by a 'resurrection' of the past" is a way to understand the melding of the Feast of Saint Mark, contemporary lampoon, and a pagan agriculture cum satire festival; see Anne Reynolds, "The Classical Continuum in Roman Humanism: The Festival of Pasquino, the *Robigalia*, and Satire," *Bibliothèque d'Humanisme et Renaissance* 49, no. 2 (1987): 306.

74. Barkan, *Unearthing the Past*, 212. Even more importantly in historical terms, Barkan notes, "The pasquinade will become an all but official medium for obstreperous forms of public debate throughout the sixteenth century. What begins as an arena of parochial dispute among

segments of the Roman people or the Curia will be exported north of the Alps by the more radically contrarian purposes of the Reformation" (*Unearthing the Past*, 213).

75. Waddington, *Aretino's Satyr*, 19; on Aretino's move to Rome, see Johannes Hösle, *Pietro Aretinos Werk* (Berlin: Walter de Gruyter, 1969), 39. Many of these poems take the genitals of the double-torsoed statue of Pasquino as a starting point, before moving on to other, often also sexual, topics, such as priestly promiscuity, sodomy, etc. In general, given the common tendencies of Humanist satire, many of the verses, as Barkan points out, "are concerned with the sexual implications of Humanist instruction—that is, the tendency of *paedeia* to be accompanied by pederasty" (Barkan, *Unearthing the Past*, 216); see Barkan also for a selection of the typical sexual insults posted on Pasquino (220–222). The fifteenth- and sixteenth-century tradition is well documented by Valerio Marucci, Antonio Marzo, and Angelo Romano, eds., *Pasquinate romane dei Cinquecento*, 2 vols., Testi e documenti di letteratura e di lingua 7 (Rome: Salerno editrice, n.d. [1983]), and Valerio Marucci, ed., *Pasquinate del Cinque e Seicento* (Rome: Salerno editrice, n.d. [1988]).

76. There are many surprising connections in the (relatively) small world of the Italian Renaissance: it was Leo X who had raised Egidio da Viterbo, Levita's patron, to the rank of cardinal, and whose death prompted the explosive emergence of the Aretinian pasquinade onto the stage of world literature.

77. This move eventually led to the attribution to him of many pasquinades written by others. In this respect, Aretino's satires resemble Levita's, in that their use of the vernacular broadened their audiences appreciably, while radically changing the tenor and appeal of the humor. One should, however, keep in mind that for Levita (and not for Aretino), the use of the vernacular was a *choice*, since Levita was a consummate stylist in Hebrew, while, as noted, Aretino apparently knew no Latin.

78. Hösle, *Pietro Aretinos Werk*, 43.

79. Aretino calls the Church "sfacciata, amorbata, affammata et vituperata," "shameless, starving, befouled and reviled"; see Hösle, *Pietro Aretinos Werk*, 52.

80. While, until recently, individual poems had appeared in various scholarly publications, there had not yet been anything like a comprehensive edition of Aretino's pasquinades. Vittorio Rossi had long ago edited an extensive selection: *Pasquinate di Pietro Aretino ed anonime per il conclave e l'elezione di Adriano VI* (Palermo/Torino: Carlo Claussen, 1891); and Sarandy Cabrera published a Spanish translation of selected pasquinades: *Sonetos lujuriosos & pasquines del Aretino: seguidos de otros sonetos lujuriosos, dudas amorosas y otras dudas amorosas de autores anónimos de tradición aretinesca y de un soneto de Giorgio Baffo* (Montevideo: Vintén Editor, 1991). Finally, however, the definitive edition was published in 2012: Marco Faini, ed., *Pasquinate*, part 2 of *Operette politiche e satiriche*, vol. 6 of *Edizione nazionale delle opere di Pietro Aretino* (Roma: Salerno editrice, 2012); see especially the section "Dal conclave del 1521 al sacco di roma," 49–113.

81. See Saad El-Gabalawy, "Aretino's Pornography and English Renaissance Satire," *Humanities Association Review/La Revue de l'Association des Humanités* [Kingston, Canada] 28 (1977): 9–19.

82. Weil, *Élie Lévita*, 69–70.

83. Nokhm Shtif demonstrates that J. Levi's suggestion that Levita was already in Rome in 1512 is almost certainly inaccurate and based on a misconstrual of information (in the prefaces to Levita's *Tishbi* and *Seyfer zikhrounes*) about how long Levita lived in Rome and how many of those years were spent in Egidio's house; cf. Shtif, "Naye materyaln tsu Elye ha-Levi's ha-mavdil lid," *Shriftn* 1 (Kiev, 1928): 156–157, and J. Levi, *Elia Levita und seine Leistungen als Grammatiker* (Breslau: Schottlaender 1888), 9.

84. Murtha Baca designated Aretino, Titian, and Sansovino the "cultural triumvirate" of sixteenth-century Venice, which then replaced Rome as "the literary, editorial, and artistic center of Italy"; "Aretino in Venice, 1527–37, and 'La Professione del Far' Lettere" (diss., UCLA, 1978), v–vi. The tradition of posting pasquinades on the statue later revived and seems now, again, periodically to thrive.

85. Weil, *Élie Lévita*, 108.

86. Jacob Burckhardt, *Die Kultur der Renaissance in Italien: Ein Versuch*, 10th ed. (Stuttgart: Kröner, 1976), 153–157. Aretino continued to flatter Charles, always hoping to be made cardinal.

87. But in naming him (in the same line), he also identifies him as "il divin [the numinous/divine] Pietro Aretino."

88. Baca, "Aretino in Venice," 23.

89. He lived outside of Venice for some months during 1541–1542, when he worked in Paulus Fagius's print shop in Isny (Allgäu).

Chapter Four

Purim Play as Political Action in Diasporic Europe and/as Ancient Persia

THE BIBLICAL BOOK of Esther was a difficult fit in both the Jewish and the Christian theological and literary traditions. As Barry Walfish points out, that hesitancy among Jews may account for the absence of the book from the Dead Sea Scrolls.[1] While ancient Jewish scholars debated whether to include the book in the canon and attempted more overtly to Judaize the book—in the Talmud and midrash, but also in the substantial so-called "additions" to the book that appear in the Greek Septuagint (ca. third century BCE),[2] ancient Christian theologians remained generally silent, although Jerome did plead—albeit against strong opposition—for the book's inclusion in the Christian canon. Unlike the early and overt Jewish textual interventions, there were no Christian commentaries on the book until those of the eighth century by Hrabanus Maurus and Peter Comestor.[3] The book was then soon theologically "naturalized" through the reimagining of Esther as a prefiguration of Mary. It was not, however, until the sixteenth century with the appearance of the dramatic tradition of Esther plays that there was a broad Christian reception of the narrative, but even then Christian theologians were wary if not outright antagonistic.[4]

In this bi-cultural context, it is not surprising that treatments of the Esther fabula were fundamentally volatile. Even so, the claim advanced by the title of this chapter, that the tradition of the Jewish Purim play itself constitutes political action, will require considerable contextualization as a quasi-preamble to the analysis, especially of the next two chapters.[5] One must first of all recognize that this politicization occurs in at least three sites: first, in the foundational document of the holiday's celebration, the biblical book of Esther; second, in the communities in which the Purim plays are performed; and third, in the plays themselves as they are enacted in performance. The multistaged and multipronged analysis of the present chapter will proceed under the constant threat of becoming protean and amorphous. There will thus be recurring discursive signposts to guide the reader through the labyrinth.

The Jewish holiday of Purim was, according to Esther 9:20–28, instituted by Mordecai to celebrate the deliverance of the Jews from Haman's genocidal plot to murder them all.[6] The text of Esther is relatively late, and its overt religious content, and thus presumably its ostensible theological authority, slight. Nonetheless, the holiday itself was well established by the second century CE, when tractate *Megillah* of the Mishnah was composed, which explains (some) details of the holiday's observance.[7] Moreover, the midrashic textual tradition that developed on the subject of the biblical book is surprisingly broad, including, in antiquity, in addition to the Talmudic tractate, the *First Targum*, *Esther Rabbah* 1 (on Est 1–2), and the *Second Targum*; then from tenth through thirteenth century, *Panim Aḥerim*, *Abba Gurion*, *Esther Rabbah* 2 (on Est 3–8), *Aggadat Esther*, *Lekaḥ Tov on Esther*, *Yalkut Shimoni on Esther*, *Midrash Aḥer*; and finally, *Midrash Tehillim*, *Yosippon*, and *Pirkei de Rabbi Eliezer* also devote some attention to Esther.[8] In the late Middle Ages vernacular traditions of Purim poems and certainly by the early modern period at the latest Purim plays begin to appear, in addition to the early custumals and the lengthy paraphrase cum commentary of the early Yiddish *Tsene-rene*.[9]

The festival itself is a joyous one, celebrating the divine protection of the Jewish people. The primary component of the celebration—appropriately for the text-based religion of Judaism—is constituted by public reading, that is, the ritual reading of the book of Esther in the synagogue. Harold Fisch notes concerning this holiday:

> Purim thus becomes, above all, a celebration of textuality itself for not only the rabbis, but also the people, for whom the Book of Esther has an enormous appeal, Purim is ultimately less concerned with commemorating a particular event than with commemoration itself—and with its relationship to textuality. . . . One could almost say that for the rabbis the significance of the Esther scroll was exhausted in the reading process itself. This would make the reading of the scroll something like a pure sign, an autonomous, self-referential act.[10]

He further remarks concerning the emphasis on writing and texts in the book of Esther, "It is thus a scroll about scrolls, about their writing and their reading."[11]

Within that practice of reading, there are some further traditional practices that are susceptible to non-normative behavior and potentially humorous enactment (the use of noisemakers—*grager*—by children and others to drown out

Haman's name each time that it is read); outside of the reading, a quasi-carnival atmosphere often obtains, with a meal as festive as circumstances allow, the production of parodies of (especially) the Talmud and its disquisitional style, not on theological matters but rather on trivial subjects such as drinking, the institution of a Purim rabbi who turns authority and sometimes propriety on its head, and perhaps most famously, a controversial directive from the (probably third to fourth century CE) Babylonian rabbi Rava: אמר רבא מיחייב איניש לבסומי בפוריא עד דלא ידע בין ארור המן לברוך מרדכי (BT *Meg* 7b), "Rava said: A person is obligated to become intoxicated on Purim until he cannot distinguish between 'cursed be Haman' and 'blessed be Mordecai.'" In order to restrict sanctioned drunkenness, however, community authorities early noted that those two key phrases ארור המן and ברוך מרדכי are numerologically equivalent (=502, as reckoned by their alpha-numeric values, i.e., *gematria*), and thus not much alcohol at all is necessary to recognize their, as it were, lack of distinctiveness. Elsewhere the Talmud also mentions entertainments and buffooneries in connection with Purim (e.g., BT *Sanh* 64b).

The centrality of the reading of the relatively brief and already rather dramatic text of the book of Esther and the general tendency toward a relaxation of strict standards of decorous behavior may well have led to the development of dramatizations of selected parts of the Esther story separate from its ritual reading. There was a gaonic tradition in the Middle East (and a similar one in Europe during the Middle Ages) of the dramatization of the Esther story in which Haman (represented by a dummy) was burned while jesters sang (BT *Sanh* 64b). Thus at least by the early modern period, there was a traditional practice of regularly circumventing the still older traditional Jewish prohibition of theatrical performance when it came to the celebration of Purim.

The Yiddish *purimshpil*, "Purim play," can be generally defined as a play performed during the Purim holidays or thereabouts for the entertainment and/or edification of the Jewish celebrants of the holiday. There is no early evidence that Jewish drama was performed outside holiday periods. In Frankfurt, the Purim "season" lasted from fourteen days before to fourteen days after Purim.[12] Thus, due to the cultural circumstances that at least discouraged theatrical performance except for Purim play, the early history of Purim plays de facto constitutes the early history of Yiddish theater.

The earliest extant material displays not just the Jewish cultural base that one would expect, but surprisingly also the direct and profound influence of the dominant surrounding culture, in particular that of the German-speaking lands, which, rather surprisingly and due to a peculiar set of circumstances, then also entails a secularized British dramatic tradition (see below). There are elements and examples of improvised comedy in the style of the Italian tradition of *commedia del arte*, the solemn Latin *acta* and German *Aktionen*, the livelier German *Singspiele*, and enlightenment drama, and in the Purim play's earliest stages, there are obvious relations to the low comedy of the bawdy German *Fastnachtsspiel* of the fifteenth and sixteenth centuries. Indeed the strongest influence on Yiddish drama of whole period, both technically and theatrically, was German drama, from the medieval plays to the bourgeois theater of the Nuremberg Meistersinger.[13]

Even so, as Chone Shmeruk explicates the issue, there were also very clear limitations on the otherwise pervasive influence of non-Jewish drama on the Purim play. For, since the Christian biblical plays of this and earlier periods not surprisingly almost always theologize, especially in treating characters from the Hebrew Bible as prefigurations or allegories of characters and/or concepts from the Christian New Testament (e.g., the sacrifice of Isaac as prefiguration of the crucifixion), Yiddish adaptations of such Christian works were conceptually impossible for both dramaturgs and Jewish audiences without excising the entire dramatic purpose of the Christian original.

The significance of the text's underlying ideology for the viability of adaptation into Yiddish may be seen, for instance, in the distinction between the Jewish treatment of Christian biblical plays and Christian secular epic. There are no Yiddish adaptations of the former, but several examples of adaptations of particular subgenres of the latter, since they did not (necessarily and always) turn on essential aspects of Christian theology, and thus just as such epics moved from one language to another across Christian Europe, they could also be adapted into Yiddish.[14]

It was not until the end of the sixteenth century that Christian secular drama seems to have exerted an influence on the incipient dramatic tendencies of the Purim play. During the last decade of that century a troupe of British comedians first toured Germany with a largely secularized repertoire (even if still primarily based on biblical narratives, that repertoire was not fundamentally theological or ideologically didactic). Itinerant English troupes continued to perform Esther plays in continental cities and towns and for German princes for decades thereafter (certainly as late as a known performance in Dresden, 3 July 1626).[15] Such troupes constituted in a significant sense a professional theater not based in or controlled directly by the Church, and especially not by the Jesuits, who had generally been the primary source of earlier dramatic performances in the German-speaking lands. These British troupes strongly influenced the development of Yiddish theater, both directly (especially in Amsterdam) and through the mediation of contemporary German drama, which likewise underwent a consequent secularizing development.

The actual techniques and means of Jewish adaptation of Christian theater from this early period are difficult to reconstruct and never transparent, due particularly to the fact that little or no contemporary German drama of the type adapted by the Jewish tradition has survived, primarily because the traveling troupes eschewed publication of their scripts in order to avoid competition from other troupes that might have appropriated their repertoire. One aspect of this type of adaptation is clear, however, and reflects a similar practice in the adaptation of medieval (secular) Christian epic for Jewish audiences: motifs and scenes deemed inappropriate for Jewish audiences were omitted and often replaced by specifically Jewish material, especially from the wealth of material unavailable to Christian biblical literary adaptations, that is, the midrashic traditions, aggadic material, and the earlier Yiddish and Hebrew literary traditions, as, for example, in the דוד אונט גליות הפלשתי "Dovid and Goliath the Philistine" (Hanau 1717), especially as it was based on the relevant passages from the Goliath episode in the Middle Yiddish *Book of Samuel.*

The earliest form of this type of drama may well have been a rhymed monologue in one act concerning the biblical Esther tale, spoken by a character in mask and/or costume. Such dramatically performed Purim poems apparently enjoyed great popularity, and by the sixteenth century there are extant manuscripts of parodic and satirical but non- or only quasi-dramatic Purim poems, such as the stanzaic poem by Gumprekht of Szczebrzeszyn from circa 1555, based on the biblical book of Esther, where the earliest known use of the term *purim-shpil,* "Purim play," is found.[16] Such monologic poems developed in time into more complex dramas based on well-known traditional narratives and including parody, satire, and even obscenity as aspects of their comic form. Despite the historical settings of the plays, there was of course no attention to "historical accuracy" in the representation of those settings, for, as was conventional in European drama of the period, historical narrative materials were commonly adapted to contemporary conditions, including topical references.

The central figure in this earliest period is the לץ "buffoon," later the מאַרשעליק/מאַרשאַליק "jester," who carries the monodrama and is central to the earlier examples of dialogic drama. This comic character was adapted from contemporary Gentile European dramatic traditions of the time, named Pickelherring in Dutch, Jean Potage in French, Signor Maccaroni in Italian, Jack Puddin' in English, and Hans Wurst in German.[17] This comic figure in the European theater was defined by his impudence, cynicism, disrespect, and often even risqué humor that spilled over into borderline or overt obscenity; he was the focus of the play's comedy, who forced his way into serious situations with respectable people and mocked them relentlessly. In addition to this character and to, for instance, Mordecai and Esther from the biblical narrative, there also developed a character who narrated parts of the plot or simply commented upon it; he was identified in the plays as the לויפֿער "messenger" or שרײַבער "scribe/writer" (conventional type-characters in drama of the time, a quasi-narrator who also takes part in the action).

Due to the paucity of documentary material, it is difficult to plot any kind of chronological development from the simple form of private chamber performance on the holiday itself to the more complex dramatic and literary forms with multifaceted productions, designed for public performance during the month of Adar, no longer confined to private houses, although still primarily (though no longer exclusively) a component of the specifically Jewish celebration of Purim. On the basis of the extant texts, it seems that the one form often ran parallel to the other, and private performances often disappeared in one locale but continued elsewhere, while large-scale professional performance for obvious reasons never developed in all Jewish communities. The developing duality of performance site (private and public) and audience (solely Jewish or Christian-Jewish mixed audience) was also matched in a pair of contrasting literary styles available to the Purim play: as the Christian biblical drama of the Reformation grew in prominence and that literary tradition became more serious, the folksy style of the German theater and of the Jewish Purim play that was directly influenced by the German theater found a parallel in the more learned prose and less prominent comic style, while continuing to include elements of both.[18]

It should be noted that the emergence of Yiddish-language Purim plays as a dramatic tradition during the period, especially in northern Italy, ran parallel to other fledgling dramatic efforts by Jews where the language of the play was not Yiddish or it is impossible to determine its language. Relatively early evidence for the performance of a Purim play comes from a surprising source: the Venetian diarist Marino Sanuto reports that on the evening of 4 March 1531, permission was granted by the Council of the Ten to the Jewish community to perform a *bellissima comedia*, "most beautiful comedy," which was to end late in the night and which no Christian was allowed to attend.[19] Sanuto does not of course identify the play specifically as a Purim play, but at that time of the year such an identification is all but certain (4 March 1531 = 5 Adar 5291), nor does he identify the language of the play, which is, in the context of northern Italian Jewish Esther plays of the period, always an interesting issue (Hebrew, Ladino, Italian, Yiddish?). One of the earliest extant Jewish Esther plays that was specifically designed for theatrical production appeared in Ferrara in 1567 in Salomon Usque's adaptation of the Esther tale to *Spanish* drama with the help of Lazaro Graziano (Gratianos).[20] This play and similar ones from the time were, however, almost certainly for the general stage and not just for Jews or Purim. Yehudah (Leone) de Sommi (1525–1592) wrote comedies, as well as dramatic theory, while leading a theater troupe at the court of the Gonzagas in Modena.[21] His Hebrew-language play צחות בדיחותא דקידושין "An Eloquent Marriage Jocularity/Farce" is the earliest extant dramatic text in that language.[22] Leone Modena worked as a director of a music academy and a dramatic troupe in Mantua.[23]

The earliest *extant* Yiddish texts that were clearly organized as dialogs, that is, overtly as dramatic texts, appear in the late sixteenth century, among them an undated Jonah play (*EYT* 85) and a play from 1598 with the superscription איין

גידיכט וואל גר חטאנו היפשן "a fine *khatonu* in good verse," whose title is שפיל פון טויב יעקליין אונ' מיט זיינם ווייב קענדליין אונ' מיט זיינן צוויי זינדלין פֿיין "Play of Deaf Yeklayn, His Wife, Kendlayn, and His Two Fine Sons."[24] While it is possible, indeed likely, that the Yiddish Purim play had existed for quite some time prior to these texts, no documentary evidence exists, and while such texts were almost certainly performed, they would likely still have constituted only of brief skits. The earliest extensive (and complete) Yiddish Purim play extant is an אחשורוש-שפיל "Ahasuerus play," the manuscript of which is dated 1697. Rather surprisingly, for almost a hundred years after that date, up to the last decade of the eighteenth century, there are in effect very few Yiddish plays extant, four of them from the two-decade period immediately following 1697: two Ahasuerus plays; a play with the title מכירות יוסף "The Sale of Joseph"; another, mentioned earlier, entitled דוד אונט גליות הפלישתי "David and Goliath the Philistine"; and the brief sketch with the unlikely title משה רבינו בשרייבונג "Description of Moses, Our Rabbi." While it is more than likely that additional plays existed, the extant corpus probably provides a reasonable sense of the relatively narrow scope of the early repertoire. That is, however, not to say that Yiddish Purim plays were rare in the sense of having been infrequently performed, but rather that plays based on the book of Esther supplied the basis for myriad adaptations during the following century, of which there are multiple textual traces, while surviving full texts are few.

This core repertoire of plays in various versions was produced countless times throughout the course of the eighteenth and nineteenth centuries (and probably already in the seventeenth century) both in German-speaking lands and the Slavic East. The older plays were adapted, revised, modified, and updated, and new ones were composed in Yiddish in both the folkloristic style characteristic of earliest two Ahasuerus plays, such as עקידת יצחק "The Binding of Isaac," יציאת מצרים "The Exodus from Egypt," שלמה מלכס משפט "King Solomon's Judgment," געשיכטע פון קניג שאול "The History of King Saul," משה רבינו לעבן אונ' טויט "The Life and Death of Moses, Our Rabbi," and the more sophisticated literary style characteristic of the chronologically third, fourth, and fifth Ahasuerus plays, specifically for Purim celebrations. It was not until the advent of the anti-Yiddish Haskalah movement, with its reformist maskilic comedies (in Yiddish!), represented especially by the works of Isaac Abraham Euchel (Itzik Eichl) and Aaron ben Wolf Halle (Aaron Wolfso[h]n) in the last decade of the eighteenth century, that the repertoire expanded substantially beyond the sphere of traditional Purim plays.[25] These anti-Purim plays of the Haskalah, intended to supplant the traditional Purim play, for obvious reasons never became part of a common community repertoire. In the nineteenth and twentieth centuries, with the massive emigration of Ashkenazic Jewry from Eastern Europe, Yiddish Purim plays came to be performed in Jewish communities around the world. Even now, in the early twentieth-first century, Yiddish-language Purim plays are still being adapted, composed, and performed in some few Jewish communities, for instance, in Brooklyn's Borough Park and in Jerusalem's Me'a She'arim.[26]

It is the Ahasuerus plays, directly based on the foundational narrative of Purim—the biblical book of Esther—that not surprisingly formed a core or family of dramatic texts in this earliest period, and they are the plays that will be the analytical focus of the three chapters concerning drama in the present volume. This core of texts was adapted, borrowed, and quasi-plagiarized within the textual family to the extent that any attempt to define the lineage of the extant plays is fraught with difficulty. The earliest representative, the text of 1697, איין שיין פורים שפיל "A Fine Purim Play," comprises fourteen folios, written in Ashkenazic cursive script and bound into a folio volume with other texts, especially letters from the collection of Johann Christoph Wagenseil. The play text was copied in Altdorf by Johann Christian Jakob, *olim* Moyshe Katz of Kraków, who was probably one of Wagenseil's convert assistants in Jewish studies.[27] The second Ahasuerus play, printed in Frankfurt in 1708, was prohibited by the Jewish authorities—perhaps due to the play's obscenity—and the copies found there locally were confiscated and burned. Two further Ahasuerus plays were published in Amsterdam in 1718, both of them with greater literary sophistication than the earlier plays: דאש שפיל פון מרדכי אונ' אסתר "The Play of Mordecai and Esther" and אחשורוש שפיל גלייך איינר אפרא "Ahasuerus Play, as an Opera" (Amsterdam 1718).[28] In 1720 in Prague, a still more serious and sophisticated Ahasuerus play was printed and performed, אקטא אסתר עם אחשורוש "The Deeds of Esther with Ahasuerus," of which there were two further editions (Prague 1763 and Amsterdam 1774).[29] The title page claims the play was performed in Prague in a regular theater with trumpets and other instruments. The actors in that production were all pupils of Rabbi Dovid Oppenheim of Prague, who also gave his consent for the performance.[30]

There are several rather striking aspects of the plots of most of the Ahasuerus plays of the period: Haman is the only *non-satirized* character; his monologue just prior to his execution and his conversation with his wife are in fact quite touching, depict an *at least momentarily* sympathetic character—not at that moment a monstrous, genocidal villain—and express genuine human emotion; the Vashti episode is altogether omitted from the two earliest extant plays, AS1 and AS2, which thus begin with the Esther story itself; in those plays, too, the comic role of the clown/fool is fused with the role of Mordecai, the plays' central figure, whose role seems still to be improvised as in contemporaneous *commedia del arte*.[31] In AS3 and AS4, on the other hand, Mordecai's role is quite serious. While one might imagine this change to have been one of a historical development from the earlier (1697–1708) to the later (1718) plays, it seems more likely that the roughly contemporary plays simply represented the parallel folk and more learned traditions or, perhaps better, the tradition of chamber performance by a strolling troupe (performing in a succession of well-to-do houses) and the tradition of theatrical performance by a quasi-resident company (at least "resident" for the period of Purim). Thus the combination of the role of the fool and Mordecai may initially have derived at least in part from a need among strolling Purim troupes for economy in casting (because of the small performance spaces in private houses and the advantage for the individual performers in having a larger percentage of the donations received from the audience).[32] These earliest chamber plays seem often, perhaps generally, to have been performed by yeshiva students in private houses in the community, some of which "troupes" traveled from town to town to perform.[33] Based on the surviving seventeenth- and eighteenth-century plays, it would be fair to surmise that AS1 and AS2 represent that chamber-performance tradition, with a mixture of the comic and the serious, always with a didactic and moral purpose.

In AS4 one finds a complexity not characteristic of AS1 and AS2, particularly in staging technique, so that it becomes clear that there were radically different production values in chamber performances in private homes and large-scale productions in theaters. The full title of AS4 makes this distinction clear from the outset: אחשורוש-שפיל אויף איינען נײַען אופן גלײַך איינער אָפערַאַ און איז אויז גיצוגין פֿון תרגום שני ומדרש ילקוט אונ' אנדרן מדרשים אונ' אויף איין זולכע מאניר גישטעלט גלייך וויא עז פֿון רעכטן קומעדיאנטן גישפילט ווערט "Ahasuerus play in a new form, as an opera, and it is also drawn from *Targum Sheni* and *Midrash Yalkut*, and other midrashim and staged in the same manner as by actual comedians." The stage directions indicate that it is not a chamber play, as seems likely for AS1 and AS2. The language is perhaps the most striking aspect of the play, which, as will become clear through the text citations that will appear in the course of the analyses here, is quite sophisticated and, just as one finds in the high Baroque plays of the German stage during this period, includes a significant number of French, Latin, and Latinate loan words.[34] A representative passage is cited here (responding to Queen Vashti's refusal to appear before Ahasuerus's banquet). My English rendering here italicizes the English words that translate the Latinate words of the Yiddish original, simply to indicate the density of their usage. The would-be grandiose *daytshmerish* (Germanizing) style of the original is also quite striking.

המן
263 אירא מאייסטעט דיזי ווארט טוהן מיר אים הערצין אויף שטייגין.
אונ' קן ניכֿט לענגיר שטיל שווייגין:
דאן איך אין הואן אוניפֿערשיטעטין לנג שטודירט.
אונ' נימר גיהערט דז איין קיניגין דעם קיניג אלזוא שימפֿפֿליך האט רעסיסטירט:
צו דעם האט זיא ניכֿט גיזינדיגט קיגן אירא מאייסטעט אליין.
זונדרין קיגן אלי פֿירשטן אונ' הערין דיא אים דען קיניגרייך זיין:
דאן איין יעדי פֿרויא ווירט דיזיש עקסעמפיל אובזערפֿירן.

אונ' אירן מאן ניכֿט וועלין פארירין:
דאן אהנא דעם איר ווילין דאהין טוט ציהלין.
איבר דיא מעניר דען מיישטיר צו שפילין:
דאן וואן דיזיז אירא מאייסטעט איזט גישעהין.
וויא זאל עש אונזרש גלייכֿין ער גיהן:
דארום טוהא איך יודיצירין.
אונ' זיא צו דעם שווערט קאנדעמנירין:
דא מיט איין יעדי פֿרויא אבזעהן קאן.
דז זיא פֿרפֿליכֿטיט איזט אירן מאן:
אונ' איין יעדיר מאן האבי צו קאמאנדירן.
אונ' נאך זיינם קאפֿף צו ארדינירין.

Your *Majesty*, these words rise in my breast, and I can no longer remain quiet. For long did I *study* in elite *universities*, and never did I hear of a queen who so ignominiously *resisted* a king. Moreover, she has not transgressed only against her *majesty*, but against all princes and nobles of the kingdom, for each and every woman will *observe* this *example* and will not wish to touch their husbands. For in any case, their will tends thereto, to act as masters of men. For when it happens to Your *Majesty*, how can it be any different for the likes of us? For that reason, I *render judgment* and *condemn* her to the sword, so that every woman can recognize that she is duty bound to her husband, and each and every man has the right to *command* and *issue orders* as he sees fit.

The effect in the Yiddish text is striking indeed. This discursive mode is obviously already learned drama in a cosmopolitan European vein. Other examples of this learned dramatic mode could be adduced: toward the end of the eighteenth century an (undated) Esther play was published with the title מרדכי אונ' אסתר "Mordecai and Esther," whose subtitle again illustrates the early tendency toward learned and indeed musical drama in the Purim play: איינע קאָמישע אָפּערעטע. אין איינען אויף צוג. פֿון ר' ליב צימבלער אין מוזיק גיזעטצט. די דעקאָראַסיאָנס פֿון איינעם אום באַקאַנטן "a comic operetta in one act; set to music by Mr. Leyb Tsimbler; set designer unknown."[35]

The first edition of "The Sale of Joseph" (printed by Johannes Wust in Frankfurt without date, ca. 1710) constitutes a prime example of rationalistic drama, produced by Berman of Limburg, performed with elaborate costumes and full sets as a *Singspiel*.[36] This play, in alternation with the anonymous comedy דוד אונט גליות הפלשתי "David and Goliath the Philistine" (Hanau 1717), was performed in Frankfurt (and later in Metz) by yeshiva students from Hamburg and Prague under the direction of Berman for the entire month of Adar. It continued to be popular, and a version of it was performed in Minsk as late as 1858.[37] This tendency toward musical drama was even clearer in the second play, "David and Goliath the Philistine," which was in fact an opera with twenty-four songs.[38]

While the Purim play originated in the Jewish community to fulfill a specifically Jewish cultural need—as a component of the celebration of Purim—the "participation" of the surrounding non-Jewish dominant culture was not confined to the profound intellectual and cultural influence on the development of the specific dramatic form of the Purim play, but extended as well to overt political intervention. While it is not always obviously marked in the plays themselves, the celebration of Purim, insofar as it intersected with the public sphere, was, like other aspects of Jewish life in Christian Europe, ultimately under the control of Christian authorities. As it extended to the regulation of Jewish theater, that control is demonstrated in the municipal documents of many communities, perhaps most clearly in Amsterdam, which in the wake of the events of 1648 (Chmielnicki's revolt against Polish rule in the Ukraine and the subsequent massacre of thousands of Jews by the rebels, and the ensuing flight of thousands of survivors to Western Europe) experienced a rapid growth of its Ashkenazic community.[39] While the extant historical documentation of seventeenth-century theater performance is understandably limited and fragmentary, especially with respect to Jewish theater, it is nonetheless sometimes surprising just how much information still does exist. In 1683 the Amsterdam Jews requested permission for the public performance of a Purim play; a similar petition from 1707 specifically indicates that such permission had been granted some years previously. The play was to be performed in the "language of the high German Jews," that is, Yiddish. Although the city council rejected this particular 1683 petition, the document nonetheless reveals an interesting fact—there was at the time already a Jewish theater operating in Amsterdam that staged performances three times a week during the Purim season to an audience of two or three hundred spectators.[40] Perhaps more significantly, these documents indicate clearly that both the Jewish community and the Christian authorities had established procedures for the municipal licensing of Purim plays; it was not a one-time event, but rather a practice already incorporated into the repertoire of governmental regulation (obviously even when such requests were denied).

Beyond the mere regulation of Jewish theater, there were at various times and places explicit attempts to suppress Purim plays altogether, sometimes by Christian authorities, sometimes by their counterparts in the Jewish community.[41] There was a widespread view—Christian and sometimes also proto-"enlightened" Jewish—that the book of Esther was anti-Christian, especially in the execution of the anti-Semitic Haman. In the Talmudic tractate *Sanhedrin* (BT *Sanh* 64b), there is mention of a pantomime associated with Purim celebration (א"נ משוורתא דפוריא), where it is also noted that in the diaspora it was a custom to burn a Haman figure tied to a ring and suspended over a fire until the rope burned through and the figure fell into the fire.[42] Early in the Christian period, however, there developed a Christian view of Haman on the gallows as a possible Jewish parody of the crucified

Jesus of Nazareth, or at the very least as a sacrificed Christian, which was particularly volatile subject matter, especially due to Purim's proximity to Easter, the period when anti-Semitic violence was historically most likely to break out. Thus such gallows were prohibited even as early as the reign of Emperor Theodosius II in 408, with specific reference to the gallows as a mimicry of the cross, with sacrilegious intent.[43] Some scholars have interpreted this edict as resulting from Christian slander of the time, while others have seen it as an accurate reflection of Jewish practice.

A clearer light is perhaps cast on the entire issue, however, when one compares the Christian biblical texts in use at the time: in the particular translations of the Hebrew text in the (Jewish and Christian hybrid) Greek Septuagint and (Christian) Latin Vulgata, Haman and his sons were in fact crucified. In the Greek text: καὶ αὐτὸν ἐκρέμασα ἐπὶ ξύλο "he [Ahasuerus] hanged him on a tree" (Est 8:7), where the verb κρεμάννυμι denotes "hang up" but likewise includes the sense of crucifixion, especially when employed in conjunction with the term ξύλον with the basic sense of "wood/tree," commonly denoting "gallows" and especially in specifically Christian usage, "cross." On Haman's sons: ὥστε τοὺς δέκα υἱοὺς κρεμάσαι Αμαν "that the ten sons of Haman be hanged" (Est 9:13). In the Vulgata: "domum Aman concessi Hester et ipsum iussi adfigi cruci," "I [sc. Ahasuerus] have granted the house of Haman to Esther, and I have ordered him to be hanged on the cross" (Est 8:7), using the explicit term *crux* "cross"; Haman's sons: *in patibulis suspendantur* "hanged on *patibula,*" (Est 9:13), the last word (here plural) originally designating a fork-shaped yoke or gibbet, to which the condemned's hands and feet were nailed; in Christian usage, however, which was obviously definitive in the Vulgata, the term generally denotes the cross.

As Horowitz points out in a different context, in Byzantine practice Jewish converts to Christianity had to renounce on oath not just Hebrew law, custom, and ceremony in general, but also, in a specific clause, both the celebration of the "festival of Mordecai," and his nailing Haman to the cross and cursing Christians.[44] A similar quasi-crucifixion seems also to have been common in fifteenth-century Italy in synagogue performances (sometimes even with Christians in attendance).[45]

In 1703 Christian authorities in Berlin forbade Purim plays altogether in order to prevent such "violations" of the Christian Holy Week. According to this injunction, the host in whose house any such play was performed, all actors, and the host's guests (the audience) were to be arrested and fined. Compliance with and enforcement of the statute was made the responsibility of the Jewish community authorities.[46] Similar statutes were instituted elsewhere as well, generally now preserved through Jewish community documentation: the Hamburg Jewish community banned performance of all Purim plays in 1728; an official warning was issued in 1747 in Fürth not to attend performances of the performing troupe that had come to town; in 1756 in Nikolsberg there were complaints officially filed about the theater; on 20 April 1768, a Bratislava rabbi issued in conjunction with Jewish community authorities the decree that מהיום והלאה זאָל קיינער ניט וואַגן גיין אין אַ קאָמעדיע "from this day forth no one is to dare attend a comedy," and no one from the community was to be seen in די קאָמעדיע-הײַזער "the comedy houses," under penalty of a fine of three *Reichsthaler*, one-third of which the person was to receive who claimed to have seen the other person at the performance.[47] In 1751 another parodistic comedy was banned in Frankfurt (this time attested in Christian documentation).[48] Unlike the AS2 (1708), copies of which survived its burning, this latter play is no longer extant, although at least its title has survived: להמן, איין יודן טייטשיש שוישפיל ווי זאלכש פון פרנקפורטר יודן האט זאלן אופגעפירט ווערדן, וועלכש אבר דמלש פון דם רט איז אונטרזאגט ווארדן "On Haman, a Yiddish play, which was to be performed by Frankfurt Jews, which was, however, at that time prohibited by the Council."[49] While none of these decrees specifically identifies a Purim play per se as that which requires regulation, all the decrees are nonetheless dated to the Purim season. It thus seems probable that it is a matter of Jewish attendance at specifically Jewish (not Christian) theater and a sign that Jewish authorities were either openly opposing Purim play or were forced into such opposition by Christian authorities.

Beyond the traditional prohibition of theatrical performance, the motivation to prevent the performance of some of the early Yiddish Purim plays may well have stemmed from their perceived indecency, which may likewise have resulted from the responsibility imposed on the Jewish authorities for the enforcement of the Christian ordinances. Rabbinical complaints about Jewish attendance of Purim plays—distinct from community prohibitions—are found throughout the eighteenth century. Other contemporary Yiddish texts that focus specifically on the ethical behavior expected of pious Jews (e.g., לב טוב, ספר עץ חיים, ספר מידות) openly condemn Purim plays as corrupting. Rabbi Jonathan Eybershitz (1690–1764) complained that Jews were attending what was called שוישפיל קאמעדיע אפערע "play, comedy, opera." Rabbi Yitzkhak Lapronti (the Baal Pakhed Yitskhok, 1679–1756), stated: אשרי מי שלא הלך לתיאטראות ולקרקסאות "Praiseworthy is the one who goes not to the theaters and the circuses." Rabbi Michael Shuer of Mannheim (1782–1809) complained that local Jews went to comedies too often. During this period in Venice it was said that at carnival season no sermon was preached in the synagogue, since no one was there to hear it. In London Rabbi Hirsh Levin (from Poland) complained that instead of going to the house of Torah, Jews went לאפרע, לפלע "to the opera, to the play."[50]

While there is no denying the widespread opposition of Jewish authorities, there is no reason to imagine the conflict as ubiquitously divisive. After all, the fact is that the authors and actors in Purim plays, wherever they were performed, were often from a yeshiva, and thus some segments of the Jewish religious elite at some level approved of—or at the very least tolerated—Purim plays, even though the idea of the theater in general might well have still been abhorrent to them. Even so, at some point the worldliness of the decorations, the costumes, and the tendency toward full-fledged operatic theater obviously became too much for the performance and indeed the function of Purim plays in private homes or the synagogue itself,[51] and it had to be moved outside,[52] where it was then perhaps no longer so immediately under the control of the local rabbi, although obviously there were exceptions even to this general practice, such as Rabbi Dovid Oppenheim of Prague, who, as noted previously, toured with the yeshiva troupe playing its repertoire.

One further motivation for opposition to—or at least a drive to control—Purim plays need be noted: the plays very often seem to have been popular and successful, whether in terms of artistic achievement or simply as entertainment. The Frankfurt theater, for instance, was very sophisticated—for the time—in its special effects of fire, machines, and thunder.[53] As noted earlier, "The Sale of Joseph" enjoyed a very successful run for the entire month of Adar in 1710 in Frankfurt, alternating with "David and Goliath the Philistine." Gentiles also attended the plays, and two soldiers had to be hired as doorkeepers to ensure order and guarantee the public safety.[54] However, as soon as Christian authorities found out that Christians were attending the production, a fine of twenty *thaler* was levied, and further performance was prohibited by the civil authorities.[55] A non-Jewish newspaper in Amsterdam noted on 25 March 1726 that there was a theater in a wooden barn in the Jewish quarter of Amsterdam that included a stage, a four-person orchestra, and a counter at which one could buy tobacco, liquor, cake, and oranges.[56]

For the range of reasons here suggested, it seems that specifically within the Jewish community, the historical anti-theater tradition was also still operative, and in some regions, the tradition of performing Purim plays seems to have been effectively suppressed: while Purim plays persisted (whether clandestinely or not) in the smaller towns of Prussia into the nineteenth century, in the course of the eighteenth century they seem to have disappeared in Berlin.[57] The fact that one of the earliest printed versions of the Ahasuerus play of 1708 (AS2) was burned in Frankfurt by the *Jewish* authorities and that the Hamburg *Jewish* community banned performance of all Purim plays in 1728 may support the view of some scholars that the obscenity of the plays (quite apparent in some of the extant plays of the period) outraged the community, but it may also simply manifest the responsibility imposed on the Jewish authorities for the enforcement of the Christian ordinances and prohibitions.[58]

There was thus a confluence of sometimes conflictual, sometimes coordinated instances of political control supervising the developing institution of the Purim play. The celebration of the festival was, as indicated in the range of community documents just outlined, obviously under the control of the *Jewish* community authorities, but, while it was not always so obvious, that celebration—like other aspects of Jewish life—was ultimately under the control of the governing authorities of the surrounding majority culture, as has also already been documented here. Beginning in late antiquity in Europe, that authority was obviously Christian. That control as it extended to the regulation of Jewish theater, particularly in the early modern period, is demonstrated in the municipal documents of many communities in the seventeenth and early eighteenth centuries, both Jewish and Christian, which regarded the plays de facto as political action that required a very specific kind of control and policing. The perceived threat to public order was due to a variety of causes: the popularity of the plays, which drew large audiences to public venues, for the control of which there was no standard provision in community ordinances; the interfaith, Jewish *and* Christian, interest in the plays, which demanded the attention of the authorities in both communities in order to control the inevitable interaction, which, while rarely or inconsistently forbidden as such, was nevertheless identified as requiring institutional control; the content of the plays, which was often perceived as obscene, which then occasioned censorship, particularly by Jewish community officials. Moreover, the overt and covert anti-monarchical and/or anti-Christian politico-religious content of the plays (particularly with respect to the Christian perception of the conventional burning of Haman's effigy as a travesty of the crucifixion) was potentially incendiary in a political sense, as well.

As has already been adumbrated in the foregoing contextualization, but as must now be specifically problematized, the foundational document of Purim play, מגילת אסתר, the biblical book of Esther, is intrinsically susceptible to overt politicization. After all, what is the plot of the story? The Persian Empire, famously conceived in the Bible as comprising 127 countries, was taken over by Jews in a tactical palace coup with strategic consequences.

In essence a Jewish minority population in exile in the capital city of a "foreign" empire stages a successful coup d'état: the empress is deposed, exiled, or executed and replaced by a mysterious foreign beauty, a commoner, a Jew, whose participation in governance bordered, in the parlance of medieval and early modern European monarchy, on that of a *regina regens*, "ruling queen," not merely that of an *uxor regis*, "[queen, insofar as] wife of the king"; two powerful ministers are denounced by a Jew (the uncle of the new empress) as conspirators plotting the assassination of the emperor and are subsequently executed; the non-Jewish vizier's diabolical will to power and murderous mania against the Jews and concomitant genocidal intrigue against the entirety of the Jewish people is uncovered by the Jewish empress's uncle, while it is she who denounces the vizier to the emperor, whereupon he is disgraced, executed, and replaced as vizier by that Jew.[59] Of the (non-Jewish) authorities *status quo ante*, there remains only the vacuous king, who is completely under the strict control of the Jewish empress and her uncle, the Jewish vizier, who move him to allow the minority Jewish population to kill seventy-five thousand of the emperor's native Persian subjects.

From the perspective of the cultural insider, the biblical text documents an ethnic, quasi-national triumph against genocide on several multiply integrated historical levels: according to *Midrash Esther Rabbah* (34 and 43), the empress Vashti was the last surviving [great-]grandchild of Nebuchadnezzar (the historical king of the Neo-Babylonian Empire who conquered Judaea and Jerusalem in 597 BCE and forced the Israelites into their first period of exile) and daughter of Belshazzar (the tyrannical and blasphemous oppressor of the Israelites in the biblical book of Daniel). In the biblical narrative, she is deposed, as is Haman (who is, additionally, executed), who represents another of the traditional enemies of Israel, for he is an Amalekite, the descendent of Agag, king of the Amalekites (Est 3:1), the desert-dwelling descendants of Esau (through his eldest son Eliphaz; Gen 36:12) who attacked and were defeated by the Israelites at Rephidim in the Sinai (Ex 17:8–10; Dt 25:18–19), after the exodus from Egypt (Gen 15:17–18).[60] King Saul was then later commanded by the Israelite God to exterminate all the Amalekites—men, women, children, and even stock animals—and his failure to do so (by sparing King Agag and some sheep, oxen, and fatlings) led to his loss of divine favor (1 Sam 15:1–35) and replacement on the throne by David. Thus in the Esther narrative two strands of traditional (proto-)anti-Semitic political authority are eliminated from the world, in addition to the seventy-five thousand Persian anti-Semites slaughtered by the Jews, as authorized by King Ahasuerus through Mordecai (Est 9:16).

On the other hand, from the perspective of the non-Jewish cultural outsider, whether anti-Semitic or not, the biblical text documents a consummate subversion of the ethnically conceived state, the ultimate palace coup, and an initially "silent revolution" that becomes anything but silent and non-violent. Just as the book of Esther thus documents revolution, Purim plays based on the Esther narrative—whatever a given Purim play's actual political content—are by definition a symbolic insurrection. The entire story is not just open to contemporary politicizing by any given playwright in any given period, it is in fact so overtly and volatilely political that a playwright would have to shun the topic altogether in order to avoid political engagement on some level.

The tradition of Purim plays has in fact *not* avoided such themes, but rather has generally accepted this underlying predisposition of the Esther narrative and made overt use of it for topical political commentary. From twentieth-century history a number of examples demonstrates this practice, including some having directly to do with the actuality of (modern) genocide: as Rabbi Joachim Prinz has pointed out, after Hitler came to power, Purim celebrations in Berlin were particularly well attended, for the story of Haman's persecutions "became the story of our own lives. . . . Every time we read 'Haman' the people heard Hitler, and the noise was deafening."[61] Hitler himself announced in a speech on 30 January 1944 that if the Nazis lost the war, the Jews could celebrate "a second triumphant Purim."[62] When Julius Streicher was led to the gallows, his last words were "Purimfest, 1946."[63] Finally, among the last Yiddish Purim plays performed by Ashkenazic Jews in Germany were those that took place in displaced persons camps after the war, performed by survivors of the Holocaust; in Landsberg in 1946 the Haman character was costumed and made up as Hitler.[64]

Such a performative construction as overtly political with specific reference to recent circumstances is also found in some of the earliest Purim plays extant, from the later seventeenth and early eighteenth centuries, an age when monarchy, international intrigue, Jews close to the throne, and deeply embedded European anti-Semitism were as real as they were in the proto-Hellenistic narrative/fiction of the biblical book of Esther.[65] It is precisely the political valence of the tradition of early Purim plays that is at issue in the present chapter, for as Jean Baumgarten remarks, "A partir du récit d'Esther, s'insinue une critique sociale qui vise à dénoncer les privilèges, renverser les hiérarchies, désamorcer les conflits toujours latents dans le ghetto juif," "Based on the story of Esther, a social critique is implied that aims to denounce the privileges, to upend the hierarchies, [and] to defuse the conflicts that always lay dormant in the Jewish ghetto."[66]

Thus far in the present chapter, one manifestation of politics in and around the early Purim play has been explored: the contemporary seventeenth- to eighteenth-century reception of Purim play as politically volatile material. In the remainder of the chapter, a second manifestation becomes the focus: the treatment of monarchy and the governmental status quo in the plays themselves. On the basis of these two distinct types of evidence, the argument is advanced that these plays functioned *as* a form of political commentary and thus of overt political activity.

The reader may have noticed that in the course of the analysis of Purim and the early Purim plays thus far, there has been no mention of either Christian or Jewish opposition specifically to the political content of the plays. Although there were at the time no *specific* legislative restrictions on the suppression of artistic expression for overtly political reasons, and thus no compulsion for contemporaries to conceal that motivation, there was likewise no precedent and thus no compelling reason for the authorities to disclose their motivation, especially if it was political in nature. That motivation seems to me, however, rather obvious. It has been pointed out by Elliott Horowitz that Jews sometimes gave "raw expression on Purim . . . to their hostility toward the symbols of what they saw as an oppressively threatening Christian environment."[67] And as Harold Fisch has indicated, the laughter of Purim is not directed at the sacred to deride it "in the name of the Carnival spirit," but is rather of a different kind: "Its main target is not the tradition of sanctity, but precisely that alien culture whose customs the celebrant adopts in his feasting and drinking. Purim laughter, in fact, tends to erase the lines of division."[68] It is simultaneously a "letting go" and a derision of the cultural outsiders, the non-Jews. Set back into the early eighteenth century—a context about which neither Horowitz nor Fisch speaks, but to which their comments are nonetheless directly pertinent—it is this last issue that is most relevant here.

For obvious reasons, all the plays share the dominant influence of the biblical source, much of the conception of characters, and among the various Ahasuerus plays even verbatim parallels in dialogue itself. Among the types of evidence for post-biblical politicization, the focus here is restricted to a few of the more important modes—first of all, the ethnic and religious identity of the characters. As has until very recently been commonly the case in literary representations of other times, places, and cultures, especially in early modern European literatures, there is no attempt in early Purim plays to historicize. There is thus, for instance, no interest in constructing Achaemenid Zoroastrians or exilic Jewish characters who would be *historically* plausible inhabitants of the Persian Empire of the fifth century BCE: Jews are portrayed simply as Jews contemporary with the play itself, while the non-Jews are not the ancient Persians of the biblical narrative, but rather more or less contemporary, early modern, European Gentiles, that is, Christians. Recurrently in the plays, when Ahasuerus's subjects are addressed or simply named, an amusingly anachronistic formula is employed, such as פריד צו אייך איר הערין פערשטן און׳ גראבין פרס ומדי. / עש זייא קריסט אדר יהודי "Peace be upon you all, you lords, princes, and counts of Persia and Media, whether Christian or Jewish" (AS1 119–120, 272–273, 554–555; AS2 118–119, 300–301, 529–530), suggesting that the speaker may turn to face the potentially mixed Christian-Jewish audience and indicating quite explicitly that the historical situation of performance in early modern Europe had been effectively conflated with the perceived tradition of ancient Persia. In AS1 Mordecai reveals the ahistorical reason why he may not bow to Haman: מרדכי:/ אוויא אוויא וויא זאל איך מיך פר דיר נייגן אונט בוקין. / דוא האשט איין קרייץ אויף דיין רוקין "Mordecai: 'Alas, alas, how am I to kneel and bow before you? You have a cross on your back' " (AS1 292–293). In AS2 (464–466) it is claimed that Jews have firearms—mainstays of the early eighteenth-century armory—and no Christian can stand against them. There is also a record from 1577 of yeshiva students performing a now lost Ahasuerus play in Brisk (Poland) in which Haman identifies himself as a גרויסער מאָסקווער פירשט "great Muscovite prince," thus, according to Shatski, probably referring to Ivan the Terrible, who was at the time remembered as a persecutor of Jews.[69]

Secondly, the representation of the king, his government, and the specific *Jewish* attitude to the monarchy must be taken into account. Obviously based on the lengthy and detailed anti-Semitic diatribe by Haman in the *Targum Sheni* of the book of Esther,[70] the Purim plays likewise include a detailed diatribe, whose purpose in context is to convince the king to permit Haman to orchestrate the mass murder of the Jews. One might acknowledge it as a quasi-epic catalog almost in the Homeric and especially the more relevant post-Homeric Hellenistic sense, as well as a textbook example of a broad range of conventional anti-Semitic propaganda. It is constructed as a description of the Jewish calendar year and the Jews' annual cycle of purportedly improper, seditious, anti-monarchical behavior. Practically every month's description includes almost as a refrain that the Jews wish the king's death, disease, or discomfort. Since, however, this speech is in Haman's mouth—that is, the play's villain and, as an Amalekite, the traditional enemy of the Jews and the prototypical anti-Semite—then his representation of the Jews' alleged attitudes and desires obviously cannot constitute *prima facie* evidence for actual *Jewish* seditious intent in the historical context of the performance. It would, logically, actually function in that context as *anti*-seditious evidence and conceivably also as didactically anti-seditious propaganda. Thus this anti-monarchical diatribe was "safe" for performance in the Jewish theater. In practice—that is, in performance—however, the diatribe becomes complicated, for its content, performative situation, and political implications are interwoven with multiple strands of cross-cultural tensions.

This speech is particularly interesting for its potential to elicit conflictual audience response—and obviously not just among the Jewish members of the audience. But the fact is that the diatribe is so detailed, so insistent, and simply so long in actual performance that it must have had a direct effect on the audience, particularly in the context of the quasi-carnival atmosphere of Purim celebration and the sporadic tradition of anti-Christian propaganda and behavior during Purim. How was the speech received by the audience? While the Jewish members of the audience were schooled to reject Haman's arguments against the Jews out of hand and to view him always and by definition as the enemy, was his malicious invention of specifically anti-governmental tendencies in the oppressed Jewish minority population altogether without resonance among Jewish audience members? On the one hand, it may well have occasioned discomfort among community leaders who were responsible for the performance, as well as for any non-Jewish members of the audience (insofar as they could actually understand the language). But it is just as likely that precisely because the speech is made by the quintessential mouthpiece of anti-Semitism, it functioned for outside observers to depict Jews as precisely the opposite of the portrait so garishly painted by Haman. Several examples from AS1 may illustrate the character of the speech; first several examples of the typically anti-Semitic accusations:

בקומין זיא אבר איין פויארן.
דען טואין זיא גאר וואל אויף לויארן.
אונ' זעהן דאש זיא זיין געלט קריגן.
(AS1 342–344)

If they come upon a peasant, they lie in wait for him and make sure to take his money.

אונ' שווערין איין יודש היידרנייאש אייד
(AS1 348; similar 359)

And they swear a Jewish-heathenish oath.

דערנאך זעהט ער דז ער מעכט איין קריסטן פינדן.
גאר וואקיר טוט ער אים בשייסן
(AS1 365–366)

Thereafter he makes sure to find a Christian; boldly he will swindle ["beshit"] him.

פר פלוכין זיא דיא קריסטן גאנז און גאר
(AS1 488)

They curse Christians up and down.

And for the sake of illustration several examples of anti-monarchial accusations:

אונ' טונין אונש אויש שפעטן אונ' אויש לאכין . . .
אונט בעטין אונט שרייאן.
גאט וואלי דען קינג אלש אום גליק פר לייאן.
(AS1 324–328; similar 356)

And they mock us and ridicule us . . . and pray and shout that God grant the king nothing but misfortune.

דער קינג זאל האבין ששה חלאים
(AS1 375)

May the king have six maladies.

אונ' האבן אויש דען קינג איין גרויש גשפאט
(AS1 382)

And they make a great mockery of the king.

און זאגין אויף דען קינג זאלין קומין דיא בועת
(AS1 467)

And say that the king ought to be afflicted with boils.

דער קינג זאל ניט לעבין
(AS1 471)

May the king die.

דער קינג זאל אום קומין דורך דען שווערט
(AS1 480)

May the king die by the sword.

און בעטין דער קינג זאל ניט רואין נאך רסטין
(AS1 521)

They pray that the king may have neither rest nor repose.

אונ' בעטין עש זאל דען קינג איבל גלינגן.
אין סומא דאש גאנצי יאר דורך טואין זיא ניקש אנדרש אלז עשין און טרינקן אונט ליגן.
אונ' טואין אונש קריסטן בטריגן.
(AS1 527–529)

And they pray that the king should have no success. In sum, they do nothing throughout the year besides eating and drinking and lying, and cheating us Christians.

דיא קינגן האט קיין חלק לעולם הבא . . . דער קינג זאל האבין אום גליק איבר אל
(AS1 827–829)

The queen will have no place in the World to Come. . . . May the king everywhere have misfortune.

In the *Akta*, the diatribe takes the form of accusing the Jews of very specific ill will and crimes against the monarchy and directly against the king personally, but not against Christians or the government in general.[71] Thus, at the end of his "report," Haman specifies that he has therein sought to provide the king with full information about the dangers presented to the monarchy by the Jews (*Akta* 1891–1892). In the diatribe itself, Haman claims that the Jews are the worst enemies of the Persian monarchy: העבן זיא קיינן פיינטר אלז אונזר פרסיאנש קינגרייך "They have no greater animosity than to our Persian monarchy" (*Akta* 1762); אייערש קיניגרייך צו פר ווינטשן אונ' פר פלוכין "They curse and execrate your monarchy" (*Akta* 1862); דא פר ווינטשן זיא אונש גנץ אונ' גאר "They curse us up and down" (*Akta* 1864); דז זיא קיין גרעשרן פיינט אלש אונזר פערסיאנרש רייך האבן אין דער וועלט "That they have no greater enemy in the world than our Persian Empire" (*Akta* 1876).

In general it is the non-Jews, particularly (but not only) Haman, in the plays who go out of their way to flatter the king and address him with laudatory and even adulatory phrases. In AS2 the most common forms are מיין אידל הוך גיבארנר קיניג "my noble, high-born king" (40 and 43) and מיין גינעדיגשטן קיניג "my most merciful king" (45, and passim). Mordecai, on the other hand, particularly in those plays in which he is an overtly comical character, shows no such fawning behavior. In AS2 he does at one point call the king מיין גינעדיגשטן קיניג "my most merciful king" (139), but then he immediately makes an obscene remark about the queen.[72] Unlike the other courtiers, he addresses the king so familiarly as to show obvious disrespect, for instance, in AS1 as קינג לעבין "king, my dearie" (AS1 1166). In his initial approach to the king in that play, he punningly pretends not to be able to distinguish the king from his servants and even his dog: וואו וואנט דער כלב זאל איך זאגין דער מלך "Where does the dog—that is, the king—live?" (AS1 169), playing on the assonance of כלב *keylev,* "dog," and מלך *meylekh,* "king." His disrespect extends to the queen, as well, as in his response to the crowning of Esther: מיר וועלין דיא קינגן בקרינן: / מרדכי: מיר וועלין דיא ארשל פישרן בקרינן "'Let us crown the queen.' Mordecai: 'Let us crown the [female] ass-pisser'" (AS1 229–230). He plays on the recurring phrase that demonstrates Ahasuerus's power and majesty:

משוררים: אסתר דיא קינגן איזט זיא גיננט.
הונדרט אונ' זיבן אונ' צוואנציג לענדר האט זיא אין אירה הנט:
מרדכי: ארשיל פישרן איזט זיא גננט.
הונדרט אונ' זיבן אונ' צוואנזיג פלעדר ווישן האט זיא אין איר הנט.
און קערט אויש דאש גנצה לנד.
(AS1 233–237)

Poet: "She is named Esther the Queen. She has one hundred and twenty-seven lands under her control." Mordecai: "She is named [female] ass-pisser. She has a hundred and twenty-seven feather-dusters under her control, and sweeps out the entire land."

Mordecai's familiarity and disrespect often become outright contempt. In AS2, in the midst of his comical tirade, which threatens to become almost exclusively anti-monarchical, he does in fact wish bad things for the king and spouts a stream of insults:

דוא בישט דער מלך איך העט דיך איאר אן גיזעהן פֿאר איין וואמפין וואשר.
פֿאר איין שטריק טרעגר.
פֿאר איין מוישב פֿעגר.
פֿאר איין הונט שלאגר.
פֿאר איין קאצין יעגר.
מאחר דאש דוא יוא דער מלך בישט.
האלט מיר דען שטעקן.
אין מארש זאלשט מיך לעקן.
אונ' ציא מיר אויז דיא שוך.
אונ' לעך מיך. . . .
(AS2 190–202)

You're the king?! I would instead have pegged you for a bowel-scrubber, a monk,[73] a seat-wiper, a dog-beater, a cat-chaser. Since you are in fact the king, hold my "stick" and lick my ass; and take off my shoes, and lick me. . . .

He moreover remarks to the king: איך ווער דיר שענקן. / אז דוא ווערשט יאר צו יאר קרענקן (AS2 231–232), "I would present you with the gift that you fall ill every year." He also offers a characterization of the attributes of the queen's beauty as an ironic opposite to the norm (in the same vein as Shakespeare's Sonnet 114):

> .... איין נעזיל.
> וויא איין טויט העזל.
> איין שטערין.
> וויא איין תחת פֿון איין בערין.
> איין פאר שינה ארין.
> אז וויא דיא מארן.
> איין פאר ציצין.
> אז וויא דיא שפיצין
> (AS2 212–219)

> . . . a little nose like a dead hare, a forehead like the ass of a bear, a pair of fine ears like the Moors, a pair of teats like barbs.

The plays include many modes of acknowledging that the depicted governmental system is corrupt. It is, for instance, not just the king who grants Haman's right to be honored and to have all people bow to him; the courtiers support this honor as deserved (e.g., שרייבער, AS2 300–305). As in the biblical text, the king makes a gift of the Jews to Haman and refuses even to take Haman's bribe (AS2 510–511), but here he goes farther and himself specifies in some detail what may be done to the Jews, revealing his own cruelty:

> דז וואו מן איין יודן גפֿינד זאל מן אים טיטן.
> צו ברענן צו בראטן אויף דער הייסן ערד.
> אונ' איין אידרן אנידר צו שלאגן מיט דעם בלוסן שווערט.
> דרייאצעהן טאג אין מרצי זאל עש זיי[ן] ביררייט.
> וואו מן איין יודן בפֿינד זאל ער ווערן גטיט:
> (AS2 516–522)

> Wherever a Jew is found, he is to be killed, burned and roasted on the hot earth, and each and every one is to be struck down with a naked sword. On the thirteenth of March, it is to be readied: wherever a Jew is found, he is to be killed.

In the *Akta*, the king goes farther still and pretends to a kind of immunity from guilt and responsibility for Haman's planned genocide, despite the fact that he nonetheless insists on his own right to approve of the plan in advance (*Akta* 1969–1988). The speech is quite interesting particularly for the condemnatory characterization of him as a willing partner and enabler of immoral deeds that can then nonetheless be attributed to others:

המן דז זאג איך היר.
האב דוא גראש אכט אויף דיר.
דוא האשט צו פיל אויף דיר גנומן.
איין גנץ פאלק אויף דיין קאפף אליין אום דז לעבן צו קומן.
נון ווייל דוא זאלכיש פיל בלוט טושט נעמין איבר דיר.
אלזו ווירט עז בוויליגט דיר.
אונ' דיין ביגער וויל איך וואל לאזין צו.
אבר מיין קיניגרייך זאל דעשינט ווענן האבן רוא.
דרום טוא איך דיז צעהן טויזנט צענטין זילבר גאר ניכט גיבערן.
אונ' זאלט מיר גלייך צעהן טויזנט מאל זא פיל דרויש ווערדן.
דאן אן דיזן היישן בלוט וויל איך קיין שולד ניכט האבן.
אונ' היריבר וויל איך אויך קיין פר אונטוואורטונג טראגין.
איבר דיין הויפט זייא דז בלוט אליין.
מיין שטול פר בלייבט און בפלעקט אונ' ריין.
זא קאנשטו נאך דיין בליבונג מיט אינן פר פארן.
דורך מיר אבר זאל קיין זיל ווערדן פר לארן.
אביר אויף דיין זיל אליין.
גיב איך זיא אלי איין היים.
אונ' מאגשט אינן נעמין אלי אירש לעבן.
אבר צו דען יונגשטן גריכט מושטו דרום פר אנטוואורטונג געבן:
(*Akta* 1969–1988)

Haman, this I here declare: be very careful;[74] you have undertaken too much, on your responsibility alone to kill an entire people. Now, because you have taken it upon yourself to spill so much blood, it will be granted to you, and I will permit your desire. But the peace of my kingdom is not to be disturbed thereby. Thus I will absolutely not accept these ten thousand hundred-weights of silver, not even if they were to become ten thousand times as much. For I want no blame for [spilling] this hot blood, and I will bear no responsibility for it. Let that blood be on your head alone. My throne will remain unblemished and pure. So you can deal with them as you wish, but on my responsibility is no soul to be lost, but by your soul alone. I give them all over to you, and you may take all their lives. But you will have to give account of them at the Final Judgment.

Mordecai's ill will for Haman is of course justified by the primary plot motivation of Haman's genocidal plan, but since Haman is the king's vizier, Mordecai's contempt is by definition likewise seditious. One might compare, for instance, his ill wishes for Haman:

אז המן זאל ווערן פֿראטה.
פֿראטה זאל ער ווערין.
אויף עשין זאלין אים דיא ווערים
דיא ווערים זאלן אים אויף עשין.

דז גאט זאל אן אים פֿר געשין.
פֿר געשן זאל אן אים גאט.
פֿריא אונ' שפאט.
שפאט אונ' פֿריא.
אז המן זאל צו ברעכֿן זייני קניא.
דיא קניא זאל ער צו ברעכֿן.
דאש הערץ זאל אים צו קרעכֿן.
צו קרעכֿן זאל אים דאש הערץ.
דז ער זאל ליידן גרושי שמערץ.
גרושי שמערץ זאל ער ליידן.
אויף דעם פֿלעקן זאל ער בלייבן.
בלייבן זאל ער אויף דעם פֿלעקן.
אז המן זאל מיך אין מארש לעקן:
(AS2 616–632)

May Haman have open sores; open sores may he have. Him may worms devour; may worms devour him. May God forget him; him may God forget. Both early and late, late and early. May Haman break his knees; his knees may he break. May his heart break in two; his heart, may it break in two. May he suffer great pain; great pain may he suffer. May he be unable to move from that spot; from that spot may he not be able to move. May Haman lick my ass.

Haman is the object of Mordecai's obscene insults almost as often as are the king and queen, often taking a form similar to that just noted, such as: המן שטעק מיר דיא צונג אין מארש ארייַן אונ' לעק מיר דען דוימן "Haman, stick your tongue up my ass and lick my 'thumb'" (AS2 678).

The king's utter incompetence is revealed of course in his misjudgment of Haman, in that he, for instance, imagines that it is Haman who is the supreme protector of the crown (AS3 805–806) and a loyal servant of the crown (AS3 985), which Haman himself is naturally more than willing to claim, even if obliquely: אין דעם קינג זיין דינשט בין איך אלי צייט שולדיג צו גין "I am always obliged to serve the king" (AS3 987).[75] When Haman's plot is revealed as affecting the queen, the king reacts predictably, viewing this act as directed against the monarchy and its law insofar as the monarchy and its law consist simply of מיין וויל אונ' גיבאט "my will and command" (AS3 1001). The king then makes a decision, as it were, based specifically on the perceived danger to the crown itself, due to the fact that the land is poorly ruled (that is, by Haman): עש שיינט דז לנדש רגירן ניט רעכֿט ווערט גיפֿירט "It appears that the government of the land is not well conducted" (AS3 1100).

In the *Akta*, the king's immediate impulsive reaction to the revelation of the plot against his life by Bigthan (Bigsn) and Teresh (Teyresh) is to promise to punish them not as they deserve, but explicitly *beyond* what they deserve: אויש דער מאסין "beyond measure" (*Akta* 626).[76] During the hilariously constructed interrogation of Mordecai during the trial of the two assassins, he again becomes the quasi-vaudeville comedian, stretching for the worst puns imaginable, many of them obscene, responding to the questions by the investigator with frivolous, comical, and, most importantly, inaccurate information about what the assassins were planning, what they said, and what he heard, until, after several pages of such bantering misinformation in response to the pitifully humorless investigator's relentless repetition of the key question, Mordecai finally gets around to telling the truth (*Akta* 801–802), at which point the investigation is immediately closed, and the death sentence pronounced. But what is the *truth*? The culprits, Mordecai, and the informed audience all know that the defendants in fact did plan the assassination; but on the basis of this farcical investigation, no court of justice could actually know that: why did the investigator reject Mordecai's innocuous testimony time after time, until, at the moment when he finally offers simply one more version of the tale—the testimony that in fact will convict and condemn the defendants—the prosecutor accepts that version without further question, and the entire legalistic sham is ended? It is not simply the case that the ruler himself is corrupt and incompetent, but also that the judiciary system—which theoretically, one might hope, ought to guarantee justice beyond arbitrary whim—is no less so.

In AS3 Mordecai and the Jews are staunch defenders of crown, as they are in the Hebrew Bible; but here that seems the whole point of the play, which opens with Mordecai's speech of *actual* praise for the king (AS3 1–18). Hatakh calls the king a גרויסער פֿירסט "great prince/sovereign" (19), while all the other courtiers chime in with fawning praise. It is in the *Akta*, however, that the king is most honorifically (self-)titled: וויר ארתקססטיס אחסווירוש פאן גאטש גנאדן ערווילטר מאגנוס רעקס. אין אסיא אפריקא. עאוראפא עט אמעריקא "We, Artaxastes Ahasuerus, by God's grace chosen great king, in Asia, Africa, Europe, and America" (*Akta* 128–129; similar 851–853).[77] Thus the political tension is always between the clear duty and action to support the monarchy and the implied undermining of that power structure by the mere existence of the parallel (Jewish) culture that does not share in the power structure of the dominant culture.

Significantly, it is only in AS3 that an issue of burning political relevance in the biblical text appears: the counter-decree issued at the end of the narrative that empowers the Jews to slaughter seventy-five thousand of their enemies (Est 9:16). Since, as indicated earlier, the Purim plays were staged not as historical dramas set in ancient Persia, but rather in the contemporary early modern society of the audience, the seventy-five thousand non-Jews slaughtered could only have been imagined by that audience as Christians of local European communities.[78] In AS3, the king empowers the Jews to seek vengeance: אונ' די אברעירז ווערט צו גשטאן דז זיא זיך מעגין רעכֿנין (AS3 1457), "And it was permitted to the Hebrews that they avenge themselves." The effect on the audience must have been sobering, particularly if any Christians were in attendance. It is little wonder that this explosively political element of the biblical narrative was omitted from most early Purim plays.

Based on the specific manifestations of political constructions in the earliest extant Purim play texts, it is quite clear that these plays did not function simply within the Jewish community as a "carnevalesque" reversal of the normal social conventions for the duration of the festival, but rather did more than merely suggest a subversion of social and political control beyond the bounds of the Jewish community. While not quite a call for revolution, the Purim play—from the earliest period of its existence, whether in the farcical Ahasuerus plays or in their more serious reflexes—quite concretely communicated the specifics of Christian repression of the Jewish community and sometimes subtly, sometimes savagely ironized the instances of authority in the Christian community. The "silent" or "passive" resistance of the oppressed in authoritarian circumstances, known from many other cultures and periods, here surfaces in an overt manner. This reality of the plays—and their consequent danger—was thus obvious to the authorities and required (and received) their constant attention.

Notes

1. Barry Walfish, "Kosher Adultery? The Mordecai-Esther-Ahasuerus Triangle," *Prooftexts* 22 (2002): 305, with references to the copious research literature on the topic (fn 2).

2. The Jewish textual tradition of the Septuagint was early infiltrated by Christian textual traditions.

3. Jacques-Paul Migne, ed., Hrabanus Maurus, "Expositio in librum Esther," in vol. 3 of *B. Rabani Mauri opera omnia*; vol. 109 of *Patrologiae cursus completus* [*Patrologia Latina*] (Paris: Migne, 1864), col. 635–670; and Peter Comestor, "Historia libri Esther," in *Adami Scoti . . . Magistri Petris Comestoris*; vol. 198 of *Patrologiae cursus completus* [*Patrologia Latina*] (Paris: Migne, 1855), col. 1489–1506.

4. Felix Rosenberg, "Der Estherstoff in der germanischen und romanischen Literatur," in *Festschrift, Adolf Tobler zum siebzigsten Geburtstage dargereicht von der Berliner Gesellschaft für das Studium der neueren Sprachen* (Braunschweig: G. Westerman, 1905), 333–354.

5. The fundamental published source for early Purim plays is the previously cited, masterful volume by Chone Shmeruk, *Maḥazot*, which includes editions of the Yiddish texts of the early corpus, as well as a comprehensive monographic introduction.

6. Some material from the introductory section of this chapter is adapted from my earlier essay "1697: The Earliest Extant Yiddish Purimšpil Is Traced to Leipzig," in *Yale Companion to Jewish Writing and Thought in German Culture: 1096–1996*, ed. Sander L. Gilman and Jack Zipes (New Haven: Yale University Press, 1997), 55–60. On the history of early Purim plays, see the often very speculative Yankev Shatski, "Geshikhte fun yidishn teater," in *Algemeyne Entsiklopedye, yidn b* (Paris: Dubnov-Fond, 1940; repr., New York: Central Yiddish Culture Organization, 1948), col. 389–414. A more recent comprehensive study is Jean Baumgarten's "Le 'Purim shpil' et la tradition carnavalesque juive," *Introduction*, 443–473; English translation: "*Purimshpil* and the Jewish Carnavalesque Tradition," *Introduction*, 359–385. A comprehensive overview of the broadly conceived early Yiddish traditions of textualities concerning Esther is

provided by Jutta Baum-Sheridan, *Studien zu den westjiddischen Estherdichtungen* (Hamburg: Buske, 1996). The absolutely fraught history of Purim celebrations by Jews in dominant Christian societies is expertly traced by Elliott Horowitz in *Reckless Rites: Purim and the Legacy of Jewish Violence* (Princeton, NJ: Princeton University Press, 2006), 1–156.

7. The Mishnaic tractate *Megillah* has nothing to say about the practices of the Purim celebration (most?) popular with practitioners, i.e. drinking, carnavalesque inversions of conventional behavior, etc. The Gemara mentions some details of such behavior, but it is never the focal point of discussion; see Harold Fisch, "Reading and Carnival: On the Semiotics of Purim," in *Purim and the Cultural Poetics of Judaism—Theorizing Diaspora*, ed. Daniel Boyarin, special issue, *Poetics Today* 15 (1994): 59.

8. For a list of the major works, see See Leila Leah Bronner, "Esther Revisited: An Aggadic Approach," in *A Feminist Companion to Esther, Judith and Susanna*, ed. Athalya Brenner, The Feminist Companion to the Bible 7 (Sheffield: Sheffield Academic Press, 1995), 177.

9. The Esther portion of the *Tsene-rene* is edited in *EYT* 98.

10. Fisch, "Reading," 55 and 60.

11. Fisch, "Reading," 60.

12. There is some evidence that there were (rarely?) also plays performed during Hanukkah; see Shatski, "Geshikhte," 402.

13. Shmeruk, ed., *Maḥazot*, 13–19.

14. See my *Early Yiddish Epic* (Syracuse: Syracuse University Press, 2014), introduction.

15. On the influence of "English plays" in early modern Germany, see Albert Cohn, *Shakespeare in Germany in the Sixteenth and Seventeenth Centuries* (London: Asher, 1865); Richard Froning, ed., *Das Drama der Reformationszeit*, Deutsche National-Litteratur 22 (Stuttgart: Union Deutsche Verlagsgesellschaft, 1895); Rudolf Schwartz, *Esther im deutschen und neulateinischen Drama des Reformationszeitalters* (Oldenburg: A. Schwartz, 1894). Slavic influence, on the other hand, seems to have been negligible on the early tradition of Purim plays.

16. Budapest, Magyar Tudományos Akadémia Könyvyára (Hungarian Academy of Sciences), Oriental Department, Kaufmann Collection, MS 397; Moritz Stern, ed., *Lieder des venezianischen Lehrers Gumprecht von Szczebrszyn* [sic] *(um 1555), Ivri taytshe shprakh denkmeler / Deutsche Sprachdenkmäler in hebräischen Schriftcharakteren*, 1 (Berlin: Hausfreund, 1922), st. 1,4; cf. also *Pariz and Viene* (1594), st. 5,5. The dramatic texts in Yiddish may also have extended as far back as the fifteenth century: Leo Landau remarks that Dr. Moses Gaster has "probably the oldest fragment of such a Purim-Spiel. . . . It may belong to the fifteenth century"; in *Arthurian Legends: The Hebrew-German Rhymed Version of the Legend of King Arthur*, Teutonia 21 (Leipzig: Avenarius, 1912), xxx. On the tradition of Purim songs, see also Evi Butzer, *Die Anfänge der jiddischen* purim shpiln *in ihrem literarischen und kulturgeschichtlichen Kontext*, jidische schtudies, vol. 10 (Hamburg: Helmut Buske, 2003), 50–60; Ahuva Belkin, "*Zmires purim*—The Third Phase of Jewish Carnivalistic Folk-Literature," in *The Politics of Yiddish: Studies in Language, Literature and Society*, ed. Dov-Ber Kerler, Winter Studies in Yiddish 4 (London: Alta Mira, 1998), 149–156.

17. Tsinberg, *Geshikhte*, 353–358.

18. The work of Ahuva Belkin has focused on the "low-culture" element in Purim plays, strangely all but denying the existence of the parallel and simultaneous tradition of the learned Purim plays of the seventeenth and eighteenth centuries: Ahuva Belkin, "'Habit de Fou' in Purim Spiel?" *Assaph: Studies in the Theatre* 2/c (1985): 40–55; Ahuva Belkin, "Low Culture in the Purim Play," in *Yiddish Theatre: New Approaches*, ed. Joel Berkowitz, Littman Library of Jewish Civilization (Oxford: Littman Library, 2003), 29–43; Ahuva Belkin, *Ha-Purim shpil: ʿiyunim ba-teatron ha-Yehudi ha-ʿamami* (Jerusalem: Mossad Bialik, 2002).

19. Marino Sanuto, *I Diarii*, 54:146; see also: Benjamin Ravid, "How 'Other' Really Was the Jewish Other? The Evidence from Venice," in *Acculturation*, ed. Myers, 32.

20. Gustav Karpeles, *Jewish Literature and Other Essays* (Philadelphia: Jewish Publication Society, 1895), 235. As Evi Butzer comments: "Die Wurzeln des jüdischen Theaters liegen—darüber sind sich die Forscher und Forscherinnen heute einig—in Italien," "The roots of Jewish theater—scholars now are agreed on that—are in Italy" (Butzer, *Die Anfänge*, 30).

21. See Kristine Hecker, "The Concept of Theatre Production in Leone de' Sommi's *Quattro dialoghi* in the Context of His Time," in *Leone de Sommi and the Performing Arts*, ed. Ahuva Belkin (Tel Aviv: Assaph, 1997), 189–208.

22. Jefim Schirmann, "Drama, hebräisches," in *Encyclopaedia Judaica*, ed. Jakob Klatzkin and Ismar Elbogen (Berlin: Eshkol, 1930), 6:17–26.

23. Israel Zoller, "Theater und Tanz in den italienischen Ghettis [*sic*]," *Mitteilungen zur jüdischen Volkskunde* 29 (1926): 596–598.

24. See Butzer, *Die Anfänge*, 61–73; Shmeruk, *Maḥazot*, 13–19, 121–127. The notion advanced first by Rosenberg (1888, 273) and accepted since then that the Yiddish Jonah play derives from an earlier Christian German play is quite troubled. Butzer, for instance, concurs with Rosenberg's notion, but then requires four pages (65–68) simply to *list* the differences between the German text and the five-page Yiddish text, which encompass all aspects of the two texts (the German text is, for instance, six times the length of the Yiddish text). The reading of the date of the "Deaf Yeklayn" text is uncertain: Rosenberg reads 1595, Shmeruk 1550, Butzer 1598.

25. On this maskilic tradition, see especially the introductory essays in the volume edited by Marion Aptroot and Roland Gruschka, *Isaak Euchel: Reb Hennoch, oder: Woß tut me damit. Eine jüdische Komödie der Aufklärungszeit* (Hamburg: Buske, 2004), 1–97.

26. On the continuing political significance of the Purim play in the post–World War II period, see Annette Aronowicz, "Joy to the Goy and Happiness to the Jew: Communist and Jewish Aspirations in a Postwar *Purimshpil*," in *Inventing the Modern Yiddish Stage: Essays in Drama, Performance, and Show Business*, ed. Joel Berkowitz and Barbara Henry (Detroit: Wayne State University Press, 2012), 275–294.

27. Leipzig, Universitätsbibliothek B.H. 18 [*olim* Leipzig, Stadtbibliothek 35], fos. 141r–153v; edited by Shmeruk, *Maḥazot*, 155–210; and *EYT* 120.

28. Shmeruk, *Maḥazot*, 330. This conception of production seems to have been the case for some others of the early Purim plays, as well, in which there are stage directions concerning instrumentation for the orchestra, for instance.

29. Shmeruk includes the eight earliest extant Purim plays, five of which were based directly on the Esther fabula. He established the convention of referring to these five plays as אחשורוש־שפּיל Ahasuerus play א (= 1) [1697], ב (= 2) [Frankfurt 1708], ג (= 3) [Amsterdam 1718], and ד (= 4) [Amsterdam 1718], and the *Akta* [Prague 1720]. Hereafter that practice will also be followed here, e.g., AS1 555 (= the Ahasuerus play of 1697, line 555).

30. Henry Malter, "Purim Plays," in *The Jewish Encyclopedia*, ed. Isidore Singer, vol. 10 (New York: Funk and Wagnalls, 1945), 280; Bernard Gorin, *Di geshikhte fun yidishn teater* (New York: Literarischer farlag, 1918), 54–55. It is the bibliophilic Rabbi Oppenheim's library of some six thousand books and a thousand manuscripts that was bought by the Bodleian Library in 1829 and still forms the core of its magnificent collection of kabbalistic, theological, Talmudic, philosophical, mathematical, and medical texts, in addition to the stunning holdings in early Yiddish texts; see Rachel L. Greenblatt, "David Oppenheim," in *The YIVO Encyclopedia of Jews in Eastern Europe*, ed. Gershon David Hundert (New Haven, CT: Yale University Press, 2008), 2:1287–1288.

31. See Tsinberg, *Geshikhte*, 358 who notes that Mordecai is the only character who can functionally be comical, since he is the only overt Jew throughout the play, and thus the only one who logically can parody Hebrew prayers, make Yiddish puns, etc.

32. That consideration may also have conditioned the omission of the Vashti episode, which, depending on staging, might have enabled a reduction of the required cast.

33. Shatski, "Geshikhte," 402.

34. On the German dramatic tradition of the period, see Richard Froning, ed., *Das Drama des Mittelalters*, Deutsche National-Litteratur 14 (Stuttgart: Union Deutsche Verlagsgesellschaft, 1891–1892); Otto Koishwitz, *Der Theaterherold im deutschen Schauspiel des Mittelalters und der Reformationszeit: ein Beitrag zur deutschen Theatergeschichte* (Berlin: E. Ebering, 1926); Franz Josef Mone, ed., *Schauspiele des Mittelalter* (Karlsruhe: C. Macklot, 1846); Heinrich Reidt, *Das geistliche Schauspiel des Mittelalters in Deutschland* (Frankfurt am Main: C. Winter, 1868); Karl Weinhold, ed., *Weihnacht-Spiele und Lieder aus Süddeutschland und Schlesien* (Vienna: Braumüller, 1875); Ernst Heinrich Wilken, *Geshichte der geistlichen Spiele in Deutschland* (Göttingen: Vandenhoeck and Ruprecht, 1872); Maximillian Josef Rudwin, *A Historical and Bibliographical Survey of German Religious Drama* (Pittsburgh: University of Pittsburgh Press, 1924); Oscar Cargill, *Drama and Liturgy* (New York: Columbia University Press, 1930); Harold Charles Gardiner, *Mysteries End: An Investigation of the Last Days of the Medieval Religious Stage* (New Haven, CT: Yale University Press, 1946).

35. Shmeruk, *Maḥazot*, 147.

36. This early edition was apparently destroyed in the fire of the Frankfurt ghetto on 14 January 1711. A second edition, by Löw Ginsburg, appeared in Frankfurt in 1713; there was also a third edition, which included a German translation; see Shmeruk, "Di 'Moyshe rabeynu bashraybung'—an umbakante drame fun 18tn yorhundert," *Di goldene keyt* 50 (1964): 296–297; Shatski, "Geshikhte," 399.

37. Malter, "Purim Plays," 279.

38. The comedy itself is rather coarse; the clown figure is initially named Lizinski, the ראטס-הער "counselor" of Goliath; later in the play, when he is sent as a spy to King Saul, he takes the "undercover name" of Hansvurst. The name Lizinski and some other vocabulary might suggest that the play originated in Bohemia; see Willy Staerk, "Die Purim-Komödie *Mekhires Yousef*," *Monatsschrift für Geschichte und Wissenschaft des Judentums*, n.s., 30 (1922): 295–296; Shatski, "Geshikhte," 399.

39. On the relevance of this migration for Purim plays in Amsterdam, see Shatski, "Geshikhte," 407.

40. Shatski, "Geshikhte," 407.

41. The general tendency to prohibit Jewish theater and circus attendance was widespread among Jews, but it was not until after the period here addressed, i.e., during the Enlightenment and the Jewish Haskalah, that the anti-theatrical movement was often also based on an antipathy to the Yiddish language (then still the general linguistic medium of the Jewish theater).

42. For more extensive information on the Christian-Jewish relations with respect to the Haman tradition, see especially the work of Elliott Horowitz, in his preliminary essay, "The Rite to Be Reckless: On the Perpetration and Interpretation of Purim Violence," in *Purim and the Cultural Poetics of Judaism—Theorizing Diaspora*, ed. Daniel Boyarin, special issue, *Poetics Today* 15 (1994): 10, 24–26, and especially his definitive book *Reckless Rites*, esp. 1–146 on the biblical text and later textual and holiday traditions.

43. Amnon Linder, ed., *The Jews in Roman Imperial Legislation* (Detroit: Wayne State University Press, 1987), 237; Horowitz, "The Rite," 10, 24–26; Horowitz, *Reckless Rites*, 17, 158–159, 214–216.

44. Horowitz, *Reckless Rites*, 28.

45. See Marianne Haraszti-Takács, "Fifteenth-Century Painted Furniture with Scenes from the Esther Story," *Jewish Art* 15 (1989): 25; Shatski, "Der kamf kegn purim-shpil in praysn in 18tn y[or]h[undert]," *Yivo-bleter* 15 (1932): 29–30. Horowitz explores in some depth the rather exten-

sive history of anti-Christian violence by Jews on Purim (*Reckless Rites*, 36–42). Butzer classifies various such traditional customs of "abusing" Haman (*Die Anfänge*, 17–19).

46. Shatski, "Der kamf," 29.
47. Shatski, "Geshikhte," 402.
48. Shatski, "Geshikhte," 397.
49. Shatski, "Geshikhte," 397.
50. Shatski, "Geshikhte," 405.
51. Haraszti-Takács suggests that there were performances in synagogues in Italy during the fifteenth century attended by both Jews and Christians; "Painted Furniture," 25.
52. Interestingly, this move resembles that of the fledgling medieval Christian drama (several centuries earlier), in the *quem quaeritis* Easter plays, which eventually had to move out of Christian churches onto the church steps and thence to other extra-ecclesiastical venues.
53. Shatski, "Geshikhte," 402.
54. On the inevitable interconnections of cultural production and state control, see also Peter Stallybrass and Allon White, *The Politics and Poetics of Transgression* (Ithaca, NY: Cornell University Press, 1986).
55. Malter, "Purim Plays," 279; Staerk, "Die Purim-Komödie, 295; Gorin, *Di geshikhte*, 50–51.
56. Renate Fuks-Mansfeld, "West- und Ostjiddisch auf Amsterdamer Bühnen gegen Ende des achtzehnten Jahrhunderts," in *Westjiddisch: Mündlichkeit und Schriftlichkeit/Le Yiddish occidental: Actes du Colloque de Mulhouse*, ed. Astrid Starck (Aarau: Sauerländer, 1994), 113. In 1793 in Siena, Italy, where the plays were performed in Italian, thus initially also drawing large Christian audiences, soldiers also had to be employed. Christians eventually were denied entrance (Shatski, "Geshikhte," 403).
57. Shatski, "Der kamf," 38.
58. See Malter, "Purim Plays," 279; Shatski, "Geshikhte," 396; Tsinberg, *Geshikhte*, 357.
59. Ahasuerus gives Mordecai a golden ring and the royal seal that Haman had previously held, thus explicitly making him his second-in-command: איך וויל מיך ביווייזן צו אייער פֿעטר קיניגליך / קומט איין הער מרדכֿי איך מאך אייך / אן מיינם רייך דער צווייטיר אן דיא קראן (AS3 1441), "I would like to show/prove myself as royal to your uncle. Come in, Sir Mordecai; I am making you second to the throne in my empire." Interestingly, the relationship between Mordecai and Esther is an ambiguous one: already in the Septuagint—ἐπαίδευσεν αὐτὴν ἑαυτῷ εἰς γυναῖκα "and he brought her up to be his wife" (Est 2:7)—and elaborated in the Talmud (BT *Meg* 13a), Mordecai is her husband, not her uncle; and according to the *Zohar* (Ra'aya Meheimna, Ki tetse, 3:275b–276b), she remains sexually faithful to Mordecai even after her marriage to Ahasuerus by means of a female spirit sent by the Shekhinah to take her place in the king's bed; see also Susan Niditch, "Esther: Folklore, Wisdom, Feminism and Authority," in *Underdogs and Tricksters: A Prelude to Folklore* (San Francisco: Harper and Row, 1987), 126–145; repr. in *Feminist Companion*, ed. Brenner, 26–46. Walfish examines this broad issue of the relationship between Mordecai and Esther as it is problematized in the textual tradition ("Kosher Adultery," 305–333). The issue becomes progressively more interesting as the exegetical tradition becomes more involved in extricating Esther from wrongdoing: if already married to Mordecai, how can one justify her adultery with Ahasuerus, especially if, as Rava bar Lima in the name of Rav says, שהיתה עומדת מחיקו של אחשורוש וטובלת ויושבת בחיקו של מרדכי "she arises from the bosom of Ahasuerus, immerses herself, and sits down in the bosom of Mordecai," connoting the sexual act in each case (BT *Meg* 13b). This marks Esther even more clearly as a mediatrix between inside and outside the palace and a liminally functional figure in exasperatingly complex ways. But that complexity is ultimately a matter of biblical-Talmudic-midrashic exegesis, while the focus in the present study is Purim play—where there is no hint that she might have

already been married to Mordecai—with attention to the tradition of Jewish sacred texts only insofar as they aid in explicating the Purim play. See below, chapter 6, on the key element of liminality in the tradition of Purim plays.

60. Although a different perspective is offered by the Deuteronomist, who claims that the "faint and weary" Israelites were defeated by the Amalekites (Dt 25:17–19).

61. Joachim Prinz, "A Rabbi under the Hitler Regime," in *Gegenwart in Rückblick*, ed. H. A. Strauss and K. R. Grossmann (Heidelberg: Lothar Stiehm, 1970), 235; cited by Horowitz, "The Rite," 11.

62. See "Hitler Sees Peril of Russia to All," *New York Times*, 31 Jan 1944, 5; and Horowitz, *Reckless Rights*, 91. I have been unable to trace what must have been the German-language original of this now widely cited quotation.

63. Philip Goodman, *The Purim Anthology* (Philadelphia: Jewish Publication Society, 1949), 374–376.

64. See Horowitz, "The Rite," 43–45.

65. Bronner notes that scholars now date the book of Esther to the late Persian or early Hellenistic period ("Revisited," 178).

66. *Le Yiddish* (Paris: Presses Universitaires de France, 1990), 108.

67. Horowitz, "The Rite," 13.

68. On the widespread and too facile identification of Purim with a vague and trivialized post-Bakhtinian notion of the carnivalesque, see Fisch, "Reading," 68.

69. Shatski, "Geshikhte," 409. As an enemy of the *Polish* state, the czar's position may complicate the present argument concerning the Purim plays' position on monarchy.

70. Paulus de Lagarde, ed., *Hagiographa Chaldaice* (Leipzig: Teubner, 1873; repr., Osnabrück: Otto Zeller, 1967), 246–248; and the commentary by Beate Ego, ed., *Targum Scheni zu Ester: Übersetzung, Kommentar und theologische Deutung* (Tübingen: Mohr, 1996), 240–255.

71. The *Akta* as a play is particularly focused on this issue.

72. Repeated later in the same speech, AS2 144. See Butzer, *Die Anfänge*, 185–187, on the metaphorical sexual language in this play, particularly having to do with Mordecai's recurring use of penis metaphors and his "penetration" of the doors/gates apparently as metaphors of the vagina.

73. On שטריק טרעגר, "rope-wearer" = monk/friar with a rope belt, cf. the usage in contemporaneous German; Grimm, *DWB*, vol. 19, col. 1589.

74. Or, less likely: "I am very concerned for you."

75. On the incompetence of the king in the biblical book of Esther, see Elsie Stern: "This overabundance of law has two striking features. First, it is inextricably tied to the will of the king. This is clear from the recurrence of the phrase 'if it please Your Majesty' in relationship to the establishment of law or royal edicts"; Elsie Stern, "Esther and the Politics of Diaspora," *Jewish Quarterly Review* 100 (2010): 35.

76. In AS3, the execution of the conspirators is described by Haman in grisly detail: by royal decree they were hanged, quartered, and the pieces of their corpses hung on four highways, the heads on iron pikes (AS3 973 ff.). As such, the punishment resembles that meted out to the rebels against the crown who instigated the attack on the Jews during the Fettmilch insurrection in Frankfurt; cf. Elḥanan b. Abraham Hellen, *The Song of Vints Hans* [*Megilas Vints*], *EYT* 100.

77. Interestingly, most of the "Yiddish" sentence is Latin: . . . *magnus rex. in asia africa. europa et america.*

78. Haman, Bigthan, and Teresh are also portrayed—as they approach their executions—as almost sympathetic characters, certainly as pious and devout ones. Did such a characterization function to prevent or foment Christian outrage, by making the culprits less monstrous?

Chapter Five

Vashti and Political Revolution

Gender Politics in a Topsy-Turvy World

WHILE THE NARRATIVE of the book of Esther seems rather straightforward and logical on its own terms, the complex Jewish textual traditions characterized in the previous chapter overlay that tale with multiple further grids of signification. It is the only book of the Bible in which God is not mentioned, and as previously noted, there is little on the surface that seems of theological import, but such an initial impression is superficial and ultimately of little relevance in the Jewish interpretive traditions of theological significance attaching to the text. According to *Midrash Esther Rabbah*, for instance, the biblical narrative of Esther explicitly expresses the divine execution of God's plan through his human instruments Ahasuerus, Vashti, Haman, Mordecai, and Esther. Ahasuerus's decisions and actions are directed by the hidden hand of God, and thus he ousts (and kills) Vashti because God wants Esther to be queen, so that she will later be able to intercede on behalf of the Jews and prevent their extermination. Ahasuerus likewise has his vizier Haman executed because God wants to reverse the king's anti-Jewish decree and save the Jews from extermination. Thus the fickle king's otherwise inexplicable behavior becomes clear if one reads the narrative as the systematic enactment or realization of the divine plan. By means of such an interpretive strategy, Vashti's execution becomes, from the level of mere human perception, a miracle, since it is necessary for the Jews' salvation.

In the midrash, Vashti is said to have inherited her great-grandfather Nebuchadnezzar's anti-Semitism and thus would have willingly joined forces with Haman to exterminate the Jews.[1] Ahasuerus and Vashti each hold their banquets in order to celebrate Nebuchadnezzar's destruction of the Temple in Jerusalem, and Vashti effectively prevents the rebuilding of the Temple during her tenure as queen, for which she is punished by death, while Ahasuerus—by whose authority Vashti is (putatively) executed—is himself punished by Vashti's death, in that his joy in life is thereby diminished.[2] Just as Vashti's descent from the evil Nebuchadnezzar inflects the narrative, so, too, does Haman's descent from Agag, king of the evil Amalekites. That narrative trajectory, begun "earlier" in Israelite history, then finally reaches closure in the book of Esther, where the last descendant of Nebuchadnezzar *and* the last descendant of Amalek are killed and their lines of descent therewith finally obliterated. Thus, while strict Christian interpretations of the book of Esther often display some level of discomfort with the lack of overt theological content and the absence of all mention of God, the post-biblical Jewish tradition of commentary had no such overt difficulty in recuperating and integrating the book into the culture's larger theologico-nationalist narratives. Leila Bronner seems to blend some aspects of both modern interpretive modes when she suggests that the classical rabbis sensed a theological deficiency in the biblical narrative and in the depiction of Esther and thus "through aggadic methods of interpretation they added the Jewish qualities they wanted her to have. They transformed her into a pious Jewish woman," and thus integrated the entire narrative into the larger theological system.[3]

Timothy K. Beal interestingly suggests that the Vashti episode constructs a frame for the Esther narrative, against which the later characterization of Esther is contrasted;[4] he also makes use of the Derridean notions of preface and supplementarity, where borders between the supplemental and the core (here: main narrative) are unstable, leaving traces, and erasure marks in the main narrative. He notes that while a royal edict "erases" Vashti ("indeed a kind of writing that erases"), there are traces that remain ("as with an ancient palimpsest"), "erasure marks that will be 'read' into the subsequent story about their replacements." Thus while Vashti refused the "status of fixed object" that Ahasuerus attempted to impose on her, Esther "fills that space from which Vashti was erased—but not entirely. Vashti is the supplement that Esther requires."[5] Interestingly, Beal seems altogether unaware of the historically and theologically charged positioning of Vashti as an integral (negative) component of Jewish cultural history, since he posits that the opening of the Esther narrative with the Vashti episode "supports an alignment of the reader with a non-Jewish woman (Vashti) as heroine in a gender-based conflict," which is of course incompatible with the Jewish conception of audience just adumbrated.[6] Thus while perceptive in many regards, Beal's reading of the text seems oblivious to the post-biblical Jewish interpretive tradition.[7]

The treatment of the book of Esther in the broad range of midrashic texts (outlined in the previous chapter) is surprisingly extensive, considering the brevity of the biblical book, perhaps indeed to insist on its theological significance, perhaps simply because in the context of an overt genocidal threat that significance is so integral to the nationalist narrative. As the present discursive context also assumes, one should likewise include the Purim plays that take the Esther fabula as their controlling narrative as further examples of this midrashic tradition.

The transformative conflicts and manifestations of revolution in these plays are multiple: the symbolic or clandestine revolution of the Jews (examined in chapter 4), the assassination attempt by Bigthan and Teresh, and Haman's attempted preemptive counter-revolution against the rising Jewish power. Moreover, one of the most intriguing aspects of two of these early Esther plays is the foregrounding of the conflict between Vashti and Esther, already at least implicit, of course, in the Bible, but here made at least momentarily the focus of revolutionary sedition. Significantly, despite the ostensive importance of the Vashti episode in the biblical tale as a narrative counterpoint to the focal character of Esther, the entire Vashti episode is, as noted earlier, simply omitted in the two earliest extant Ahasuerus plays (AS1 of 1697 and AS2 of 1708), which, while incidentally acknowledging the former existence of Vashti as queen, nonetheless begin the narrative with the king's search for a new queen or indeed even after his having chosen Esther. In the chronologically third and fourth such extant dramas (AS3 and AS4, both printed in Amsterdam in 1718), however, Vashti plays not just the minor role known from the biblical text, but at some points early in the plays seems on the verge of taking over the plays and the narratives altogether. She is in any case essential to the explicitly political nature of these dramas' plots.

These two plays differ in myriad other ways from the first two extant Ahasuerus plays, both of which are rather simpler in conception. In the later plays, however, Mordecai is not at all simply the Jewish incarnation of the comic characters of Hans Wurst and Pickelherring of the contemporary Christian stage, not the foul-mouthed and fouler-gestured ne'er-do-well who will do almost anything to make a joke based on sexual innuendo, as is the character of Mordecai in those two earlier plays. Nor is he simply the holy sage of the biblical text. Indeed he is here even more extensively and explicitly characterized as the consummate statesman and court diplomat.

Not surprisingly, the character of the biblical Esther drew a great deal of attention—much of it approving—from twentieth-century feminism. More recent evaluations have been rather less enthusiastic in that respect. Indeed Elliott Horowitz comments: "Modern feminists . . . often regard the more passive Esther with disdain."[8] Susan Niditch notes that Esther "is an altogether appealing portrait of women's wisdom for the men of a ruling patriarchate, but hardly an image meaningful or consoling to modern women."[9] Susan Zaeske has, however, attempted to claim the book of Esther as a "rhetoric of exile" and Esther herself as only initially subordinate to male power while later transforming into an independent leader of her people.[10] Bronner notes that feminist scholarship has sometimes "glorified Vashti to the detriment of Esther" and joins Zaeske in her claim that Esther only starts out as a "docile" character, while progressively moving from "obeying to commanding. It is she who commands the fast, develops a plan and implements it. Ultimately, she institutes the festival of Purim. Esther takes charge."[11] I would simply point out that Esther's would-be feminist credentials, as it were, are rather thin: she is after all the winner of the Miss Persian Empire contest, the—at least initially—reluctant opponent of anti-Jewish genocide, goaded by her *former* male guardian (Mordecai) to approach her *current* male guardian (Ahasuerus) with a petition. In fact it requires a very generous reader to impute much initiative to her at all, even in the late stages of the narrative.

In the end, however, terms such as "feminist" or "proto-feminist," which are so essentially embedded in the political discourse and social structures of our own culture and so anachronistic for a twenty-five-hundred-year-old literary character, seem all but irrelevant to the texts at issue here. That is, at the same time, not to elide the issue of gender in the text tradition of the Esther fabula, for it sometimes seems that precisely that issue is of essential importance in its various guises along the trajectory of the multiple interpretive traditions.

In any case, there is no deterioration of Esther's role from the biblical text to the Purim plays.[12] In the absence of Mordecai the clown (of the quasi-slapstick tradition of AS1 and AS2), she is not the butt of her stage uncle's insatiable drive for the cheap, prurient snicker. King Ahasuerus is still the typical dull-witted fairy-tale king of the biblical text, who would dearly love to do the right thing, if only he were able to figure out what that might be. Lacking that gift of basic morality and even more basic intelligence, however, he simply does whatever anyone and everyone tells him to do, repeats what they say, thinks (insofar as he is capable of thought) what they think, and then imagines that he was the clever one to begin with, all the while being misled and manipulated by those around him.[13] The frequently anti-monarchical position of the early Purim plays is interesting because it takes the traditionally anti-monarchical biblical text—whose king *is* after all evil *and* ineffective *and* a willow bending to evil influence, who is opposed, mocked, and manipulated by the Jews (for the sake of their own survival!)—and repositions the dramatic action in a contemporary, early modern European setting.

The whole narrative complex thus is multi-layered, and it is of course this complexity that made it still interesting for the eighteenth-century Purim audience, and makes it still interesting for contemporary readers. As noted in the previous chapter, while the first two of the extant Purim plays are obvious examples of a tradition of folk drama, both AS3 and AS4 are just as obviously examples of sophisticated Baroque drama. Each of the formally divided acts of AS4 is, for instance, preceded by a staged tableau that visually previews the plot of the act. In these two plays, characteristically of the high drama and *Staatsaktionen* of European drama of the period, Queen Vashti is pitted against the king, and—as is known to informed members of the audience—also against the future Queen Esther, with the two in the conventional roles of female court rivals.[14]

An essential part of these plays' sophistication is an overt problematization of the function of female beauty (particularly in its power to disable the king)—certainly not as a proto-*feminist* critique of its social role in a patriarchal society, but a quasi-modern (or at least *early* modern) view nonetheless, particularly as it examines how beauty functions in male-female relationships and especially how those relationships are explicitly acknowledged as overt power relationships. In this respect the Purim plays make explicit what the biblical text only implies: the king's ultimate incompetence as a ruler is even more sharply accented by his own lust and his overt and vociferously expressed inability to focus on much of anything besides female beauty, at any time of the day or night. Consequently, more specific analysis of Vashti's role is called for here, which will require occasional, tactical plot summary, since these particular texts are no longer performed in any community, are untranslated, and are not widely read in the original Middle Yiddish.

The primary conflict between Vashti and the king arises from the issue of female beauty and the gender-defined "ownership" or control of it. This issue is of some significance in the *Midrash Esther Rabbah*, where Ahasuerus, in a dispute with his banquet guests, claims that Vashti is the most beautiful woman of all, which prompts their desire to see her (*MER* 42). As was conventional in the post-biblical Jewish interpretive tradition, the king's consequent order that Vashti appear at his banquet before his courtiers, wearing a crown, was interpreted not to mean that the crown was to symbolize her majesty as queen, but rather to mean that she was to wear *only* the crown and thus display herself naked and thus as the king's beautiful, possessed female object (*MER* 34).[15] It is indeed the courtiers who specify that she is to be naked, and the king willingly complies: אָמְרוּ לוֹ הֵן וּבִלְבַד שֶׁתְּהֵא עֲרוּמָּה. אָמַר לְהוֹן הֵן וַעֲרוּמָּה "They said to him: Yes, provided that she is naked. He said to them: Yes, naked" (*MER* 42).

Vashti ultimately rejects the king's gender-defined attempt to co-opt her beauty as his possession and deflects the voyeuristic and possessing male gaze of the courtiers by refusing to participate in the king's display of her beauty.[16] In attempting to dissuade the king from his order that she appear naked, Vashti sends him three messages: first, that if the banqueters were to find her beautiful, they would kill the king in order to possess her, while, on the other hand, if they were to find her ugly, then the king would be disgraced. So he would gain nothing either way. In her second message, she reminds him that he was the stable-master for her father, Belshazzar (קוּמֵיס אִיסְטַבְלָאטִי שֶׁל בֵּית אַבָּה הָיִיתָ) and was thus accustomed to ordering harlots (זוֹנוֹת) to come before him, and that he has not changed his debauched ways (לֹא חָזַרְתָּ מִקִּלְקוּלְךָ) (*MER* 43). He seems incapable of understanding the significance of either of these messages, so she sends him a third, indicating that even Nebuchadnezzar executed condemned prisoners with their clothes on, so Ahasuerus is consequently even less respectable than was Nebuchadnezzar. He finally comprehends this message and is, predictably, enraged by it. A second motivation for the king's immoral request is provided by the *Midrash Rabbah*: it is only because of his drunkenness at the banquet that he orders Vashti to appear naked, and likewise his drunkenness causes his rage when she refuses (*MER* 55).[17]

In any case, the king wishes to display his wife's reputedly spellbinding beauty to the courtiers, as the Purim plays make explicit, in such a way that no one could imagine that that beauty was the result of or even enhanced by jewelry or elegant clothing (AS4 185). The king himself is depicted as a slave of female beauty. Memukhan (Memukh) says the king gave Vashti his טרוא "troth" because of her beauty (AS3 280 ff.); Hatakh (Hesekh) says that the king טעט איר שאנהייט מער ליבן אז אונז אלין "loved her beauty more than he did all of us" (AS3 289). Significantly, Vashti's beauty continues to function at court even after she is gone; for just as the king was unable to admire it in morally acceptable fashion while she was at court, he is unable to function as king after she leaves: he is literally disabled. He apparently even contemplates suicide—at least he claims not to be able to live without her, which in context seems more than mere hyperbolic bluster and is perhaps to be taken more seriously in that genre and time period than it might be, for instance, in twenty-first-century situation comedy.[18] But then of course, as the fundamentally patriarchal gender-ideology of the narrative demands, as soon as such a king sees an as yet un-possessed beauty such as Esther, he immediately forgets the previously possessed beauty. For, like Vashti, Esther is also represented as supernaturally beautiful: Mordecai specifically claims that Heaven granted her such beauty (AS3 370).[19] Thus the king's courtiers manage to save the kingdom *and* the conventions of patriarchy by preventing the lovesick king from summoning his longed-for Vashti back from exile, which, as they explicitly remark, would have destroyed normal gender relations by encouraging wifely disobedience among the broad populace.[20] This particular issue is treated far more seriously and at greater length in the post-biblical textual tradition (*Megillah*, *Midrash Rabbah*, and the Purim plays) than it is in the Bible.

Additionally, as the audience knows—precisely from that detailed post-biblical tradition—Vashti's rehabilitation would also have opened the door to her own further political ambitions, which must now be addressed, for such aspects of the *effect* of female beauty (by definition passive and obedient to patriarchy) on male political authority, while themselves traditional, are here transformed by the added complication of *active* female participation in the political process. Significantly in these Purim plays, while Vashti is obviously condemned and exiled (or explicitly executed, as in AS4),[21] her political sedition is not *overtly* condemned as "female intrigue," that is, as the conventional behind-the-scenes machinations that are traditionally (misogynistically) construed as "typical" female intrusions into the (necessarily) male sphere of political action. As Barry Walfish points out, there was general agreement among medieval interpreters that Ahasuerus was justified in punishing Vashti as he did, in order to quash all inclination toward insurrection even at the beginning of his reign.[22]

Vashti's refusal to obey the king's overt command at the banquet (i.e., that she make an appearance wearing her crown) denies the patriarchal construction of the category "wife" as male possession under absolute male control, which is in this case—involving the king and queen—thus immediately construed as an act of treason and lèse-majesté. In AS3 the courtier Memukhan says that since she refuses to obey the king's command, she should be banished, for fear that she will incite other women to disobedience. Thus it is extrapolated that any and every other woman who disobeys her husband should suffer the punishment that Vashti will suffer (AS3 100–107, 149 ff., 231 ff.). In AS3 she is condemned in absentia, but after line 411 she simply exits the stage and disappears from the plot, mentioned only a few more times in the course of the trial of Bigthan and Teresh. In AS4, as already noted, she is executed.

Vashti's own response to her downfall is directly political: she identifies the kingdom from which she is to be banished as her own (AS3 155–156) and, echoing Bigthan's defense of her, explicitly denies the strictly gender-based identity of a queen's actions with any other woman's: האט דען איין קינגין ניט מער רעכֿט. / אלז איין אנדרי פֿרוא דיא דא איז שלעכֿט (AS3 165–166), "Does a queen then not have more extensive rights than another woman who is a commoner?" In her long speech protesting her banishment (AS3 169–190), she focuses especially on her personal pain and the inability of her wealth and nobility to change the verdict:

יוא וואל אורטייל קיגין רעכֿט אויז ביזן הערצין גקומין.
אבר דז רעכֿט דז האבט איר אליין וועק גנומין.
אבר די נייט איז אל לנג גישטאקין אין אייער הערצין.
דרום טוט איר מיר אן זעלכֿין שמערצין.
אבר דאך איך דא בין איבר וואונין.
אך עלענט וואר צו בין איך גקומן.
עז טוט מיר ניקז העלפֿן מיין זילבר אודר רוטיר גאלט.
מן טוט מיך יאגין אין ווילדן וואלט.
אך ביגתֿן אונ' תרש ביקלאגיט מיין אונגיפֿאל.
איך פֿעריכֿט מיך דז עש אייך אך נאך טרעפֿין זאל.
אך וויא בין איך גזעסין אין קוטשין אונ' ביהנגין וואגין.
נון טוט מן מיך אויז דעם רייך ארושר יאגין.
אך שאנט אונ' שמאך וואש מיר טוט גישעהן.
וויא קאן איך דז לענגיר צו זעהן.
היר איז דז קינגש קרון.
גוויש ווערט ער בקומן זיין לון.
אונ' טוט עש אחשורוש זאגין.

עש זאל ווערין ביצאלט אין קורצין טגין.
אך וויא ווער איך פֿר שטוסין אויז מיינם לאנד.
אונ' מוז גין דא איך בין אום גיקאנט.
אך המן מעכֿט בגתֿן אונ' תרש מיין גלייטש מנין זיין.
אזו וואלט איך מיך ניט רייכֿר ווינשן אין מיין בטריבטי פיין:

Indeed an unjust verdict comes from evil hearts. But it is justice itself that you yourselves have taken away. Envy, however, has ever lodged in your hearts. It is for that reason that you cause me such pain. But I have here, after all, been overcome. Alas, the calamity to which I have come! My silver and red gold are of no aid to me. I am being forced out into the savage forest. Alas, Bigthan and Teresh, lament my unhappy fate! I will conduct myself such that you will also be affected. Alas, how I have ridden in carriages and draped palanquins! Now I am being driven out of the empire. Alas, it is shame and dishonor that is happening to me! How can I watch any longer? Here is the king's crown. He will surely get his comeuppance. And tell Ahasuerus: it will be paid in the very near future. Alas, how I am cast out of my own land and go where I am unknown! Oh, Haman, may Bigthan and Teresh be my attendants? I would not wish to be richer than that in my aggrieved pain.

She is granted Bigthan and Teresh as retainers to accompany her into exile. She refers to the king's disloyalty to her and to her high-born status: אך קינג איז דאז דיא טרוא דיא איר מיר האבט גישווארין. / אך ווער איך דאך פֿון אזו איין הוכֿיר שטאם ניט גיבארין (AS3 193–194), "O, king, is that the loyalty/constancy that you swore to me? O, if only I had not been born to such a noble family!" As if it were a transition between the fallen queen's fortunes and the fortunes of the rising queen-to-be, the *shrayber* retrieves the queen's crown from the ground (where Vashti has cast it) and takes it to the treasury, to preserve it for another queen, who at this point has not yet been identified (AS3, 196).

Thus far in the drama there has been no more than a slight elaboration of Vashti's role as known in the biblical text, not an unusual practice in dramatizations of conventionally schematic biblical narratives. But after her initial defiance of the king in the biblical text, Vashti quietly disappears, while in *Targum Sheni* she steps into a somewhat more active role by frequently criticizing the king's intelligence (e.g., *ad* Est 1:12).[23] In the Purim plays, however, the political import, indeed the entire significance of the Vashti episode is suddenly transformed. In AS3, she openly conspires with Bigthan and Teresh—the two courtiers who in the biblical text plot the assassination of the king, here identified as קיניגש קאמירלינגן "king's chamberlains" (AS3 544) but later called "princes" by the king himself (AS3 1113–1117)—to overthrow the monarchy, specifically, as she makes explicit, because of the corruption and immorality of this particular king. Vashti thus becomes the primary agent of a peculiar and interesting attempt at political revolution. Her association with the would-be assassins begins earlier in the narrative, for Bigthan defends Vashti (AS3 108–115), claiming that banishment is inappropriately extreme in the case of a queen. He and his confederate, Teresh, consider this punishment the result of a conspiracy of the court against the queen (AS3 124–140) and seek a means of aiding her. As is later revealed, their loyalty to her is plausible by reason of her past sponsorship of them at court: גדענגט ביגתֿן אונ' תרש וויא דז איך אייך האב טון אויף ברענגין "Remember, Bigthan and Teresh, how I have raised you up / sponsored you" (AS3, 387).

Vashti herself justifies the conspiracy to assassinate the king as רעכֿינונג "vengeance" (AS3, 386 ff.)[24]; she claims that she would do it herself were she not a woman; otherwise, she says, זוא וואלט איך דען קיניג נעמין דז הערץ אוז זיין לייב. / אונ' וואלט עש אויף שטיקר שניידן. / אונ' וואלט עש פֿאר דיא הונד ווארפֿין מיט פֿריידן (AS 395–397), "thus I would like to take the king's heart out of his body and cut it in pieces and joyfully throw it to the dogs." She promises Bigthan and Teresh a reward for killing the king (AS3 391). Teresh explicitly commits Bigthan and himself to do so as service directly to the queen (AS3 408).[25] While the biblical assassination plot by Bigthan and Teresh must logically have also been part of a larger plan to overthrow the government, the specific details of that plan are not made explicit in the gapped biblical narrative. In the Purim plays, however, it is clear that Vashti intends not just to avenge her own personal humiliation, but also to displace the government of Ahasuerus and his court by taking over the ruling function herself.

It is at the same time quite interesting that she is not made part of Bigthan and Teresh's trial and execution as one of the co-conspirators. While the audience knows of her role, because of her explicit and on-stage plotting with Bigthan and Teresh, *they* never reveal her participation in the conspiracy during the trial. When the king notes that Bigthan and Teresh wanted to poison him and asks them directly if anyone else is party to the plot, they simply refuse to speak, and thus Vashti is never openly charged with sedition (AS3 590–591). Later Mordecai even says explicitly that he does not know who was responsible for advising Bigthan and Teresh to attempt the assassination: אבר דר איז מיר און ביקענט דר איז צו זעלכֿין זאכֿין האט גיראטין אן "but he is unknown to me, who counseled such things" (AS3 635). The letter to Vashti, confiscated from Bigthan and Teresh, which is read aloud by the *shrayber* in the presence of the court and which implicates the two men explicitly in the plot, does not mention Vashti (AS3 580–586). Even so, there is some inconsistency in the play, which indicates that Vashti's underlying seditious role was well understood, even if it did not merit explicit mention during the trial: first, Bigthan and Teresh did in fact mention her name during their initial conspiratorial conversation together, overheard by Mordecai, which is after all precisely what led to their arrest in the first place (AS3 490). Much later, during Ahasuerus's fateful sleepless night, the *shrayber*, in the midst of his reading from the chronicle, mentions Vashti's "era" and her nurturing of the two princes, Bigthan and Teresh, at court (AS3 1113–1117). The king responds that Vashti did wonderful things (1117); the *shrayber* continues reading about the treachery of Bigthan and Teresh and then explicitly states either that Vashti was part of the conspiracy or that it was undertaken for her benefit (perhaps the ambiguity of the preposition דוריך is not accidental): זיא האטין דוריך ושתי איין גרוש פֿאראט פֿאר (1119), "by means of / for the sake of Vashti, they had planned a great act of treason."

Just as interestingly, in AS4, Vashti is *not* explicitly involved in the conspiracy to assassinate the king.[26] But this play also adds a detail that transforms the whole perception of the relationships among the primary characters at the Persian court. In the process of justifying her refusal to comply with the king's drunken and salacious order, Vashti's first reaction is hope that the king's honor might cause him to reconsider such an order unbefitting a king (AS4 297).[27] She focuses on the fact that the king's *class* origin makes it impossible both for him to conduct himself morally and for her to obey him—he had, after all, been her royal grandfather's stable-boy (BT *Meg* 12b; in *MER* 43, as noted previously, he is stable-master), and it had only been by means of his marriage to her that he had become king, which consequently made such demands on her all the more inappropriate:

וויא דאש ער בייא מיינם עלטר פֿאטר שטאל קנעכֿט גיוועזין:
אונ' דורך מיך איזט ער קומן [צ]ו זאלכֿין עהרן.
דרום זאל ער זאלכֿש פֿון מיר ניכֿט ביגערן:
אלז דאן זאל ער פֿון זאלכֿן גידאנקין אב שטיהן.
(AS 224–226)

> Inasmuch as he was a stable-boy of my grandfather's, and through me he has come to such great honors, therefore he should not demand such things of me. Consequently he ought to distance himself from such thoughts.[28]

Ahasuerus responds that Vashti's disobedience is due to האפֿרט "arrogance" (AS4 247), that is, inappropriate pride before the king; and thus he refuses even to respond to her attempt to problematize the issue in terms of class *origin*, as opposed to current class *affiliation* and gender/power relations.

He continues to heap abuse on her, saying that this defiance will cost her her life (AS4 250) and that her refusal to obey his command constitutes a פֿרעבֿיל "iniquity" (AS4 259). Haman then delivers a lengthy and rhetorically florid speech about lèse-majesté and the dishonoring of both monarch and monarchy by Vashti (AS4 263–280).[29] The king responds, calling Vashti a בעשטייא "beast" (AS4 283) worthy of the death sentence suggested by Haman, and says that he must punish the commission of lèse-majesté: אונ' דען אפֿרונט פֿון מיינר מאייסטעט רעכֿין (AS4 286) "and avenge the affront to my majesty."

Knowing well this former stable-boy's irrational lustiness, Vashti asks the king not to kill her, specifically because of her beauty, the likes of which he will never find anywhere else. She intriguingly also adds that she deserves to be spared because of her טוגנט "virtue" (AS4 343–345).[30] At one point she hints that she is to be sent to a nunnery: שיקן זיא מיך אין איין נונין קלווישטיר אניין "they are placing me in a nunnery" (AS4 350);[31] but in fact the stage directions indicate quite another fate: המן נימט פֿון איר דיא קרוין. אונ' שלאגט איר דאש הויבט אב (*ante* line 372), "Haman takes the crown from her and strikes off her head."

Significantly, Vashti's initial response to the possibility of her banishment is rooted in class considerations: פֿאר שטוסין אויש מיינם רייך / אך וויא טוט מן מיר דאז אורטייל אזו אום גלייך (AS3 155), "Expelled from my kingdom! Alas, such an unjust sentence is being passed on me!" Her opposition and explicit comments signal an obvious condescending class resentment and *imply* a move to restore some conception of a traditional aristocratic order to the Persian dynasty. But it is to be recalled that in this particular play (AS4) Vashti *does not* explicitly participate in Bigthan and Teresh's plot to assassinate the king. In AS3, on the other hand, where she does participate in the conspiracy, this particular class conflict in the royal family as represented in AS4 is neither explicit nor implied.

In the larger scheme of things, however, class and racial identification is nonetheless of primary importance in both plays. Esther's social status is, for instance, *definitively* low: she is a Jew, a foreigner, an exile, and thus—like Ahasuerus in the midrash and AS4—not born as a member of the Persian royal class. Immediately after Vashti's having taken off her crown in AS3, Esther comments very pointedly on the social and political consequences of her identity:

די שלאווירנייא מיין פֿעטער דז גיבט אונש פֿיל צו קלאגין.
וועלכֿיש מיר עברעירש אלי טאג מוזין מער שפאט פֿאר טראגין.
פֿון דיא פרסיאנר ועלכֿש נאך אן וואקשט אלי טאג.
אונ' אונזר פֿאליק ישראל ניט דאר קיגין אויף מאג.
אביר דאך אונזר זינט די מאכֿין די שווערי פלאגין.
וועלכֿש מיר מוזין מיט גידולט פֿאר טראגין.
איך טוא האבין גרושי פיין אין מיינם הערצין.
ווייל דיא פרסיאנרש אן מיין פֿאלק טון גרושי שמערצין:
(AS3 199–206)

Slavery, my uncle, gives us a great deal to lament, from which every day we Hebrews have to endure more mockery from the Persians, which increases every day. And our people Israel can do nothing against it. But it is our sins that cause these heavy afflictions that we must bear with patience. I have great pain in my heart; for the Persians cause great pains to my people.

Later she claims: איך בין דאך איין ארמי דינשט מייט גיבארין "I was after all born as a poor servant girl" (AS3 379), among the exiled Jews who serve in שלאווירנאיי "slavery" (AS3 337); she prays for an end to the exile and to their slavery simultaneously.[32] After Vashti's dethronement, Haman promises the king a new wife who will be עבין "suitable" for him (AS4 426).[33] It is difficult in context to decide whether there is irony involved here; that is, does Haman's term "suitable" denote a commoner, since that is after all what Ahasuerus *was* and of course also what Esther at this point still *is*? For thus they would indeed be a match. Or is Haman speaking here in a more general sense, in which the king and Esther are to be king and queen of Persia, in which positions their class *origins* would have become insignificant? In performance, an actor's tone or gestures might well have decided this ambiguity or perhaps further emphasized the ambiguity as such. In any case, Esther refers to Ahasuerus as אליר גינעדיגשטר קיניג "most merciful king" and says she is not worthy of the honor of marriage to him (AS4 518), commenting that he is of high birth: דאן אירי מאייסטעט זיין פֿון הוהן שטאמן. / איך אבר פֿון שלעכֿטין אונ' אונאדליכֿן זאמן "For Your Majesty is of a noble house, while I am of common and non-noble seed" (AS4 520–521), thus indicating her ignorance of his class origin or perhaps adding another ironic note. Ahasuerus also comments on what might as well be acknowledged as a *yikhes* motif as much as it is a class motif:[34]

פֿיר וואר דיא יונג פֿרויא איז מיר עבין.
דיא קרון פֿון רייך וויל איך איר געבין:
דרום ברינגט היהער דיא קיניגליכֿי קרון.
אונ' ערהיבט זיא אויף ושתי טראהן:
(AS4 522–525)

The maiden is indeed appropriate for me. I wish to give her the empire's crown. Bring, therefore, the royal crown here, and elevate her up onto Vashti's throne.

The king thus also makes explicit that Esther is taking the place of Vashti on the throne. The chancellor likewise comments on Esther and the status motif: דעם גינעדיגין קיניג וואר זיא ליב אונ' עבין. / דרום האט ער איהר דיא קראן פֿון ושתי געבין "She was beloved to and fitting for the merciful/clement king. Consequently he gave her Vashti's crown" (AS4 1607–1608).

As already problematized in the previous chapter, in contrast with the anti-monarchical tendencies of AS1 and AS2, in the plays AS3 and AS4 Mordecai and the Jews are staunch defenders of the crown, as they—problematically—already are in the (anti-monarchical) biblical text, but in the Purim plays it seems one of the focal issues of the text. In AS3 and AS4 then, the political tension is always between the clear duty to support the monarchy and the implied undermining of that power structure by the mere existence of a parallel (Jewish) culture that does not share in the power structure or the culture of the dominant society. The pro-monarchical position is broad-based, including even the formerly "outsider" Jews, Mordecai and Esther, but significantly excluding the court "insiders," Vashti, Bigthan, and Teresh, who attempt to dethrone and/or assassinate the king, although *not* in order to replace monarchical rule with another mode of governance.

Is there additionally a superimposition of *gendered* behavior here on political action? That is, does Vashti's revolutionary scheme also signify as a female rebellion against male authority in general and against the male authority in her own life (her king/husband)? And simultaneously, is Esther, a Jew who resists her ethnically based social oppression but a woman who does not resist her gender-assigned subordinate position in the patriarchal order, to be construed as a character who supports the monarchy? The play's internal dynamic and ideology must be definitive in determining the valorization of Vashti's revolution—she *must* lose in order to make way for Esther. Vashti is not here a valued character, not a model of behavior, but neither is she represented in the Purim plays as an overtly villainous or even trivial character. By means of the retention of Vashti in the dramatic tradition in AS3 and AS4 (as opposed to her exclusion from AS1 and AS2) and the expansion of her biblical role into an explicitly political one—even in these first decades of the *extant* tradition of Ahasuerus plays—the authors of the plays have radically changed not just the conventional narrative (taking into explicit account the midrashic tradition) but also the dramatic possibilities of the play. The stage directions clearly indicate that this is not folk drama or even a chamber play as in the earliest extant plays; here the language is complex, formal, non-colloquial, with an overabundance of Yiddishized Latinate and French words (as, one might note, was common in other francophile European vernacular dramatic traditions of the period). It is learned drama, and with its cultural and political sophistication, the Yiddish Purim play has already in the early eighteenth century become modern drama. In its insistence on the significance of female participation in the plot on issues of class and ethnic identity, it seems indeed to have become *very* modern drama in a pan-European sense that is not found in Christian European drama for another half century. While already a century later than Shakespeare's work, these plays, so essentially dependent on both the midrashic tradition and the contemporary non-Jewish dramatic traditions, manifest a necessarily middle ground of cultural tensions between the inside and outside, between Jewish and Christian cultures. The early Yiddish Purim play comprises in and of itself a field of cultural translation that enabled the beginnings of Jewish drama. In the next chapter its in-built in-betweenness must be further examined from yet another perspective.

Notes

1. Nosson Scherman and Meir Zlotowitz, eds., *Midrash Rabbah: The Five Megillos; Ruth/Esther*, ArtScroll Series (Brooklyn: Mesorah Publications, 2011), 12.

2. According to the midrash, the ultimate cause of Vashti's death was: מְנַּחַת לַאֲחַשְׁוֵרוֹשׁ לִיתֵּן רְשׁוּת לִבְנוֹת בֵּית הַמִּקְדָּשׁ "she did not allow Ahasuerus to permit the Temple to be built," saying to

him: מַה שֶׁהֶחֱרִיבוּ אֲבוֹתַי אַתָּה מְבַקֵּשׁ לִבְנוֹת "What my ancestors destroyed, you seek to build?" (*MER* 55). The idea is that even though Cyrus, who preceded Ahasuerus on the throne, had allowed the reconstruction of the Temple to begin, Ahasuerus halted it due to Vashti's influence (in Ezra 4, however, Gentiles request that the Persian authorities halt the construction, and it is in fact halted by royal order).

3. Bronner, "Revisited," 197.

4. One might note, however, that it can actually only be reckoned as half a frame, since once Vashti disappears from the narrative, she does not return.

5. Timothy K. Beal, "Tracing Esther's Beginnings," in *A Feminist Companion to Esther, Judith and Susanna*, ed. Athalya Brenner, The Feminist Companion to the Bible 7 (Sheffield: Sheffield Academic Press, 1995), 89, 100, 105–106.

6. Beal, "Tracing Esther's Beginnings," 88.

7. One should note that such blind spots are typical for theoretically informed interpretations by Protestant theologians of recent decades, who in this respect interestingly seem to continue the tradition of the founders of the Reformation in seeking "direct" access to the biblical text without the mediation of subsequent interpretive traditions—except their own. The same could be said for Beal's *The Book of Hiding: Gender, Ethnicity, Annihilation, and Esther* (London: Routledge, 1997), which is a brilliantly argued book with insights derived from social, cultural, and feminist theory of (primarily) the 1980s (thus, even when published, rather dated). There he makes no use of Talmud, midrash, Rashi, Ibn Ezra, or any part of the tradition of Catholic theology and none of either Jewish or Catholic extra-theological literature. It is impressive in its philological and extra-philological explication of the Hebrew-language biblical text, but the deracinated text is treated as a proto-Protestant monolith without connection to any real society except that of the late twentieth-century West, via Derrida, Cixous, Bhabha, Irigaray, Freud, Lacan, and Butler. One might take his bizarre representation (in his postscript) of the focal texts of the present chapter as emblematic: *Purimschpiels*, a word not Yiddish, not Hebrew, not German, and not even English.

8. Horowitz, *Reckless Rites*, 58.

9. Niditch, "Folklore," 39.

10. Susan Zaeske, "Unveiling Esther as a Paradigmatic Radical Rhetoric," *Philosophy and Rhetoric* 33 (2000): 204, citing Michael V. Fox, *Character and Ideology in the Book of Esther* (Columbia: University of South Carolina Press, 1991), 197–203. Interestingly, the long tradition of viewing the book of Esther as a book written in and of the Jewish exile has recently been challenged by Stern, "Esther," 24–53.

11. Bronner, "Revisited," 195.

12. Mordecai's speech of appeal to Esther to intercede with the king is based on his conception of the strength of women (AS3, 914 ff.); the play also ends with Mordecai's comment about a people saved by women: אזו ווערט איין שטאם דר ליזט דורך איין פֿרוא "thus a tribe is redeemed/saved by a woman" (AS3 1482). In AS4 (454), Mordecai nonetheless claims: דאן דיא ווייבר גאר לייכֿט פֿון זינין זיין "Indeed women quite easily become irrational."

13. In her study of Crescas Caslari's Judeo-Provençal *Esther*, Susan L. Einbinder, notes: "Crescas's depiction of King Ahashverus presents a striking portrait of mental instability exacerbated by alcoholic excess and a tendency to alternate angry (often drunken) outbursts with despondency. That text notes ominously the effects of his drinking and rage, which lead directly to at least two executions—Vashti's and Haman's"; Susan L. Einbinder, "A Proper Diet: Medicine and History in Crescas Caslari's *Esther*," *Speculum* 80 (2005): 445.

14. In AS4 this opposition is made quite explicit: in the lengthy description of the tableau before line 29 the two queens are positioned on each side of Ahasuerus; later, when Esther be-

comes queen, the text notes that she is taking Vashti's place: ערווֿיהליט ווארט אן איהרי שטאט "was chosen in her place" (AS4 36); likewise in *Midrash Rabbah*, Esther becomes queen תַּחַת וַשְׁתִּי "in place of Vashti," as a spatial, metonymic replacement (*MER* 63).

15. According to BT *Meg* 12b: the king's order for her to appear naked on the Sabbath was punishment for her having made her Jewish maidservants work naked on the Sabbath; according to Rabbi Yose bar Chanina, she had leprosy and thus did not wish to appear naked; or, alternately, a *baraisa* (extra-Mishnaic oral tradition) claims that her reason was that the angel Gabriel had caused her to grow a tail.

16. See Alice Bach, *Women, Seduction, and Betrayal in Biblical Narrative* (Cambridge: Cambridge University Press, 1997), 131; Cristelle K. Baskins, "Typology, Sexuality, and the Renaissance Esther," in *Sexuality and Gender in Early Modern Europe: Institutions, Texts, Images*, ed. James Grantham Turner (Cambridge: Cambridge University Press, 1993), 39.

17. In AS4, Ahasuerus admits that he is drunk (also noted later by Hatakh in his delivery of the king's order to the queen that she must be naked; AS4 175–194).

18. He complains that he cannot live without Vashti: וויא קאן איך נון לענגיר זונדר ושתי לעבין "How can I now go on living without Vashti?" (AS3 248, 227, 229–230); he claims that his scepter and crown are useless without Vashti (AS3 243–245); and even: דז רייך איז אינין ווינג איר מויארן איין גפֿאלן "the empire has collapsed within its walls" (AS3 244). In AS4, the king is also quite depressed about the loss of Vashti (AS4 394 ff., and the stage direction immediately preceding).

19. Interestingly, according to Rabbi Yehoshua ben Korcha (BT *Meg* 13a and 15a), Esther has a greenish complexion and seemed beautiful to the king only as a result of divine intervention.

20. In AS4, Haman delivers a lengthy speech about what lessons are to be learned from Vashti's example, including a general admonition to women to respect their husbands (AS4 376); the *loyfer* also delivers a speech about the lessons of Vashti's example for women (AS4 388–393):

אונ' דיא זאך צו פופליצירין.
דאש איין יעדי פֿרויא זיך וויש צו רעגולירין:
אירן מאנש ביפֿעהיל גיהורזאם נאך צו קומן.
זונשט ווירט איר וויא ושתי דאש לעבין ווערדין גינומין:

> And to proclaim the matter: that each and every woman know how to control herself and to comply obediently with her husband's commands. Otherwise she will lose her life, as happened to Vashti.

21. Interestingly, the *Midrash Rabbah* makes Vashti's execution for disobeying the king's command significant in terms of Jewish history of *longue durée*: as the last surviving representative of the Babylonian dynasty, Vashti's death functions to punish both her and her ancestors (*MER* 40). While it is not made explicit in the Bible that Vashti is executed, rabbinical commentary assumes that she was: e.g., BT *Meg* 11b, *Pirkei de Rabbi Eliezer* 49.

22. Barry Dov Walfish, *Esther in Medieval Garb: Jewish Interpretation of the Book of Esther in the Middle Ages* (Albany: State University of New York Press, 1993), 195–196.

23. Lagarde, *Hagiographa Chaldaice*, 237–238.

24. This is, significantly, the same justification sought (and in one case the same word used) by Haman later in his plot against Mordecai and the Jewish populace in general: he wants revenge on Jews because it was a Jew who brought about deaths of his comrades, Bigthan and Teresh:

דש דיזי צווייא קאמיראטין איר לעבין איזט ווארדין זוא שענדליך גינומין.
אונ' איזט אליש איבר דען מארט בעשטיאלישי יודין הער גיקומן:
איך וויל מיך אן אים רעוואנשירין.
זאלט איך אויך דא דורך מיין לעבין פֿרלירין:

"Because the lives of these two comrades [or: chamber-counselors] were so ignominiously taken, and because their murder was altogether due to bestial Jews, I want to take vengeance on him, even if I were to lose my life as a result" (AS4 697–702). He additionally desires vengeance for his parents: .עש איז נון צייט אום מיין עלטרין איר בלוט צו רעכֿנין "It is now time to avenge the blood of my parents" (813). He thus links the narrative's entire range of villains, great and small, together as a band: himself, Bigthan, Teresh, and Vashti.

25. Bigthan and Teresh later plot when and where to carry out the assassination: they want to do it in chambers with a hammer or axe, but are dissuaded by the presence of guards there (AS3 476).

26. The conspiratorial conversation between Bigthan and Teresh takes place in her absence and without mention of her participation (AS4 530 ff.).

27. Her lengthy complaint of injustice begins at AS4 303.

28. Hatakh also comments to Ahasuerus that since the king had been Vashti's grandfather's stable-boy, he should not dishonor her by such a humiliating command (AS4 238). Later there is another reference to her grandfather, again in comparison to Ahasuerus, both of whom often drank wine, while only Ahasuerus ever harms anyone while drinking. By implication then, class identity has directly to do with morality (AS4 307). The issue of class arises, even as it ironically intersects with the tasks of Haman's unexpected and, as he deems, inappropriately required service to Mordecai: דז איך הער המן קאווילר זאל דיך פוצין אונ' שערין "That I, *Sir* Haman, must be your valet and barber" (AS3 1202).

29. Interestingly, in AS3, Haman describes the relationship of the king and queen as: אחשווירוש טיראן פֿון זיין קינגין "Ahasuerus the tyrant of his queen" (AS3 1406). Esther then kneels before the king (AS3 1423).

30. Interestingly, Vashti suggests that her punishment by the king is actually divine punishment for her having forced Jewish girls to work on the Sabbath (which, as noted earlier, is the interpretation of BT *Meg* 12b); but in accepting her punishment willingly, she hopes, she may perhaps still earn admission to paradise (AS4 312–316).

31. In *Bovo d'Antona*, the hero's villainous mother, Brandonia, is also punished and removed from society and thus further political relevance by confinement in a nunnery.

32. Esther later again remarks: דען איך בין דעם קיניג זיין שלאבֿין "For I am a slave of the king" (AS3 1249).

33. This term, עבין "appropriate, suitable, equal," had been the conventional term employed in precisely such literary situations concerning the suitability of the partners of a potential marriage match in both Yiddish and (in its cognate form) German since the High Middle Ages, when that suitability (however defined) or lack thereof served to motivate entire epic narratives, as in the Middle High German epic *Das Nibelungenlied*, Brünhild's belated recognition that Gunther was not her equal. Similarly in the Middle Yiddish epic *Pariz and Viene*, the king vehemently rejects the marriage suit by the son of one of his vassals; see chapter 7. The term is also used by Ahasuerus about Esther (AS4 522).

34. The term יִיחוּס conveys a broad range of meanings within the Jewish community, dealing with prestigious lineage, based on the high valuation of rabbinical learning, community status, moral character, piety, and wealth.

Chapter Six

The Political Liminality of Mordecai in Early Ashkenaz

In the Esther fabula as constituted in the Bible and the post-biblical traditions, it is Mordecai who ultimately enables the Jewish survival of impending annihilation, and it is precisely his character as the consummate border dweller and intermediary between inside and outside, between the Jewish community and the surrounding non-Jewish majority culture, that is decisive and definitive. It is ultimately his mediation that actually enables the salvation of the Jews, but it additionally enables whatever partial integration into non-Jewish culture and political power they achieve, and in the end that integration and power are not insignificant. In a larger context, it is his role that enables the *narratable* exilic cultural life of the Jews. Without this opening to the outside, they would have been annihilated by Haman's genocidal villainy. Even though the rabbinical notion of the *Megillah* is one of hermetically sealed Judaism as the path to preservation, the narrative itself actually resists that message and tells quite a different tale. To step back for a moment from the biblical and Talmudic texts and their immediate historical settings in order to put them into a yet larger historical context, it is after all Mordecai's openness to the outside that becomes especially poignant in the age of the Purim play in the late seventeenth and early eighteenth century, when so-called "court Jews" were playing the quasi-Mordecai role at numerous aristocratic courts across Central Europe, for the spatial positioning of both Mordecai and Esther reflects, in addition to their narratological significance, their political, politicized ethnic and moral positioning in relation to Gentile culture. And insofar as Ashkenazic culture of the late medieval and early modern period was open to contact and exchange across the cultural borders to Christian society, Mordecai represents that impulse. In a significant sense, it was Mordecai, the eternal inhabitant of the gateway between Jewish and Gentile culture, the legendary speaker of seventy languages, who had the ear of important personages on both sides of the divide and embodied the mode of cultural translation that is the focus of the present study, especially as his character appears and is developed in early modern Purim plays.

The narrative of the biblical book of Esther is in many ways essentially liminal, and that is precisely how it must be seen to function not merely in the troubled Christian tradition but also in the far less problematic post-biblical Jewish tradition. One of the earliest comprehensive and, in the long-term, effective theorizations of the cultural function of liminality grew out of Victor Turner's rethinking his own anthropological field work in West Africa and emplotting it according to a conceptual suggestion made by Arnold van Gennep concerning social rites of passage, such as coming of age, marriage, or social promotion, which logically consist of three states—the initiand's states and affiliations both preceding and following the ritual, but also including that in-between state in which the initiand belongs to neither of those "permanent" social groups, but rather is temporarily excluded from all "normal" social affiliations.[1] The passage of the initiand from the initial position in the social structure to the final position is enabled by means of the intermediate isolation from both of those positions located on the margin or threshold of them both. Here the initiand is functionally part of no structure at all. Such liminal persons—the boy about to become a man, the betrothed bride-to-be, the dead but still unburied—escape the classificatory systems that position them in cultural space defined by law, custom, and convention. In the course of several decades of further anthropological work, Turner developed this notion of liminality into an effective, if ultimately limited, tool of social analysis.[2] Even early in his work, Turner posits the possibility that the initiand, the liminar, may not necessarily be in transition to another and better state of existence, for he notes the relevance of non-transitionally marginalized outsiders: "Members of despised or outlawed ethnic and cultural groups [who] play major roles in myths and popular tales as representatives or expressions of universal values."[3] If liminality can be construed as not necessarily temporary, then its social implications are immediately far more significant, for in suggesting that marginalized *groups* can also definitionally and productively be classified as liminars, it opens the possibility for a conception of that group as a politically active social formation capable of specific social action.

Turner's work seems particularly relevant in coming to terms with the social function of the Jewish festival of Purim, which, as Jean Baumgarten perceptively observes, both is positioned liminally in the Jewish calendar and functions liminally in a cultural sense:

Purim took place on the fourteenth and fifteenth days of the month of Adar (February–March), which marks the passage between two seasons, *tkufas teyvet* (winter) and *tkufas nison* (spring). The holiday occurs quite precisely between the end of the one season and the beginning of the other. It is in this interstitial space that the moment of the Jewish carnival occurs, a time of collective rejoicing and festive celebrations in honor of this symbolic death and resurrection. It is a time of transition in which there is expressed a yearning for reversal and destruction, as well as a performative fury, which in the *Purim-shpil*, in addition to music and dance, takes the form of laughter and parody.[4]

The narrative situation of the originary text of the festival of Purim, that is, the biblical book of Esther, is likewise by definition liminal in its essentially exilic character. As Elsie Stern in quite another context expresses it: the book of "Esther responds to the ongoing, existential realities of the diasporic experience: political and theological insecurity, the demands of dual loyalties, the challenge of creating a meaningful Jewish life outside the land of Israel."[5] To define what may already be rather obvious: a diasporic people under the political rule of an alien culture necessarily negotiates practically all conditions and practices of life on a daily basis: policing community behavior, cultic practices, traditional foodways, clothing, courtship and marriage, language, literary practice, and so on. The diasporic individual and diasporic community are always in the middle between a now distant "home" culture that provides legitimation for continued "insider" cultural practice and the insistently present alien culture that generally threatens multiple aspects of the continuing integrity of the community's identity. To be in exile is by definition to be liminal. Moreover, according to *Midrash Esther Rabbah*, Rabbi Pinchas and Rabbi Chama bar Gurion taught that Esther was a foundling, since her father died before her birth and her mother immediately thereafter (*MER* 61), which marks her as liminal even from the beginning of her life.

The liminal obviously signifies spatially, and however else one might wish to construe the Esther story, it is first and foremost a discourse of semiotic spatial constructs that depends very directly on what is inside (the court), what is outside, and what is on the liminal border between them, in what amounts to a limbo-like field of action and negotiated transfers and crossings of borders and designated spaces, some constituting smaller restricted spaces (e.g., Esther's banquet) within larger restricted spaces (the royal precinct).[6] While this spatial construct is already implicit in the biblical text of Esther, which establishes the festival of Purim—the only Jewish liturgical holiday originating in the diaspora, where it must by definition be liminal—evidence for the significance of space is particularly prevalent in the densely woven textual web of the post-biblical traditions.[7] In this broad range of texts the character of Mordecai becomes the border inhabitant par excellence, and the spatial and conceptual liminality becomes determinative of the Esther fabula's potential for meaning.

Moreover, as a Jew, Esther is an ethno-cultural outsider who marries into the Persian royal house. She must later pointedly decide to cross the line to reveal her own ethnic identity to the king, overtly by illegitimately entering the throne room to draw the king's attention forcibly, in order to save the Jews. Mordecai, on the other hand, while also a Jewish outsider, is, from his ubiquitously acknowledged position at the palace gate, capable of discovering the plot against the king, specifically because he inhabits that inter-cultural space created explicitly by his knowledge; as already noted, he knew seventy languages and thus understood the overheard conversation of the conspirators against the king.[8]

The villainous character, Haman, also crosses boundaries, for he, too, is a foreigner, an Amalekite,[9] who also crosses in and out of the king's court and presence, but does so without the barriers experienced by Esther (who, as both Jew and woman, is doubly marginalized and admissible only under even more circumscribed conditions than is Haman) and Mordecai, who is necessarily outside, excluded from the court, at the door *and* necessarily on the outside of that gate (at least it is so in the Bible, although not in all of the Purim plays, where he is sometimes a courtier of the king). Mordecai's spatial positioning is also explicitly conceived metaphorically by *Midrash Esther Rabbah*: he is the one who stood בַּפֶּרֶץ "in the breach" (*MER* 59), that is, functioned as the intercessor, and is thus likened to Moses, since both were humble and stood in the breach for and taught Torah to their people.

After her integration into the court as queen, Esther changes the constellation of space-power by setting up the banquet with the king and his vizier in her quarters, thus undermining the *Staatsaktion* and male power configuration of the opening sequence of the biblical book of Esther, where the king has his lengthy banquet in the restricted "public" (i.e., male) space of the royal court, while Vashti has a corresponding, parallel banquet in her "private" women's quarters for the ladies of the court. While private, Esther's later banquet is nonetheless also clearly political, and it is a political space that is in some ways under her own control, also because she has a secret—a state secret—that will change the course of national politics and rearrange the constellation of power and authority in the kingdom, such that Haman is *out*, Mordecai *in*, and Esther's authority in the palace all but absolute.

One might indeed conceive of the Esther fabula in general as a semiotic spatial construct, one that is already implicit in the biblical text, for it seems defined by gates and doors, borders and boundaries. As an outsider who marries into the Persian royal house, Esther is taken from her excluded (Jewish) community into the very heart of Persian elite culture, from the unspecified site of marginalized Jewish residence into the imperial palace complex. Initially, however, she is admitted only into the interstitial, engendered liminal territory of the royal harem (בֵּית הַנָּשִׁים literally 'house of women,' Est 2:9)—that domestic zone of the household's women who are forbidden to other men—where she and the other wives-for-a-night of the Persian emperor are oiled and scented for a year (שִׁשָּׁה חֳדָשִׁים, בְּשֶׁמֶן הַמֹּר, וְשִׁשָּׁה חֳדָשִׁים בַּבְּשָׂמִים, וּבְתַמְרוּקֵי הַנָּשִׁים 'six months with oil of myrrh, and six months with with feminine spices and ointments'; Est 2:12), before they are individually admitted to the royal presence for a single night before being shunted back into the limbo of the harem.[10] She must later decide to recross that boundary between her quasi-insider but still gender-defined, liminally outsider space and the prohibited insider space of the ruling (male) elite, entering the throne room to gain the king's attention, in order to reveal her own essential, ethnic identity in hopes of saving her people from extermination (Est 4:11–16). Effectively this movement also entails not simply the crossing of a gender-defined boundary but also an ethnically defined one, for while the harem may have conventionally also been non-Jewish territory, Esther's presence there even as a crypto-Jew has changed that status (at least for the informed reader, and eventually for the king, his vizier, and the court, when they are informed of Esther's ethnicity). But without question the male space of the palace is seemingly a strictly Persian and not a Jewish space, although the presence of the Amalekite Haman in this rabidly ethno-sensitive narrative complicates the issue. It is in fact precisely Esther's transgressive crossing of that boundary that undoes its ethnically defined status, for in outing herself as a Jew, Esther de facto renders the harem not a Jewish space per se of course, but at least a space in which a Jew is permitted, and as it turns out in the remainder of the narrative, that same transformation takes place in the imperial court itself, where after her public identification of her ethnicity, she becomes not the emperor's "queen-for-a-night," but queen indeed, soon to be accompanied by her uncle Mordecai as vizier.[11] In order to accomplish all this, however, she must after all first cross that designated boundary *unsummoned*, that is, as an act of personal will and in defiance of custom if not law, for which she requires the overt and insistent prompting of Mordecai (Est 4:8), who—better than anyone else in the narrative (with the possible exception of Haman)—understands borders and liminalities and their importance, and especially why the political transgression of them—under prescribed conditions—is also important and sometimes vitally necessary.

The function of Mordecai as a creature of the border requires some unpacking, which itself requires some philological spadework and thus necessarily also the reader's patience. As the texts tirelessly emphasize, Mordecai is a creature of the פֶּתַח in the Hebrew text, the תְּרַע in the Aramaic *Targum*, the טאָר in the Purim plays, that is, the "gate": Aramaic תרע בית מלכא "gate of the palace [=king's house]" or תרע דמלכא "gate of the king," which translates the Hebrew פֶּתַח הַבַּיִת "gate of the [king's] house." This usage was influenced by the Hebrew idiom שַׁעַר הַמֶּלֶךְ "gate of the king," as found in Est 2:19, 2:21, 4:2, 4:6, and 6:12.[12] Mordecai inhabits this interstitial space not accidentally but essentially, as a key characteristic of his nature: he is so frequently, recurrently, almost constantly referred to as the "one who sits at the king's gate"—in the biblical book of Esther, the *Targumim*, *and* the early Purim plays—that the almost tedious repetition of that information practically becomes a surname.[13]

As has long been a commonplace of biblical study, the use of gates in the Hebrew Bible is itself overdetermined in its community function and cultural significance. Koehler and Baumgarter's lexicon details the range of connotations, including the seventh entry for "שַׁעַר הַמֶּלֶךְ in Susa: a) gate of the palace, Est 4, 2.6; b) rooms/premises directly proximate to the gate, Est 2:19–21; 3:2–3; 5:9–13; 6:10 . . . 'the entire body of officials, civil servants, and residents of the palace, as well as the building; also the seat of government (although excluding the personal sphere of the ruler)."[14] The city gate and/or king's gate is thus, in biblical narrative, one of the focal points of significant action, as a few examples might illustrate: upon approaching Sodom, the angels find Lot sitting at the city gate (Gen 19:1). Samson's "recovery of his strength is symbolized by the tearing up of the city gates," as pointed out by Mieke Bal, for instance, who also notes that in the case of Boaz and Ruth there is a "trial at the gate," which is in general the community site of common juridical proceedings in the Bible.[15] Another customary conception of the community function of the gate appears in *Yalkut Shimoni* (*Esther* § 1053), where Esther arranges for Mordecai to be stationed at the gate in order to give wise advice as needed (more or less as Daniel was at the gate of Nebuchadnezzar in his day: וְדָנִיֵּאל בִּתְרַע מַלְכָּא "and Daniel was in the gate of the king" [Dan 2:49]).

The surprising density and contours of this usage in the biblical text of Esther may be illustrated by a few further examples:

וּבְהִקָּבֵץ בְּתוּלוֹת שֵׁנִית וּמָרְדֳּכַי יֹשֵׁב בְּשַׁעַר־הַמֶּלֶךְ:
(Est 2:19)

When the virgins were gathered together the second time, Mordecai was sitting at the king's gate.

2TargEst:[16] when virgins gathered a second time, ומרדכי יתיב בתרע בית מלכא "and Mordecai sat at the gate of the king's house" (repeated again a few lines later).[17]

בַּיָּמִים הָהֵם וּמָרְדֳּכַי יֹשֵׁב בְּשַׁעַר־הַמֶּלֶךְ קָצַף בִּגְתָן וָתֶרֶשׁ שְׁנֵי־סָרִיסֵי הַמֶּלֶךְ מִשֹּׁמְרֵי הַסַּף לִשְׁלֹחַ
וַיְבַקְשׁוּ יָד בַּמֶּלֶךְ אֲחַשְׁוֵרֹשׁ:
(Est 2:21)

And in those days, as Mordecai was sitting at the king's gate, Bigthan and Teresh, two of the king's eunuchs, who guarded the threshold, became angry and sought to lay hands on King Ahasuerus.

וְכָל־עַבְדֵי הַמֶּלֶךְ אֲשֶׁר־בְּשַׁעַר הַמֶּלֶךְ כֹּרְעִים וּמִשְׁתַּחֲוִים לְהָמָן כִּי־כֵן צִוָּה־לוֹ הַמֶּלֶךְ וּמָרְדֳּכַי לֹא יִכְרַע
וְלֹא יִשְׁתַּחֲוֶה: וַיֹּאמְרוּ עַבְדֵי הַמֶּלֶךְ אֲשֶׁר־בְּשַׁעַר הַמֶּלֶךְ לְמָרְדֳּכָי מַדּוּעַ אַתָּה עוֹבֵר אֵת מִצְוַת הַמֶּלֶךְ:
(Est 3:2–3)

> And all the king's servants who were at the king's gate bowed down and did obeisance to Haman; for the king had so commanded concerning him. But Mordecai did not bow down or do obeisance.[18] Then the king's servants who were at the king's gate said to Mordecai, "Why do you transgress the king's command?"

2TargEst: when all others די בתרע בית מלכא "who were at the gate of the king's house" bowed to Haman, Mordecai did not.[19]

> וּמָרְדֳּכַי יָדַע אֶת־כָּל־אֲשֶׁר נַעֲשָׂה וַיִּקְרַע מָרְדֳּכַי אֶת־בְּגָדָיו וַיִּלְבַּשׁ שַׂק וָאֵפֶר וַיֵּצֵא בְּתוֹךְ הָעִיר:
> וַיִּזְעַק זְעָקָה גְדֹלָה וּמָרָה וַיָּבוֹא עַד לִפְנֵי שַׁעַר־הַמֶּלֶךְ כִּי אֵין לָבוֹא אֶל־שַׁעַר הַמֶּלֶךְ בִּלְבוּשׁ שָׂק:
> (Est 4:1–2)

> When Mordecai learned all that had been done, Mordecai rent his clothes and put on sackcloth and ashes, and went out into the midst of the city, wailing with a loud and bitter cry; he went up to the entrance of the king's gate, for no one might enter the king's gate clothed with sackcloth.

2TargEst: Mordecai came as far as the palace of the king, for no one was permitted to enter the gate of the palace of the king, ואתא לקדם פלטרין דמלכא "and he went up in front of the gate of the king" (when) dressed in sackcloth.[20]

> וַיֵּצֵא הֲתָךְ אֶל־מָרְדֳּכָי אֶל־רְחוֹב הָעִיר אֲשֶׁר לִפְנֵי שַׁעַר־הַמֶּלֶךְ:
> (Est 4:6)

> Hathach went out to Mordecai in the open square of the city in front of the king's gate.

2TargEst: Hatakh goes to find Mordecai to find out what is the matter, he "went toward Mordecai to the main square of the city, which was in front of תרע בית מלכא 'the gate of the king's palace.'"[21]

> וַיְהִי בַּיּוֹם הַשְּׁלִישִׁי וַתִּלְבַּשׁ אֶסְתֵּר מַלְכוּת וַתַּעֲמֹד בַּחֲצַר בֵּית-הַמֶּלֶךְ הַפְּנִימִית נֹכַח בֵּית הַמֶּלֶךְ
> וְהַמֶּלֶךְ יוֹשֵׁב עַל-כִּסֵּא מַלְכוּתוֹ בְּבֵית הַמַּלְכוּת נֹכַח פֶּתַח הַבָּיִת; וַיְהִי כִרְאוֹת הַמֶּלֶךְ אֶת-אֶסְתֵּר
> הַמַּלְכָּה עֹמֶדֶת בֶּחָצֵר נָשְׂאָה חֵן בְּעֵינָיו וַיּוֹשֶׁט הַמֶּלֶךְ לְאֶסְתֵּר אֶת-שַׁרְבִיט הַזָּהָב אֲשֶׁר בְּיָדוֹ,
> וַתִּקְרַב אֶסְתֵּר וַתִּגַּע בְּרֹאשׁ הַשַּׁרְבִיט.
> (Est 5:1–2)

> On the third day Esther put on her royal robes and stood in the inner court of the king's palace, opposite the king's hall. The king was sitting on his royal throne inside the palace opposite the entrance to the palace; and when the king saw Queen Esther standing in the court, she found favor in his sight and he held out to Esther the golden scepter that was in his hand. Then Esther approached and touched the top of the scepter.

2TargEst: Esther prays in the inner court of the palace and is overheard by the king who is "staring toward תרע ביתא 'the gate of the house'"; when Esther goes to the king to ask for mercy, she first is seen when she then stood בתרע בית מלכא "at the gate of the royal palace" opposite the palace (itself), as the king was seated on his royal throne in his palace בתרע בית מלכא "at [facing] the royal gate." The king saw Queen Esther standing דרתא "in the courtyard."[22]

וַיֵּצֵא הָמָן בַּיּוֹם הַהוּא שָׂמֵחַ וְטוֹב לֵב וְכִרְאוֹת הָמָן אֶת־מָרְדֳּכַי בְּשַׁעַר הַמֶּלֶךְ
(Est 5:9)

And Haman went out that day joyful and glad of heart. But when Haman saw Mordecai in the king's gate . . .

2TargEst: Haman ויצא ונפק המן מלוות מלכא "leaves the presence of the king"; later when Haman wishes to have Mordecai bow to him, מרדכי יתיב בתרע בית מלכא "Mordecai is sitting at the king's gate," studying Torah and refuses to bow.[23]

וְכָל־זֶה אֵינֶנּוּ שֹׁוֶה לִי בְּכָל־עֵת אֲשֶׁר אֲנִי רֹאֶה אֶת־מָרְדֳּכַי הַיְּהוּדִי יוֹשֵׁב בְּשַׁעַר הַמֶּלֶךְ׃
(Est 5:13)

Yet all this does me no good, so long as I see Mordecai the Jew sitting at the king's gate.

2TargEst: מרדכי יהודאי דיתיב בתרע דמלכא "Mordecai the Jew who was sitting at gate of the king."[24]

וַיֹּאמֶר הַמֶּלֶךְ מִי בֶחָצֵר וְהָמָן בָּא לַחֲצַר בֵּית-הַמֶּלֶךְ הַחִיצוֹנָה לֵאמֹר לַמֶּלֶךְ לִתְלוֹת אֶת-מָרְדֳּכַי עַל-הָעֵץ אֲשֶׁר-הֵכִין לוֹ
(Est 6:4)

And the king said: "Who is in the court?"—Now Haman had just entered the outer court of the king's palace, to speak to the king about having Mordecai hanged on the gallows that he had prepared for him.

2TargEst: Haman is standing לדרת בית מלכא "in the courtyard of the king."[25]

וַיֹּאמֶר הַמֶּלֶךְ לְהָמָן מַהֵר קַח אֶת־הַלְּבוּשׁ וְאֶת־הַסּוּס כַּאֲשֶׁר דִּבַּרְתָּ וַעֲשֵׂה־כֵן לְמָרְדֳּכַי הַיְּהוּדִי הַיּוֹשֵׁב בְּשַׁעַר הַמֶּלֶךְ אַל־תַּפֵּל דָּבָר מִכֹּל אֲשֶׁר דִּבַּרְתָּ׃
(Est 6:10)

Then the king said to Haman, "Make haste, take the robes and the horse, as you have said, and do so to Mordecai the Jew who sits at the king's gate."

2TargEst: The king specifies to Haman which Mordecai is to be honored: דיתיב על תרעא דילי "to the Jew Mordecai who sits at my gate," repeated then verbatim in reply to Haman's claim that there are many in the world who are named Mordecai. Haman then continues his pose of ignorance: "The gates of the king are many, and I do not know of which gate [תרע] you have spoken to me"; the king replies: תרעא דעלין מבית נשיא ועד בית מלכא "Did I not tell you only the gate from which one passes from the harem to the palace?"[26]

וַיָּשָׁב מָרְדֳּכַי אֶל־שַׁעַר הַמֶּלֶךְ וְהָמָן נִדְחַף אֶל־בֵּיתוֹ אָבֵל וַחֲפוּי רֹאשׁ׃
(Est 6:12)

Then Mordecai returned to the king's gate. But Haman hurried to his house, mourning and with his head covered.

2 TargEst: after Mordecai's ride of honor, he returns to his place בתרע פלטירין דמלכא "at the palace gate."[27]

As is thus obvious, while the figure of Mordecai is already liminally defined in the book of Esther itself, that status becomes further enhanced in the *Targum Sheni*, where he becomes the veritable denizen of the gate. As will become clear, however, it is in the early Yiddish Purim plays that the figure of Mordecai finally becomes the essential creature of the border, where it is that spatial and conceptual liminality that becomes determinative of the text's potential for meaning. Beyond the mere naming of Mordecai as "the one at the king's gate" in the various seventeenth-century Ahasuerus plays, his liminality, interstitiality, in-betweenness becomes definitive of the entire performance, identifying a necessary quality of his character and of the story and its cultural significance in historical Judaism.[28] There is after all very little action per se in the Purim plays; indeed "action" seems to consist primarily in the recurring dramatic establishment of positional and spatial relationships, that is, a going in and out, crossing lines back and forth, identifying and re-identifying Mordecai as "at the gate," naming who is inside, who is outside, who is allowed to go in and out, and so on. As Harold Fisch remarks about the Esther tale, "We are once again in the realm of semiotics" (68–70). Indeed, as I have earlier suggested, it is the spatial aspect of that "realm of semiotics" that constitutes the very story itself.

The textual evidence from the earliest Ahasuerus plays of Mordecai "at the gate" is abundant, indeed practically ubiquitous. Haman so identifies him: אונד אויך דער מרדכי דער דא זיצט אין טאר "and also Mordecai, who there sits in/at the gate" (AS1 435). In one of Haman's anti-Jewish diatribes, he indicates that among the wicked Jews is צו פֿאר אויז דען שעלמישן יודן מרדכי. דער דא זיצט אונטר דעם טאר "above all that mischievous Jew Mordecai, who sits there beneath the gate" (AS2 380); and again: אלש דען בין איך קומן אונטר אייאר טאר. / דא זיצט דער שעלמישר יוד מרדכי מיט לאנגי האר "Then when I was passing beneath your gate, there sits the mischievous Jew Mordecai with his long hair" (AS2 384–385); and yet again: אונ' (מרדכֿי) דער דא זאס אם טוהר "and (Mordecai) who sat at the gate there" (AS4 47). In a rage at another moment, Haman comments on Mordecai at the door: זוא לאנג איך זעה זיצן מרדכֿי פֿור דער טיר: " as long as I see Mordecai sitting before the door" (AS4 1560). In the *Akta*, a remark by Haman even suggests that Mordecai's position at the gate is permanent, even definitive, and is the sole blemish on Haman's own power and position; Haman comments to his wife, Zeresh: דז איך דען יודן מרדכי אויז דען קיניגליכן האף ניכט קאן פר טרייבן. / דען ער זיצט אין דז קיניגליכי טאר. "... that I cannot drive the Jew, Mordecai, from the royal court, for he sits in the royal gate" (*Akta* 2212–2213).

This association is made apparent even in the stage directions: אומד מרדכי על הפתח ועונה "Mordecai stands by the door and replies" (*ante* AS1 155); וחוזר ואומר להתוך בתוך הפתח "And again he says to Hesekh, within the gate" (*post* AS1 155); ובא לפתח ואומ' "And goes to the door and says" (*ante* AS1 168); גיט מרדכֿי אן דיא פֿפֿארט אונ' זעצט זיך אנידר "Mordecai goes to the gate and sits down" (*ante* AS4 765).

Similarly, Esther identifies Mordecai not just by means of his familial relationship to her, but repeatedly through his spatial positioning vis-à-vis the court: she instructs Hatakh, for instance: גיא צו מיין פֿעטר מרדכֿי אין טאר אריין. / אונ' פֿראג אים ווארום דז ער טוט וויינן אונ' שרייאן אונ' ברומן "Go into the gate to my uncle Mordecai and ask him why he is weeping, shouting, and yowling" (AS2 557); and similarly a few lines later: גיא צו מיין פֿעטר מרדכי אין טאר אניין "Go into the gate to my uncle Mordecai" (AS2 581).

Later when the king is reminded of Mordecai's having saved him from the assassination conspiracy, it seems that even in the royal chronicle read aloud to the king, Mordecai is identified as the one who sits at the gate: אלש דען דער יוד מרדכי דער זיצט אונטר איירן טאר . . . "When thus the Jew Mordecai who sits beneath your gate . . ." (AS2 717). Indeed it seems that the king is well aware of Mordecai's identifying epithet, for when he instructs Haman to honor Mordecai, he specifies that the Mordecai in question is the Mordecai "at the gate": דען מרדכי דער דא זיצט אונטיר מיין טאר. / זאלשטו עהרין גאנץ אונ' גאר: "You are to show the greatest honor to that Mordecai who sits there beneath my gate" (AS1 979–980); דען יודן מרדכי דר דא זיצט אונטר מיינם טאר "The Jew, Mordecai, who sits there beneath my gate" (AS2 750); המן דיזן מרדכי דער דיא אפֿיציע האט אונטר מיינם טאר "Haman, that Mordecai whose office is beneath my gate" (*Akta* 2311).

Interestingly, gates and doors function more generally in a semiotic system of favor and power in the Purim plays, such that being "led to the door," for instance, connotes banishment, exclusion, ejection, even discharge from service. Thus in Haman's anti-Semitic tirade, the claim that in the month of Iyyar the Jews free their servants is expressed in the earliest extant play as: פירן זיא איר קנעכט אונ מיידן צו דער טיר "They lead their manservants and maidservants to the door" (AS1 461); and in Haman's derogatory listing of Jewish customs in the third play: אונט אוך אין דר מאנהייט פֿון מאיו[ס] טונין זיא דיא מיידן אונ' קנעכֿטין צו דער טיר גינעהן. "And also in the month of May, they bring their maidservants and manservants to the door" (AS3 736). This metaphor for discharge from service is similarly employed when Haman comments on his attempt to escape after having been condemned by Ahasuerus and Esther: המן בורח ואומר / . . . / מוז א[יך] לויפן צו דער טיר "Haman flees and says: ' . . . I must run to the door' " (AS1 *ante* 1095–1096); אונ' ווען עש גיט אום מיר. / אלז דען וויל איך לויפֿן צו דער טיר "And when my life is on the line, right then I'll run for the door" (AS2 796–797). Likewise, when the time comes for Haman's execution, the *shrayber* (who seems in charge of the operation) expresses it thus: איך וויל דיך פירן צו דער טיר "I'll lead you to the door" (AS1 1395).

The spatial indicators concerning Mordecai are not surprisingly more complex still. Even when there is no explicit mention of the gate, for instance, Mordecai is still identified as one who "hangs around" the courtyard, as Bigthan remarks: איך זיך דעם טרונצין יוד אלי צייט אין דען הויף ארום גין "I see the impudent Jew always walking around in the courtyard" (AS3 493).[29] The directions of "in" and "out" as the means to approach Mordecai are everywhere apparent. Esther, for instance, orders: התוך דוא גטרייאר דינר מיין. / גיא צו מיין פעטיר מרדכי הריין "Hatakh, my loyal servant, go inside to my uncle Mordecai" (AS1 838–839; repeated 864–865 and 877–878). In an altogether different context, however, Mordecai again positions himself liminally: דרום וויל איך ניט לאנג דרויזן שטאן. / אונ' וויל ליבר אויף קבר אבות̃ אניין גאן "Thus I do not want to stand outside for a long time and would prefer to go inside the ancestral tomb" (AS2 600–601), followed by the stage direction קומט מרדכי אניין "Mordecai comes inside" (AS2 *ante* 602). Likewise he conceives of his position as metaphorically liminal, in that having sat at the gate in ashes for a long time, he needs cleaning up before he can be honored: אויך בין איך צוועלף און צוואנציג וואכין אין דיא עשין גזעשין "I have also been sitting for twelve and twenty weeks in the ashes" (AS1 997). In another context, extending the metaphor even further, he conceives of a crudely expressed sexual position as somehow quasi-liminal: דז זיא מיך זאל לאזן ליגן אין דער מיטן "So that she let me lie in the [=her] middle" (AS2 605). After a long night of wandering the streets distraught over the fate of his people, Mordecai comes before the court, when, across that political and semiotic divide, פון אינין ווינג ווערט גירופין / ווער דא "from inside there is a call: 'Who's there?'" (AS3 *ante* 1091).

The door/gate thus functions definitively to divide the royal court from the rest of the world and to distinguish the insider status of those close to the throne and thus having influence on the king from that of those who are excluded from that positionally defined status. The proximity to and crossing of the boundary between the king and the people is a mark of distinction, as is clear in Haman's insistence that it is an insult to him to have to assist Mordecai in making himself presentable at court: אזו לנג גיא איך בייא דען קינג אויש אונט איין "for such a long time have I been going in and out of the king's presence" (AS1 1007), employing a figure of speech also common in German usage of the period in identifying a person's habitual and familiar practice. Haman thus claims also to have "gone in and out" at other aristocratic courts: מיט גראבֿן אונ' פֿערשטן בין איך אימר גאנגן בייא טאבֿל אויז אונ' איין "At the courts of dukes and princes I have always gone in and out at table [=dined with them]" (AS2 988). Indeed Haman expresses his power at court by means of the metaphor that all doors open to him: קיין טירן זענין פֿאר מיר גישלאסין אין דען גנצין האף "No doors are closed to me in the entire court" (AS3 1084). Simply to be in the presence of the king not surprisingly seems itself to convey some level of power, and thus Haman begs to be admitted to the king after his condemnation: פר דען אידלן קינג וואלשטו מיך לאזין טרעטין "Would that you would allow me to approach [= step before] the noble king" (AS1 1107; similarly also 1111); Ahasuerus responds likewise with a spatial expression akin to that introduced above as a metaphor of dismissal: המן גיא וועק פון מיר. / אבר איך שט[וש די]ך צו דער טיר "Haman, go away from me, or [lit. but] I will knock you to the door" (AS1 1117–1118). Esther later responds in identical manner to Haman's request (AS1 1141–1142), and in the second play, the metaphor repeats; Ahasuerus rejects Haman's further pleas for mercy, threatening similarly: המן גיא וועק פֿון מיר. / אודר איך גיב דיר איין שטוס דז דוא פֿאלזט ביז צו דער טיר "Haman go away from me, or I will give you a knock so that you fall all the way to the door" (AS2 891–892; cf. also AS2 978–979).

With respect to Mordecai's essential cultural liminality as it signifies politically, one of the most significant scenes in the Purim plays is the depiction of his discovery of the assassination plot against Ahasuerus, in which quasi-midrashic improvisation illustrates the basic principle of Mordecai's essential liminality. The biblical text remarks: בַּיָּמִים הָהֵם וּמָרְדֳּכַי יֹשֵׁב בְּשַׁעַר־הַמֶּלֶךְ "In those days, as Mordecai was sitting at the king's gate." While in that position, it is he who discovers the plot of Bigthan and Teresh—who are themselves there indeed identified as מִשֹּׁמְרֵי הַסַּף "guardians of the threshold"—against the Persian monarch, Ahasuerus (Est 2:21–23).[30] While the biblical text says no more about the circumstances or the specifics of the discovery, as it rushes headlong to have the traitors executed, the *First Targum* provides more information: Mordecai is said to be sitting "among the Sanhedrin, which Esther set up for him at the queen's gate" (בתרע מלכתא), and it is specifically there and while so engaged that he hears the plot against the king's life.[31] This Sanhedrin theme introduces the key issues of justice and judgment, as is common in the Bible, where, as noted earlier, the city gate is the site of community business dealings, including the rendering of justice by village elders, judges, or priests. In AS4 for instance, Mordecai is predictably at the gate, where he is said by Haman to יודיצירן—punning on "judge/do justice" and "be Jewish": מרדכֿי דען זיא גיזעטץ האבין אן איהר טאהר צו יודיצירן "Mordecai, whom they have placed at their gate to render justice / be Jewish" (1026).[32] The association of the gate with performing the duties of a judge is acknowledged by Ahasuerus in a comment to Mordecai in AS1:

מלך: . . . דוא זאלשט זיצן הינטר מיין פפורטין אונ' טיר.
און זאלשט זוא וואל ריכטן ארם אז רייך.
אלי גלייך.
איך זאלשטו אויש שפרעכין איסור והתר. . . .
(AS1 247–250)[33]

King: "You are to sit outside my gates and doors and judge both poor and rich, all alike. You are also to pronounce prohibitions and permissions."

Concerning the scene where Mordecai uncovers the conspiracy against the king, the Talmud notes that Rabbi Yochanan is cited as identifying the conspirators as טרסיים "Tarsians"—that is, from Tarsus, the ancient trade center near the Mediterranean on the southern coast of Asia Minor, indeed the seat of a satrapy of the Persian Empire—and their language as לשון טורסי "Tarsian," and therewith the Talmud has done with the episode (BT *Meg* 13b). In AS4, however, this moment seems merely the pretext for a further characterization of Mordecai's liminality not just in the ancient and distant setting of Persia, but in the eighteenth-century Central European present of the Purim play as well, where, in plotting to kill Ahasuerus, Bigthan and Teresh couch their overtly seditious phrases in *Latin*: מיטאמוס מאנוס אין רעגם = *mittamus manus in regem*, "let us lay hands on the king" (AS4 536) and פֿענענא אקצידאמוס רעגעם = *veneno occidamus regem*, "let us kill the king with poison" (AS4 542). Despite the fact that the language is obviously Latin, however, it here is still identified, as in the Talmud, as טארסיאר שפראך "Tarsian language" (AS4 551). In the *Akta*, the language spoken by the conspirators is designated לעק דיין נארש [*lek-dayn-narsh*] "lick-your-rass" (*Akta* 778), a comical and quasi-punning contortion of what one would expect in conventional Yiddish of the period as the designation of Latin—לאטייניש [*lataynish*], much of the humor of which would have derived from the audience's recognizing that the language spoken by the conspirators was in fact Latin and not, for instance, Tarsian, whatever they might otherwise have imagined that to be. In AS4 Mordecai is said to understand the language, since he understands the speech of all lands (AS4 573–574), possessing that ultimate linguistic liminality and inhabiting the linguistic space on the edge of all cultures (as noted earlier in the Talmud's attributing to him a knowledge of seventy languages, BT *Meg* 13b), without culturally "belonging" to any of them. He is thus depicted as the ultimate cosmopolitan, an identification that has historically been an expression of bigotry against Jews and frequently twisted into a motivation for nationalistic or ethno-centrically based persecution.[34] Later in the same play (AS4 1615–1616), it is said that Mordecai understands all languages because he is an elder from Jerusalem.

In any case, however, in the Purim play the conspirators are obviously open to identification as Christians (Catholics ?) since Latin-speaking,[35] and thus here it is indeed eighteenth-century European Christians and not eighteenth-century European Jews who are overtly anti-monarchical, seditious assassins, plotting the overthrow of Christian monarchs, while it is precisely Mordecai's essential liminality—ensconced at the gate and understanding all languages—that enables the salvation of the king (across the linguistic, religious, and cultural divide, inside the palace) from assassination, and ultimately then also the salvation of the marginalized Jewish populace from genocide.

Beyond the liminal portal between the imperial court and the sphere of the commoners, as has thus far been discussed, there is a still more powerful such "portal" that is introduced in the texts and comes in for a great deal of linguistic and semiotic play: the gallows, which functions quite literally as the constructed mechanism by means of which a condemned prisoner crosses from the present life to the hereafter, one of the most significant thresholds in Victor Turner's theorization of the liminal. Appropriately, it physically positions the condemned between heaven and earth. In both the biblical text and the Purim plays, the identity of the condemned seems to be fluid or at least negotiable, since Haman's intention that Mordecai hang on the gallows specifically constructed for him is undone in the king's ultimate order to hang Haman himself there (cf. Haman's speech on the topic: AS1 1188–1326).[36] This is thus one border that Mordecai does not cross in the plays, for here he is strategically replaced by Haman.

As briefly noted earlier in the chapter when the issue of liminality was introduced, while Mordecai is a quintessentially liminal character, other characters fully participate in the texts' insistence on a general semiotics of spatial positioning. Indeed, the plays seem absolutely obsessed by multiply imbricated grids of spatial positioning. Thus Haman, too, is necessarily a creature of the interstices and a constant crosser of boundaries; as already noted, he, like Mordecai and Esther, is also non-Persian. He, too, crosses in and out of the king's presence, as he explicitly says of himself as a mark of distinction, but he does so generally without the barriers experienced by Esther, who is admissible only under certain, gender-dependent conditions.[37] As Mordecai's essential rival, it makes sense then that Haman, too, is a creature of the gate/door, as was just noted with respect to Haman's assuming the position on the liminal gallows intended for Mordecai. There are thus recurring commands issued in the plays concerning Haman's positioning, such as "let him in" and "send him out/away."[38] When he comes to the court early in the morning, for instance, the stage directions specify: המן דופק אצל הפתח "Haman knocks at the door" (AS1 *ante* 943),[39] which sets in motion a response from the inside: סופר הולך אצל הפתח "the *shrayber* goes to the door" (AS1 *ante* 945), and the king orders that if it is Haman, he be let "in" הריין (AS1 954); likewise in the second play: ווען המן איז דער מאן. / זאל ער ניט לאנג דרויז[ן] שטאן. / אונ' זאל גישווינד אריין גאן "If Haman is the man, let him not long remain outside, and he ought to come inside quickly" (AS2 731–733).[40]

Esther's position is likewise a matter of spatial positioning that simultaneously operates on ethnic, cultural, class, gender, and political levels. As an ethnic and thus class outsider, she is soon incorporated into the court as what might initially seem a permanent insider (but, like Vashti, her permanence is gender-conditioned, so she could theoretically be summarily expelled, exiled, or executed, literally at the king's pleasure), who now identifies and establishes her own presence, expressed in part spatially at and within the court: specifically, she takes the place of Vashti: אבר אסתר דורך גאטש גינאד / ערוויהליט ווארט אן איהרי שטאט "But by God's grace Esther was chosen in her place" (AS4 35–36). Her incorporation is clearly indicated by the directions issued to her as she enters the court for the first time. At first she hesitates at the door: בלייבט שטין דיא מלכה ביי דער טיר "The queen remained standing at the door" (*ante* AS2 253) and must be admitted by the king's order: דרום זאל זיא זיך ניט לאנג אום זעהן. / אונ' זאל זיך צו מיר הער גינעהן "Therefore she ought not look around for too long, but ought to approach me here" (AS2 262–263); likewise in the *Akta*: זא קומט אסתר אונ' בלייבט שטין בייא דער טיר / וואמאר המלך / זאגט דער מלך / אליר שענשטי פרינצעסן. ווארום בלייבט איר שטין בייא דער טיר. / גיא זיא אוועניק הער צו מיר: / זא גיט אסתר ווייטר אהין אונ' קניט לפני המלך . . . "Thus Esther came and remained standing at the door. And the king said the king said:[41] 'Most beautiful princess, why do you remain standing at the door? May she approach me somewhat more closely.' So Esther went farther inside and knelt before the king" (*Akta ante* 573–*ante* 575). Later in the *Akta* when Esther enters the court uninvited, Ahasuerus reassures her: דוא דרפשט דיך ניכט צו פירכטן דז דוא בישט מיינה גבאט איבר טרעטן. / אונ' בישט אהני ברופין. אין מיין קיניגליכן האף גטרעטין "You need have no fear because you transgressed my command and entered my royal court without a summons" (*Akta* 2169–2170).

After she has become queen, Esther stages a banquet in the defined female space of her quarters—a second "insider" female space, supplemental to the definitively liminal female space of the harem—to be attended only by male invitees: the king and his vizier. Thus she reverses the gender-conditioned rules of banquets and guests, since in the beginning of the biblical book, Vashti's banquet was attended by women only (1:9), while Ahasuerus's banquet was attended by כָל־הָעָם הַנִּמְצְאִים בְּשׁוּשַׁן (1:5) "all the people present in Susa," although traditionally it is understood that only men were in attendance, that is, until Ahasuerus commanded Vashti to display herself at the festivities (1:10–12). In any case, the space of Esther as queen is clearly not identical to the king's space: hers seems to be private, unlike his public, political sphere. Guests must be invited to enter here, too, however, as is also the case with the king's space: the *shrayber* conveys the invitation to Haman to enter Esther's space and banquet (AS3 1228–1230); Hatakh specifies that Haman is expected to come אין דען האף "into the court" (AS3 1236), in this case, Esther's space, for the banquet. Ahasuerus acknowledges the reversal of gender/power priorities and the roles of king and queen when he goes to Esther's banquet at her invitation and enters her designated space: אלזו וועלין מיר צו אונזר קינגין גינעהן. / ווייל זיא עש ביגערט אזו זאל איר וויל גישעהן "Thus let us approach our queen. Since she thus desires it, then let her will be done" (AS3 1245–1246). Esther then extends the image by exercising the authority as ruler of this, her, court, by inviting in all the important court personages: אלי דיא אידלן פֿון מיינם האף. / דיא זאלין קומן אין דען זאל אום מיין ווילין צו טאן "All the nobles of my court, they are to come into the hall, in order to do my will" (AS3 1254–1255).

Although further examples could be adduced from the early Purim plays, the general tenor of the present argument should by this point be clear, such that the argument may be concluded by a brief return to the theoretical conception of the liminal. Turner suggests that cultural meaning is generated at the boundaries of culture. From there we have but a short step to more overtly political theory.

While for Turner the strictly pragmatic political sense of the liminal is no more than "a subversive flicker," since it is almost immediately resorbed into the service of the norm,[42] as already noted in the introductory chapter of this study, for Homi Bhabha, among others, interstitial spaces constitute radically different sites of resistant, even subversive and counter-hegemonic creativity and innovation. In the specific discursive context in which Bhabha operates, however, having to do with, among other things, the formation of political identities, the significance of the creativity spawned by the space bleeds over into specifically political issues and the formulation of "strategies of representation or empowerment" in resistance to "shared histories of deprivation and discrimination."[43] Clearly this space is not one whose primary identifying feature is its effective isolation from the spaces that surround it, as is necessary in the strict construction of Turner's rites of passage model, but rather its necessarily permeable boundaries that not only allow passage into the interstitial elements from the surrounding spaces but actively engage, absorb, and develop those elements into a hybrid innovation. The conception of the movement through the liminal stage, as conceived by Turner, as predominantly ameliorative in nature, resulting in the initiand's post-liminal enhanced status is likewise absent from Bhabha's state of "hybridity," in which value is not a matter of the hierarchization. The specificity, the "localness" of political formation can be the defining feature:

> The social articulation of difference, from the minority perspective, is a complex, on-going negotiation that seeks to authorize cultural hybridities that emerge in moments of historical transformation. The "right" to signify from the periphery of authorized power and privilege does not depend on the persistence of tradition; it is resourced by the power of tradition to be reinscribed through the conditions of contingency and contradictoriness that attend upon the lives of those who are "in the minority."[44]

That space in which cultural hybridity is produced is then not merely vaguely "creative" or "anti-structural," as Turner suggests, but in fact the site of overt political activism: "the intervening space 'beyond,' becomes a space of intervention in the here and now."[45]

Thus we may return to the marginalized ethnic group—Ashkenazic Jews in early modern Europe—that via annual ritualized drama symbolically experiences the transformative liminalization from exclusion to inclusion, from political insignificance to effective imperial rule. The holiday is brief, the performance briefer still; the transformation ephemeral, the hybridity always in tension with the eternal power of tradition, the liminality permanent. The plays make overt use of contemporaneous Christian drama, are often staged in playhouses open to the general public, and apparently are often somewhat too enthusiastically attended by Gentiles; more than one text identifies itself as an opera, and one even lists the orchestra's elaborate instrumentation. Mordecai and Esther—and the eighteenth-century Ashkenazic celebrants of Purim—are poised on a point, liminally balanced betwixt and between. Significantly, that single point may function spatially as the threshold not of a single but of multiple cultural axes. It is a point produced by means of multiple modes of cultural translation, whether from Gentile dramatic traditions or Jewish midrashic exegetical traditions, and the negotiation of cultural borderlands of community political authority, permissible gendered behavior, and the spatial constructs of power. The early Yiddish Purim play positively hums as a site of cultural production, and the character of Mordecai is the conduit through which that cultural translation takes place.

Notes

1. Van Gennep, *Les rites*, trans. Vizedon and Caffee, 65–68, 10–24.

2. Cf., for instance, Victor Turner's *The Ritual Process: Structure and Anti-structure* (Chicago: Aldine, 1969); *Dramas, Fields, and Metaphors; Symbolic Action in Human Society* (Ithaca, NY: Cornell University Press, 1974); *Image and Pilgrimage in Christian Culture: Anthropological Perspectives* (New York: Columbia University Press, 1978); *From Ritual to Theatre: The Human Seriousness of Play* (New York: Performing Arts Journal Publications, 1982); *Celebration, Studies in Festivity and Ritual* (Washington, DC: Smithsonian Institution Press, 1982); *On the Edge of the Bush: Anthropology as Experience* (Tucson: University of Arizona Press, 1985); *The Anthropology of Experience* (Urbana: University of Illinois Press, 1986); *Blazing the Trail: Way Marks in the Exploration of Symbols* (Tucson: University of Arizona Press, 1992).

3. Turner, *The Ritual Process*, 110.

4. Baumgarten, *Introduction*, 366–367. On this relation among calendar, cosmos and carnival, see Claude Gaignebet, *Le carnaval: essais de mythologie populaire* (Paris: Payot, 1974).

5. Stern, "Esther," 27.

6. Kenneth M. Craig, Jr. interestingly notes that "instead of a linear sequence of events, the Esther plot unfolds by reversals—not changes or breakdowns, but specific 180 degree turns"; see *Reading Esther: A Case for the Literary Carnivalesque* (Louisville, KY: Westminster John Knox Press, 1995), 81. In general one might note that Craig's study resembles Beal's in its provocative but "Judaically-challenged" interpretation of biblical texts.

7. See Daniel Boyarin, who notes that Purim is an outsiders' holiday that has been incorporated into the liturgy to be celebrated by insiders and that "Purim is the text of Diaspora par excellence," thus establishing Jews in the larger historical world outside of Israel; see Daniel Boyarin, introduction to *Purim and the Cultural Poetics of Judaism—Theorizing Diaspora*, special issue, *Poetics Today* 15 (1994): 1–8. The importance of liminality in conceptions of this holiday may also be noted in its function in other early Purim plays: the מכירות יוסף "The Sale of Joseph" deals overtly with multiple "national" border crossings, the limbo-like existence of immigrant/slaves, etc. Likewise, in the דוד אונט גליות הפלשטי "David and Goliath the Philistine," the central episode in the conflict between the liminally adolescent David and the villain Goliath focuses on the duel that occurs in the determinative liminal space between the two armies, that transformational zone of action that defines heroism.

8. וְהָיָה יוֹדֵעַ בְּשִׁבְעִים לָשׁוֹן "and he knew seventy languages"; BT *Meg* 13b. The issue is pointedly topicalized earlier in the conspirators' conversation, when they express their doubt that he can understand them (AS3 1118–1124).

9. Since the Amalekites as conceived in Genesis were likely nomadic Canaanites, they were in the book of Esther not, for instance, to be imagined as the ancestors of the Persians, and thus are necessarily also foreign at the Persian court.

10. See, for instance, Kristin De Troyer, "An Oriental Beauty Parlour: An Analysis of Esther 2.8–18 in the Hebrew, The Septuagint and the Second Greek Text," in Brenner, *A Feminist Companion*, 51, with reference to W. F. Albright, "The Lachish Cosmetic Burner and Esther 2.12," in *A Light unto My Path: Old Testament Studies in Honor of Jacob M. Myers*, ed. H. N. Bream, R. D. Heim, and C. A. Moore (Philadelphia: Temple University Press, 1974), 25–32. The situation is in some ways reminiscent of the narrative frame of ألف لَيْلَة وَلَيْلَة *1001 Nights*, although the post-coital fate of the serial wives is famously rather different in that narrative.

11. Again much as Shahrāzād in *1001 Nights*, whose stint as queen-for-a-night is extended to successive nights and then apparently to permanent queenship, while it is her father (and not her uncle) who is—and was from the beginning—vizier.

12. The Hebrew Bible is cited from תורה נביאים וכתובים *Biblia Hebraea Stuttgartensia*, ed. A. Alt et al., 2nd ed. (Stuttgart: Deutsche Bibelgesellschaft, 1967); the English translation of the Bible is RSV. The *Targum Sheni* is cited from Lagarde, *Hagiographa Chaldaice* [hereafter: 2Targ Est], with consultation of the commentary by Ego, *Targum Scheni*, 141–333; other editions consulted include David Moritz, *Das Targum Scheni zum Buche Esther: nach Handschriften herausgegeben* (Crakow: J. Fischer, 1898); and Leo Munk, *Targum Scheni zum Buch Esther: nebst variae Lectiones* (Berlin: J. Benzian, 1876).

13. Avraham ben Meir ibn Ezra indeed claims that Mordecai was positioned at the gate by order of the king and is prohibited on pain of death from leaving the palace gate without permission: *ad* Est 3:4 in both of his commentaries, the first printed in editions of the *Mikraot gedolot*, the second in *Vayosef Avraham: hu perush ha-Raba' al Ester*, ed. Joseph Zedner (London: D. Nutt, 1850); see also Walfish, *Esther in Medieval Garb*, 158. A seemingly incidental usage in an early seventeenth-century book demonstrates just how ubiquitous and automatic was the veritable obsession with gates and doors, inside and outside, and in general, spatial positioning in the book of Esther: on the final page of the midrash-influenced version of the book of Esther in the Middle Yiddish *Tsene-rene*, the so-called "women's Bible," the letters ח and ת are once printed substantially larger than the surrounding letters, which was traditionally interpreted as a designation of their function as gates—to admit good people, both rich and poor, to the Purim festival instituted by the book of Esther. See Jacob ben Isaac Ashkenazi of Janov, *Tsene-rene* (Hanau 1622), ed. in *EYT* 98, 563.

14. Ludwig Koehler and Walter Baumgartner, 3rd ed. by Johann Jakob Stamm, *Hebräisches und Aramäisches Lexikon zum alten Testament* (Leiden: E. J. Brill, 1990), Lieferung IV, 1493 (translation mine).

15. Mieke Bal, *Lethal Love: Feminist Literary Readings of Biblical Love Stories*, Indiana Studies in Biblical Literature (Bloomington: Indiana University Press, 1987), 49, 78, 81. Bal sees this liminal zone as one of "'mixtures,' transgressions of clear limits, like the one between the public and the private that Ruth so blatantly transgresses when she goes back to the field where she had been gleaning the day before, only to go to the center of the field, the threshing floor, which, by a strange mixture, is also Boaz's bed. The trial at the city gate, at the entrance to the female domain, where two men debate the question of who dares to take the woman, is the *place* of the mixture" (83). On Boaz, she notes, "Assuming this position as a mediator, participating in collective heroism, Boaz constitutes himself the gate he wished to enter" (86).

16. The *Targum* passages are here generally summarized with selective citation only.

17. Lagarde, *Hagiographa Chaldaice*, 243.

18. According to *Midrash Esther Rabbah*, Haman embroidered a צֶלֶם "[idolatrous] image" (generally: "cross") on his clothing so that bowing to him was in effect bowing to an idol (*MER* 66).

19. Lagarde, *Hagiographa Chaldaice*, 244.

20. Lagarde, *Hagiographa Chaldaice*, 251.

21. Lagarde, *Hagiographa Chaldaice*, 252.

22. Lagarde, *Hagiographa Chaldaice*, 256.

23. Lagarde, *Hagiographa Chaldaice*, 257.

24. Lagarde, *Hagiographa Chaldaice*, 257.

25. Lagarde, *Hagiographa Chaldaice*, 258.

26. Lagarde, *Hagiographa Chaldaice*, 259; similarly in BT *Meg* 16a.

27. Lagarde, *Hagiographa Chaldaice*, 259. Bernard Grossfeld cites further instances of Mordecai at the gate: BT *Meg* 16a; *LekaḥTov* 6:10, 106; *Aggadat Esther* 6:10, 62; see Bernard Grossfeld, *The Two Targums of Esther, Translated with Apparatus and Notes*, The Aramaic Bible 18 (Edinburgh: T and T Clark, 1991), 72.

28. Timothy K. Beal uses the term "betweennesses" to characterize salient aspects of the book of Esther; see *The Book of Hiding*, 3.

29. According to the *Midrash Rabbah*, וּבְכָל יוֹם וָיוֹם מָרְדְּכַי מִתְהַלֵּךְ לִפְנֵי חֲצַד בֵּית הַנָּשִׁים "Day after day Mordecai walked around in front of the courtyard of the harem" [to keep track of Esther] (*MER* 61). This activity is already "spatially" conceived, with Mordecai in relation to Esther, the court, and the king.

30. The *Targum Sheni* identifies the two would-be assassins as בגתנא ותרש תרין סריסוי דמלכא מן נטרי מניא "Bigthan and Teresh, two of the king's eunuchs who guarded the vessels," as the text's editor indicates in a footnote, the translator of the *Targum* construed the Hebrew root סף here not in its common connotation as "threshold" but in its equally common connotation as "bowl" (Lagarde, *Hagiographa Chaldaice*, 243). Characteristically, during the hyper-official interrogation (עקסאמיני *Akta ante* 638) of Bigthan during the trial, he interestingly identifies his profession as איין טיר שטיער "a doorman" (*Akta* 642); later Teresh says that he is himself from איראביא "Arabia" and that his job is איין טיר שטיאר "a doorman," just as Mordecai (*Akta* 695–698). In the Talmud, Bigthan and Teresh identify their motivation for regicide as a lack of sleep: since Esther has become the king's bed companion, he has become so sexually active that they must fetch him water to drink all night long (BT *Meg* 13b). In AS3 522, Mordecai acknowledges that forces larger than himself are working through him, when he states that Heaven brought him to the place where he overheard the seditious plot of Bigthan and Teresh.

31. Bernard Grossfeld, ed., *The First Targum to Esther: According to the MS Paris Hebrew 110 of the Bibliothèque Nationale* (New York: Sepher-Hermon, 1983), 13. Barry Walfish notes that while the biblical text provides no motive for the insurrection by Bigthan and Teresh, the medieval commentaries fill in this gap by attributing jealousy to them because of Mordecai's promotion over them or replacing them, among other reasons; Walfish, *Esther in Medieval Garb*, section: "Bigthan and Teresh's Motives for Plotting to Kill the King," 177–178.

32. Commonly the word's connotation also extended to include "to make Jewish," i.e., circumcise, as in the modern Yiddish ייִדישן, but it is unlikely that the Purim play would site that ceremony at the Persian palace gate.

33. The corresponding scene in AS2, AS3, and AS4 is similar.

34. Interestingly, such Semitic linguistic prowess *qua* cultural liminality was already depicted as a political liability by the early Roman playwright Plautus in his proto-anti-Semitic

portrayal of the character Hanno, a Phoenician-speaking Carthaginian and thus—from a rabidly unsympathetic Roman perspective—an ancient linguistic and quasi-cultural "cousin" of the Jews (Plautus, "Poenulus," lines 990–1040).

35. Educated Christians of the period, whether Protestant or Catholic, would have theoretically been capable of some level of conversation in Latin, of course, as would theoretically any high-ranking officials at court, but the maintenance of Latin as the liturgical language of Catholicism, while it was on principle rejected by Protestants in favor of the vernacular, may here at least suggest that the conspirators are conceived as Catholic.

36. The larger reversal of fortunes of Haman and Mordecai is expressed variously; Esther, for instance, remarks: מיין פֿערשט שענקט אן מרדכֿי דיא קינגליכֿן גאבין. / פֿון המן זיין הערשאפֿט אונ' רייך פֿון גוטין האבין "My prince grants to Mordecai the royal gifts, from Haman his authority and wealth of fine possessions" (AS3 1467–1468).

37. Interestingly, however, as Tsinberg points out (*Geshikhte*, 329), in the beginning Vashti appeals to Haman to save her life, and after he refuses, she asks the chancellor to be admitted to the king to beg for mercy (i.e., the same mode of intrusion into the royal presence that Esther executes later to save the Jews, with the clear contrast between Vashti's selfish attempt to save herself versus Esther's self-endangering attempt to save her people); later Haman himself begs both Esther for his life and then the chancellor for admission to the king's presence to beg for his life. Thus in duplicating the actions of the two previous such petitioners, both women, Haman is quasi-feminized and, like Vashti, subjected to the ultimate exclusion through denial of admission and condemnation to remain outside of the gate.

38. The quasi-stage directions in AS3 are also interesting in this respect, because they (as conventional) specify "out" as *onto* the stage, i.e., into view, while "in" is to go offstage and out of view; the spatial conception of the production stage thus reverses the political conception of space.

39. Cf. also: קלאפּט המן בשער המלך "Haman knocks on the king's door" (*Akta ante* 2279).

40. Repeated by the *shrayber*: ווען המן איז דער מאן. / אזו זאל ער ניט לאנג דרויזן שטאן. / אונ' זאל גישווינד ארייַן גאן "If Haman is the man, then he ought not long remain outside, and ought to come inside quickly" (AS2 734–736).

41. This phrase of the stage directions appears in both Hebrew and Yiddish, thus doubled in the text.

42. Turner, *From Ritual to Theatre*, 44.

43. Bhabha, *Location*, 1.

44. Bhabha, *Location*, 2.

45. Bhabha, *Location*, 7.

Chapter Seven

Feudal Bridal Quest Turned on Its Jewish Head

SANDRA SILBERSTEIN HAS demonstrated on the basis of late twentieth-century courtship tales, collected in an oral history project, that such narratives necessarily participate in a nexus of social relations that function in larger and socially more significant contexts.[1] As is the case in any complex of social relations, courtship articulates with a culture's multiple social formations and is thus always dialectical, negotiable, in process, and thus ever expressive of the economic and socio-political relations of the participating parties. Contemporary courtship narratives do not, Silberstein argues, necessarily tell us much about "what happened," but rather express what the narrators assume to be appropriate components of a discussion of courtship; they are not to be understood as "statements about psychological reality, but as articulations within shared ideologies," or, to use C. Wright Mills's terminology, articulations of a shared "vocabulary of motive with which communities of people explain their actions to each other."[2] One's membership in the community is made manifest by one's conforming to the community's rules not just of courtship, but also and especially of story-telling about courtship.

A similar function of courtship tales is found, *mutatis mutandis*, in a variety of medieval European literary traditions. In each case the courtship narratives function within the acceptable social code of the culture while at the same time somehow commenting on and critiquing that code. To bring this issue into the focus of the present study: when the courtship narratives—as distinct from historical courtship praxis—of one such medieval community are culturally translated, that is, borrowed by and adapted for another contemporaneous community, such that they become integrated into that borrowing community's *literary* praxis, that adaptation generally necessitates the change not just of "external" aspects of the narrative, but indeed a radical transformation of the embedded cultural code that enables a particular mode of narrated courtship. If that cultural translation for some reason does not take place, then the resulting borrowed text functions in the borrowing community as a marked Outsider text, a narrative about the Other, not about members of the borrowing community and not necessarily relevant to their personal or community practice.

In several of the epic genres that crossed the linguistic and political boundaries of Europe quite freely during the High Middle Ages and late Middle Ages, the motif of courtship, wooing, *Brautwerbung*, "bridal quest," or, as its all but exclusively uni-directional, transitively engendered patterns of behavior in Christian literature makes the more appropriate term, "wiving" (for this last term most effectively conveys the direct denotation of dominant gender-power relations of the practice) recurs as a motif of focused significance.[3] While narratives of courtship and marriage are common, popular, and culturally important in many periods and cultures, it is a particular use of the wiving motif, one of the most productive and widespread narrative motifs known from medieval European epic, that is at issue here, for it topicalizes a politically significant plot structure that is directly tied to interests of the ruling elite.[4] Since feudal political rule is conceived as most nearly perfect when it approximates permanence, unproblematic dynastic succession (which presupposes an heir of, among other considerations, acceptable dynastic lineage) is a necessity. Wiving thus appears in narratives as a means to that end of enabling an unmarried, potentially ideal ruler to realize that potential. Representatives of existing social structures (vassals, councillors, relatives) inform him of the availability of potential socially and politically appropriate brides and offer him the requisite opportunities to demonstrate his worthiness (to her guardians) to gain her as bride, thus very concretely activating and demonstrating both the depicted culture's conception of ideal ruler and the depicted prince's qualities that make him just such a ruler. Successful wiving thus not only accomplishes the ostensive purpose of providing the ruler with an appropriate wife as the bearer of an heir, but also qualifies and certifies the ideal ruler as such, reconfirms the entire social structure of rule, the gender-power constellation, and the wiving procedures themselves.

There are multiple possibilities for the realization of this motif in the narrative: by means of direct petition by the suitor to the prospective bride's male guardians for the bride, by means of deceit and treachery, by abduction (with or without the woman's consent), by violent means, including war and military siege, and even, in exceptional cases in particular narrative modes, by means of independently acting women who make themselves available to appropriate bridegrooms.[5] This structure of wiving praxis thus becomes one of the primary means to represent class and intra-class status relations in medieval epic, which itself functioned most often as an explicitly political component in the cultural program of the feudal ruling elite in medieval Europe. The concrete task is enacted through the process of identifying, negotiating for, and fetching a bride appropriate to the prince or king. That suitability is largely reckoned by the rank in the feudal hierarchy or hierarchies of the two parties or families involved. In the narratives, this process regularly results in some combination of several of the following activities: elaborate calculations of relative rank, careful weighing and frequent rejection of internal and external proposals, wars of vengeance for insults real and imagined, negotiation and contracting of marriage, abduction of the desired bride, and military expedition to recover an abducted female family member.

The specific form of the realization of this motif depends rather strictly on the sub-genre of epic in which it is employed. Those relevant to an analysis of the motif in early Yiddish epic are conventionally designated heroic epic, minstrel epic (*Spielmannsepos*), courtly epic, and Renaissance (romance) epic.[6] Until the period of the Renaissance, the literary tradition most relevant to the earliest corpus of Yiddish epic is Middle High German, and thus for the medieval period, it is that tradition on which I first focus; then in the sixteenth century, Italian epic becomes relevant for Middle Yiddish epic.[7]

It will be necessary to deal in considerable detail with the construction and practice of wiving in the Christian literary tradition alongside the Yiddish treatment of the issue, not as a vaguely relevant "background" to that treatment, but rather as the direct underlying form of wiving as it informs a broad swath of contemporary (late medieval and early modern) Western and Central European epic narrative that incorporates wiving motifs. Medieval and Renaissance European epic was an international cluster of genres, and most early Yiddish narratives in which the wiving motif appears overtly participate in this international tradition and thus have Christian texts as their direct or indirect sources. In the necessarily Jewish cultural context of these narratives' audience, however, such texts can obviously no longer fulfill the cultural function of legitimizing the feudal social structure as the culture's own inner structure, nor of glorifying the aristocratic elite or authorizing the dynastic claims of any given royal family, historical or fictional—as authorizer or patron of the text's literary production—as wiving had (generally) done in Christian epic. Rather, in those Jewish texts where the represented context of Christian feudal culture and institutions (royalty and aristocracy and their courts, castles, and palaces) *is* retained, the insistence on appropriate social rank as prerequisite to marriageability necessarily undergoes radical transformation into a vehicle of social commentary and analysis of external Christian or internal Jewish class and status problematics.

To state the thesis of the argument to be presented here quite clearly, before the evidence is adduced: as witnessed by the extant early Yiddish epics, it seems that the selection of Christian epics to be adapted into Yiddish depended directly on the central function of wiving as the narrative's primary motivator, albeit generally with a peculiar twist, or rather with a range of peculiar twists. In the early Yiddish literary tradition, there are five extensive examples of quasi-secular epic that are relevant to the motif under examination: דוכוס הורנט *Duke Horant,*[8]ווידווילט—איין שיין מעשה פֿון קעניג ארטיס הויף *Vidvilt—A Fine Tale of King Arthur's Court,*[9] בבֿא דאנטונא *Bovo d'Antona,*[10] פאריז אונ' וויענה *Pariz and Viene,*[11] and the prose adventure tale מעשה בריעה וזמרי *The Tale of Briyo and Zimro,* which originated within Jewish culture and was thus not translated or adapted across such cultural boundaries.[12]

The issue of wiving in Yiddish epic and its various source traditions will here be treated through analysis of the various extant epic sub-genres. In the few medieval German texts conventionally identified as representative of the genre of *heroic epic*, the motif of wiving plays an important role, and despite the fact that there is no example of this genre extant in early Yiddish, the German tradition is still relevant here because of shared patterns of narration between this German sub-genre and those represented in early Yiddish. In the Middle High German *Nibelungenlied*, for instance, one need only think of Siegfried's unusually diffuse and protracted suit for Kriemhild (*aventiure* 2–9), the Burgundian wiving expedition to Iceland that provided Gunther with Brünhild as bride (*aventiure* 6–8), and the Hunnic wiving expedition (by proxy) to provide Etzel with the widowed Kriemhild as bride (*aventiure* 20).[13] There are multiple modes of wiving represented in the narrative: by proxied petition (Etzel for Kriemhild), by quasi-courtly love service (Siegfried for Kriemhild), by war games dominated by cunning and deception (Gunther for Brünhild), and by implied or threatened armed combat (both Siegfried's and Gunther's suits). Inappropriate marital matches, whether real or imagined, in fact motivate Siegfried's murder and thus much of the epic's plot. In the Middle High German *Kudrun* epic, as well, one might refer to the multiple petitions by Hartmuot, Herwîc, and Sîfrit (especially *aventiure* 10–15) for Kudrun, which again present a broad spectrum of types of wiving episodes, and which in themselves motivate the entire epic plot.[14]

The medieval German genre in which the wiving motif is most important is the so-called *Spielmannsepos,* "minstrel epic," where in some cases, wiving again effectively motivates the entire plot by means of its function as the vehicle of the text's politically charged "message."[15] As Christian Schmid-Cadalbert has indicated, there is logically and predictably a tripartite structure of wiving narrative: the preparation for the expedition, the journey itself, and the return home with the bride and the wedding.[16] According to Ingeborg Schröbler, there are indeed six components of the narrative structure of *Brautwerbung* in medieval German epic narrative: vassals advise their lord to marry; courtship takes place via proxy/envoy; courtship involves *List,* "deceit/strategy/artifice"; a bower scene takes place involving the proxy/envoy and the bride-to-be; the bride is abducted by means of deceit; the abduction party is pursued by the maiden's male guardian, leading to combat and eventual resolution.[17] In the primary example of minstrel epic in Middle High German, *König Rother*, for instance, wiving is the motor for the entire plot, which it would be useful to summarize briefly, because of its display of practically all possible attributes of an overtly political wiving narrative: King Rother of Rome lacks a bride, is convinced of the appropriateness of the daughter of King Constantin of Constantinople, and sends a proxy to present his petition. The bride's father not only rejects the suit (because of Rother's alleged unworthiness of the honor of the match and its attendant political benefits), but also imprisons the wiving party (because of the perceived personal and political insult constituted by the inappropriate proposal itself). Rother as king of Rome, the emperor of the West, the latter-day *Imperium Romanum*, is thus denied his universalist claims and honor, in this obvious reference to the political ambitions of the Holy Roman emperors of the Hohenstaufen dynasty contemporary with the epic's period of composition. Rother responds by summoning a court council from all his territories, launches a second expedition, this time not one of petition and not yet one of military action, but now one of *List*, in order to free his ambassadors, taking with him, among others, the giants Widold and Asprian. He himself joins the party incognito, as the warrior Dietherich, who insinuates himself into Constantin's court and through his wisdom, honor, justice, and generosity—the idealized cardinal virtues of the medieval monarch—actually goes far toward usurping the function of the actual king, many of whose vassals defect in order to serve Rother/Dietherich. In this respect he has de facto already defeated Constantin, without a single stroke of the sword. He wins the love of the princess, frees his ambassadors, and—in order to prove directly and unequivocally to Constantin his superiority—he also defeats and captures the Muslim general who besieges Constantinople. After he and the princess flee clandestinely to Rome, a counter-move by Constantin—defined by the requisite treachery instead of legitimate warrior's skill—manages to recapture the princess, so that Rother must return to the East, this time, finally, at the head of an army. In the meantime, Constantin has allowed the Muslim leader to escape, who has then captured the city and thus coerced Constantin's promise of his daughter as bride. Rother again defeats the Muslims, is finally recognized by Constantin as the legitimate ideal ruler, is granted the princess, and returns to Rome, where their son, Pippin, the future father of Charlemagne, is born, and thus the political function of the text to legitimize the hegemonic claims of the Western over the Eastern Imperium, even from the time of the pre-Carolingian period, is made explicit (like so much else in the narrative, this entire sequence is purely fictional, despite the few [quasi-]historical personages involved).[18] Rother is thus represented as not only the legitimate ruler of Europe but also its divinely appointed protector against Byzantine "pretenders" and the so-called "infidel" Muslim, constructed as the ultimate enemy of Christendom. In the *Spielmannsepos* in general, wiving episodes function as integral elements in political programs, even if not always so clearly part of Hohenstaufen imperial political ideology, as is the case in *Rother*.

While there is no translation or adaptation of *Rother* into Yiddish, the oldest extant quasi-secular epic in Yiddish, *Duke Horant*, initially seems to represent the classic Christian feudal wiving tale, transferred with a few minor cultural adaptations into Yiddish.[19] Ironically, however, *Horant* has no extant Christian source text, nor is there any actual evidence that such a text ever existed. In the Yiddish narrative, Duke Horant, a vassal and wiving proxy of King Itene of Denmark, Lombardy, and the German lands (among others), the quintessential Western European Christian imperial monarch, sails east to the exotic lands of Hagene the Savage, the Christian king of Greece, to gain the hand of his daughter Hilde in marriage, taking with him, among others, the giants Witolt and Asprion. He plans quite conventionally to accomplish his task by any means necessary, *explicitly* including stealth, bribery, lies, murder, and war. But, disguised as a merchant, the vassal gains access to the princess and wins her attention to his quest by means of his sweet singing, and *not* by those other means earlier envisioned (and commonly employed in such missions). The Yiddish text fragment lacks the narrative's conclusion, and thus the precise form of the resolution of the proxy-suitor's quest in the wiving episode is indeterminable, although if true to type, it would seem likely that Horant would somehow manage to leave Greece with Princess Hilde, probably by stealth, and that they would be pursued by her father, King Hagene, who would probably have ample opportunity to demonstrate the aptness of his byname "the Savage"; reconciliation and compensation via property exchange would most likely follow at some point, whether after or instead of hostilities. But all that is mere speculation, based on the pattern of other such narratives, for in fact the Yiddish fragment breaks off in mid-courtship.

In this earliest quasi-secular wiving epic in Yiddish, there is nothing in the text that demonstrates a specifically and identifiably Jewish reconception of the wiving motif.[20] There is moreover no evidence that any of the (royal or aristocratic) characters is conceived as anything other than Gentile. It seems then that *Horant* was a narrative derived from outside the experience and culture of Ashkenaz and would have clearly been perceived as such by its Ashkenazic audience. One might somewhat anachronistically designate it "escape literature" for that audience, although to be fair one would likewise have to acknowledge that the purported Middle High German source text would have functioned in the same way for the vast majority of its fourteenth-century, post-courtly audience of non-royal and non-aristocratic Christians, for whom such (quasi-) courtly narrative was culturally as alien as it would have been for their Jewish neighbors.

Among the quasi-secular epics in early Yiddish, *Horant* seems the only one to present a conventional praxis of narrative wiving as outlined above by Schmid-

Cadalbert and Schröbler. But *is* the wiving praxis of this text in fact so canonically conventional? It is after all Horant's singing ability that distinguishes him from other heroes and enables him to carry out the wiving expedition successfully (if indeed one might project ultimate success onto the fragmentary text). The entire wiving expedition seems predicated on Horant's supernatural singing abilities. As early as stanza 8 of the poem, Horant is already identified as the בש זינגשטא, which most likely means "best sensed = most prudent," but the idiom is obscure, and there is a conceivable possibility that it means "best singing."[21] But regardless of the interpretation of that particular phrase, even as the mission is still in its planning stages, King Itene views Horant's singing ability as the key to the successful accomplishment of his wiving embassy: מיט דימא זושן גזנגא ברעכטשט דו מיר די מגט חר דן · / איך וולדא דיר אלז' ריכא גובא געבן · / דו מוכטשט אומר וול מיט ורוודן לעבן: "If you were to bring me home the maiden by means of your sweet singing, I would give you such rich gifts that you would live joyously ever after" (*Duke Horant*, st. 31, 2–4). As noted earlier, Horant journeys to Greece to present his king's marriage suit, and while still at sea he gives evidence of the supernatural character of his singing:

זי בֿורן אל גריכטא אוף דש ווילדא מיר.
הורנט אונ' זין גזילן איין גרוש קריפֿטיגש היר.
הורנט הופּ אוף אונ' זנק.
דש עש דורך די וואולקן קלנק:

ער זנק אימא אלזא לווטא נן קומא אונש דער צו טרושטא.
אן דיזמא טגא הויטא דער די יודן אוף דעמא מיר ערלושטא.
אין ג' נאמן בֿרן וויר.
זינר גנדן גערן וויר:

דא בגונדא ער אלזא לוטא אונ' אלזא זוש̌א זינגן·
דש די מירמינא צומא ש̌יפֿא בֿגונדא אלא דרינגן·
אונ' די ויש̌א אין דעמא בודמא·
שוואומן אלא אובנא:
(st. 62–64)

> They sailed directly [or: well prepared] out onto the savage sea, Horant and his comrades, a great and mighty host. Horant began to sing, so that it resounded up through the clouds. He sang so clearly [or: loudly]: "Now, on this day, today, may He come to comfort us, who delivered the Jews on the sea. 'In God's name do we fare; his mercy do we desire.' "[22] Then he began to sing so clearly [or: loudly] and so sweetly that the mer-men began to rush toward the ship, and the fish in the depths all swam to the surface.

While he bewitches the creatures of the sea with his song here, later, in the royal gardens in Greece, when he serenades Princess Hilde while she stands on the battlements, he bewitches her, as well as the birds in the air and the wild boars in the woods; he says:

איר שולט אוור ועכטן לן·
איך קן ויל בש גווינן די מגט וול גטן·
מיט דעם זושן גזנגא מין·
ברינגא איך אונש דש מעגטין:

ער הופֿ אוף אלזא לוט איין שטימא אונ' [זנק·]
דש עש זא ונקליכן דורך די וולקן דרנק·
אונ' דש די קליינן בֿוגלין·
איר וליגן מושטן לושן זין:

אונ' בגונדן אלא צו דער לינדן דרינגן·
זי הורטן אלֿזא גערנא דען קונן הורנדן זינגן·
אונ' דש די ווילדן עבר שווין·
איר וואוילן מושטן לושן זין:

נו ווש די יונגא קוניג' אן איינר צינא גגן·
זי הורטא דען זנק זא גערנ' ער דוכטא זי זא וול גטן·
זי שווייק אלזא לנגא·
נוך דעמא זושן גזנגא:

אונ' דא דער זנק זא [ ][23] בֿור [ ] איין גנם
דא שפר' די קונגינ' צו איינר הירצוגן טוכטר לובזם·
נן הורטא איך ני בש זינגן·
נוך איין קעלא זא זושא ארקלינגן:

דו שולט דורך מינן ווילן צו דער לינדן גן·
אונ' [ ] מיר דעמא בֿורשטן [ ] דען זושן זנק דא הבא גטן·
איך וולדא אין אלֿזא גערנא זחן·
מוכטא עש מיט בֿוגן גשחן:
(st. 159–164)

"You are to leave off your fighting. I can win the lovely maiden much better: with my sweet voice I will bring the maiden to us." He began to sing in such a clear [or: loud] voice that it resounded so marvelously up through the clouds and halted little birds in their flight—they all began to rush to the linden tree, so eagerly did they listen to bold Horant sing—and the wild boars had to give up their rooting around in the ground. Now the young queen had gone up to the battlement. She listened so happily to the song; it seemed so lovely to her. She quietly listened for a long time to the sweet song. And when the song so sweetly before [. . .] had ended, then the queen said to the worthy daughter of a duke: "Now, I have never heard better singing nor a voice sound so sweet. You are to go for my sake to the linden tree and tell the lord for me [. . .] has sung there the sweet song, I would very much like to see him, if it could be done with propriety."

Princess Hilde sends her attendant to ascertain the identity of the singer, offering ten thousand marks of gold and a beautiful maiden as a bed companion that very night in exchange for a private concert (st. 169). As noted earlier, Horant refuses both the monetary reward and the bed companion (who seems to be construed as the princess herself) and uses the invitation as an opening to invite the princess to come to speak with him in the garden, where he will sing for her.[24] She comes and in response to his query admits that she has come for the sake of his magnificent singing and דורך ווילן "for entertainment's sake."[25] His singing then again spellbinds both her and the natural world in general (birds and wild boars; st. 183). After he again refuses her gifts, one of them then presents the other with a ring—perhaps he presents a ring from his king (st. 188)[26]—and he introduces his lord's marriage suit, claiming that הבא [איך ויל] וול גזונגן דו שטולצא קונגינ' · דש מוכט ניכט גליכן דעמא ליבן הירן מין · ער זינגט [ויל בש] דין איך הבא גטן (st. 192, fol. 36r), "While I may have sung well, most noble queen, that cannot equal my dear lord. He sings much better than I did." While he also claims that King Itene is handsome, noble, generous, and powerful, the would-be groom's singing ability forms an integral component of the marriage suit itself, which seems to have precisely the desired effect on the maiden, who first offers herself to Horant (who again declines, claiming a prior amorous commitment; st. 171 and 195). The deteriorated state of the manuscript renders the following stanzas only partially legible, but it is there clear that if she marries Itene, Horant promises to sing for her, to which she apparently agrees, adding: איך וויל אלזא גערנ' ליישטן אל דש ווילן דין (fol. 36v), "I will very happily do all that you wish" (st. 197, 2). The subsequent couplet is all but illegible: דינר [ ] וויל איך [ ]ן · [ ] מק איך ניכט אנפערן "Your [. . .] I will/wish [. . .] may I not do without," which Peter Ganz, Frederick Norman, and Werner Schwarz creatively reconstruct (in their bizarre ad hoc transcriptive mode) as "dinr <b^{c}t'> wwil 'ikh <gww^{c}r>n. <dins> . . . <zngs> mq 'ikh nikht <'n>p^{c}rn,"[27] that is, more or less: "I will grant your requests; I cannot do without your sweet singing."[28] Horant's singing is the primary instrument of the success of his marriage suit, whether in fact he convinces Hilde to marry Itene because of the king's own merits or simply so that—bewitched by Horant's singing as she clearly is—she could thus be near Horant and hear his singing with some frequency.

In this context of Horant's supernatural musical abilities as an essential qualification as hero and wiving proxy, it might be useful to address this issue in a somewhat larger cultural context, because as it turns out, Horant's praxis is pertinent to practically the entire tradition of early Yiddish epic wiving. The coupling of musicianship with epic heroism is of course not unique either to early Yiddish epic or even to medieval European epic in general. The Jewish and Christian cultural model of the quasi-supernatural powers of singing and musicianship is obviously King David, וּנְעִים זְמִרוֹת יִשְׂרָאֵל (2 Sam 23:1), "the sweet psalmist of Israel," whose singing soothed Saul during his bouts of insanity (1 Sam 16:17–23;

cf. also the Middle Yiddish *Book of Samuel*, st. 293–300, 350–351, 400, 448).[29] Significantly, however, David's musical abilities are noted in the biblical narrative among the essential identifying characteristics *of a hero* (1 Sam 16:18)—he is skilled as both a musician and a warrior, strong, intelligent, handsome, and favored by God.

Likewise in the non-Jewish epic tradition, musical ability recurs as an essential trait of the hero; one need look no further than Homer's uncanny scene in Akhilleus's tent when the Greek embassy arrives by night to present their desperate petition for him to return to battle, and they find him, the greatest warrior alive, not, of course, performing his own glorious heroic deeds on the battlefield but rather those of others, on the lyre:

τὸν δ' εὗρον φρένα τερπόμενον φόρμιγγι λιγείῃ
καλῇ δαιδαλέῃ, ἐπὶ δ' ἀργύρεον ζυγὸν ἦεν,
τὴν ἄρετ' ἐξ ἐνάρων πόλιν Ἠετίωνος ὀλέσσας·
τῇ ὅ γε θυμὸν ἔτερπεν, ἄειδε δ' ἄρα κλέα ἀνδρῶν. (*Iliad* 9.186–189)[30]

They found him delighting his spirit with a beautifully and cunningly made, clear-toned lyre, on which there was a silver bridge—this he took from the spoils, when he had destroyed the city of Eëtion. And he was delighting his soul with it and singing the glorious heroic deeds [κλέα] of men.

Another fundamental association of music in Western cultural traditions is found in the poetic tradition of erotic verse, which was in antiquity and the Middle Ages performed to musical accompaniment. The direct link of supernatural musicianship to a hero dates at least to the ancient myths of Orpheus, whose fame as a musician hero in Western literature rivals David's, and tales concerning whom are stitched together from various often enigmatic references in a broad range of ancient writers and whose character then became the subject in later quasi-encyclopedic digests, such as Apollodorus's Βιβλιοθήκη and even Ovid's *Metamorphoses*.[31] While Orpheus generally seems to have been construed as having had more significance in mystery religious cults than in heroic conception, he was nonetheless one of the Argonauts who journeyed with Jason to Colchis to win the Golden Fleece, and thus by definition one of the greatest Greek heroes of the legendary heroic generation preceding the "lesser" heroes of the Trojan War. Above all, Orpheus was known as a musician whose singing and musicianship were supernatural, and although Hermes was reputed to have invented the lyre, Orpheus was said to have perfected it. His singing could bewitch both humans and the natural world, including fish, birds, and wild animals, even to the extent that they danced to his tunes.[32]

In the Middle Ages Bartholomaeus Anglicus acknowledges the curative powers of music, as well as its abilities to excite erotic passion.[33] In one of her famous letters to Abaelard, Heloise likewise recognizes this power in a very practical sense in the case of Abaelard himself: "Duo autem, fateor, tibi specialiter inerant quibus feminarum quarumlibet animos statim allicere poteras, dictandi videlicet et cantandi gratia . . . atque hinc maxime in amorem tui femine suspirabant," "Moreover, I confess that you possessed two special talents by means of which you could immediately entice the spirit of any woman, namely composing verse and singing . . . and for that reason women heaved great sighs for love of you."[34] Moreover, the figure of Tristan that emerges from the tradition of courtly romances by Beroul, Thomas of Britain, Gotfrid von Straßburg, and others borders on the same conception of quasi-supernatural musical abilities found in the myths of Orpheus: Tristan plays a stunning range of musical instruments to accompany his mesmerizing voice, such that King Marc employs Tristan to sing and play for him at night when he is troubled and cannot sleep, just as King Saul had so employed David.[35] On his first voyage to Ireland, Tristan takes along his harp, which stands him in good stead in gaining access to Queen Iseut, who is the only person who can heal his poisoned wound. Impressed by his musicianship, she engages Tristan as the musical tutor of her daughter, Princess Iseut. Later when he returns to Ireland to sue for the hand of the princess as bride for his uncle, his musicianship need not again play an explicit direct role, since it has already done so in the previous episode and thus carried over into the wiving episode.[36]

Horant's supernatural singing ability and his uniting that ability with the role of a warrior thus had long precedent. The tertiary role as wiving proxy whose success depends on his supernatural singing ability seems not to have been anticipated by more ancient traditions, but is certainly clear in the actions of Tristan, and this trait had, by the time the Yiddish epic was copied, already long been part of the pan-Germanic tradition of the broadly known character of Horant himself (in the Kudrun narrative cycle): the tale of the courtship of Princess Hilde, including Horant's singing ability, seems to have been familiar throughout Germania by the sixth or seventh century, as demonstrated by a carved stone figure from Stenkyrka in Gotland (Sweden).[37] The Old English canon likewise knows the tale well: the poem "Widsið" mentions the central characters known from *Kudrun*—Heoden, Hagena, and Wada (i.e., the Itene, Hagene, and Wate of *Horant*)—while the poem "Deor" mentions "Hoerrenda . . . leoðcræftig monn," "Horant . . . the man skilled in song."[38] The medieval Icelandic politician and antiquarian author Snorri Sturluson summarizes the tale in chapter 50 of the *Skáldskaparmál* of his *Prose Edda*,[39] and the Danish ecclesiastical historian Saxo Grammaticus mentions the tale in chapter 5 of his *Gesta Danorum*.[40] Despite the widespread familiarity of the Horant motif, it did not—except in *Horant*—become a model of epic wiving praxis, but rather remained a particular and peculiar example without direct evidence of further influence on the larger subgenre.

Among the primary representatives of a third medieval epic genre, courtly epic, the Old French Arthurian romances of Chrétien de Troyes—the source of the basic form and content of this genre throughout European literary traditions of the medieval period—wiving functions less as the basic narrative motivator of an entire episode or indeed an entire epic than simply as the means to the (still necessary) marriage that supplies, sometimes seemingly almost incidentally, the narrative's hero with a bride—usually one whom he has somehow saved or served in the course of the narrative.[41] But in all such cases, the political requirements of appropriate rank are—again almost incidentally—met, or the match is simply rejected. The fact that such marriages both take place and are socio-politically appropriate in such a seemingly automatic fashion does not compromise the normative political requirements of this mode, but in fact reinforces them: in this genre they have (generally) become automatic, no longer necessarily requiring the focused attention of the narrative itself, for the essential political foundation of the practice and its principles are unquestioned. In the establishing preface to the Middle High German *Parzival* by Wolfram von Eschenbach (based in part on Chrétien's unfinished *Perceval, le Conte du Graal*), for instance, Parzival's father, Gahmuret, while voyaging to foreign lands almost incidentally happens upon the unmarried Queen Belakâne, who is besieged by multiple armies, including that of Isenhart, who has died as a result of her rejection of his suit for her. Gahmuret wins her as bride by defeating the besieging armies and thus rescuing her. Later, after he has abandoned her (which seems just as automatic, since she is Black and Muslim and thus according to medieval Christian ideology ultimately unsuitable as bride for a Christian European knight), he wins the European Christian Queen Herzeloyde as bride through his triumphant performance in the pre-tournament on the eve of an actual tournament, staged specifically to provide her with a husband.[42] Gahmuret seems initially uninterested in a wife, but ultimately acquiesces; in courtly epic it often seems that wiving is an activity in which the hero engages at best reluctantly, briefly, but necessarily successfully.[43]

An even more convoluted conception of bridal quest or wiving is found in the fourteenth- or fifteenth-century Old Yiddish Arthurian romance *Vidvilt*.[44] One might do better here to leave aside the term "wiving" and coin a term to designate the practice here introduced as "husbanding," which effectively stands the genre on its head in comparison to Thomas Kerth's description of the normative practice:

> The overwhelming majority of bridal quests are structured solely from the perspective of the wooer, and logically so, since in most cultures it is, at least officially, the male who initiates the courting ritual. The main conflict in the quest does not concern the willingness of the bride to accept the proposal of her wooer, but whether the prospective father-in-law deems the wooer of suf-

> ficient status to marry his daughter. The bride herself is almost always a relatively passive figure in these negotiations. . . . The elevation of the bride to a subject of the action demands that the traditional analysis of the text based upon the bipolar conflict of status between wooer and father in the bridal quest be reconsidered to include a third point in a triangular competition to assert prominence.[45]

That triangulation becomes precisely the issue in the Old Yiddish *Vidvilt*. In the narrative's establishing prelude, at Pentecost (the pre-conflictual setting of harmony and equilibrium typical for the beginning—and often also the ending—of an Arthurian romance), a mysterious knight appears outside Arthur's castle on what initially almost seems a wiving expedition, suggestively offering Queen Guinevere the intimate gift of a belt, even more suggestively extended to her on the upraised "tip of his lance" (st. 139; he refuses to enter the castle and thus offers the gift to her from horseback outside the castle wall), which after consultation with Arthur's council is rejected (on the grounds that kings are to grant unsolicited gifts, not receive them), which prompts the knight to take offense and challenge the entire court to combat. Sir Gawain accepts the challenge, is defeated, and is thus obligated to accompany the knight, who leads him over the course of a month-long forced-march ride to the Otherworld, where the knight's purpose finally becomes clear—to fetch as a husband for his daughter the greatest knight at the court of the world-famous King Arthur, that is, Gawain. What initially seemed a wiving expedition by a potentially marriageable knight thus turns out to have been a matrilocal "husbanding" expedition by the father of a marriageable princess, which seriously disturbs the equilibrium of the Arthurian world by placing its best knight, Gawain, who is also the renowned womanizer of the genre, in the magical Otherworld (from which there is allegedly no return, even for a consummate hero such as Gawain), bound to a—from the necessarily masculist perspective of the narrative—cumbersome and obstructive marriage.

Later—after Gawain has indeed laboriously managed to return to Arthur's court, which (years later) draws his son, Vidvilt (the narrative's actual protagonist), after him from the Otherworld—Vidvilt is likewise fetched from Arthur's court, also by a mysterious stranger, but this time *not* the father of, but rather the lady-in-waiting of a marriageable princess, this one named Lorel, and not for the immediate purpose of marrying the princess but instead first to save her and her entire kingdom from a giant and his demonic mother, who has apparently killed (although in fact only bewitched) Lorel's father for having rejected another wiving suit (by the giant). Only after having rescued the princess and (avenged) her father would Vidvilt be granted the princess as bride, for Lorel has now been promised to anyone who would save her mother and rescue/avenge her father. Thus in taking on the quest, Vidvilt is effectively fetched as (potential) husband by his future bride's lady-in-waiting, who functions as proxy in a husbanding quest in much the same way as his maternal grandfather had fetched his father (albeit under radically differing circumstances). Along the way from Arthur's to Lorel's court, Vidvilt successfully champions another maiden (st. 49,1–57,2),[46] who consequently presents her own marriage claims on Vidvilt with some vigor. He refuses to marry her because in his view he has, in taking on the initial quest, already committed himself as future husband to Lorel. Consequently, after his arrival at the court of Lorel's father, she and Vidvilt are betrothed (st. 64,11–68,2). In addition to his primary task, numerous other adventures obstruct the marriage, however, and Vidvilt must along the way reject a further marriage proposal tendered by a king whom he has saved from a dragon, who offers him the reward of his daughter in marriage (st. 96,1 ff.). Vidvilt again refuses the offer explicitly because he has promised himself to Lorel, despite the fact that he is ultimately cured of his debilitating wound (received in battle with the dragon) by this king's daughter. During the period of enforced muteness imposed on him by the defeated giant's mother (st. 109,13–126a,5), however, that king goes ahead with his plan for the wedding and invites marriage guests, among them Vidvilt's (long separated) parents, Princess Lorel and her family, and Arthur and his court. Having finally fulfilled his vow of silence, Vidvilt speaks with Lorel, whose now restored father reminds him of his betrothal, while the other king insists on Vidvilt's obligation to his daughter. In a scene of juridical decision, Arthur decrees that Vidvilt is to marry Lorel. Thus Vidvilt, as Lorel's successful champion, does finally marry her (st. 109,13–126,5). This spousal expedition, whose trajectory spanned practically the entirety of the Vidvilt section of the narrative (the majority of the epic), is, as was also the case with his own father's fetching by the mysterious knight (who was to become Vidvilt's grandfather) in the prelude to that primary narrative, in fact an overt "husbanding" expedition that comprises several offers of marriage to the groom by the potential brides or their agents or proxies, precluding any and all active wiving engagement on his part.

It is difficult to classify Elia Levita's Old Yiddish בבא דאנטונא Bovo *d'Antona* in terms of its epic sub-genre: while it displays some few affinities to the courtly epic, it is generally post-courtly in conception and likewise exhibits clear anticipations of the *romanzo cavalleresco* of the sixteenth-century Italian tradition.[47] In any case, it turns very specifically on the issue of the noble hero's marriage, although not in the form typical of wiving as represented in minstrel epic or courtly epic.[48] Even so, nowhere in this text is wiving the central narrative focus, and although wiving expeditions do occur in the text, the narrative's hero, Bovo, never conducts one but is instead himself, much like Vidvilt, the object of the husbanding attentions of more than one would-be bride.

Although Bovo belongs to the high aristocracy, the fickle fortune typical of the genre temporarily makes of him a purchased slave and stable-boy of a foreign king, whose aggressive daughter, Druzeyne, makes overtly erotic advances toward him, leading eventually to their mutual love and marriage at the tale's conclusion. Bovo initially "wins" her in a tournament, only immediately to have to save the entire kingdom from the besieging Muslims of the Suldan, "sultan," which results in his lawful betrothal to the princess by the willing king, but he is then immediately betrayed into the Suldan's hands, to whom Bovo's nemesis at court has contrived to send him on a Uriah-gambit mission. The Suldan then gives him the choice between conversion to Islam or death, only to allow his rescue from execution by his own (the Suldan's) aggressively amorous daughter, Margarete. The hero eventually escapes prison and returns to Europe to seek Druzeyne, only to find her wedding feast in progress, since she is being forced to marry against her will, as a result of a conventional wiving expedition. Bovo rescues her and escapes with her to a forest idyll, where eventually twins are born to them. Ill fortune then separates Bovo and Druzeyne, such that each thinks the other dead. After further adventures, Margarete writes to Bovo that her father, the Suldan, is dead and that a rival is now, via a conventional (martial) wiving expedition, attempting to force marriage on her. Bovo rescues her, and on the condition of her conversion to his faith, they agree to marry. Druzeyne hears of the wedding, comes to the wedding feast with the twins, "rescues" Bovo from this "inappropriate" marriage, and marries him herself, having made explicit to Bovo that each of them has now rescued the other at the last moment from marriage outside their own mutual vow of fidelity (st. 633). As a typical example of the non-European female Other, Margarete is personally and politically active and openly and even aggressively operates in the interest of her own pleasure (st. 234),[49] and despite having loved and pursued Bovo for several hundred stanzas, she is immediately prepared to marry his foster brother, Teyrets, the European consolation prize, as it were, when, at the epic's conclusion, Bovo becomes unavailable to her through his marriage to Druzeyne (st. 636).[50]

As noted earlier, there are no positively valued or successful wiving expeditions or episodes in this narrative, whose primary female characters are, moreover, as active as men in pursuing their spouses, sometimes unconventionally so, since on the model of Christian epic, Christian women are conventionally passive (despite the notable exceptions of, for instance, Brünhild and Herzeloyde, noted above, who nonetheless do not *actively* pursue marriage), while Muslim women—if and when they appear there—are both aggressive and overtly sexual, conforming to the obviously already functional patterns of proto-Eurocentric characterization.[51] That pattern seems clearly operative here, as well, except that, significantly, Druzeyne too is quite active in her pursuit of Bovo as lover and later as husband.[52]

While neither the hero of this narrative nor any overt and conventional wiving proxy exhibits any musical abilities, there is nonetheless an interesting twist on that issue in this text, for in keeping with the dual motifs of musicianship and disguise by means of which marital interest is to be elicited, in *Bovo* Druzeyne journeys to the impending wedding celebration of Bovo and Margarete while disguised as a beggar/musician, who considers: אוב איך איין פפֿעניג קונט איין נעמן · / מיט מיינר לייער וויל איך דא אום ווינדן · אונ' וויל דריין זינגן מיט מיינן קינדן: (st. 617, 5–8), "Perhaps I can earn a penny. I will go around with my lyre and sing with my children." She first plays at the inn in order to pay for her room and board (618), and then:

צו מורגש שטילט זי זיך בֿור דעם פאליש דאר·
אונ' הוב אן מיט איר לייער צו קלינגן·
אונ' איין ליד הט זי גימכֿט גנץ אונ' גאר·
בֿון בבֿא אונ' דרוזייאנה ווש זי דריין זינגן·
אונ' וויא זי אין איינם וואלד גילעגן וואר·
אונ' בֿון מקברון אונ' פעלוקן מיט אלי דינגן·
אונ' וואש זי מיט אננדר האטן גיהנדילט·
דא זי אים לאנד ווארן אום גיוואנדילט:
(st. 619)[53]

> In the morning, she took up a position in front of the palace and began playing her lyre and singing a song that she had composed that was all about Bovo and Druzeyne, and how she was living in a forest, and about Makabrun and Pelukan and everything else, and what they had done with each other as they made their way through the land.

Bovo hears the song and wishes to question the foreign musician, but predictably she escapes back to the inn (st. 620–621), where she prepares her sons to lure Bovo to the grand scene of anagnorisis (st. 624–635), which eventually leads directly to their long-awaited marriage. Druzeyne thus assumes the role as quasi-"husbanding" proxy whose actions bring about the marriage between the object of the suit and the proper bride, who is in this case, herself, although her disguise that masks her race, class, and profession effectively displaces that identity even more effectively than, for instance, did Horant's assumed disguise. Her disguise also includes musicianship and public performance, not in the Tristan-Iseut mode, since the text does not suggest that Bovo taught her to sing and play, although some hint of mentorship does arise in the detail that he taught her how to mix and use the preparation that turns her skin black (a component of her musician's disguise). Her musical skills are not identified as supernatural, but her performance does have precisely the character necessary to draw Bovo's attention, that is, the intimate bit of information shared only by Bovo and Druzeyne that reveals her identity to him.[54] Thus Druzeyne's mission leads successfully to marriage by means of a journey to a foreign court, disguise, singing, *List*, and a recognition scene, all as components of an elaborate "husbanding" quest.

To move to the genre of Italian Renaissance epic of the fifteenth and sixteenth centuries, the relevant Christian exemplars are Boiardo's *Orlando Innamorato* and the quasi-continuation of that lengthy fragment by Ariosto's *Orlando Furioso*, which are likewise of primary importance for the single extant example of a Middle Yiddish *romanzo cavalleresco*, the *Pariz and Viene*.[55] In this subgenre, just as in courtly epic, love in its courtly or hyper-courtly sense dominates much of the narrative. As C. P. Brand notes on *Orlando Furioso*, "The love affairs of paladins and pagans and of many of those that they meet, wayfarers, inn-keepers, damsels in distress, are recounted so frequently and at such length that the poem comes to resemble an anthology of love stories."[56] Even so, wiving as such plays a subdued (but still essential) role, although wiving expeditions in a strict sense are quite rare. With one exception, they appear only in the stories of ephemerally introduced characters (in a narrative characterized by a veritable flood of such characters) and are *explicitly negative* models of wiving, since they result in violent and destructive military expeditions, due to the conventional paternal rejection of the suitor's petition, as, for instance, in the story of Lydia and Alcestes (*Orlando Furioso*, 34, 16–43).[57] Interestingly, however, there is one courtship narrative that involves two of the epic's central characters and is thus essential to the plot: the courtship of Bradamante and Ruggiero, which in fact functions as the subplot by means of which this sprawling, proto-picaresque tale finally achieves closure. It involves a significant number of the typical components of the normative wiving sequence. Even after several thousand stanzas of their ongoing courtship, that standard sequence suddenly begins officially, as it were, with the presentation by the groom of a suit to the bride's parents (canto 44), which is necessarily rejected, because a better match—with a landed and Christian knight, in this case, Leo, the son of the emperor of Constantinople—is planned by the parents. The former Muslim Ruggiero has, however, already converted—specifically for the purpose of gaining the Christian maiden as bride (as is usually the case in such epic conversions of the otherwise "noble heathen" Muslim heroes)—and now embarks on a period of quasi-exile during which he gains both the eternal friendship of Leo (canto 45) and the crown of Bulgaria (canto 46), rendering him acceptable to Bradamante's parents, resulting in the concluding wedding (canto 46). Thus even in this epic sub-genre where wiving as such plays a far less prominent role than in other epic forms of the later Middle Ages and Renaissance, a stereotypical wiving episode can still be enacted and integrated into the central plot. Most importantly, in the case of the match between Bradamante and Ruggiero, Ariosto quite specifically engages in the conventional practice of legitimizing the political authority of his patron and lord, the Ferrarese Duke Alfonso d'Este, by means of providing his featured ancestors, Bradamante and Ruggiero, with a glorious and heroic paean. Even at this late date the conventional political purpose of epic wiving continues to function clearly and explicitly.

The sub-genre "Renaissance epic" represented, as noted earlier, in Middle Yiddish by the sixteenth-century פאריז אונ' וויענה *Pariz and Viene*, is a post-courtly, non-Arthurian romance about the love of the hero, Pariz, a noble knight and son of a councillor at court, and Viene, the daughter of his king, Dolfin.[58] Due to the politically conditioned impossibility of the marriage of a princess and a vassal, Pariz ultimately chooses self-exile rather than facing the king's wrath at his marriage suit (presented by Pariz's father), during which time he has many adventures, including, finally (in Turkish disguise), the rescue of King Dolfin from Mamluk captivity in Egypt. In the meantime, Viene has steadfastly refused any another marriage match, insisting on her own right of consent. Dolfin promises his daughter as a reward to his rescuer, thus accepting an unknown but at least nominally noble and ostensibly Muslim Turk as a son-in-law, while he had refused on principle his own Christian vassal's son (st. 691). In agreeing to the "Turk's" request for Viene's hand in marriage, however, Dolfin quizzically acknowledges that he cannot and will not force her to marry (st. 642)—although at this point in the narrative he had already imprisoned her for several years for precisely that noncompliance with his will. When the "Turk" reveals himself as Pariz, however, Dolfin ultimately agrees to the match, and Pariz and Viene are married.

It should be noted that the ubiquitous insistence in such epic texts on class status as determinative of the suitability of marriage partners has nothing specifically and directly to do with any imagined Jewish identity of the characters or any imagined ייחוס- "lineage"-motif—since precisely that same motif is of primary importance in general in Christian courtly epic and even in the specific "source" texts of Yiddish epic. Nonetheless, when those Christian motifs appeared in a Jewish cultural context such as Yiddish epic, they may well have taken on a radically different valence for the Ashkenazic audience. In *Pariz and Viene*, for instance, even Viene—whose erotic interests are long thwarted by her father's status-conscious conception of wiving—expresses her own version of (conventional) class prejudice when she discovers that Pariz is the disguised knight who has championed her: she praises God that he is noble and not a peasant (st. 218–219). But only then does her nurse and lady-in-waiting, Isabele, disabuse her of even this self-serving level of naiveté, pointing out to Viene that she is after all royal and that no matter how noble Pariz may be, he is not only not royal, but indeed the son of an actual vassal of her father and thus by no means of a status appropriate for marriage to her (st. 220).

Everyone involved in this complex matrix of relationships knows the rules of (genre-defined) wiving and has his or her own self-serving application of them, which in every case is rigid within its own definitional strictures. More than once, however, Viene claims that her father will have to consult with her before arranging a marriage (st. 274, 276, 283–284, 315), her expectation apparently being that her father will accede to her will.[59] In the event, he does not consult with her, although he does not in fact force her into marriage with his preferred son-in-law, but it likewise turns out that she is quite mistaken in imagining that as a consequence of his not so forcing her he will also allow her to exercise her own will in choosing a partner. Instead, as already noted, he has her imprisoned. However else one might interpret such parental behavior, it is most certainly not to be imagined as a conventional variation on the standard Jewish *yikhes* motif; indeed one might well identify it as monstrous and inhuman.[60] In any case it is a representation of a Christian-conceived wiving-status motif as something otherworldly, indeed something quite non-Jewish in the extreme. It is not accidental that the Jewish author of the Middle Yiddish *Pariz and Viene*, unlike Levita in *Bovo*, never teases the audience with hints that any of his protagonists might be Jewish.

Of paramount interest in this epic is the mode of initial courtship, which is carried out by the suitor, Pariz, by means of musical performance. As such, it constitutes the most extensive episode of courtship via musicianship in the early Yiddish epic corpus. While he later engages in more (genre-conditioned) conventional displays of martial skills in tournaments as a means to demonstrate his knightly prowess and thus gain her love, even at the point of his introduction into the narrative, the hero's musical abilities deserve immediate mention alongside his conventionally heroic martial prowess:

דער דוזיג יונג דער היש פּריז
ער וואר נון לעכֿט בֿון בֿיפֿציהן יארן.
ער האט איין שטערק גלייך וויא איין ריז
דענוכֿט וואר ער גערן און בֿור ווארן.
זיין אידלקייט גאר וואל ביוויז
דש ער זיין צייט ניט האט ור לורן.
אין לייאן שרייבן האט ער טון שטודירן
דרויף האט ער בֿור לענגשט גישערפֿט זיין הירן:

אונ' אך אין אלן זייטן שפּיל
אונ' אין זויטן אידל דינגן.
עז אים אין הערצן וואל גיפֿיל
ער קונט וואל טאנצן אונ' אך שפּרינגן.
דר צו האט ער גילערנט ויל
דיא נוטן בֿון דער שולפֿא זינגן.
קיין לושטיג שטוק האט ער ניט אויז גילושן
דש ער ניט קונט אלז וואל אויז דער מושן:
(st. 32–33)

That youth was named Pariz. Now, he was some fifteen years old. He was as strong as a giant but was happily without entanglements. His nobility well demonstrated that he had not wasted his time. He had studied reading and writing. He had long since sharpened his mind therein, and also in the playing of all stringed instruments and in such noble things his heart took great delight, he could dance well and also leap, and he had learned much about music from singing solfège. There was no charming or lovely thing that he could not do exceedingly well.

With the aid of his trusty companion, Odoardo, Pariz turns his musical abilities to the use that seems almost conventional in early Yiddish epic, that is, to serenade the beloved (Viene) in her father's castle:[61]

מאן שפריכט וואל אך וויא גלייך אונ' גלייך
דש זעלביג שטעץ גיזעלטציך גערן.
ער קונט וואל אך אויף שפילי זאייטן
קיין בעשירן שלעגר ואנד מאן ניט אין ווייטן:

נון האטן זי אין איינש גיבוייט
זי וואלטן גין מיט אננדר שלאגן.
וואר עז אורגיל הארפף אודר איין לוייט
דש ווייש איך אויך נון ניט צו זאגן.
פריז מיט זיינם גיזעל דער טרוייט
צוואו שטונד אי עז ביגאן צו טאגן.
גינגן זי הרוייש מיט אירן בעשטן וואופֿן
אונטר די קאמר דא וויענה וואז אינן שלופֿן:

אונ' ווארן שלאגן אזא זוישן
דש איז איין קראנקש העטן מאכֿן גינעזן.
גאר אופֿט ווארן זי זי אזו גרוישן
גאר וואל גיבֿיל איר אך דש ווען.
זיא קונט אבר צו מולט ניא וואוישן
ווער די גוטן שלעגר ווערן גיוועזן.
דער קויניג דער הורט אך דז גישלעג גערן
אבר ער וואלט יא וואוישן ווער זיא ווערן:

דש זויס גישלעג אים וואל גיפֿיל
אז ניא מין וואז גיהוירט אויף זאייטן.
דש אין נון דוכֿט קיין אנדר שפיל
דש ווער דר בייא ניט ווערט צוואו מייטן.
(st. 51,5–54,4)

It is indeed also said that two like things gladly consort together: he could also play stringed instruments well; no better musician was to be found far and wide. Now they together decided that they would go play together. Whether it was organ, harp, or lute, I cannot tell you. Two hours before day began to break, Pariz and his trusted companion went out with their best weapons beneath the chamber in which Viene slept. And they played so sweetly that they could have healed a sick person. Very often did they greet her thus; very well

> did it also please her. She could, however, never recognize who the good musicians were. The king was also delighted to hear the playing, but he did indeed wish to know who they were. The sweet music—whose like has never again been heard on stringed instruments—pleased him well, so that it seemed to him that no other playing was worth two mites.

Since Pariz and Odoardo make a point of keeping their identity secret, King Dolfin then organizes a court dance and invites all musicians to play, hoping—as it turns out, in vain—to recognize his favorite musicians among them (54–56). Eventually the king has an ambush laid to capture the musicians when they serenade the princess the next time. After a street battle that leaves six of the king's men wounded and four dead, Pariz and Odoardo nonetheless escape (st. 63–72), and איר האנדל דער בליב גאנץ פֿור בורגן (st. 73,2), "their affair remained quite secret."

The emotional effect of the music is quite obvious in the delight of both Viene and her father, although secondary effects on them are rather different. Clearly for Dolfin, his inability to identify the musicians—even at the very walls of his royal castle—transforms the issue into one of power politics, which leads him to lay the ambush to capture the musicians, resulting in the slaughter of his palace guard, which then causes the entire affair to be construed as open rebellion, in response to which the king predictably orders the musicians tracked down and killed. Their benign and soothing behavior as musicians would have earned them a reward—as hirelings, of course, and certainly not as appropriate suitors of the princess, especially were the king to find out that it was Pariz who was the instigator of the serenading.

For Viene the delight with the music also led to an interest in the identity of the musicians but then further to the realization that the musicians were singing specifically to her and בֿון אירר ליבשאפֿט וועגן (st. 59,6), "for the sake of her love," which quite transformed her own participation in the situation, which had therewith become no longer merely a matter of aesthetics but one of erotics. The effect of this realization was immediate and dramatic:

> זיא נאם זיכֿש אן אין זוילכֿר מושן
> דש איר וואר דש הערץ אין בֿוייער ברענה
> דש זויס גישליג האט אירש זו טון אנצוינדן
> איר גרושי ליבשפֿט קוינט מן ניט דר גרוינדן:
> (st. 81,5–8)

> It affected her so seriously that her heart was inflamed. The sweet playing had so enkindled her heart that the depth of her great love could not be fathomed.

It seems at this point that Old Yiddish epic has entered new territory, for suddenly the conventional binary available to express female participation in amatory relationships—that is, the aggressively active and open lust of Druzeyne (and, to a lesser extent, Margarete) in *Bovo* and the passive, devoted, and chaste—is transcended.[62] Viene has become a typical amatory heroine of Renaissance epic, for whose sake the Renaissance language of eros makes its entrance into the Yiddish language (if it had not done so before; cf. chapter 2, above):

איר הערץ ווז ולייש אונ' ניט אויז שטיין
קיין אייז העט אירז קענן דר קעלטן.
אזו הט אירש גיווערמט אונ' מאכֿן ברענן
אליין דער דינשט און דש זי וואז דען דינר קענן:

דז זי נורט וואושט דז איר צו ליב
מן הט גישלאגן אונ' גיזונגן.
אזו איין הולד אין אירן הערצן בליב
קיין זולכֿן הט ניא מייד צו יונגן.
אונ' דז גיבערד דז זיא נון טריב
הב איך ואר דר צילט מיט מיינר צונגן.
דאז שטעכֿן וור בירייט איר לייד צו טרוישטן
דו וואור אלז ערשט גיוועשט נורט צו דעם בישטן:

דש שטעכֿן וואש גיוועשט איין שטרוך
דז דו מאכֿט אויףּ שלאגן די ולאמן.
ור וואר עז איר די זיל אויז צוך
אונ' אופּט שפראך זי צו אירר אמן.
אז גוֹט שטעץ איז אים הימל הוך
אזו גיוויש זיין די דו קאמן.
אין ווייש גיקלייט אונ' אזו ורישליך שטרייטן
די דו זו זיס אופּט שלוגן מיט אירן זייטן:

ער הוט די לאנץ טון אין מיך שטעקן
דז ער מיין הערץ שיר הוט טון טיילן.
עז איז נון פֿאל אין אלי עקן
מיט אייטל הערטי שארפּי פּיילן.
אונ' ביז איך אין ניט קאן אנטפלעקן
ווערן מיר מיין וואונדן נימר היילן.
דער קאן ניט אנדרש זיין אז אידלש בלוטן
אן זיינר גרושן שטערק אונ' ווערק זו גוטן:

(st. 107,5–110)

Her heart was flesh and not of stone. No ice could have cooled it: so much had the [lover's] service alone—without her knowing the servant—warmed it and made it burn. From the fact that she but knew that someone had played music and sung for her sake, such an affection remained in her heart—no maiden had ever had such affection for a young man, and the behavior that she now

> displayed, I told earlier with my own tongue. The tournament was organized to comfort her in her sorrow. At first all of that resulted in nothing but the worst.[63] The tournament functioned like straw that made the fire flame up. In truth her soul left her, and she often said to her nurse: "As God is ever in the high heavens, you may be just as certain that those who came there clothed in white and fought so boldly, were the ones who often here so sweetly played on the strings. He has thrust his lance into me so that he has almost split my heart in two. It is now full in all its parts with nothing but hard and sharp darts. And until I can discover who he is, my wounds will never heal. Because of his great might and very good works, he can only be of noble blood."

Later, when Dolfin returns home and reports on the outcome of the tournament in Paris whose purpose was to determine the realm's most beautiful woman, his words describing Viene's victorious champion in the tournament have a—by this point in the narrative—predictable effect:

דיא וארן וויענה הערץ רעכֿט אנצוינדן:

אויףֿ דיזי ווערק וואר זיא ביטראכֿט
ווער דו מויכֿט זיין דער אידל הערן.
דער אזו מיט גוינשטקליכֿר מאכֿט
זיא האט ביהאלטן בייא דער עירן.
זיא שוויג אזו ביז עז וואורד נאכֿט
איר פיין וואז זיך אוימדר מערן.
אין אירן הערצן וואז זיא עז אלז טראגן
אונ' צו איזבעלה וואז זיא אזודר זאגן:

או ליבי או טרוייטי שוועשטר מיין
וואז זול איך טון וויא זול איכֿש האלטן.
בֿון שטונד צו שטונד מירט זיך מיין פיין
דש ווייזט דיר וואל מיין בויז גישטאלטן.
איין ולאם קאם אין מיין הערץ היניין
אונ' נוימר לוט זי מירש דרקאלטן.
איך הב דיר אופֿט גיזגט מיט מונד ביטר
וויא מיך אים הערצן ליבט איין אידלר ריטר:

אונ' איך האלט גיוויש קיין אנדרר ניט
אז דען מיר הוט בֿון גיזגט מיין עטן.
איז דער זו זויס גישלאגן הוט מיט
דען פפֿוייפֿן אורגלן טרומבעטן.
דער דוזיג הוט מיך בֿור וואר גישמיט
אין דיקי ענגי אייזיני קעטן.
מיט ייעמרליכֿן טוט ווערט ער מיך וינדן
קומט ער ניט באלד מיין הערץ אוףֿ בינדן:

איך ווייש דש ער מיך הוט הולט
די גוטן ווערק טונן מירש ווייזן·
אונ' ווען איך אין ניט ליבן זולט
זו מוישט וואל זיין מיין הערץ אויז אייזן·
(st. 149,8–153,4)

They quite inflamed Viene's heart. She was thinking about who the noble lord might be, who had preserved her honor with such benevolent might. She remained thus silent until night fell. Her suffering was ever increasing. She was bearing it all in her heart, and she thus said to Isabele: "O, my dear and beloved sister! What am I to do? How am I to bear it? Hour-by-hour my pain increases. That is proven to you by my poor appearance. A flame has entered my heart and never lets it cool. I have often said to you with bitter words how a noble knight loves me in his heart.[64] And I think for certain that the one of whom my father has spoken is none other than the one who played such sweet music with pipe, organ, and trumpet. That one has indeed shackled me with thick and tight iron chains. Unless he soon comes to unbind my heart, he will find me miserably dead. I know that he is true to me. His fine deeds prove it to me. And if I were not to love him, my heart would have to be of iron."

When Viene later, in the first *recognitio* scene, confronts the still reticent Pariz with the objects that she has stolen from his underground vault and that demonstrate his clear connection (if not identity) with her tournament champion, her first words confess that her heart is still aflame and maintain that his is, too (st. 256, 5). When she then details her "case" that Pariz is himself her secret admirer, it is his role as singer/musician that she mentions first (followed then by his championing her cause as the white knight in the tournament in Paris; st. 257, 6–258, 4). His initial singing and serenading of her is for her the identifying act that won her love and likewise defines his love.

The final example of early Yiddish heroic wiving to be considered here lies beyond any overt link to the literary traditions of wiving in the majority culture surrounding Ashkenaz, for the Old Yiddish מעשה בריעה וזמרי *The Tale of Briyo and Zimro* is a radically different kind of text and focuses quite clearly on the issue of wiving, albeit without reference to the motif as realized in Christian epic. This text, while narrating a heroic tale, differs substantively from the Yiddish variants on Christian epic discussed thus far, most strikingly in the fact that it is a prose tale, not a verse epic, and its origin is almost exclusively in Jewish and not Christian literary traditions.[65] The requisite king is Hurk(e)nis, whose chief court legal advisor and judge, Zimro, sees Briyo, daughter of the chief priest, Feygin, is spellbound by her beauty, and they immediately and rather undramatically fall in love, leading to Feygin's rejection of successive marriage proposals presented by the community's four elders, formally and properly acting on Zimro's father's behalf, by the king on Zimro's behalf, and again by the king at the prompting of his son, Zimro's boon companion, all explicitly because Feygin wishes to avoid dishonor through accepting into the family someone of lower (e.g., non-priestly) social rank.[66] As he argues to the king, "Dear my lord king, would you advise me to join myself to a lower lineage than my own? All Jews will ridicule me!"[67] As is a recurring motif in such narratives (in the first and last presentation of Zimro's marriage suit), he specifies that he would rather kill his daughter himself than give her to Zimro: איך וועלט זיא אי דר טרענקן "I'd rather drown her" (*EYT*, p. 360 and, similarly, p. 362). Feygin himself acknowledges that he is willing to risk defiance of the king and indeed die for that defiance in order to prevent the marriage. The king then does condemn him to death for his obstinacy, although in fact Feygin is not actually executed. Briyo and Zimro vow never to marry anyone but each other and seal their vow with what proves to be a fatal kiss, which leads to her death (דרום זול קֿיינר אייניש קוסן · ווען איינר בֿון איינום הין וועק גֿיט "For that reason, no one should kiss another person when departing"; *EYT*, p. 365), while Zimro's death results from another kiss, which ultimately then leads, rather surprisingly, to their wedding in Paradise.

On the basis of the wiving praxis of the Yiddish epics and the heroic prose tale "Briyo and Zimro," here analyzed, it seems possible to draw some preliminary conclusions both about the Jewish treatment of this motif and about some strategies employed by the Jewish writers in their cultural translation of the motif. In the translation and transformation into Yiddish of medieval Christian heroic narrative in which wiving functioned overtly to legitimize the feudal political structures, Jewish authors developed several strategies of adaptation, but one overarching tendency is clear: it seems that they generally avoided those texts in which the feudal wiving motif in its overt political function is the primary motor of the plot. Beyond the single instance of *Duke Horant*—the earliest quasi-secular epic adapted into Yiddish—there is no evidence of the existence in Yiddish of Christian epics such as *König Rother* in which wiving so functions. Among the other extant Yiddish texts in this cluster of epic genres, what one finds is the result of a kind of quasi-editorial pre-selection such that from the perspective of the normative Christian pattern, wiving practice in Old Yiddish epic is consistently unorthodox.

If indeed the Old Yiddish *Duke Horant* was adapted from a no-longer-extant Christian source text, then, despite the fact that the fragmentary nature of the text precludes any conclusions about the ultimate outcome and thus the comprehensive mode of wiving praxis in that narrative, the fragment itself already seems non-normative, for what is extant there presents a bridal quest conducted not by a diplomatic embassy or a commando detachment that will win the bride by means of negotiation or surgical-strike abduction, respectively, but rather by a wiving party that has assumed the theatrical roles of both political exiles and merchants and whose chief agent operates by unorthodox means to win Princess Hilde's favor, not through diplomatic or martial skills, but by means of his magical, otherworldly ability to sing. Admittedly, even though the canonical bridal-quest epic *König Rother* makes use of the merchant gambit, the musical motif complicates the Yiddish text's relationship with that mode. And as already noted, the character slot of marriage broker as aristocratic and supernaturally talented singer is not unique to the Yiddish adaptation but indeed essential to the pan-Germanic Horant tradition, where that character is all but ubiquitously defined by his supernatural singing ability. This trait in the Yiddish text is then obviously not peculiar to it, nor the result of the Jewish poet's invention. But the familiarity of Horant's peculiar ability does not render it any less non-normative—within the larger tradition of wiving-epic—as a negotiating tool employed by a wiving proxy.

In *Vidvilt*, the anti-wiving mode takes a different tack: the spouse fetched is not the bride but the groom, and the spouse is then not fetched—as conventionally—by a designated vassal proxy, but rather in one case by the bride's father, and in the other by an aristocratic lady-in-waiting of the prospective bride's court. The initial Gawein episode is nothing less than a matrilocal groom quest, when the hero's future maternal grandfather journeys to Arthur's court to fetch home the most promising of the Arthurian knights, Gawein, as husband for his daughter. The quest of the epic's eponymous hero is, as noted above, defined not merely by his normative defeat of a succession of bewitchments, giants, and dragons, but also by his managing to negotiate the complicated path through the marriage proposals aggressively asserted by a succession of nubile royal/aristocratic women, all of whom in fact have genre-defined claims on him that would have provided sufficient cause for marriage in any medieval courtly epic. Just as Vidvilt's father was actually called out, defeated in battle, and thus "legally" fetched home (quasi-abducted) by the bride's father, so, too, Vidvilt is—even as he fulfills the canonical duties of the questing knight—with respect to normative wiving behavior, antinomial: even as knight-champion, he is in an overt sense the passive object of female groom-questing, and at the narrative's conclusion—where a king typically distributes brides to the deserving knights—King Arthur "distributes" Vidvilt as groom to one of the deserving maidens.

Likewise in *Bovo d'Antona*, it is again the groom who is the object of marital courtship: Bovo is courted successively by two aggressively amorous women, one problematically, obliquely, and not quite compellingly identified as Jewish, the other a Muslim, both interested in marriage, and both offering kingdoms as part of the marriage settlement, and in each case also defined by the socio-political superiority of the woman: they are the daughters of a king and sultan, respectively, while he is the (initially dispossessed) son of a mere duke. In a still more pragmatic sense, however, in the narrative confrontation of the characters: Bovo is the stable slave purchased by King Arminio, who then becomes the sexualized plaything of Princess Druzeyne, who makes a point of having him assigned to serve at her banquet, where she uses her position of power to manipulate him such that he is in a physically (as well as socially) vulnerable position so that she can force her lustful affection on him (e.g., in stealing a kiss under the table; st. 111). Later she accosts him in the stables and in a lengthy scene bullies him with her openly sexual attentions, kissing him again and even opening her blouse and shaking her naked breasts at him, suggestively and vulgarly deeming them "fine little titties" and irresistible "mouthfuls" (st. 135–136). She elopes with him while they are betrothed but not yet officially married and has vigorous intercourse with him by a spring under the open sky (st. 350), after which she and Bovo cohabit during the remainder of their flight, during their stay at the castle of Count Orayon, and later in the forest, where she ultimately bears twin sons (st. 441–444).

Bovo is also the object of the aggressively amorous attentions of the Muslim princess, Margarete, who, interestingly, is not characterized as nearly so sexually aggressive as Princess Druzeyne, although she is nonetheless not in the least reticent in advancing her interests; she actively engages in the political affairs of the sultan's court, saving Bovo from the gallows, negotiating a temporary reprieve for him, in order to give her time to convert him to Islam (so that she can marry him), and providing him with provisions while he is imprisoned. After his escape from prison and return to Europe, she summons him by international courier to rescue her from the marital and martial intentions of a neighboring king, who is conducting a conventional wiving venture, after which she offers herself to Bovo as bride and indeed converts from Islam in order to make herself eligible for that marriage. This sequence of actions clearly functions as a gender-inverted model of a wiving expedition. She thus mixes both the conventionally active male role in wiving and the unconventionally active female role.

Only in *Pariz and Viene* do the typical features of the wiving motif as found in a conventional Christian plot initially seem to be preserved, particularly in the father's rejection of the groom because of his specifically defined social status beneath that deemed acceptable for marriage, in this case because he is the bride's father's vassal. But the agency demonstrated by the bride-to-be undermines that conventionality altogether, since Viene rejects her parent's assumed right to decide her marital fate outright and then resolutely suffers the consequences of that rejection: she is hardly the conventionally passive maiden whose quasi-purchase is negotiated by the patriarchs of the groom's clan and her own. Nor is Pariz the typical groom: although he must rescue his bride as imprisoned "damsel in distress," before that rescue he must first rescue her father, who is imprisoned in an Egyptian dungeon. The bride is, however, imprisoned by her own parents in the dungeon of their home castle, and the hero is one of their vassals. His bridal quest, as it were, is thus peculiarly constructed, since the knightly deeds that he performs in order to win his bride do not *directly* enable his winning her or freeing her from prison; in each case, the actions performed that enable the courtship are anonymous or performed in disguise. Initially he and his comrade, Odoardo, serenade the princess and indeed the entire castle from the street by night and without ever identifying themselves, winning the affection of the princess; Pariz, disguised as the "White Knight," then wins the tournament in Vienne, accepting the prizes from the hands of Viene herself (st. 98); as the champion of Viene, he then later wins the tournament in Paris that was organized to determine the most beautiful woman in the entire French realm; later, while in self-exile and disguised as a Turk, he frees her father from prison in Egypt, in reward for which her father grants him Viene as bride. Not until the scene of anagnorisis in the dungeon and the following scene in which her father acquiesces to the marriage of Pariz and Viene is the hero's identity finally established for all.[68] It thus almost seems that the incognito Pariz repeatedly functions as his own wiving proxy. It is hardly a conventional bridal quest.

The central focus on wiving in *Briyo and Zimro* occurs in a strictly Jewish cultural context without direct connection to any Gentile tradition and thus without reference to the dynastic interests of representatives of feudal society.[69] This "abscncc" of a feudal substrate does not produce a motivational void in the narrative, as it would if the political impulse to wiving were simply subtracted from a narrative such as *König Rother*, however. Instead the entire social impulse toward courtship/marriage/wiving is manifested in one of its authentically (medieval) Jewish literary refractive forms: as a *yikhes* motif,[70] which necessarily demonstrates a radically different conception of wiving and a different view of the articulation of the literary and social function of wiving, which in the present analytical context presents an intriguing juxtaposition to the conventional mode of Christian wiving. The issue is complicated by means of the specific constellation of relationships that condition the presumed lack of "suitability" of the two partners. Unlike in the conventional case in Christian epic (e.g., *Paris e Viena*), where (the father of) one of the aristocratic partners is the actual or supposed vassal of the (father of the) other, in this staunchly Jewish tale, Briyo is the daughter of the כֹהֵן הַגָּדוֹל "high priest," Feygin, while Zimro is the finest Torah scholar, and thus also the chief judge, of the land; he is the grandson of a great lord of the people, "second only to the king." Obviously Feygin is constructed as the villain of the narrative insofar as he prevents the marriage of the lovers and thus ultimately although indirectly brings about their deaths. At the same time, however, one must note that, not surprisingly, much is going on beneath the narrative surface. After all, as high priest, Feygin is well aware of the rule that a בת־כהן "daughter of a priest" who marries a non-priest loses membership status in the priestly caste for herself and her descendants (since that status passes through the father). A marriage to Zimro would thus diminish both the social and the cultic status of his daughter and her offspring, and thus also his own current social status. In thus understandably opting to retain those various instantiations of status, he is, one might argue, acting both responsibly and legitimately, except insofar as in so doing he opposes the trajectory of the narrative as love story.

While one might initially be tempted to imagine that Yiddish adaptations of "exotic" Christian epic—as opposed to the "familiar" world of wiving in *Briyo and Zimro*—functioned in Jewish society only as a fantasy literature of the exotic world of the Christian aristocracy, the conditions of literary reception and cultural translation are here more complex, in precisely the same way as earlier suggested for the non-aristocratic, post-courtly Christian reception of courtly epic. For although *Briyo and Zimro* has its origin within strictly Jewish traditions (and exerts no later influence beyond those traditions), the specific details of its historical setting are undoubtedly almost as foreign to sixteenth-century European Ashkenazic culture as any Arthurian romance would have been. There had at that time been neither Jewish king nor high priest in Israel for one-and-a-half millennia, so that the specific *historical* form and function of those roles at the end of the Second Temple period (as in part, apparently, depicted in the tale) were no longer known or even *empirically* accessible to sixteenth-century Jews.[71] For a sixteenth-century Ashkenazic audience, the ancient priesthood was an institution that touched their lives at most only very tangentially, although it is not to be denied that it still had very obvious textual (and thus ultimately also very real) significance. With the destruction of the Second Temple by the Romans in 70 CE, the Temple cult in a practical sense came to an end, which (by means of a lengthy and complex process) precipitated the rise of the rabbinate as the central religious force in Judaism.[72] The conflict between Feygin and Zimro, that is, between the high priest and the Torah scholar who is empowered to judge the people in a quasi-rabbinical court, is then immediately obvious to twenty-first-century readers. The priestly opposition to the rabbinate and to marriage ties with a Torah scholar would have been perceived by the sixteenth-century audience as *legally* comprehensible but *socially* obstructive, since in fact no principle of Talmudic law would thus have been transgressed. As surely as the Arthurian *Vidvilt* was fantasy literature set in a fantasy world, so, too, did *Briyo and Zimro* take place—in some significant sense—in a fantasy world,[73] despite its centripetal Jewishness.

It does not seem accidental that of the literally scores of pre-courtly, courtly, and post-courtly Christian epics more or less "available" for adaptation into Yiddish in the fourteenth through sixteenth centuries, it was *Duke Horant*, *Bovo d'Antona*, *Pariz and Viene*, and *Vidvilt* that were chosen.[74] The representation of spousal quest in early Yiddish quasi-secular epic certainly functions as a significant motif across the genre and might well indicate a common Jewish approach to this literary issue during this period, and not simply a reactive Jewish rejection of the Christian praxis. The entire plot of *Horant* is predicated on a wiving expedition. *Bovo* begins with a catastrophic May-December marriage that (via murder) is quickly replaced by a lust-match; the eponymous hero later rescues his beloved at the last minute from an unwanted marriage and then comes close to marrying her before apparently losing her, almost marries a second princess before the first returns to rescue and marry him, leaving the abandoned second princess to marry his second-in-command. The tale of *Vidvilt* begins with a groom quest that brings together the eponymous hero's parents, while his own defining quest is predicated on the condition set at its initiation that its successful completion will put him in possession of the hand of the princess of the rescued land, although along the way, he is offered marriage with three further rescued maidens *qua* potential brides, and in the end it takes King Arthur himself to decide which of the competing finalist bachelorettes will have him.[75] The entirety of the plot of *Pariz and Viene* focuses on the systematic overcoming of the obstacles in the way of the eventual marriage of the title characters, that is, the anything but conventional princess and her (father's) intrepid vassal.

If the severely reduced Middle High German genre of *Spielmannsepik* is one essentially defined by wiving, one might almost propose early Yiddish quasi-secular epic as a genre defined by *anti-wiving*, subtly adapted to undo the wiving process conventional in Christian epic, not by altering the plots of specific source texts, but rather by means of culling or pre-selection of particular narratives for adaptation into Yiddish that are already provided with questionable anti-wiving practices, "husbanding" quests substituted for wiving quests, and by the insistent and recurring role, for instance, of socially transformative singing as a mode of wiving.

While many epics in the medieval and early modern Christian repertoire focus on marriage, not all or even most have that as their primary motif. It thus seems unlikely that this motif only accidentally dominates the corpus of early Yiddish quasi-secular epic. While it may well be the case that it was a motif of great interest to the Ashkenazic audience, some caution and some consideration of other causes for the choice of this particular subset of Christian epic for adaptation into Yiddish might be salutary here. Two of the primary plot motivators of medieval and early modern Christian epic were the theologically driven quest for the Holy Grail (variously construed in narrative of the period as the cup from which Jesus of Nazareth and his disciples drank at the Last Supper or as a quasi–horn of plenty that supplies devout Christians with sacral food and drink, among other possibilities) and the (in part) theologically based quest for the bloody slaughter of Muslim enemies in battle after battle and the imperialistic conquest of Muslim territory in the centuries-long, intercontinental conflict of Christendom and Islam. The Jewish literary response to the first of these two epic modes was complete silence, as it was also to the second, with the exception of Levita's *Bovo*, as will be treated in the following chapter. The elimination of entire—*and essential*—such sub-genres of Christian epic (based on their primary plot motifs) from the pool of texts available for adaptation into Yiddish would then in large part leave the subset of epic narratives driven by wiving or marriage as that pool of Christian epic acceptable for adaptation. Within that vast available pool, however, only certain texts were chosen for adaptation into Yiddish, in which the convention of spousal quest was subversive or at best antinomial, with unconventionally active brides and/or fetched grooms. It seems almost as if, parallel to the underlying insistence on the principle of primogeniture in the biblical book of Genesis that is then all but systematically undermined by the succession of foundational myths of the culture, in early Yiddish epic the conventional modality of marriage narrative is just as insistently undermined by the component epics chosen to populate the genre. Quasi-editorial pruning and thus cultural translation take place then not through radical revision of the motifs in the Christian source texts themselves, but rather by means of a strict pre-selection of which texts are appropriate for such cultural translation and integration.

Notes

1. Sandra Silberstein, "Ideology as Process: Gender Ideology in Courtship Narratives," *Gender and Discourse: The Power of Talk*, ed. Alexandra Dundas Todd and Sue Fisher, Advances in Discourse Processes 30 (Norwood, NJ: Ablex, 1988), 125–149.

2. C. Wright Mills, "Situated Actions and Vocabularies of Motive," *American Sociological Review* 5 (1940): 904–913; cited by Silberstein, "Ideology as Process," 129.

3. The term "wiving," not so incidentally, has a literary tradition in English dating back to the Old English period; cf. Joseph Bosworth and T. Northcote Toller, "*Wífian*," in *An Anglo-Saxon Dictionary* (Oxford: Oxford University Press, 1898; repr., 1980), 1218–1219. The term has historically carried both a transitive sense—the subject male "wives" an object female; and also a middle sense—a man "wives" for himself, i.e., obtains a wife *for his own use*, and additionally, rather surprisingly, one may also "wive" for another; thus, according to the *OED*, the verb "wive" may be used both intransitively and transitively to mean "to take a wife, get married, marry, furnish with a wife, obtain a wife for, to marry *to* a wife."

4. The medieval institution of marriage and its ubiquitous literary refraction of feudal social history from the High Middle Ages and late Middle Ages has been the subject of much scholarly attention in the course of the last century and a half in the field of medieval studies. Most manifestations of the motif have been studied thoroughly from the broad spectrum of scholarly methodologies through which humanistic studies have passed during that time. Among the more important studies that define the issues, see Christopher N. L. Brooke, *The Medieval Idea of Marriage* (Oxford: Oxford University Press, 1989); Charles Donahue, Jr., "The Canon Law on the Formation of Marriage and Social Practice in the Later Middle Ages," *Journal of Family History* 8 (1983): 144–158; Georges Duby, "Le mariage dans la société du haut moyen âge," in *Il matrimonio nella società altomedievale*, Settimane di studio del centro italiano de studi sull'alto medioevo 24 (Spoleto: Presso la sede del centro, 1977), 15–39; and Georges Duby, *Le chevalier, la femme et le prêtre* (Paris: Hachette, 1981). On the general wiving praxis of heroic narrative, see Viktor M. Zhirmunskiĭ, *Narodniĭ geroicheskiĭ epos* (Moscow/Leningrad: Akademia Nauk, 1962), 114–123; and Zhirmunskiĭ, "The Theme of Heroic Courtship," in *The Study of Russian*

Folklore, ed. Felix J. Oinas (The Hague: Mouton, 1975), 39–48. On the historical background of the practice in the Germanic tradition, which formed the primary cultural source for later literary adaptations in that tradition, and also on the variety of possibilities for the literary realization of the motif in Germanic literatures, see Friedmar Geißler, "Brautwerbung," 421–425, and "Brautwerbungssage," 425–428, in *Reallexikon der germanischen Altertumskunde*, 2nd ed., vol. 3 (New York: Walter de Gruyter, 1978); and his much broader study of the motif in a variety of European and non-European traditions in *Brautwerbung in der Weltliteratur* (Halle: Niemeyer, 1955); Xenja Ertzdorff and Marianne Wynn, eds., *Liebe-Ehe-Ehebruch in der Literatur des Mittelalters*, Beiträge zur deutschen Philologie 58 (Gießen: Schmitz, 1984); and Willy van Hoecke and Andries Welkenhuysen, eds., *Love and Marriage in the Twelfth Century* (Leuven: Leuven University Press, 1981). My *Brides and Doom: Gender, Property and Power in Medieval German Women's Epic* (Philadelphia: University of Pennsylvania Press, 1994), 58–67, 187–218, 239–254, 263–264, also focuses on the specific issues here relevant, particularly the literary praxis of wiving.

5. Since the woman is legally subordinate to a male guardian, her consent as such does not disallow the legitimate use of the criminalizing term "abduction" if she is removed from the guardian's control without *his* consent. See also, on the more general concept of consent in medieval marriage, Christian Gellinek, "Marriage by Consent in Literary Sources of Medieval Germany," *Studia Gratiana* 12 (1967): 555–579.

6. One of the most useful summaries of the *communis opinio* on courtship/wiving in the so-called *Spielmannsepos* is found in Christa Ortmann and Hedda Ragotzky, "Brautwerbungsschema, Reichsherrschaft und Staufische Politik: Zur politischen Bezeichnungsfähigkeit literarischer Strukturmuster am Beispiel des 'König Rother,'" *Zeitschrift für deutsche Philologie* 112 (1993): esp. 324–325, which has informed my further distillation here.

7. Despite the obvious problems inherent in the traditional genre taxonomy conventional in the field of medieval German (and Yiddish) studies—i.e., minstrel/heroic/courtly epic—I make use of those terms and categories here without further analysis, since my specific interest in this chapter is not dependent on a new theorization of epic genres. Those issues have been so thoroughly treated in recent decades that Sarah Bowden's otherwise interesting recent argument that positing bridal-quest epic as a genre per se is "historically unfounded . . . theoretically questionable" and an "unnecessarily restrictive mode of reading" seems rather belated; see Sarah Bowden, *Bridal-Quest Epics in Medieval Germany: A Revisionary Approach* (London: Modern Humanities Research Association, 2012), 165.

8. This Yiddish epic, almost certainly based ultimately on a German literary tradition, although no German text is extant, is found in a manuscript from the Cairo genizah (Ben Ezra synagogue in Fustat), now in the Taylor-Schechter collection, Cambridge University Library (T.-S. 10K22), the oldest known collection of Yiddish texts (dated 1382), fos. 21r–42v. The poetic texts are edited by Eli Katz, "Six Germano-Judaic Poems from the Cairo Genizah" (diss., UCLA, 1963); see also *EYT* 5–9; *Horant* is translated in Frakes, *Early Yiddish Epic*, 159–180. Unless otherwise indicated, *Duke Horant* is here cited from the manuscript. See also Shmeruk, *Prokim*, 33–37, 48–49, 97–120, 133–139, 182–189; Baumgarten, *Introduction*, 132–139.

9. A fifteenth-century adaptation of Wirnt von Gravenburg's thirteenth-century Middle High German *Wigalois* (while the German text is conventionally entitled *Wigalois*, its eponymous hero is consistently named Gwîgâlois, as he will be identified hereafter). The narrative proved extremely popular among Ashkenazic audiences and went through numerous Yiddish adaptations in poetry and prose over the course of three and a half centuries. The anonymous poet of the earliest Yiddish version composed more than twenty-one hundred rhymed couplets (probably in northern Italy; Cambridge, Trinity College, F.12.44), following Wirnt's plot

rather closely through the first three-quarters of the narrative (abbreviating much and generally eliminating specific Christian reference), before offering quite a different conclusion. No adequate scholarly edition of the text has been published; to be consulted are Irving Linn, "Widwilt, Son of Gawain" (diss., New York University, 1942); and the transcription by Leo Landau into a Roman alphabet, quasi-Middle High German form, *Arthurian Legends or the Hebrew-German Rhymed Version of the Legend of King Arthur* (Leipzig: Avenarius, 1912); excerpts from three versions of the early *Vidvilt* tradition are edited in *EYT* 80, 111, and 112 (453–60, 692–713); translated in Frakes, *Early Yiddish Epic*, 181–237. While Wulf-Otto Dreeßen initially argued against the *Wigalois* as the source text of *Vidvilt* ("Die altjiddischen Estherdichtungen: Überlegungen zur Rekonstruktion der Geschichte der älteren jiddischen Literatur," *Daphnis* 6 [1977]: 28), he later came to argue *for* that relationship: "Wigalois—Widuwilt: Wandlungen des Artusromans im Jiddischen," in *Westjiddisch: Mündlichkeit und Schriftlichkeit/Le Yiddish occidental: Actes du Colloque de Mulhouse*, ed. Astrid Starck (Aarau: Sauerländer, 1994), 84; see also Dreeßen, "Zur Rezeption deutscher epischer Literatur im Altjiddischen—Das Beispiel 'Wigalois'—'Artushof,'" in *Deutsche Literatur des späten Mittelalters: Hamburger Colloquium 1973*, ed. Wolfgang Harms und L. Peter Johnson (Berlin: Schmidt, 1973), 116–28; Susanne Knaeble, "Ironische Distanzierung im Fokus intellektuellen Erzählens. Der westjiddische *Widuwilt* als Rezeptionsgegenstand," in *Ironie, Polemik und Provokation*, ed. Coral Dietl, Christoph Schanze, and Friedrich Wolfzettel, Schriften der internationalen Artusgesellschaft 10 (Berlin: Walter de Gruyter, 2014), 85–108; Matthias Däumer, "Das Lachen des verbitterten Idealisten. Parodie und Satire im *Widuwilt*," in *Ironie, Polemik und Provokation*, ed. Coral Dietl, Christoph Schanze, and Friedrich Wolfzettel, Schriften der internationalen Artusgesellschaft 10 (Berlin: Walter de Gruyter, 2014), 259–285; Astrid Lembke, "Ritter außer Gefecht. Konzepte passiver Bewährung im *Wigalois* und im *Widuwilt*," *Aschkenas* 25 (2015): 63–82. As with other early Yiddish epics and their proposed "sources," *Vidvilt* is not a translation of the *Wigalois* or even a close paraphrase. Indeed the final third of the two narratives is altogether different. The one may thus be considered the "source" of the other in only a very restricted, even peculiar, sense.

10. Cited from Levita's edition of 1541.

11. Cited from the Verona 1594 edition.

12. The earliest source of the narrative is in the manuscript: Munich, Bayerische Staatsbibliothek, Cod. hebr. 100, fos. 67r–73v (copied by Isaac b. Judah Reutlingen; cf. Sarah Zfatman, *Ha-siporet be-yidish me-reshitah ad "shivḥei ha-besht" (1504–1814)*, 2 vols. [Jerusalem: Hebrew University, 1983], 15–18, 33–34, 45–46). The text has been edited by Max Erik, *Vegn altyidishn roman un novele*, 147–178; Frakes, *EYT* 67; translation in Frakes, *Early Yiddish Epic*, 419–430. See also Elias Shulmann, *Sfas Yehudis-Ashkenozis ve-Sifruso* (Riga: Levin, 1913), 155–171; Max Erik, "Vegn 'Mayse Briye ve-Zimre,'" in *Shriftn fun yidishn visnshaftlekhn institut* [filologishe serye] 1 (Vilnius 1926), = *Landoy-bukh: Dr. Alfred Landoy tsu zayn 75stn geboyrntog dem 25stn november 1925* (Vilnius: Kletskin, 1926), col. 153–162; Israel Tsinberg [Zinberg], "Oys der alt-yidisher literatur," in *Shriftn fun yidishn visnshaftlekhn institut* [filologishe serye] 3 (Vilnius: Kletskin, 1929), col. 173–184; Yitskhok Shiper (Ignacz Schipper), "A yidishe libe-roman fun mitl-elter: tsushtayer tsu der geshikhte vegn dem ufkum fun mayse briye ve-zimre," *Yivo-bleter* 13 (1938): 232–245; Erika Timm, "Zwischen Orient und Okzident: Zur Vorgeschichte von 'Beria und Simra,'" *Literaturwissenschaftliches Jahrbuch*, n.s., 27 (1986): 297–307.

13. In addition to his initial challenge to the Burgundians, simply to take their kingdom (and Kriemhild) from them by force (*aventiure* 3), his military service to the Burgundians against the invading Saxons (*aventiure* 4), as counselor to Gunther and recurring, multivalent proxy for him in *his* suit for Brünhild (*aventiure* 6–10), Siegfried's suit, as it were, and the service

performed for its sake extend over almost the first third of the epic. The entire wiving situation surrounding Brünhild is non-normative: she is a ruling queen and has no discernible male guardian; the groom's worthiness is to be demonstrated in war games with Brünhild herself—a male victor wins her as bride, while a vanquished suitor is killed.

14. In general on wiving praxis in these two texts, see the earlier studies by Otto Zallinger, *Die Eheschließung im Nibelungenlied und in der Gudrun* (Vienna: Hölder-Pichler-Tempsky, 1923); and "Heirat ohne 'Trauung' im Nibelungenlied und in der Gudrun," *Veröffentlichungen des Museum Ferdinandeum in Innsbruck* 8 (1928): 337–359; and Eckart Loerzer, *Eheschließung und Werbung in der "Kudrun"* (München: Beck, 1971); Lynn Thelen, "The Internal Source and Function of King Gunther's Bridal Quest," *Monatshefte* 76 (1984): 143–155; and Thomas Grenzler, *Erotisierte Politik—Politisierte Erotik: Die politisch-ständische Begründung der Ehe-Minne in Wolframs "Willehalm," im "Nibelungenlied" und in der "Kudrun"* (Göppingen: Kümmerle, 1992). And, as noted above, the wiving praxis of these two texts is the central focus of my *Brides and Doom.* The standard text editions are *Das Nibelungenlied,* ed. Helmut de Boor [nach der Ausgabe von Karl Bartsch], 21st ed., rev. by Roswitha Wisniewski (Wiesbaden: Brockhaus, 1979); and *Kudrun,* ed. Karl Bartsch, rev. 5th ed. (Wiesbaden: Brockhaus, 1980); due to the established tradition of editorial manipulation and distortion of the *Kudrun,* however, the diplomatic edition by Franz H. Bäuml is to be preferred: *Kudrun: Die Handschrift* (Berlin: Walter de Gruyter, 1969).

15. The best contextual treatment of the issues relevant here is found in the extensive studies of Michael Curschmann, *Der Münchener Oswald und die deutsche Spielmännische Epik* (Munich: Beck, 1964), esp. 101–114 on *König Rother*; and *"Spielmannsepik": Wege un Ergebnisse der Forschung von 1907–1965* (Stuttgart: Metzler, 1968), passim (cf. indices und *Braut/Brautwerbung*), specifically on *König Rother,* 25–34 and 74–76; and also Christian Gellinek, *König Rother: Studie zur literarischen Deutung* (Bern: Francke, 1968). The following analysis adheres to the stringent restriction of the use of the term *Spielmannsepos* that has come about especially due to Curschmann's definitive study.

16. Christian Schmid-Cadalbert, *Der Ortnit AW als Brautwerbungsdichtung: Ein Beitrag zum Verständnis mittelhochdeutscher Schemaliteratur,* Bibliotheca Germanica 18 (Bern: Francke, 1985).

17. Ingeborg Schröbler, *Wikingische und spielmännische Elemente im zweiten Teil des Gudrunliedes* (Halle: Niemeyer, 1934), 59.

18. The standard text edition is *Rother,* ed. Jan de Vries, 2nd ed. (Heidelberg: Winter, 1922).

19. The narrative has generally been so classified, such that in Claudia Bornholdt's recent study, a plot summary of *Horant* is simply included along with those of other such narratives: *Engaging Moments: The Origins of Medieval Bridal-Quest Narrative,* Reallexikon Der Germanischen Altertumskunde—Ergänzungsband (New York: Walter de Gruyter, 2005), 184–187.

20. Gabriele Strauch points out the similarity between Horant's function as royal marriage broker and the traditional role of the specifically Jewish marriage broker (*shadkhen*), especially the fact that Horant is himself already committed to another lady, loyal to his lord, and strictly professional in his behavior: he refuses Hilde's three offers: of meeting her in her boudoir, of betraying his mission and marrying her himself, and of a bed companion for the night (st. 165–175); cf. Strauch, *Dukus Horant: Wanderer zwischen zwei Welten* (Amsterdam: Rodopi, 1990), 67–68, 77. Strauch's suggestion that the transfer of the golden ring (st. 188) reflects the conclusive act of betrothal as conducted by a *shadkhen* is troubled, since the manuscript is damaged at that point, making it impossible to tell whether it is Horant or the princess who bestows the ring, an essential issue in Jewish praxis. Moreover, the ring is given early in the negotiations when the princess still imagines Horant not as proxy suitor for his king, but as himself the suitor; so the gift of the ring at this point in the tale cannot logically function to seal her

betrothal to his king; on this point see also Wulf-Otto Dreeßen, "Horant als *Schadchen*?" *Jiddistik-Mitteilungen*, no. 23 (April 2000): 2–4. In any case there is no indication in the text that Horant is anything other than a conventional aristocratic wiving envoy empowered by his lord to negotiate a marriage with an eligible princess on his behalf; no hints of any specifically Jewish convention or practice of wiving are to be discerned.

21. See the similar usages in st. 163,3 and 193,3, where the meaning can only have to do with "better singing," albeit without the troubling superlative adjectival form. See the textual note in *EYT* (p. 35) on the interpretations by Jean Fourquet, "Ernest-H. Lévy et le Dukus Horant" [review of Fuks, *The Oldest Known Literary Documents*], in *Études Germaniques* 14 (1959): 50–56; and Peter Ganz, Frederick Norman, and Werner Schwarz, eds., *Dukus Horant*, Altdeutsche Textbibliothek, Ergänzungsreihe 2 (Tübingen: Niemeyer, 1964), ad loc.

22. This sentence is borrowed from a famous Middle High German Crusader song, the ironic wit of which usage here would not have been lost on the Jewish audience. See John Julian, *A Dictionary of Hymnology* (London: Murray, 1915), 564.

23. The manuscript is frequently damaged such that it cannot be read; such places are marked with square brackets in the text; in the translation I try to the extent possible to construct sense around the gaps without falsifying the extant textual evidence.

24. The manuscript is troubled at the point where the bed companion is offered (the last line of fol. 34r).

25. Or perhaps: "of my own free will."

26. Or so it seems; the manuscript is here again very difficult to decipher (fol. 35v).

27. Ganz, Norman, and Schwarz, *Dukus Horant*, F. 72, p. 195. By the time I examined the manuscript in 2002 (under incandescent as well as ultraviolet light), its state of deterioration prevented any such speculative reconstruction.

28. As is inevitably the case with all such reconstructions, the sense well fits the context, but the question is always whether that plausibility results from the reconstruction or the reconstruction from the "logic" of the text, written—one ought always to keep in mind—in a form of a language that no one (and certainly none of the "reconstructing" scholars) has spoken for more than six centuries.

29. The Yiddish book is edited by Felix Falk, *Das Schemuelbuch des Mosche Esrim Wearba: Ein biblisches Epos aus dem 15. Jahrhundert*, Einleitung und textkritischer Apparat von Felix Falk, aus dem Nachlaß herausgegeben von L. Fuks, 2 vols. (Assen: Van Gorcum, 1961) [facsimile of Augsburg 1544].

30. David B. Monro and Thomas W. Allen, eds., *Homeri Opera*, vol. 1, *Iliadis libros I–XII continens*, 3rd ed. (Oxford: Clarendon, 1920), 180.

31. On the Orpheus tradition, see John Block Friedman, *Orpheus in the Middle Ages* (Cambridge: Harvard University Press, 1970; repr., Syracuse: Syracuse University Press, 2000).

32. Pseudo-Apollodorus, Βιβλιοθήκη 1.3.2, and Ovid, *Metamorphoses* 11; see also Euripides, Ἰφιγένεια ἐν Αὐλίδι 1212 and Βάκχαι 562. The medieval (Christian) connections of David and Orpheus as hero-musicians are explored by Friedman, *Orpheus*, 148–155.

33. Bartholomaeus Anglicus, *De proprietatibus rerum*, ed. Christel Meier et al. (Turnhout: Brepols, 2007), lib. 19, cap. 131; see Heinz Meyer, "Bartholomäus Anglicus, 'de proprietatibus rerum'. Selbstverständnis und Rezeption," *Zeitschrift für deutsches Altertum* 99 (1988): 237–274.

34. *Abélard. Historia Calamitatum*, ed. Jacques Monfrin (Paris: J. Vrin, 1962), 115.

35. On Tristan's musical abilities and their social function, see Merritt R. Blakeslee, *Love's Masks: Identity, Intertextuality and Meaning in the Old French Tristan Poems* (Woodbridge: Boydell and Brewer, 1989), 26–38.

36. Gottfried von Straßburg, *Tristan*, ed. Reinhold Bechstein and Peter Ganz (Wiesbaden: Brockhaus, 1978), vol. 1, *aventiure* 11 and 12.

37. See Erik Nylén and Jan Peder Lamm, *Bildsteine auf Gotland* (Neumünster: Wachholtz, 1981; 2nd ed., 1991); and Victor Millet, *Germanische Heldendichtung im Mittelalter: Eine Einführung* (Berlin: Walter de Gruyter, 2008), 245, with photograph.

38. "Widsið," lines 21–22, in *The Exeter Book*, vol. 3 of *The Anglo-Saxon Poetic Records*, ed. George Philip Krapp and Elliott van Kirk Dobbie (New York: Columbia University Press, 1936), 150; and "Deor," lines 39–40, ibid., 179.

39. Finnur Jónsson, ed., *Edda Snorra Sturlusonar* (Copenhagen: Gyldendal, 1931), *Skáldskaparmál*, c. 50.

40. Jørgen Olrik and Hans Henning Ræder, eds., *Saxonis Gesta Danorum*, 2 vols. (Copenhagen: Levin og Munksgaard, 1931 and 1935), here, vol. 1, c. 5.

41. An early example of a meticulous, politically astute study of this cluster of issues in Old French courtly epic is Andrée Kahn Blumstein, *Misogyny and Idealization in the Courtly Romance*, Studien zur Germanistik, Anglistik und Komparatistik 41 (Bonn: Bouvier, 1977). Kathryn Gravdal then provided the necessary critical perspective on one of the more salient aspects of wiving praxis: "Chrétien de Troyes, Gratian, and the Medieval Romance of Sexual Violence," *Signs: Journal of Women in Culture and Society* 17 (1992): 558–585; see also Betsy Bowden, "The Art of Courtly Copulation," *Medievalia et Humanistica*, n.s., 9 (1979): 67–86. On the general literary context of wiving in the courtly tradition as it was culturally translated from Old French into Middle High German, see Joachim Bumke, "Liebe und Ehebruch in der höfischen Gesellschaft," in *Liebe als Literatur: Aufsätze zur erotischen Dichtung in Deutschland*, ed. Rüdiger Krohn (München: Beck, 1983), 25–45.

42. On the issue of the representation of Islam and the erotic entanglements of Christians and Muslims in medieval Christian epic, see my *Vernacular and Latin Literary Discourses of the Muslim Other in Medieval Germany* (New York: Palgrave, 2011), chaps. 4–5, 59–122; *Parzival*, in Lachmann, ed., *Wolfram*, *aventiure* 1 and 2. The wiving situation of Herzeloyde is obviously also anything but normative, due to her own independence in staging the tournament, insistence on Gahmuret as the winner of the pre-empted tournament, and thus practical coercion of him into marrying her (*aventiure* 2).

43. There are numerous reasons for such reluctance, the most significant of which is the hero's conventional devotion to knight errantry, roaming the countryside and engaging in one adventure after another to prove his valor, by which means he also demonstrates his service to his lady. Upon his marriage, that principal motivation of his life is either simplified or complicated—depending on one's perspective—by having a wife (who, at least in courtly epic, is frequently identical with the lady whom the knight devotedly serves/has served). The seemingly infinite series of adventures with giant after Muslim after sorcerer, rescuing maiden after maiden, is now interrupted by his new marital ties to one single woman and one single castle as home. This complication appears recurrently in the courtly epic as a significant motif: in Chrétien's French and Hartmann von Aue's German *Erec* and *Yvain/Iwein*, for instance, and even in Wolfram's treatment of Gahmuret's two marriages, the first of which is unsatisfactory, the knight claims, because it inhibits his ability to engage in sufficient jousting (although he first justifies abandoning that wife because of her being a Muslim); thus as a condition to his second marriage he insists on a prenuptial agreement that permits him to schedule one tournament per month (*Parzival*, *aventiure* 2, 96, 25–97, 12).

44. The representation of wiving in *Vidvilt* closely approximates that of its Middle High German "source," Wirnt von Gravenberg's *Wigalois*, except in the episode with Count Moral and his daughter (*Wigalois, der Ritter mit dem Rade*, v. 8533 ff.), which is substantially less elaborate than in *Vidvilt*, especially with reference to matters of wiving. For a comparison of

the basic narrative content of *Wigalois* and *Vidvilt*, see Wulf-Otto Dreeßen, "Zur Rezeption deutscher epischer Literatur im Altjiddischen: Das Beispiel 'Wigalois'—'Artushof,'" *Deutsche Literatur des späteren Mittelalters—Hamburger Kolloquium 1973*, ed. Wolfgang Harms and L. Peter Johnson (Berlin: Schmidt, 1975), 116–128. The *Wigalois* is a heterogeneous narrative based indirectly on several Old French narratives, perhaps known to Wirnt primarily through the oral tradition, as he claims in the text's epilogue (11,686 ff.), although one portion of the narrative follows the twelfth-century *Le Bel Inconnu* of Renaut de Beaujeu rather closely.

45. Thomas Kerth, *König Rother and His Bride: Quest and Counter-Quests* (Rochester, NY: Camden House, 2010), ix–x.

46. Named Elamie in the Middle High German text but unnamed in the Yiddish text.

47. On this genre classification and the narratives assigned to the genre, see Baumgarten, *Introduction*, 163–206.

48. On some aspects of the historical institution of marriage in (Christian) Venice, contemporary with Levita, see Stanley Chojnacki, "The Power of Love: Wives and Husbands in Late Medieval Venice," in *Women and Power in the Middle Ages*, ed. Mary Erler and Maryanne Kowaleski (Athens: University of Georgia Press, 1988), 126–148.

49. See the excellent studies of the politically and militarily active female character epic, by Margaret Tomalin, *The Fortunes of the Warrior Heroine in Italian Literature: An Index of Emancipation* (Ravenna: Longo Editore, 1982); and Lillian S. Robinson, *Monstrous Regiment: the Lady Knight in Sixteenth-Century Epic* (New York: Garland, 1985).

50. One should note that the name טיירץ "Teyrets" (in the Tuscan texts, Terygi/Tedrise) is a homophone of תירוץ "pretext, justification, answer to a complex question." At the conclusion of the narrative, he certainly does become the convenient solution to a touchy situation.

51. As argued in chapter 8, below.

52. A further unexpected complication arises in the text's complex play with the ethnic identity of Druzeyne—Jewish or Christian? Despite that ambiguity, there is no overt problematization of the marriage at the narrative's conclusion between a possibly Jewish Druzeyne and an ostensibly Christian Bovo, so one might at that point conclude that Druzeyne is *not* Jewish, or perhaps some readers (as suggested but not compellingly argued by Ruth von Bernuth, "Zwischen Kreuzrittern und Sarazenen") might further wonder whether Bovo, too, is tactically conceived as Jewish.

53. The description of their lives is extended for another half-page in the late sixteenth-century manuscript of *Bovo*: Jerusalem, National Library of Israel, Ms. Heb. (2)8° 7565, fol. 61rv.

54. Much as such details are key elements of identification in other famous scenes of recognition, such as the scar on Odysseus's leg or the construction of the marriage bed in Homer's *Odyssey* 23.

55. Text editions: Matteo Maria Boiardo, *Orlando Innamorato*, ed. Aldo Scaglione, trans. Charles Stanley Ross (Berkeley: University of California Press, 1989; and Ludovico Ariosto, *Orlando Furioso*, ed. Santorre Debenedetti and Cesare Segre (Bologna: Commissione per i testi di Lingua, 1960).

56. C. P. Brand, *Ludovico Ariosto: A Preface to the "Orlando Furioso"* (Edinburgh: Edinburgh University Press, 1974), 57.

57. The astonishingly complex and convoluted plot is characterized by an ironic (but for all that no less rabid) devotion to *entrelacement* as a principle of plot construction. On *entrelacement*, see Tzvetan Todorov, *Introduction à la littérature fantastique* (Paris: Seuil, 1970), 146; Claude Bremond, *Logique du récit* (Paris: Seuil, 1973), 34, 132; William Ryding, *Structure in Medieval Narrative* (The Hague: Mouton, 1971), 139–154; and my "Metaphysical Structure as Narrative Structure in the Medieval Romance," *Neophilologus* 69 (1985): 481–489.

58. Erika Timm observes, "Darüber hinaus behandelte er aber als Zentralthema—was man vom *Bovobuch* noch nicht sagen konnte—ein auch im Selbstverständnis der aschkenasischen Gesellschaft hochsignifikantes Problem, die Partnerwahl bei der Heirat," "He moreover treats as a central topic—which cannot yet be said of the *Bovo-bukh*—a problem of great significance in the self-image of Ashkenazic culture: the selection of a spouse," in *Paris un Wiene* (Tübingen: Max Niemeyer, 1996), cxxx.

59. Although at one point she does also concede the opposite (st. 476). Cf. Timm, who notes that since the period of the final editing of the Babylonian Talmud (at the latest), it was conventional that a Jewish bride possessed the right of consent to marriage (BT *Kid* 2b, 41a; also Rashi on Gen 24:57, from *Genesis Rabbah* 60). She further notes nonetheless that cases of a bride's choosing her husband against her father's will are few, although here, too, the Talmud recognizes the marriage of non-minor partners as legal and without sanction (*Paris un Wiene*, cxxx–cxxxi).

60. Timm's remarks on love as a legitimate basis for choosing a partner, on the affirmation of *körperliche Selbstverwirklichung*, "corporeal self-actualization," as a manifestation of a Renaissance ideal, and the happiness of his daughter as Dolfin's primary concern (directly based on social and economic status), while interesting and potentially relevant, are left without clear articulation with either the text or the Jewish cultural environment of early sixteenth-century Italy (*Paris un Wiene*, cxxxi). It is indeed hard to imagine how a twentieth-century scholar could imagine a father who imprisons his daughter in a dungeon on rations of bread and water *for years* on end because of her refusal to marry his choice of bridegroom as unproblematically concerned with her happiness!

61. The positioning of the singer and listener, knight and lady, is not accidental: the field of courtly operation of the lady is conventionally inside the castle, while the knight's is outside the castle. That socially conditioned positioning becomes most clear when the lady functions as audience of the knight's prowess, generally by observing his skills on the battle- or tournament-field just outside the castle walls from her viewpoint at a castle window or on the battlements. There are complex elements of a courtly "female gaze" involved in this type scene. See my "The Female Gaze and the Liminal Window in Medieval Epic," in *De consolatione philologiae: Studien zur älteren und neueren deutschen und skandinavischen Literatur und Sprache. Festgabe für Evelyn Firchow*, ed. Anna Grotans et al. (Göppingen: Kümmerle, 2000), 85–100. Here, obviously, as was also the case with Hilde and Horant in *Horant*, the woman is an "ear-witness" of the knight's musical prowess as demonstrated outside the castle.

62. In *Briyo and Zimro* (see below), Briyo's conventional chastity is compromised by her permitting Zimro to kiss her (a thousand times!), and the conventional mode of passivity in the female beloved is likewise modified in her reaction to Zimro's kisses: דא קוסט ער זיא טויזנט מול אונ' זיא אין אווך (*EYT* 361) "Then he kissed her a thousand times, and she kissed him also." It is precisely their transgressive passion that is identified in the text as the cause of both their deaths.

63. The word בישטן is ambiguous, the superlative either of גוט "good" or בויז/ביז "bad/evil," the latter choice here seeming better suited to the narrative context, although one might well entertain the possibility of a necessary ambiguity.

64. One might prefer: "how I love a noble knight in my heart," which can, however, be construed only by means of syntactic violence.

65. Timm also notes that there is no evidence of a German source and indeed no compelling internal indication of a Hebrew source ("Beria und Simra," 82).

66. In medieval and Renaissance Christian epic, any given lady introduced into the narrative would immediately be assumed beautiful, noble, and wealthy, while a knight introduced into such a narrative would be assumed handsome, noble, and wealthy, such that if one of the required characteristics be mentioned, the others automatically follow. Interestingly, in the very

non-Christian *Briyo and Zimro*, that—or a similar—convention also appears, such that Briyo is beautiful, honorable, and wealthy, while Zimro is handsome, noble, and wealthy. Briyo's beauty is so great in fact that her father reifies it: איך הב זיא נוך ויל שׂוינר צו חֵפֶץ "I have a much more beautiful *thing*" (*EYT*, p. 359; my emphasis), referring to her. The narrator comments: דיא וואר דיא איניקליך שוין מענשא · דש ניא קיינר מיט אווגן גיזעהן הט · איר שונהייט איז ניט צו שרייבן "She was the most essentially beautiful woman that anyone had ever seen. Her beauty is indescribable" (ibid.). Likewise, Zimro שוינישט אונ' דער קלוגישט קנאב אישט אין דעם לנד "is the most handsome and wise/noble lad in the land and kingdom" (*EYT*, p. 360); while the more modern Yiddish sense of the word קלוג "wise, clever, smart" might also be relevant here, it seems in this particular context that the older and more formulaic sense of "noble" likewise deserves mention—cf. Matthias Lexer, *Mittelhochdeutsches Handwörterbuch* (Leipzig: Hirzel, 1872–1878; repr., Stuttgart: Hirzel, 1979), vol. 1, col. 1637. Interestingly, however, Briyo is also identified as זער דעמויטיג אונ' גר ורום "very humble and (piously) honorable," which characteristics then set her quite apart, for instance, from the heroines of (both Christian and Yiddish) romance epic; one should note that the connotation of the modern Yiddish reflex of ורום (פֿרום), along with the modern German *fromm*, ought not to mislead into imagining that that sense was the exclusive connotation in Old or Middle Yiddish, or even Middle High German, in both of which languages the word *included* the modern connotation of piety but also generally had more to do with those attributes characteristic of the nobility: "stalwart, competent, honest, decent, good, felicitous, distinguished, noble, valiant, courageous"; see my explication of the term in *Early Yiddish Epic*, xvi–xvii.

67. *EYT*, p. 360; Frakes, *Early Yiddish Epic*, 423.

68. This liminal period of the knight's quasi-anonymous transformation—quite conventional in classic courtly romance—is thus prolonged far more extensively than it was, for instance, for Lancelot in Chrétien's *Le Chevalier de la Charette*, for Yvain in *Le Chevalier au Lion*, or for Parzival in Wolfram's *Parzival*.

69. Dauber's recurring designation of the text as "chivalric romance," despite the utter absence in the text of all reference to or deployment of either the historical or the literary worlds of chivalry, is baffling; see Dauber, *Demon's Bedroom*, 37, 213 and passim.

70. Zinberg (*Geshikhte*, 76) notes that in *Pariz and Viene* essentially the same *yikhes* motif is found as in *Briyo and Zimro*. The cultural contexts—Christian feudal versus Jewish—nonetheless immediately give them radically different valences.

71. Timm's insistence that Feygin's rejection of Zimro as son-in-law expresses his desire to maintain a closed priestly lineage as a manifestation of the conflict between the Pharisees and Sadducees beginning in the Maccabean period simply ignores the evidence of the text, the sixteenth-century European cultural context, and, as she herself notes in passing, the fact that Jews of the medieval and Renaissance periods had *no* access to any information about the very existence of such a conflict in antiquity ("Beria und Simra," 56–59).

72. Simon Schwarzfuchs, *A Concise History of the Rabbinate* (Oxford: Blackwell, 1993); Schwarzfuchs, "Rabbi, Rabbinate," in *Encyclopaedia Judaica*, 2nd ed., edited by Michael Berenbaum and Fred Skolnik (Detroit: Macmillan Reference USA, 2007), 17:11–19.

73. One might likewise note that the specific historical form, function, and period of origin of the papacy was empirically inaccessible to Jews—and Christians—of the sixteenth century, as is clear from the character of the pope as a secular ruler inserted into the Second Temple period in this narrative, several centuries before the papacy existed.

74. There may well have been others, no longer extant.

75. Astrid Lembke's compellingly argued thesis, that the Yiddish poet's conception of heroism in the case of Vidvilt requires community engagement more than individual prowess, is here also relevant ("Ritter außer Gefecht," esp. 82).

Chapter Eight

The Other of Another Other

Yiddish Epic's Discarded Muslim Enemy

THE RELATIVELY FAMILIAR modes of Christian European depictions of the Muslim Other becomes more complicated when a Jewish perspective is added, looking athwart the Christian literary tradition through the literature of co-temporal Ashkenazic Jewish culture of the period, which was, with some important exceptions, in large part co-territorial with and, as is becoming more and more clear through the scholarly work of recent decades, in constant and direct cultural interchange with Christian culture in the German lands and northern Italy. While only a small segment of the relevant literature will be considered in depth here—the genre of later medieval and early modern Yiddish quasi-secular epic—that segment is of singular importance, since it is precisely in the literary genre of secular epic that one finds the most extreme views in *Christian* literature.

One of the most commonly cited examples is the Old French *Chanson de Roland*, in which Muslims are represented as bestial not just in behavior but even in anatomy (monstrous semi-humans with spikes growing out of their backs or horn-like skin; *Chanson de Roland* 3214–3264), as treacherous in their essence, as polytheistic worshipers of idols, as slaughtered in their martially incompetent hordes of hundreds of thousands by a mere handful of Christian heroes, as potentially valuable and individuated human beings only via conversion to Christianity. Such a concentration of negative characteristics is quite rare in the depiction of any given Muslim, and in any case there is a great deal of variation in the representation of Muslims over the course of the ensuing centuries in Christian epic. But one may at the same time make the factual statement that nowhere is a Muslim—with the possible (and very rare and restrictive) exception of Saladin—represented in Christian epic as a morally positive or even neutral character *without conversion to Christianity*, that is, without eliding his/her identity as a Muslim.[1]

Jewish epic traditions, which were developing parallel to and in some cases directly dependent on the Christian ones during the late medieval and early modern periods, are thus especially intriguing. The Jewish epic tradition is a hybrid—as ultimately are probably all epic traditions—although in the case of the Jewish tradition the mechanisms of hybridization are historically more accessible, for unlike in many other national traditions, the contributing components in Jewish epic are not just vaguely identifiable or reconstructible but in fact directly accessible to textual analysis. Not surprisingly, medieval and early modern Jewish epics participate in the pan-European epic tradition that spans the length and breadth of European national literary traditions and are particularly strongly influenced by medieval and Renaissance German and Italian epic traditions, such that not just motifs and plots are adapted, but in many cases metrical forms, verbal style, and even epic vocabulary are calqued and borrowed directly.[2] At the same time, however, Jewish epic is also firmly grounded in the lengthy Jewish intellectual tradition based on biblical narrative, aggadic (narrative) materials from the Talmud, and especially post-biblical commentary and homiletic traditions.

Before we proceed to the analysis of the corpus of Jewish epic and its representation of Muslims,[3] however, it is first necessary to adumbrate a fundamental cultural distinction that characterizes Jewish culture and thus distinguishes Jewish epic from its co-temporal Christian counterparts. The subsequent analysis itself will then have to take this distinction into account at every step, which will require recurring explanatory gestures to obstruct the automatic assumptions schooled by training in the scholarship on the literature of the Christian Middle Ages.

While Jews were as directly affected by the rise of Islam as were Christians, since the early waves of Muslim conquest swept through territories populated by each group, Jewish culture, already adapted to diasporic conditions for some centuries, which necessarily included living under the political control and subject to the periodic anti-Semitic zeal and violence of Christian hegemony, did not suffer the wholesale cultural upheaval and disruption that Christian communities throughout the eastern Mediterranean, North Africa, and Spain certainly did. It would be quite inaccurate to pretend that Jewish life continued as it had before the Muslim conquest, for it certainly did not. Nonetheless, as Yaron Peleg points out (in his study of a much later period and a much different situational context, which is nonetheless pertinent here, as well), "the distinction that always existed between Western cultures, such as those of England and France, and Eastern cultures, such as those of Egypt and Persia, for instance, was less clear in the case of European Jews, who were never fully regarded as an integral part of Western culture by other Europeans nor indeed by themselves for much of their history in Europe."[4] Moreover, as Mark Cohen's ground-breaking study of medieval Jewish culture under the political control of both Christianity and Islam indicates, a fundamental distinction is necessary:

> A comparison between Islamic and Christian polemics with Judaism should yield substantial insight into the attitude toward and treatment of the Jews of Islam. To anticipate our conclusion: neither the Christian preoccupation with the intellectual struggle against Judaism nor the bellicose Jewish response to Christian polemics has a counterpart of similar intensity in the Judaeo-Islamic context. Combating Judaism and Jewish interpretations of Scripture was essential in Christianity; it was incidental in Islam.[5]

With some further provisos and qualifications, essentially the same could be said about the propaganda war between Christianity and Islam, as opposed to Judaism versus Islam: in the latter case, there was little purpose for political propaganda, and thus there was little.

Even so dedicated an anti-Muslim scholar of Islam as Bernard Lewis points to the key issue that distinguishes the Christian and Muslim attitudes toward Jews:

> If we compare the Muslim attitude to Jews and treatment of Jews in medieval times with the position of Jews among their Christian neighbors in medieval Europe, we see some striking contrasts. . . . In Islamic society hostility to the Jews is nontheological. . . . It is rather the usual attitude of the dominant to the subordinate, of the majority to the minority, without that additional theological and therefore psychological dimension that gives Christian anti-Semitism its unique and special character.[6]

As Cohen's analysis demonstrates, the underlying motivations for ideological conflict are decisive: while historical Christianity seems by definition more or less constrained to carry on ideological war with Islam, there is no such compulsion on either side in the relation of Judaism and Islam.[7]

Conditions and quality of life must always be treated as local phenomena, and there certainly were significant and well-known but non-systemic examples of Christian tolerance and Muslim intolerance, but in general, as Cohen's reexamination of these issues has demonstrated, the historical evidence in general supports the long-standing scholarly consensus that during the length and breadth of the Middle Ages, Jews lived less persecuted, more prosperous, and freer lives with more social, religious, economic, and general cultural opportunities under the rule of Muslim governments than Christian ones.[8]

A second essential point is that while Jews were in terms of their own traditions and ethnic history obviously as closely linked to the biblical lands as were Christians, there were no deep-seated cultural aspirations toward immediate Jewish reconquest and independent political rule of those territories, nor, obviously, was there any logistical possibility of such reconquest by the scattered communities of Jews; although in the centuries following the Muslim conquest of the Iberian peninsula, there were some exceptional cases of Jews who became high-ranking governmental and even military leaders in the Muslim government, nowhere did any independent Jewish political entity exist and thus no Jewish military. As a result of these conditions of Jewish life in both Muslim- and Christian-controlled territories, the Jewish view of Islam was different in kind and not just in degree, from the Christian view.[9] Under Islamic rule both Christians and Jews were classified and treated as اهل الكتاب "people of the book" and were thus اهل الذمة, who were free non-Muslim subjects living under Muslim governmental control, who, in exchange for paying a capital tax, enjoyed protection and safety. Thus while they ranked hierarchically below the level of Muslim subjects, they nonetheless enjoyed in a qualified sense a privileged status above those ethnicities not deemed "people of the book" that was guaranteed them by the tenets of Islamic religious law itself. There is no question but that there was tension between Muslims and Jews in lands under Muslim control, which erupted periodically in violence against Jews, but there never (until the recent past) seemed to develop the systemic anti-Semitism that had arisen quite early among Christians. The central point here is that Muslims did not function as the essential Other in Jewish culture, nor did Jews so function in Islamic cultures; neither thus functioned as did Muslims in Christian epic, as that ubiquitous opposite of the Self essential to self-definition.[10]

In order to get at the early Jewish usage in epic, which is grounded in a radically different cultural context and thus signifies in quite a distinct manner than was the case in the surrounding Christian culture, it will be necessary to examine semantic fields and patterns of usage not just in the historically relevant German and Italian texts on which early Yiddish quasi-secular epic was based, but also in the specifically Jewish textual tradition that informs the broad range of Jewish epic texts. This mode of argument may thus almost seem to lead us astray before returning us to the issue; I ask the reader's patience. For the Jewish epic tradition may not simply be identified as yet another branch of this pan-European system, for it also draws on its own *literary* tradition of heroes that at the end of the European Middle Ages already stretched back some two millennia, ultimately based on biblical narratives, but in most cases drawing more heavily on later Talmudic and midrashic narrative traditions than on the Bible itself.

In the hybridized—quasi-secular and midrashic—corpus of Jewish epic, there are four identifiable strategies developed by Jewish authors to deal with the issues surrounding the representation of the cultural Other. These strategies are clearly differentiated according to whether the text in question belongs to the subgenres of midrashic or quasi-secular epic. In each case, the source material and its relation to the epic text requires careful attention. The first strategy is characteristic of midrashic epic, where the Other is always in some sense a historical, usually biblical Other (e.g., Philistines), the identity and valuation of which is already established for the Yiddish author by the received Jewish textual and interpretive tradition. There is, however, even in the face of that established tradition, some possibility of adaptation. In quasi-secular epic—in all cases Jewish adaptations of Christian epic—are found the other three strategies of treating the representation of the Other. Here one can distinguish gradations in the degree to which the Jewish adapters are willing to adopt the anti-Muslim praxis of the Christian authors of their source texts: they may attempt fully to eradicate the Christian system of representing the Muslim Other, including most or all details of that representation; or, secondly, they may retain some of the exoticizing details of that system, but eliminate their central function as motivator of the plot, thus undermining the ideological system as such; or, thirdly, they may adopt the Christian system and its component elements intact.

Before proceeding to a consideration of these strategies in the quasi-secular epics adapted from Christian sources, however, midrashic epic requires some attention, for this epic tradition, in large part an internal Jewish one on which the Christian tradition nonetheless impinged in significant aspects, established an overarching set of norms for the narrative representation of the cultural Other that developed from quite different historical circumstances than did the Christian construction of the Muslim as Other. Midrashic epic is represented by numerous texts from the Old Yiddish tradition, such as the אברהם אבינו "Our Father Abraham" (*EYT* 5); the mid-sixteenth-century ספֿר מלכים [מלכים־בוך] *Book of Kings*,[11] ספֿר דניאל *Book of Daniel*,[12] and ספֿר שמואל [שמואל־בוך] *Book of Samuel*;[13] the late sixteenth-century עקידת יצחק "Binding/Sacrifice of Isaac";[14] and various paraphrases of the Esther scroll.[15] These texts are clearly based on narrative materials from the Bible, but also make not just incidental use of later Jewish literary traditions of Talmud, biblical commentary, and midrashic narrative, as well as the co-temporal (late medieval/early modern) European (especially German) epic tradition. This last tradition was especially important in the formation of the peculiarly medieval heroic ethos of the epic characters in these texts. These epic recastings of the stories of, for instance, David, Solomon, and Daniel, have no real politico-ideological equivalent to the Christian-Muslim conflict as characteristic of medieval Christian epic. The embedded political conflicts of the narratives—based especially on a similar insider versus outsider cultural identification defined by religious affiliation—do, however, offer paradigms for constructing the outsider as Other and thus also some ground for comparison with the Christian texts, which will become particularly relevant in the consideration of Yiddish quasi-secular epic.

Throughout the biblical books of Samuel and in the Middle Yiddish epic adaptation, it is the Philistines who constitute the primary political, ideological, cultural, and military enemy of the Israelites. In the Yiddish text they are conventionally designated by a term from the Germanic component of Yiddish that is familiar to readers of medieval German epic: דער הייד/די היידן *der heyd/di heydn*, cognate with Middle High German *der heid/die heiden*, "the heathen(s)."[16] The term clearly represents the Philistines as having a distinctive status, for, rather surprisingly, none of the other numerous Gentile military opponents of the biblical Israelites (e.g., Moabites, Edomites, Jebusites) are so designated. This distinctive usage for the essential enemy parallels the practice in medieval Christian epic, where Muslims are by definition "the heathen(s)," while representatives of other non-Christian cultures, such as Jews or non-Muslim Asians who appear in travel literature, are only very rarely so designated. The Philistines are, however, so often thus named in the Yiddish *Book of Samuel* that "heathen" comes to define their identity, just as it does for Muslims in medieval Christian secular epic.[17]

This terminological usage as a reflection of the political and military conflict between the Jews and the Philistines is clearly illustrated in a single stanza:

מִיט אלזוא גרושן קרעפֿטן ער דיא לאנד ביצוואנג
דש זיא אים מושטן דינן אויבר אירן דאנק
דיא יודן אונ' דיא פְּלִשְׁתִּים דיאווארן ניט צו שיידן
זיא שטריטן שטענטיקליכן דיא יודן אונ' דיא היידן:
(st. 248)

> He imposed his will on the country with such great strength that they had to serve him against their will; the Jews and the Philistines [*plištim*] could not be kept apart; they fought each other constantly, the Jews and the heathens [*heydn*].

Interestingly, this phenomenon of nomenclature has no basis in the Hebrew text of the biblical book of Samuel, where there is no differentiated system of naming non-Israelites, such that the Philistines would be designated by a pejorative term, while other ethnicities would simply be designated by their customary ethnic identifiers. Instead, there is no more than the relatively rare but recurring designation of the Philistines as עֲרֵלִים *arelim*, "uncircumcised" (e.g., 1 Sam 14:6, 31:4; 2 Sam 1:20).[18] This characteristic of the Philistines, indicating (among other things) their outsider status with respect to the cult of Yahweh, recurs in the Bible, gaining prominence already in the story of Samson, where his father questions whether he cannot find a bride among the Israelites instead of seeking one among the פְּלִשְׁתִּים הָעֲרֵלִים *plištim ha-arelim*, "the uncircumcised Philistines" (Judges 14:3).

The issue of circumcision as an indicator of insider versus outsider status becomes a key signifier in the Yiddish midrashic epics. In the Bible, David is to pay a bride-price to King Saul of one hundred foreskins of Philistines killed in battle: אֵין־חֵפֶץ לַמֶּלֶךְ בְּמֹהַר כִּי בְּמֵאָה עָרְלוֹת פְּלִשְׁתִּים "the king desires no marriage present except a hundred foreskins of the Philistines" (1 Sam 18:25), although when the narrative actually comes to that point in the action, David in fact kills two hundred (מָאתַיִם) Philistines, whose foreskins were then delivered to King Saul (1 Sam 18:27). In the *editio princeps* of the Yiddish *Book of Samuel*, David pays, however, not with Philistine foreskins, but, if the text is taken literally, with toes: דו זולט אויש שלאגן דיא צֵין צווישן דעןביינן "you should strike/knock out the toes between the[ir] legs" (st. 417,2). While one might also construe the form צֵין *tsen* as "teeth," it is here almost certainly, as Layb Fuks glosses in German as "Zehen . . . mhd. *zêhe, zê*," that is, "toe(s)," which, when occurring between the legs of men, can only be a euphemism for penis, which in context offers a slightly different take on the genital mutilation only hinted at in the biblical prescription of foreskins which are "taken," one would imagine, by means of post-mortem sword- or knife-work on the battlefield, where, one might likewise imagine, the precise surgical technique that is circumcision was unlikely to have been very carefully performed. The early sixteenth-century manuscript tradition that predates the *editio princeps* of the Yiddish *Book of Samuel* provides a slightly different anatomical route to a similar goal: the manuscripts read here ביצים Hebr. "eggs/testicles."[19] The play of cultural identity via cultic mutilation, as opposed to the parodic non-cultic mutilation of the dead Philistines, as that mutilation intersects with patriarchal clichés of virility and castration, merely suggested in the biblical text, are made more explicit in the Yiddish text, while still retaining some metaphorical distance. One should note, however, that the effective sign of Philistine male Otherness and the concretization of the pejorative designation of their ethnicity as "the uncircumcised," that is, the foreskin, whether separately excised (as in the biblical text) or removed while still attached to the amputated "toe" (as in the *editio princeps*), disappears from the narrative as represented in the manuscript tradition of the Yiddish *Book of Samuel*, where the ביצים "testicles" alone obviously do not bear that sign but rather only testify to the castration of the (already dead) enemy.

Before proceeding, however, it would be useful to recall, incidentally, that whatever the semantic usage of the biblical text that structures the discourse of the Other, with the Philistines as the quintessential enemy of the broad range of narratives that lead, inevitably and teleologically, to the founding of the Davidic monarchy, there was little compelling *contemporary* geo-political relevance, for instance, for sixteenth-century Jews in the Rhineland, the Danube Valley, or the Veneto, since they could not and did not fear or despise Philistines in any concrete manner. They certainly recognized the cultural, metaphorical significance of the Philistines as perhaps the most essential of biblical Others, but there were for them no actual sixteenth-century Philistines as enemies, as there were, for instance, Muslims *qua* constructed essential Other for sixteenth-century Christians. The modern recycling of the Latin geographical designation *Palestina* and its adjectival derivations to designate the non-Jewish inhabitant of the geographical region as a *Palestinian* (Hebr. פָּלֶשְׂתִּינָאִי *palestinai* / Arab. فلسطيني *filastīnī*) had obviously not yet come about to reconnect with the ancient traditions of distorted Otherizing.

In any case, the biblical usage of עֲרֵלִים *arelim*, "uncircumcised," relatively infrequent as it is, and not so clearly or consistently pejorative, thus does not directly parallel the use of Yiddish הייד "heathen" in the Yiddish *Book of Samuel*, although it could still conceivably have functioned as a secondary model for the development of the usage in the Yiddish text, alongside the primary German Christian model of *heid*. In any case, here, too, as in the Christian texts' *heid*, the Yiddish reflex הייד is employed to designate the enemy who is constructed as the most dangerous in terms of the text's depicted culture.

In addition to that particular term, there are some few further specific details in midrashic epic of this same kind of deprecation of outsiders, particularly based on religious practice. In the Yiddish *Book of Samuel* itself, in the course of the type-scene of heroic boasting before battle, David calls Goliath טויבֿילישר מאן "devilish man" (st. 368,3) and טויבֿיל אויש דער הֵילן "devil from Hell" (st. 369,1), which recalls the specific usage of Christian epic in designating (usually) individual Muslim enemies in battle as "devils" or "devilish/demonic." But this latter expression in the Yiddish text seems almost to be a formulaic phrase, used commonly also in the Yiddish *Book of Kings* (st. 470,3; 482,1; 483,2), where there is no reference to Philistines or any other ethnicity, but rather quite explicitly to demons from Hell, over whom King Solomon in fact has control.[20]

One of the common means to suggest the Otherness of Muslim warriors in German Christian epic—by providing them with non-courtly weapons (especially clubs, often designated *stang*, "pole")—*seems* also to have a reflex in the Yiddish *Book of Samuel*, for in addition to his sword, Goliath also prominently carries a weapon identified in the Yiddish text with the same etymon, as an immense שטאנג "pole" (st. 331,4); but in the subsequent stanza, it is noted that this pole is provided with an iron tip, so that it should probably be more specifically identified as the חנית "spear" of the biblical text (1 Sam 17:7). In general one must take great care in assigning moral valuations to the hero's weaponry, for primitive weapons are by no means exclusively negative in medieval Christian epic, although pejorative instances clearly outnumber their appearances in the hands of positively valued (but generally still young and unproven) heroes. The difficulties inherent particularly in such texts as the Bible, which theoretically at least must for religious reasons cross cultural and linguistic boundaries with its value system strictly intact, are obvious even in the present context, for the biblical text insists on a completely different valuation of weaponry in this conflict, such that Goliath is the fully equipped and experienced warrior, while David rejects the heavy and ill-fitting armor offered by King Saul and goes into battle armed only with the shepherd's weapons that he has in the past used successfully against the bear and lion: staff, stones, and sling. He represents then the hero from the realm of "nature" in conflict with animal enemies from that realm, while Goliath is the hero from the realm of "culture" (or technology), in keeping with the general tendency of the biblical narrative to cast the Israelites as the unsullied natural innocents in opposition to the urban and technologically superior Philistines. David then seems almost characterized as the primitive warrior, except—and this is theologically perhaps the most telling point—that his technologically unsophisticated equipment merely serves to emphasize the ultimate source of his strength and victory, that is, from the perspective of the narrative—the Israelite God, whose favor can, the narrative thus insists, bring victory even to the young, weak, inexperienced, and ill-equipped warrior.

Even so, the Yiddish text—here in direct opposition to the biblical text—does slightly accommodate the medieval heroic ethos, for after his earlier struggles with the animals, David proclaims אויף מיין טרויאן עש זול מיר ניט מער גישעהן דאש איך וויל איין שטרייט און שווערט ביזעהן "I swear it should never again happen to me that I go into battle without a sword" (st. 326,3–4), and he takes a fine one along on his father's errand to the Israelite army, where he will in fact fight and kill Goliath. And even after having refused Saul's weaponry and stripped off the borrowed armor, the text specifies that he girds on his sword (זיין ויל גוטש שווערט נאם ער אן זיין זייטן "he took his very good sword on his side"; st. 356,3) and wears it into battle against Goliath. Nonetheless, here too, as in the biblical text, he fells the giant with the sling and stone and then cuts off his head with the enemy's sword, not his own (st. 374–376). Based on the biblical source, there is a clear, as it were "historical" reason for David's lacking a sword (in the technologically more primitive Israelite culture): וְחָרָשׁ לֹא יִמָּצֵא בְּכֹל אֶרֶץ יִשְׂרָאֵל כִּי-אָמְרֻ פְלִשְׁתִּים פֶּן יַעֲשׂוּ הָעִבְרִים חֶרֶב אוֹ חֲנִית "Now there was no smith to be found throughout all the land of Israel; for the Philistines said, 'The Hebrews must not make swords or spears for themselves'" (1 Sam 13:19). Deprived of smiths, the Israelites thus initially have few standard weapons in their wars with the Philistines.

There are some few other passages in midrashic epic where a slight hint of deprecation of foreign cultures appears, often with direct reference to their religious practices. In the Yiddish *Book of Samuel*, when David's son Amnon rapes his half-sister Tamar, it is said that Amnon took Tamar's honor אלש דיא לוייט טון יענהאלב דעש מֵיר "as do people beyond the sea" (st. 1359,4). It is not clear whether this is a reference simply to assumed barbarity or to the documented practice of sibling marriage among royals known elsewhere from the ancient eastern Mediterranean littoral, especially Egypt. In any case, there is no such explicit statement in the biblical text, where Tamar herself says, כִּי לֹא־יֵעָשֶׂה כֵן בְּיִשְׂרָאֵל "For such a thing is not done in Israel" (2 Sam 13:12), without reference to what is done outside of Israel.

Another such momentary glimpse of criticism of foreign cultural practice is found in the Old Yiddish "Our Father Abraham" (ca. 1382), where the Mesopotamians are frequently designated היידן "heathens" (lines 293, 396, 409, 412). It is said in the course of the story of Abraham's rejection of the Mesopotamian gods and the statues that represent them: די היידן די דא וורן די הטן איינן טומן זיט "The heathens who were there had a dumb/foolish/naïve custom" (line 66; cf. also line 300).

In the Yiddish *Book of Samuel*, in his hymn of praise to God, David says about other religions:

איך צווינג זיא מיט גיוואלט זיא קירן וויא דיא שוויין
איך לוש איר לעבן קיין זיא מוישן דר שטוכן זיין
זיא שריאן צו אירן אפגוטן זיא האלפֿן אין ניא
איר נארהייט מוש איך שפוטן איך בין שטערקר מער ווען זיא:
(st. 1726)

> I compel them by force—they squeal like pigs. I leave none of them alive: they have to be stabbed. They cry out to their idols—they never help them! I must mock their folly. I am mightier than they.

Finally, in a fifteenth-century Yiddish Esther narrative, a strategy not seen elsewhere in early Yiddish materials appears to express valuation, in that the categories of female beauty and its absence are expressed as שון "beautiful" versus שווארץ "black" (line 39).[21] The text also makes use of היידן "heathen" in that naturalized ostensibly valueless mode that became the standard in the bigotry found in medieval German texts. When Mordecai and Haman are traveling, they are in היידן לאנט "heathen land" (line 282), which here seems to mean no more than "in a foreign country," that is, away from home. In general, since the narrative takes place in Persia, most of the surrounding population would logically be Gentile, and such subjects of the Persian empire are here designated היידן "heathens" (lines 683, 687, 729, 1056). But there is at some level still an edge of moral valuation, since the term differentiates between people on the basis of belonging to the in- or out-group.

The Yiddish *Book of Kings* addresses the focal issues in a number of ways, especially in connection with Solomon's penchant for foreign wives. In the Yiddish text, the enigmatic Shimei (שְׁמְעִי) advised Solomon against marrying Pharaoh's daughter (while in the Bible his marriage is simply reported without comment; 1 Kings 3:1–2), because she was Gentile (גויָה) and because it was thus sinful: ווען ווער דא גויָה נימט קיין גוטש דר בֿון קומט אן לייב אונ' אן זֵיל עז אים ניט ורומט: "for who[ever] marries a non-Jew, no good comes of it; not for body or soul is it of any value" (st. 165,3–4). While the word גוי[ה] *goy*[*e*] has become a pejorative word not often used in polite company in Israeli Hebrew, its use in Yiddish (whether of the earlier period or currently) has not been so politically inflected but means simply "Gentile." While Shimei lives, Solomon follows his advice against exogamy, but immediately after his murder/execution by Solomon (as directed by David, for an earlier insult; 1 Kings 2:8–9), then Solomon sends for Pharaoh's daughter and marries her (st. 166). In the Yiddish text she plays the predictable role as religious subverter and temptress (מיט איר הט ער ויל קורץ ווייל "with her he was much entertained"; st. 167,1), hanging a sheet painted with stars above their bed, so that when Solomon wakes in morning, he thinks that it is still night and stays in bed with her, which means that he misses morning prayers, as does everyone else, since he keeps the keys to the Temple under his pillow (st. 170). She does this מיט אירן לישט "in her fraud" (st. 167,4) and דא מיט האט זיא דען קויניג זער ביטרוגן "therewith she betrayed the king greatly" (st. 168,2). Solomon's sins mount in ensuing stanzas, all traceable to this illicit marriage: דא בֿור זוינד זיך קויניג שְׁלֹמֹה דא ער פַּרְעֹה טוכטר נאם "earlier King Solomon sinned when/because he married Pharaoh's daughter" (st. 180,1). The sin results in the coming of the angel Gabriel from Heaven to plant a reed on the edge of sea, around which develops an island, on which a city is eventually built in that רוימישן לאנדא "Roman land" (st. 181,2), from which Jews were subsequently to suffer greatly (a midrashic commonplace).

A second episode of Solomonic exogamy reported in the Yiddish *Book of Kings* concerns the Queen of Sheba, which ultimately also results in the rise of yet another destructive enemy of the Jews. In the Bible (1 Kings 10:1–13; 2 Chronicles 9:1–12), there is no hint of the sexual attraction and marriage that define the post-biblical narrative, where the Queen of Sheba appears as the characteristically female Other with monstrous attributes: she is sexually aggressive and has, among other things, legs as hairy as a man's.[22] In the Aramaic *Targum Sheni* (no earlier than sixth century) to the book of Esther, Solomon remarks to the Queen of Sheba: מתיב מלכא שלמה ואמר לה שופריך שופרא דנשי וסערך סער דגברא וסער לגברא שפר ולאתתא גנאי "King Solomon began and said: 'Your beauty is the beauty of women, but your hair is the hair of men. Now hair is beautiful for a man but a disgrace/obscenity for a women.'"[23] In the *Pseudo-Ben Sira*, the queen's hairiness is remedied with a depilatory that removes the hair and makes her טהר "pure," implying not just that her skin is therewith made smooth but that she herself is ritually purified.[24] There may also be some suggestion in her hairiness of not merely a lack of conventional femininity but a surfeit of masculinity, already indicated in the queen's aggressively independent sexuality ("the very model of a phallic woman"[25]), that is, a transgressive masculinity in the female and thus a threat to patriarchy, which must apparently be remedied, here conveniently by means of a depilatory that restores the "feminine" form. The depilatory is made from lime and arsenic, which is also mentioned in various Hebrew sources, as well as Qurʾānic commentaries, although the motif is absent from the Queen of Sheba episode in the Qurʾān itself.[26]

In the Yiddish text, the objectification of the Queen of Sheba is immediate. When she comes before Solomon, his first words are not *to*, but *about* her: he comments first on her beauty and then on her hairy legs (st. 509). She is immediately the sexual aggressor who makes clear her intentions: נון וואר זיא ווארן לושטיג דיא

קויניגין בֿון שְׁבָא · זיא ווער גערן גילעגן בייא דעם שונן קויניג דא "Now she had become aroused, the Queen of Sheba; she would have liked to lie with the handsome king there" (st. 522,1–2). As it turns out, the king is as willing as she is, but that desire comes about or at least comes to be expressed only as a response to her impetus. As is generally the case in epic tales of royalty, sexual union functions to subordinate the woman to the male-controlled status quo, and thus it is enacted, here, too. But Solomon additionally insists on "normalizing" this female Other in another way before her subordination is sealed sexually: he makes the sexual union that she so ardently desires dependent on her first depilating her hairy legs (st. 523). He makes a chalky depilatory that not only removes the hair, thus "feminizing" her, that is, altering the natural condition of her body by cosmetic means, according to a Solomonic (i.e., male-defined) aesthetic of beauty, but also rather surprisingly turns her skin—only now intimated to be dark—white (st. 524,3). While the expected result of a depilatory is skin made smooth by the removal of hair, this depilatory is explicitly described as chalky: איין קארזיף מיט קאליך ווייך "soap/abrasive[27] with soft chalk" (st. 524,1). It would then perhaps not be surprising that her legs would become white after he daubs them with the substance (st. 524,2), but the effect seems not a matter of lightening via the application of a white layer of chalk, for it is not simply her legs that turn white: זיא ווארד דר בֿון גלאט אונ' העל גאנץ איבר אירן לייבא "she became smooth and bright over her entire body" (st. 524,3). Since the text has not identified her race or skin color beforehand, the narrative here almost suggests the same kind of sudden and unexpected racial metamorphosis that sometimes accompanies the conversions of Muslims in medieval Christian epic. Immediately following her chemically induced racial metamorphosis here, in fact in the next line, after having smoothed and whitened the queen's body and thus "normalized" it, Solomon abruptly takes sexual possession of it, which the text expresses as קויניג שְׁלָמָה גאר ביהענדא גיוואן ער זיא צו איינם ווייבא "Quite quickly King Solomon won/took her as bride" (st. 524,4). Yet another layer of "normalization" occurs then, for the idiom of "wife-winning" is the common euphemism for the sexual act. She is then not simply made a sexual partner, but wived and thus subdued, controlled, subjected to the dominant society's norms, after having met the preconditions of depilation and whitening, that is, enforced gender and racial "normalization."

The prediction/report of the disastrous results of this exogamous and thus by definition illicit union is delayed only until the next stanza: דוך העט קויניג שְׁלָמָה ניט רעכֿט גיטון · בֿון איר קאם נְבֿוכֿד נֶצַר ער זולט זיא האבן לושן גון "King Solomon had indeed done wrong: from her came Nebuchadnezzar; he should have let her go / left her alone" (st. 535,1–2). Nebuchadnezzar (Nebuchadrezzar II) is of course the Babylonian ruler who conquered Judea and destroyed the Solomonic Temple on which the text of the book of Kings had just expended so much descriptive detail. Interestingly, while the catastrophic results of exogamy could hardly be more clearly expressed, it is nonetheless בֿון איר "from her" that Nebuchadnezzar comes, and *not* from his ancestral sire, Solomon. In this case then, even in a patriarchal culture in which lines of descent as a rule comprise male names only (as in the recurring genealogies of the book of Genesis), it is the mother alone who is identified as having produced the child, perhaps as a result of gender prejudice, because it is here a matter of a destructive descendant. The fundamental moral point is underlined several more times in the course of the next few dozen stanzas (especially again st. 580–598, where the idols of Solomon's wives *and* his enjoyment of his wives are again emphasized).

Later in the book, the story of King Asa is recounted: the militantly pious reformer king of Judah who appears in two passages in the Bible: 1 Kings 15:10–24, where his reforms and wars against the Kingdom of Israel are narrated; and 2 Chronicles 14–16, where the scope is rather more broadly conceived, such that his defense against an attack by זֶרַח הַכּוּשִׁי "Zeraḥ the Cushite" is mentioned. The latter *nomen gentis,* כּוּשִׁי *kushi,* designates in ancient Hebrew the populace of the southernmost territory known to Jews in antiquity, conventionally associated with the region of the upper Nile, that is, the northern Sudan. In the Septuagint, the term is translated as Aἰθίοψ "Ethiopian." Conventionally the Hebrew term, as also the Greek, designates a black African.[28] The Yiddish *Book of Kings* obviously does not restrict its source material exclusively to the biblical book of Kings, but also makes use of the book of Chronicles, from which it incorporates the African invasion of Zeraḥ; the biblical כּוּשִׁים "Cushites" are then here designated "Moors": אויף אין קם גיצוהן דער קוניג אויז מארן לנט / מיט טויזנט מול טויזנט מן אלזו קרעפֿטיגר הנט "The King of Moor-land marched against him / with a thousand times a thousand men, thus with a powerful hand" (st. 723,1–2); דא מורדט גוט דיא מארן זיא ולוהן לעשטרלייך "There God killed the Moors; / they cursed blasphemously" (st. 726,1); קוניג אֲרַם הושטו גידינקט גוט הושטו גילון / דער דיר הוט גיהולפֿן בייא דען שווארצן מארן "King Aram, do you remember, you have forsaken God, / who helped you against the black Moors" (st. 734,2–3).

An interesting specification of ethnic detail that initially seems almost to undermine the simple insider-outsider ethnic dichotomy suggested in the Yiddish use of the term היידן "heathens" is found in the midrashic epic based on the biblical book of Daniel. In the Bible, after Daniel has interpreted Nebuchadnezzar's dream and won royal favor for himself and his three Israelite companions, the text introduces the typical turn of events: the biblical text reads: גֻּבְרִין כַּשְׂדָּאִין . . . קֲרְצֵיהוֹן דִּי יְהוּדָיֵא "Chaldean men [*or*: certain Chaldeans] . . . maliciously accused the Jews" (Daniel 3:8), providing no more information about the identity of the Chaldeans. The Middle Yiddish *Book of Daniel* is both far more specific and less precise: נון ווארן די היידן אונ' די גוים גנץ ניט וואל דראן "now the *heydn* and the *goyim* were not at all pleased by this."[29] Obviously it is not possible simply to understand both היידן as "heathen" and גוים as "non-Jews" here, since the two do not seem either to be strictly synonymous or mutually exclusive. In an important sense, however, it has thus far simply been taken for granted that in the Jewish texts the two terms are more or less synonymous—the former derived from the Germanic component of Yiddish and the latter from its Semitic component—since they have not been juxtaposed in this manner and thus there has been no necessity to differentiate between them. Ultimately it may well still be the case here that they function as approximate synonyms, for otherwise what two non-Jewish ethnic groups would the sixteenth-century European Ashkenazic author of the Yiddish *Book of Daniel* have imagined as living in Babylon in the sixth century BCE and as being sufficiently distinct that they required separate ethnic designations? Interestingly, while they, as non-Jews, curse and blaspheme against the Jewish God, which marks them definitively and negatively as the Other, they are not otherwise characterized negatively (whether in appearance, behavior, or values).

After having surveyed the biblically inflected but clearly independent tradition of the conception of the Other in midrashic epic, which is in large part to be understood as an integral component of an inner Jewish cultural tradition dominated by biblical narrative but especially by post-biblical interpretive and narrative traditions, there remains the second, quasi-secular, sub-genre of Jewish epic, where the situation, both in terms of literary discourse (including dominant literary influence) and ethnic identity of the Other, is quite distinct. While it is necessary in some analytical situations to maintain a definitional distinction between the genre of epic (necessarily in verse) and heroic tale (in prose), in the present context the two categories may be tactically collapsed into an amalgam of heroic narrative, which in the Jewish tradition comprises several further sub-categories: (1) the legends of Greco-Roman antiquity, such as the Hebrew Alexander novel ספר תולדות אלסנדרוס המקדוני *The Book of the History of Alexander the Macedonian*; (2) chivalric narrative, including the late thirteenth-century fragment of a Hebrew King Arthur prose tale ספר השמד הטבלה העגולה [קיניג אַרטוס] *The Book of the Destruction of the Round Table (King Arthur)*,[30] and many of the early Yiddish quasi-secular epics—the late fourteenth-century *Duke Horant*, the fifteenth- to sixteenth-century *Vidvilt*, and the early sixteenth-century *Bovo d'Antona*; (3) Yiddish Renaissance epic, such as the later sixteenth-century *Pariz and Viene*; and (4) fantasy-adventure tales, such as *Briyo and Zimro*.

The Hebrew *Alexander* novel is a rather close translation/adaptation of the Latin *Historia de preliis* by Archpriest Leo of Naples, which was based on a Syriac (i.e., Christian Aramaic) source text.[31] Both the Christian Latin source and its Jewish adaptation participate in the long literary tradition of tales of "Wonders of the East," in which the Outland is indeed made outlandish, populated by as broad a range of exotic Others as the author has interest in mining from the tradition and incorporating into the work at hand. The broad scope of texts that grew out of the Alexander legend in the centuries after his extraordinary life (e.g., hagiographical biography, military history, adventure romance, heroic epic), which made secondary cultural contact between Greeks (and via them in the ensuing centuries the rest of Europe) and Asian cultures, in the south as far as the borders of India and farther north almost to the borders of China. By "secondary" cultural contact I do not mean contact as a process that leads to any deep knowledge by either culture of the other culture, that is, by Greeks or Macedonians of Persians, Egyptians, Syrians, Scythians, or the various peoples of India and central Asia: while the conquered peoples came to know Greek culture at least in the form in which it was represented by Alexander's military and administrative systems (and their hybridized Hellenistic derivative forms), and some individual Greeks without question came to know the cultures of the conquered, there was never any systemic impulse on the part of Greek culture to know the culture of the Other except as an exoticized caricature. Via the Alexander tradition, the Greek "invention of the barbarian"[32] during the Greco-Persian wars of the sixth century BCE extended its discursive range to include, potentially, any and all [non-Greek] Others anywhere in the world then known to Hellenistic culture.

In the Hebrew adaptation of the Alexander romance thus the "populace" of Asian territories is constituted, for instance, by monstrous women with teeth as sharp as those of wolves and as large as those of boars, or who are as hairy as camels, or by those who, like the naked race of Oxidraces, live not in constructed dwellings but in holes in the earth, are as black as ravens, and are, from the assumed Hellenistic perspective, inevitably, foolish.[33] Even so, while the accumulation of such exoticizing detail in the Hebrew text is certainly not without significance, the details are not systematically articulated into a *design* that functions to exoticize and denigrate entire ethnic groups. Trivial as that distinction might on the surface seem, it can be argued that in word choice and nuance the Hebrew text is systematically and demonstrably less orientalizing than its source text, and thus in fact represents the second adaptational strategy indicated above—while eliminating the "system" of ethnocentrically motivated denigration, significant details of that system are retained.

Medieval knightly epic, particularly Arthurian epic, provides perhaps the clearest illustration of this second representational strategy, for in the broad Christian tradition of such narrative, Muslims conventionally play quite significant roles that are central to the plot—for example, as invaders, witches or evil magicians, or bewitched monsters who must be subdued as part of the hero's quest. Unfortunately, the tiny extant prose fragment of the Hebrew Arthurian romance *The Book of the Destruction of the Round Table* is simply too brief to provide any indication of a representational strategy—if indeed there were any relevant material to be included—and in fact no evidence pertinent to the present topic.

In turning to the early Yiddish reflex of chivalric romance, we find that precisely the same strategy of eliminating the systemic prejudicial depiction of the Other that characterizes the medieval Hebrew *Alexander* novel is even more strongly present in the Old Yiddish *Vidvilt*, for instance, particularly in contrast with Wirnt von Grafenberg's Middle High German *Wigalois*, from which much of the Yiddish narrative was adapted. In the German text, the entire character of the narrative's arch-villain, Rôaz von Glois, is constructed around his essential identity as a Muslim, caricatured in the manner conventional in Christian epic: feigning friendship, he gained access to a neighboring Christian king's castle and then treacherously murdered most of its inhabitants, including the king, and took over the kingdom (lines 3705–3743), leaving its subjects to suffer in fiery Hell-like torment. In the brief passage that introduces him, treachery becomes an essential aspect of his characterization.[34] Rôaz is designated *der heid*, "the heathen," so often that line-by-line, page-by-page, this epithet (which often seems almost a cognomen) comes to constitute his entire identity.[35] He is the essential enemy of Christendom, who has given his life and soul to a devil: "er hât durch sînen zouberlist / beidiu sêle unde leben / einem tiuvel gegeben," "in exchange for magic powers, he sold both soul and body to a devil" (lines 3656–3658). One of Rôaz's knights of Glois, who is himself identified as "der selbe tievels trût," "the minion of the same devil" (line 6577), bears a shield on which "Machmêt . . . der heiden got," "Muḥammad . . . the heathen god" (lines 6572–6575), is depicted. When the hero Gwîgâlois enters Rôaz's castle, his amulet (which contains a Christian prayer) and crucifix prevent the devil from approaching him (lines 7340–7341). The exotic material culture of the orientalized East defines Rôaz's castle of Korntin and the tomb that he prepared for himself and his wife, Japhîte (lines 8228–8289). Her life is one of unrelenting orientalized luxury and pomp (lines 7395–7467) in her castle "in der grôzen Asîâ," "in great Asia" (line 7446). According to the narrator's judgment, her virtues do have a limit, however:

> deheiner slahte gebreste,
> der ie an deheinem wîbe wart,
> des was ir lîp vil wol bewart,
> wan daz si ungetoufet was (7462–7465)
>
> Any flaw of any kind that any woman ever had was quite far from her—except that she was unbaptized.

That characteristic determines all response to her, even at her own death, when the narrator coldly comments: "wær si niht ein heidenîn, / sô müese ich klagen ir jâmers nôt," "if she were not a heathen, then I would have to lament her suffering" (7752–7753). At her husband's death, she cries out to her putative god Muḥammad:

si sprach, wâ nu Machmêt?
dîne helfe ich ie hêt
ze ganzem trôste und dîn gebot;
Machmêt, vil süezer got,
ich hân dich geminnet ie;
wem hâstu mich nu lâzen hie?
er lît tôter hie vor mir,
den ich bevalch mit dienest dir,
sît ich sîn kunde alrêrst gewan. (7714–7722)

She said: "Where are you now Muḥammad? I always had your help, along with full trust and your power. Muḥammad, most benevolent god, I always loved you. To whom have you abandoned me here? He, whom by my service I entrusted to you since the time that I first knew of him, lies dead here before me."

In perhaps the most telling turn of phrase, after their deaths the narrator comments on Japhîte and Rôaz: "hie lâgen samet vieriu tôt: / zwô sêle und zwêne lîbe," "here lay four dead: two souls and two bodies" (lines 7755–7756). Before he can be buried,

Rôaz der wart verstolen dan
zehant von der tievel schar
daz sîn dâ niemen wart gewar
unz daz man in ûz solde tragen (8136–8139)

Rôaz was then stolen away by a troop of devils, so that no one noticed it until he was to be carried out [for burial].

After the death of Rôaz, Gwîgâlois himself delivers a sermon of more than twenty lines, providing the basic articles of the Christian faith (lines 8142–8165), to Rôaz's surviving retinue, which converts the "noble heathen," Adân, whose pietistic "confession of sin" then extends another forty lines (lines 8167–8206). Adân later hears another sermon, this time by a bishop who then baptizes him (lines 9500–9519). In the course of his "confession," Adân participates in his own Othering when he remarks "swie gar ich sî ein heiden," "although I am altogether a heathen" (line 8219). Later, when he accepts a vassal's responsibilities from Gwîgâlois, he again so identifies himself, using almost the same words, but makes a further significant claim: "swie ich sî ein heiden, / ich gestên iu zaller iuwer nôt / michn irre es danne der bitter tôt," "although I am a heathen, I will support you in all adversity, unless bitter death then hinders me" (lines 8523–8525). Therewith he acknowledges the expectation of faithlessness and treachery conventionally imputed to Muslims, while at the same time claiming that he can overcome that putatively innate character trait.

In the Old Yiddish *Vidvilt*, on the other hand, none of this ideology of bigotry is present: the poet has systematically eliminated its systemic structure and all but a few of its details. While the Rôaz of the *Wigalois* is a monstrous Muslim, in *Vidvilt* the corresponding but unnamed villain is simply the giant son of a sorceress, without reference to religious or ethnic identity. The sorceress herself has a horde of female minions, however. In one of the manuscripts it is said: זיא ווארן שווארץ אן מושן / זיא ווארן דש טויבליש גנושן "They were exceedingly black; they were the Devil's companions."[36] As noted earlier, it is a cliché of Christian epic to depict any and all Muslims as racially black, and their designation as the Devil's companions also gives one pause. But in the Yiddish text, neither the women nor their mistress are in fact identified as Muslims.[37]

Even so, before proceeding, it might be pertinent to contextualize the seemingly incidental but significant use in *Vidvilt* of the motif of black skin as a means of negative characterization. As has already become clear from the earlier discussion of the depiction of the Queen of Sheba, it is not without precedent in medieval Jewish literature that black skin appears as a sign of physical ugliness and/or deformity, even if not as a necessary identifying feature of Muslims. In the late twelfth-century *maqāma* from Sephardic Spain מנחת יהודה שׂונא הנשים "The Gift of Judah the Misogynist," by Judah ben Isaac ibn Shabbetai, there appears:

> . . . אִשָּׁה מְצֵרָה. כְּעוֹרֵב שחוֹרָה. שְׂפָתֶיהָ כְּנֹאד עַל נֹאד נְפוּחִים. וּשְׂעַר בְּשָׂרָהּ קוֹסים כְּסוּחִים. כָּסּוּ פָנֶיהָ חֲרוּלִים. מַבְרַחַת יוֹנְקִים וְעוֹלְלִים. כִּי הָיְתָה בְּעֵינֵי כָּל בְּזוּיָה. וּשְׁמָהּ רִצְפָּה בַּת אַיָּה.
>
> . . . a quarrelsome hag, black as a crow, with lips like two inflated bladders—anyone who saw her would gasp. The hair on her skin was like stubby brambles, and her face was covered with nettles—something to make infants and babes recoil. She was repellent to all. Rizpah bat Aiah was her name.[38]

H. Schirmann suggests that that woman was in fact an African Black and that the representation of the woman as such and the direct connection of that identity to repulsiveness constitutes evidence of *Christian* influence on Judah ibn Shabbetai.[39] Raymond Scheindlin comments:

> It is possible, however, that the woman was simply dark-skinned. For, while Arabic writing does not generally depict the Negro as disgusting, it is a convention of Arabic love poetry that courtly ladies are pale-skinned. In this context, Rizpah's dark skin would mean simply that she is uncouth.[40]

With respect to the Jewish poet's use of the cliché of European epic of the devil's bride, which in Christian epic conventionally sometimes designates a Muslim woman, sometimes simply any active, independent female character who does not submit to patriarchal control, again one must note that in the Yiddish text the women are not Muslim.[41]

With the exception of these few instances, none quite conforming to the conventions of anti-Muslim caricature, the entire ideologically based Christian versus Muslim conflict and the bigoted depiction of Muslims consequent thereon that is of fundamental importance to the German narrative has simply and systematically been excised from *Vidvilt*. Such a massive reconceptualization of the epic and one of its primary motivations for heroic action in the narrative cannot have been inadvertent or casual, and its narrative consequences are quite obvious to the reader, for without the monstrous Muslim villain, another plausible motivation must be found for the devastation of the landscape and people whom the epic's hero must rescue. Quite plausibly in the context of Arthurian epic, the Yiddish poet recasts the villain's motivation such that it derives from his having simply been rejected as marriage suitor of the displaced king's daughter, a common enough occurrence in courtly romance (and minstrel epic).

In the post-biblical Jewish texts addressed thus far, ethnically Other characters have generally been marginal to the primary plot (except perhaps in the *Alesander* novel, where they are at least frequent, if not central), and specifically Muslim characters, demonized in the Christian originals, have been deemphasized or eliminated altogether. In the Middle Yiddish *Pariz and Viene*, however, the anonymous poet retains the primary Muslim character of his Tuscan "source" text.[42] But in that text the normative Christian conception of Muslims is fundamental: the Tuscan narrator designates Muslims "quella perfida canaglia," "this nasty/perfidious rabble" (Ivii.r) and "infideli," "infidels" (Hiii.v) and uses the same term for the Soldano (Hiiii.r), while Paris calls Muslims "questi cani," "these dogs" (Iv.r), and King Dolfino calls them "quelle cani," "those dogs" (Ivii.v)[43] and "quella maladeta gente crudele senza alcuna remissione," "this cursed and unremittingly cruel race" (kiiii.v); espionage against Muslims is at one point identified by the narrator as "santo seruitio," "holy service" (Hiiii.r); Viena says of Paris while still unrecognized in his disguise as a Turk, "che non siate nato de nobil natione," "you who are not born of a noble nation" (ki.r).

In the Yiddish adaptation, on the other hand, while the Turkish Soldan (sultan) is retained as a significant individualized Muslim character, he is depicted not as an anti-Christian caricature, but rather simply as an unusual character, perhaps indeed simply "foreign," but neither he in particular, nor Muslims in general become the caricatured perfidious and monstrous creatures of the Tuscan text. Some familiar motifs are nonetheless present, even though they appear rarely, rather than dominating every mention of Muslims: in Muslim-controlled Turkey, for instance, it is said that souls are lost (st. 489); the Soldan fights eternally with Christians (st. 492–495); while the Soldan himself does make use of treachery, his instrument thereof is a Christian traitor (st. 526); it is claimed that not to help a Christian held in captivity by Muslims, at this point called הינט "dogs," is a sin (st. 598). In the end, however, as already treated in some detail in the previous chapter, while Viene's elitist (Christian) father, King Dolfin, has long rejected his Christian vassal's son (Pariz) as a son-in-law, he is perfectly willing to accept a noble Turk (st. 691). Or at least so it seems, for in fact this "Turk" is not really a Turk at all, but rather Pariz in disguise, so the entire issue is adroitly sidestepped in the process of resolving the class/status conflict in the hero's bridal quest.

Intrained epic expectations sometimes appear in unexpected places. The Soldan captures Dolfin as a spy in Muslim territory and immediately intends to kill his prisoner but is dissuaded by his advisors (ווייזי "wise men"), who counsel that imprisonment would better serve his desire for vengeance: ויל ערגר דש ער לעבט אין לייד אונ' מרטר "much worse that he live in agony and torture" (st. 531,8). The narrator then deems the prisoner דען ארמן דולפֿין "the poor Dolfin," only almost immediately to find a sense of justice in Dolfin's imprisonment, specifically because of his earlier refusal to allow the marriage of Pariz and Viene and the imprisonment of his own daughter for refusing to marry the suitor whom he favors. The narrator here cleverly makes use of the convention common in romance of announcing a change of focus from one character or subplot to another, by thus "leaving" Dolfin to suffer in prison, while the plot turns to Pariz:

אים גישאך רעכֿט ביי מיינם לעבן
דש ער פריז ניט וואלט וויענה געבן:

אין לוש איך אין דער קייך גאר שוואך
אז ער ליש זיין טוכֿטר אונ' קינדן.
אונ' פריז וויל איך גין זוכֿן אך.
(st. 537,7–538,3)

> It served him right, by my life, because he would not give Viene to Pariz. I will leave him quite weak in prison, as he left his daughter and child. And indeed I will go looking for Pariz.

While one might impute to the narrator some lack of consistency on whether Dolfin deserves imprisonment and discomfort, the Soldan's action of capturing and imprisoning an enemy spy might seem to a non-partisan observer hardly villainous but in fact both proper and commendable for a head of state.[44] At the same time, however, the fact that he then decides on the basis of counsel to spare the life of the spy only momentarily seems virtuous, since its grounding motive (vengeance through torture) is hardly so. It seems then that this is not a programmatically negative depiction of a character based on race or religion, but rather a somewhat nuanced portrayal of a character motivated by multiple and often conflicting impulses; that is, there is at least a hint of complex character depiction, even in a sixteenth-century genre not known for such complexities and certainly not for any tinge of realism.

Similar to this situation in the sophisticated narrative of *Pariz and Viene*, the far more plebeian chapbook tradition, represented by, for instance, the Yiddish פארטונאטוס *Fortunatus* (1699), offers in the course of its two hundred pages practically no evidence of a bigoted representation of the Muslim characters, who nonetheless play quite extensive and significant roles in the narrative.[45] Even so, there is some distant hum of the ideology that is ever present in Christian narratives. When the eponymous hero, for instance, steals the sultan's magic cap and refuses to return it, even though the sultan courteously requests it and gives Fortunatus every opportunity to avoid an "incident," he simply refuses to do so (fol. 35–36). Is that act of defiance merely another instance of the insolence of the arrogant trickster hero of this text, or does it function as a sign of disrespect for the Muslim political leader? Or both? The "Prester John" motif, ubiquitous in Christian travel literature and cosmography from the High Middle Ages up through the first era of modern European imperialism (ca. 1750), also appears briefly here (fol. 32r) but is not further developed.[46] One wonders just how well acquainted a Jewish audience of the time would have been with that motif. At one point in the tale a non-European people is designated דיא בארבארישי לייט "the barbarian people" (fol. 33r), while another is identified by the already familiar term היידן "heathens" (fol. 37v). The reader is also taken on a brief, whirlwind tour of the clichés of the "Wonders of the East" discourse (fol. 34r–v). Only once, however, does an example of the bigotry associated with those clichés appear: אונ' וויזט דז דיא היידן קיינם טייטשן ווערדר טרייא נאך האלד זיין זונדרן זיא זינט פֿון נאטור גינייגט דען זעלבן שאדין צו טון "and know that the heathens are neither faithful nor well-disposed to any German but rather by nature tend to do injury to him" (fol. 32v). While one might make a facile gesture to the German culture that provided the "source" text for the Yiddish adaptation and thus deny or deemphasize Jewish responsibility for such a blatant example of stereotypical ethnic bigotry, one must always be aware of context, and Yiddish authors seem to have made a systematic effort to eliminate such assumptions and claims from their works, even those minimally adapted from Christian texts. Here the Yiddish author obviously chose not to elide the judgmental remark.

It would be useful to take stock of the situation thus far surveyed before proceeding to the final text to be considered. In the brief fragment of the Hebrew *Lanzelot* romance and in the fifty pages of the Yiddish *Duke Horant*, in neither of which Muslim characters appear, there is no anti-Other (and thus no anti-Muslim) prejudice otherwise characteristic of Christian texts in the sub-genres of Arthurian romance and bridal-quest epic. In the longer texts, *Alesander*, *Vidvilt*, and *Pariz and Viene*, where non-Europeans and Muslims play significant roles, perhaps a dozen anti-Muslim clichés appear in some three hundred pages of text, while in corresponding Christian texts one often finds that many examples per page. One might thus conclude that the issue is one of little importance to the Ashkenazic authors and audiences. I would suggest on the contrary that such systematic attention to its elimination indicates just how important the issue was and how focused was their attention on excising it from their texts. Just as the Christian authors and audience seemingly reveled in the anti-Muslim bigotry, the Jewish authors and audience apparently abhorred it.

One relevant early Yiddish text remains to be examined, however, and in the present context it is rather explosive: the Old Yiddish *Bovo d'Antona*, adapted and reworked by Elia Levita in 1507 in Padua[47] and published by Paulus Fagius in Isny im Allgäu in 1541, probably on the basis of a Tuscan ottava rima version of the immensely popular, originally Anglo-Norman romance *Bueve de Hantone*.[48] The Yiddish adaptation was one of scores of adaptations of this text across the face of Europe from England to Armenia, and from Spain to Russia. The Yiddish *Bovo* narrative then became a cottage industry in itself: over the course of the centuries it was reprinted and reworked in more editions and versions than can probably now be reconstructed. That textual history demonstrates a broad-based popularity in the Yiddish-reading audience that is scarcely to be found in early Yiddish literature beyond such core texts of the tradition as Jacob ben Isaac Ashkenazi of Janov's צאינה וראינה *Tsene-Rene* (Hanau 1622) (a biblical paraphrase with integrated traditional commentary) or the anonymous aggadic/folktale treasury איין שוין מעשה-בוך *A Fine Book of Tales* (generally known as the *Mayse-Bukh*, Basel 1602). In any case, the *Bovo* epic is the only early Yiddish text that demonstrates the fourth representational strategy suggested at the outset: the full acceptance and reproduction of the bigoted discourse of Christian epic.

This situation is particularly unusual, since it was especially at this period that recent scholars have posited a broader amelioration of the negative representation of Muslims in European literature.[49] John Patrick Donnelly suggests that in epic of the High Renaissance, there is no sense that Europeans are racially superior to Muslims.[50] Antonio Franceschetti suggests that this improvement in the attitude toward Muslims was due to Andrea da Barberino (ca. 1371–ca. 1431).[51] Gloria Allaire notes that while the traditional mode of characterizing Muslims remains essentially intact, "in Italian texts the Saracen characters do receive a more humanized, less evil or bestial representation than in the chanson de geste."[52] Like Franceschetti, Allaire proposes a concrete cause for this change: "Closer contacts with real Muslims in [the late] thirteenth and early fourteenth centuries experienced by Italian missionaries, merchants, and pilgrims would have further encouraged the humanizing process," especially as war became the less dominant mode of contact between Christians and Muslims.[53] She offers no actual textual evidence for the posited "humanization," however, and she seems to forget the Christian paroxysms of venomous invective following the Muslim conquest of Constantinople in 1453 and the conquest of Hungary and the Balkans—precisely in the period that she is discussing. As a corrective to this conventional echoing of such apologetical notions, Nancy Bisaha points out that calls for Crusade continued right up to the Reformation and that Crusade propaganda dominated the careers of many Humanists, while combat itself was almost incessant on both the large and small scale, although no actual continent-wide Crusades as such were mounted.[54] Even in the works of a thinker such as Petrarch, the Turks are portrayed as barbarians from the perspective of ancient Rome on its enemies.[55] While Bisaha's thesis is unquestionably correct, she nonetheless notes that not all Humanists were so negative: Coluccio Salutati (fourteenth century) expressed admiration for the Turks and compared them to ancient Romans; Giovanni Mario Filelfo even wrote *Amyris* (1476), an epic on Mehmet II, the conqueror of Constantinople.[56] It would be salutary to acknowledge that such attitudes had very concrete effects on Christian relations with Islam during the period, for as Daniel Vitkus remarks, the gross misrepresentations of Islam in European documents "are also 'real' in the sense that any such representation has a material and ideological impact as a historical phenomenon: it is a mode of perception that shapes the way people think and therefore the way they act."[57]

In order to determine Levita's role in constructing the image of the Muslim Other in his Old Yiddish epic, it would be particularly pertinent to compare his text with his "source" text. Unfortunately, either because that source has not been identified or because Levita so radically adapted the narrative that none of the potential source texts is particularly close to Levita's in content, a simple comparison as such is not possible. The text most often proposed as his source, as well as a second, chronologically proximate text, are thus here adduced at least as analogues.[58]

In this epic Muslims again play a significant role, and their depiction participates explicitly in the system of anti-Muslim bigotry characteristic of Christian epic. The systemic nature of the anti-Muslim bigotry of the Yiddish adaptation is demonstrated by a range of examples from the text. Very often the significance of the Yiddish examples becomes clear only in direct comparison to the analogous Tuscan texts, for the motifs are present in both but seem indeed to have a sharper edge of bigotry in the Yiddish text.

One of the primary opponents faced by Buovo in the Tuscan epic is the Soldan and his son Luchaferro (1480, V, 18, 6–8; Palladino, *Buouo*, [a7vb]), who, as Muslims, are designated by the terms "pagano," "pagan" (1480, VI, 26, 5 and Palladino, *Buouo* [a8ra]) and "traditor," "traitor" (1480, VI, 30, 4 and Palladino, *Buouo*, a8vb), "quella gente falsa e dispietata" "this false and impious people" (1480, VI, 34, 1), and "sarracini," "Saracens" (1480, VI, 35, 8). But in the 1480 Tuscan text, these designations are not repeated so often as to become definitive of the characters or their ethnicity, while in Palladino, after the appearance of the Soldan and his son Luchaferro, the terms "pagano" and/or "traditor(e)" recur only occasionally. In Levita's Yiddish adaptation, however, just as was the case in the Middle High German *Wigalois*, Muslims are to an even greater extent designated as היידן "heathens," in fact so often that the term and its conception simply become definitive of their existence.[59]

In keeping with the typical Christian construction of Muslims as anatomically Other, Luchaferro is identified as both a "pagano," "pagan," and a giant: "corpo suo era grandissimo," "his body was huge" (1480, V, 20, 3–4); "Era gigante questo homo," "this man was gigantic" (Palladino, *Buouo*, [a7vb]); and "Luno ochio da laltro hauea lontano / Un palmo o píu" "the one eye was distant from the other a palm's width or more" (Palladino, *Buouo*, [a7vb]). When Luchaferro fights, he is like a dragon (1480, V, 31, 1).

In Levita's adaptation, however, the description of the son of the Suldan of Babylonia[60] becomes more explicit in its active incorporation of the Christian system of anti-Muslim bigotry:

נון וואש דיש זעלביגן שולדאנש זון.
דער העשליכֿשט מאן דער ניא וואש גיבורן.
ער האט איין גישטאלט אז איין דראקון.
אונ' האט גרושי אויגן אונ' גרושי אורן.
ווער אין נורט זאך דער ולוך דאר בֿון.
ער וואר ויל שווערצר וועך די מורן.
אונ' האט איין בערטליין ווי די גיישן.
אונ' לוציפֿר וואר ער גיהיישן:
(st. 145)

Now, this same sultan's son was the ugliest man who had ever been born. He had a form like a dragon[61] and had huge eyes and huge ears. Whoever even so much as saw him took to his heels. He was much blacker than the Moors and had a little beard like a goat, and Lutsifer was his name.

In the Tuscan text of 1480, King Erminio, Buovo's future father-in-law, responds quite brutally to the suit of Luchaferro for his daughter's hand in marriage:

Bruta e orribel bestia dolorosa,
io credo che tu venisti da l'inferno,
che pari un demonio bruto e scherno.

Tu mi par per certo un satanasso:
ananti ch'io ti desse mia figliola
con un coltello gli daria fracasso,
certamente gli segaria la golla. (1480, V, 26, 6–27, 4)[62]

You brutish, horrible, deplorable beast who seems a brutish and scornful demon—I think that you have come from Hell. You certainly seem to me a devil:

> before I would give you my dear daughter, I would give her a blow with a knife and surely slit her throat.

He later adds that he would rather let his daughter be eaten by dogs than marry Luchaferro (1480, V, 36, 2).

In the Yiddish text, too, the Christian king would rather kill his daughter than allow her to be married to the Muslim suitor, whose caricatured Muslim גיילקייט "lust" is duly noted by the text (st. 153,6). Levita passes up no opportunity to add orientalizing detail: Lutsifer, for instance rides an elephant into battle (st. 153,1) and uses a steel pole as a weapon, as opposed to the "civilized" sword, lance, and shield of knights (st. 154–156). The Muslims are hewn down like dogs (st. 157,7; they are later killed like dogs, st. 184,8).[63] Holy war has been in progress for some time, and the brother of Bovo's beloved, Druzeyne, was in the past killed in battle in טערה די מורי "Moor-land" (st. 163,7).[64] In Palladino's text, the Soldan(o) calls on "macometo," "Muḥammad" (*Buouo*, b2va), who is identified as his god ("suo dio macone," "his god Muḥammad"; b3rb). Likewise, in the Yiddish text the Suldan swears by מאחמיט "Muḥammad" (st. 187,5), and later the warrior Passamonte (פאשאמונט) calls on מאחומיט "Muḥammad" for aid in battle but dies before he can finish pronouncing the name (st. 603,3), characterizing this putative deity as powerless. The Suldan is also an irresponsible and cowardly leader who abandons his men in battle and flees (st. 191) in a manner characteristic of the conventional representation of Muslim cowardice in Christian epic. The Christians slaughter the Muslims to the last man (st. 195–197).

As the Suldan in his incompetence is depicted as a caricatured Muslim military and political leader, so his daughter Margarete is represented as a typical example of the female Other insofar as she all but automatically falls in love with the European hero (Palladino, *Buouo*, b2vb). In the Yiddish text she is aggressive (sexually and otherwise) and gives orders to her father, the ostensive leader of the Muslim world, as if a servant; she saves Bovo, the typically desired European male hero, for her own personal pleasure (st. 241–243). Her character is quite typical of the genre in general and this romance in particular, as Rana Kabbani points out concerning the English adaptation of the Anglo-Norman original:

> The romance of *Sir Bevis of Hampton* contains the prototype of the enamoured Saracen princess. She is ready to serve her knight with slavish devotion. He inspires ardent desires in her, and this is because she is inherently lusty. Muslim princesses are the wooing women of medieval temptations scenes, who walk unbidden into bedchambers and proffer their bodies only to be virtuously refused. These seductresses will even forsake their religion for love of the knight. Josian swears to Sir Bevis that she will embrace Christianity if he would only embrace her. He agrees with missionary zeal, and she becomes a "good" Saracen when converted.[65]

In the Yiddish adaptation the character of the Muslim princess is no less accommodating. Kabbani points to the insight by Dorothee Metlitzky that in such works it became standard for Christian knights to defeat the Muslim leader with the help of the latter's wife or daughter: "What seems important in this framework is not the military defeat of the enemy but 'the degradation of the sultan or emir through the enmity and treachery of his own kin.' "[66]

Later in the Tuscan epic of 1480, after Buovo has been taken captive by the Soldan (via the status-driven machinations of a Christian kinsman of his beloved), the Muslims, recognizing Buovo's great nobility, attempt to entice him to convert to Islam ("deventar pagano," "become pagan"; VIII, 16, 3) and the worship of their putative god "Macon" (VIII, 41, 6 and 8), offering him the reward of the Soldan's beautiful daughter in marriage.[67] In Palladino's text, conversion to Islam is expressed as "renegare / E ritornare al nostro dio," "recant and return to our god" (*Buouo*, b2vb) and "Mia figlia vole che tu si campato / Lassia iesu macon vogli adorare," "My daughter wants you to stay alive. Disavow Jesus; desire to worship Muḥammad" (b3ra); Buouo responds that he has no desire to exchange a living for a dead god. In the 1480 recension, Buovo responds, " 'Tu felone Soldano, / vo' tu ch'io creda ne la fede ria? / Io voglio prima morir che renegare," "You felon, Soldano, you want me to believe in a wicked faith? I would die before recanting" (VIII, 16, 5–7), and calls Islam "le vostre fede torte," "your twisted/unjust faith" (VIII, 17, 4). To the repeated offer of the daughter as incentive for conversion, Buovo replies, "Di questo no curo io," "That does not interest me" (VIII, 28, 6). The daughter pleads, and he replies, "Indemoniato / nel padre tuo el diavolo gli ha parte; / in anima e in corpo l'è perduto," "The Devil has taken possession of your father; in soul and body, he is lost" (VIII, 31, 5–7). Levita again sharpens the prejudicial representation. To a battlefield challenge that he convert to Islam, Bovo responds: איך שיש אין דיך אונ' אין דיין גלאבן "I shit on you and your faith" (181, 7).[68] Later he is to be spared and given the Suldan's daughter as bride, but only if he converts, which he again refuses to do (243, 245, 251).

The cliché of medieval Christian epic that Muslims are by definition racially black appears when Buovo/Bovo at one point disguises himself as an Arab physician by smearing himself with a compound supplied him by a dishonest pilgrim, which functions to disguise his appearance: "negra come carbone," "black as charcoal" (IX, 51, 6–7) and "ello fu sì negro deventato, / che parea d'un saracin nasciuto," "he became so black that he seemed a born Saracen" (X, 4, 5–6).[69] Later, in order to get to his arch-enemy, the ailing Dudon, he assumes the disguise of a famed physician, blackening his face by means of a method such that people "parean pur in Oriente nati," "appear indeed born in the Orient" (XVII, 15, 5–8).[70] Levita's narrator comments on the technique: גלייך אז איין מור וואר ער גיקלייט "he was disguised/fitted out exactly as a Moor" (st. 564,5).[71] On the one hand, this motif constitutes a recognition of the scientific acumen of Muslim culture, particularly with respect to the practice of medicine, such that a "Muslim appearance" constitutes as it were one's medical credentials. On the other hand, the motif demonstrates a characteristic orientalism in the description of clothes and skin color. Bovo's blackface routine differs both in its details and its larger cultural context from the racism of nineteenth- and twentieth-century blackface comedians in the United States, but within its context, it is no less racist.

Still later in the tale, Drusiana/Druzeyne, who—explicitly in the Yiddish text—had learned the technique from Bovo, blackens her own skin and that of their children in order to disguise them obviously not as Muslim physicians but as beggars so that incognito they might test their father's attitude toward her and them after their long adventurous separation (XVIII, 32, 5–6). And in the Yiddish text:

דא מן זיך מיט מאכֿט שווארץ אז איין קול.
דא שמירט זי זיך אונ' איר קינדר אונטר אירן אויגן.
אונ' רעכֿט ווי איין בעטלרין וואר זי זיך קליידן.
(st. 615,5–7)

> Therewith one made himself black as a (lump of) coal / then she smeared herself and her children under the eyes / and quite like a beggar was she disguised/fitted out.

There are several inconcinnities in the explicit identification of Muslims and Bovo's blacking up. It seems that Druzeyne's blackening her and her children "under the eyes" functions synecdochically for the whole face. It is not, however, here made explicit that so disguised they are then necessarily construed as specifically *Muslim* beggars, as the physician was earlier in the text necessarily so ethnically perceived (st. 615). Or is it the case that one assumes that all beggars are Muslims? Or that Muslims look like beggars or vice versa? Or is it simply that since they are in fact in Babylon, a disguise as a beggar should take into account that beggars are likely to be locals? The laconic mode of the text implicitly poses but answers none of these questions.

At the conclusion of the romance, not surprisingly, a marriage takes place, as is conventional in the genre. Buovo/Bovo rescues the Soldan/Suldan's daughter, Malgarita/Margaríta/Margarete—who has repeatedly been his benefactor in the past—from foreign invasion and usurpation, and accepts her offer of marriage in return. In the Yiddish text, it is explicitly indicated that the hero's relatives do not object to his marriage to the Soldan/Suldan's daughter (st. 590–591), but the common cliché of Christian epic (and of course of historical Christian societies) in such situations arises, that is, that the Muslim must convert before the marriage can take place, since otherwise the marriage would not be legitimate.[72] While Palladino explicitly mentions the conversion of Margaríta (*Buouo*, f2ra), in the Yiddish adaptation, Margarete expresses the issue in a far more interesting manner in terms of Christian-Muslim cultural history, for she makes her conversion explicitly dependent on the European man's *desire*: דו וואלשט ניט טרעטן אין מיינן גלאבן · נון וויל איך אין דען דיינן ווילטו מיך הבן "You did not want to convert to my religion. Now I wish to/will convert to yours, if you wish to/will have me" (st. 610,7–8). And Bovo replies, also significantly: ווילטו דש טון · זא וויל איך דיך נעמן גאר און גר גערן "If you wish/will do that, then I wish/will take you quite willingly" (st. 611,1–2).[73]

In the end, however, this entire plot motif is sublated, for Buovo/Bovo's betrothed, Drusiana/Druzeyne, presumed dead, returns with their twin sons, and the hero's Muslim bride-to-be Margaríta/Margarete is simply disposed of by marrying her to the next best European knight,[74] Buovo/Bovo's right-hand man, Terygi/Tedrise/Teyrets, which she is immediately willing to do, her eternal love for Bovo apparently being easily transferred to the stranger, since after all her passion is depicted as "only" that of an apparently irrational and thus passion-driven Muslim, illustrating the long-lived European literary principle that a Muslim is so eager to marry a Christian/European that one is generally as good as another. In both texts the issue is treated almost as if automatic. Buovo simply tells Tedrise to put the wedding ring on her finger: "Vedi, Tedrise, io ho preso partito: / a Malgarita pon l'anello in dito," "Come, Tedrise, I have made a decision [*or:* taken a stand]: place the ring on Malgarita's finger" (XIX, 51, 7–8), and the marriage follows automatically (XX, 2, 1–2).

Before returning to Europe in the Tuscan text, Buovo stays with Tedrise fourteen months (XX, 9, 4), during which time "tutti i pagani ha fatto baptizare," "he baptized all the Muslims" (XX, 12, 1; cf. also Palladino, *Buouo*, f2vb). In the Yiddish text, that conversion is apparently not voluntary, for Bovo helps Teyrets to *conquer* a suitable number of lands in Muslim territory, specifically those that had previously belonged to Margarete's father (the Suldan), in order to support him and his new wife appropriately, after which Bovo returns to Europe (st. 640). In Palladino's text, Terygi is left with his new former-Muslim bride as ruler of her former-Muslim lands, explicitly identified as sultan: "Lassio Terygi e soldan chyamato," "I leave Terygi, named as sultan" (*Buouo*, f2vb).

Thus in its final stanzas the epic, which has been consistently anti-Muslim throughout, suddenly transforms into what to all appearances seems a conventional crusader/conversion epic, when, for all intents and purposes, Bovo and Teyrets lead a European military expedition from Italy to Babylon to defeat a Muslim military force and establish by conquest a Christian colony in Muslim territory. They are—like so many foreign conquerors before and since—(conveniently) invited by a local political instance, here a Muslim princess, to invade, but the invasion and the military and political result—a kingdom of converts to Christianity, ruled by a Christian king and his converted, formerly Muslim, wife—provide an idealized Crusader conclusion to the romance.

The situation of Terygi/Tedrise/Teyrets and Malgarita/Margaríta/Margarete at the conclusion of *Bovo* almost suggests "what might have been" imaginable before Gahmuret's departure from Zazamanc near the end of the first *aventiure* of Wolfram's *Parzival*: a Christian hero and (formerly) Muslim bride ruling newly conquered (and perhaps formerly) Muslim territory beyond the borders of Christendom. Surprising or not in its conclusion, the romance of Buovo/Bovo as a whole is thus quite consistent with the anti-Muslim ideology conventional in the pan-European genre. The Yiddish adaptation is, additionally, both much more explicit and more extreme in that ideology and, in the context of the broad tradition of Jewish epic, quite aberrant, for otherwise in the Jewish epic tradition there is quite simply no systematic *pattern* of bigotry to be discerned, such as that found in Christian epic. While some few details remain that almost certainly derive from the ideological structure characteristic of Christian epic, the Jewish examples seem only to be scattered remnants of that tradition that have been deemphasized and all but eliminated from the Jewish texts. There does remain, of course, the one radical exception—Levita's *Bovo*—the only one of the Jewish epics whose author is well known. One can attach an author's (or perhaps a scribe's) name to some few of the other texts, but *Bovo* was written by the internationally famous Elia Levita, as problematized above in chapter 3, one of the early modern Jewish intellectuals often deemed by scholars most eligible, as it were, to be reckoned as a "Jewish Humanist." Yet he was also the author/translator/adapter of the rabidly bigoted representation of Muslims in the *Bovo d'Antona*. Moreover, as earlier noted, there were not a few contemporary (Christian) Humanists who were just as rabidly anti-Muslim.

The obvious conditioning factors of the Jewish reception of Christian literature in the production of Yiddish texts are not demonstrably different in Levita's *Bovo* from those of the other texts discussed, except as they pertain specifically to Levita, who lived in the Veneto (Padua and Venice) a half century after the Turkish conquest of Constantinople and as the Turkish military and political administrative presence moved seemingly inexorably northward through the Balkans toward the latitude of Venice directly across the Adriatic.[75] The Turks were literally next door and moving ever closer and contesting Venetian possessions and trade monopolies throughout the eastern Mediterranean. During Levita's adulthood there were two major wars fought by Venice against the Ottoman Empire: the second Ottoman-Venetian War (1499–1503, only a few years before he wrote *Bovo*), which resulted in the Ottoman capture of some Venetian-controlled Aegean islands and some Venetian strongholds in the Peloponnese; and the third Ottoman-Venetian War (1537–1540, just before he published the text's first edition), which brought the Ottoman capture of most of the Cycladic and Sporadic Islands and the remaining Venetian strongholds in the Peloponnese. As is known from the wealth of surviving Venetian documents of the time,[76] life certainly went on, but there was an almost constant state of alarm during Levita's many decades in the Veneto. While he was serving as Hebrew and Aramaic scholar-in-residence in Cardinal Egidio da Viterbo's palace (during his years in Rome interspersed between his periods of residence in Venice), at the end of February 1518, the pope received a threatening letter from the sultan and in response sent four cardinals on missions to the four Christian states most likely to support a papal crusade. Levita's patron, Egidio, was thus sent to Spain on 16 March as a papal legate,[77] bringing the ongoing conflict between the Islamic and Christian realms, and specifically the Turkish crisis, home to Levita in a very personal way.

The connections were also textual and philological, however, and thus spoke more directly to Levita's professional interests. During the period when he served as Egidio's tutor in Semitic languages and lived in his Roman palace, the cardinal commissioned a Qur'ān translation by Iohannes Gabriel Terrolensis.[78] Egidio's interests in Qur'ān and Kabbalah were thus obviously simultaneous and supported by a hired staff of experts in both fields.[79] Some of the notes in the Qur'ān translation not surprisingly demonstrate as much interest in Hebrew as in Arabic, which might suggest that Levita had some hand in this project as well, since it was executed at the same time and under the same roof as was his own work.[80] Egidio himself was deeply engaged in political polemic and political action that grew out of his vested interests in religion and politico-theological perspectives. In 1517, for instance, he wrote a treatise against the Jews, and as Robert Bonfil points out, unlike Erasmus, who thought the "cult of Hebrew" among Christian Humanists would just reinforce Jews in their convictions, Egidio was among those who thought this subfield of scholarly endeavor was key to converting the Jews to Christianity.[81]

While Egidio's Qur'ān project was an effective tool for the philological study of the text, it nonetheless displays typical traits of the Christian anti-Muslim propaganda of the period, even though it lacks the "vicious denunciation of the Qur'ān that exists alongside all the philology that we find in the twelfth-century texts—no cursing of Muhammad as a *mendax*, no snide dismissals of the Qur'ān's . . . fables."[82] But in the end one finds there essentially the same modes of polemic that characterize anti-Islamic Qur'ān work elsewhere in Christian society.[83] This connection between Levita's intellectual experience in Egidio's palace and his own sensibility vis-à-vis Islam, as expressed in his Yiddish epic *Bovo d'Antona*, is striking. To make the one a direct function of the other would be to employ a simplistically conceived biographical interpretation as a blunt instrument; let it instead be merely suggestive of the intellectual milieu in which Levita worked.

While Levita had already written a first draft of *Bovo* in 1507 (as he notes in the preface to the 1541 printed edition), which pre-dates his sojourn in Rome, the connection may still be of twofold relevance: his concurrence with Egidio on this issue may have drawn the two together or at least provided them common ideological ground.

Levita's portrayal of Muslims in *Bovo*, so radically different from the rest of the tradition of Yiddish epic, thus may be due to a particular mode of reception on Levita's part, to some aspect of his own experience, or to other factors, probably no longer ascertainable.[84] The representation of Muslims by Jews—one "Other" (from the hegemonic Christian point of view) by another "Other"—one could say, undermines the Christian narrative norm. But since these Yiddish texts existed outside the realm of Christian reception, that norm itself is not applicable. The Jewish conception of this problem is quite simply different. In any case, *Bovo* seems a glaring exception to what one might otherwise recognize as a basic principle of early Yiddish epic, that of religious and ethnic tolerance.[85]

Notes

1. This issue is key; cf. Jerold C. Frakes, *Vernacular and Latin Literary Discourses of the Muslim Other in Medieval Germany*, New Middle Ages Series (New York: Palgrave, 2011), 157–158.

2. See esp. Erik, *Vegn altyidishn roman* and Tsinberg, *Altyidishe literatur*, chap. 3, 61–102.

3. This is in general an issue that has practically not been examined in Yiddish literary history. See, however, the brief and general comments by Arnold Paucker, "Yiddish Versions of Early German Prose Novels," *Journal of Jewish Studies* 10 (1959), esp. 155–157, where the representation of Muslims in the early Yiddish *Oktavianus* is briefly discussed.

4. Yaron Peleg, *Orientalism and the Hebrew Imagination* (Ithaca, NY: Cornell University Press, 2005), 4. Indeed as Ivan Davidson Kalmar and Derek J. Penslar point out in their introduction to *Orientalism and the Jews* (Waltham, MA: Brandeis University Press, 2005), Jews have themselves been construed by Christians as components of the Christian image of Islam: ". . . the Western image of the Muslim Orient has been formed, and continues to be formed in inextricable conjunction with Western perceptions of the Jewish people" (xiii).

5. Mark R. Cohen, *Under Crescent and Cross: The Jews in the Middle Ages* (Princeton, NJ: Princeton University Press, 1994), 145.

6. Bernard Lewis, *The Jews of Islam* (Princeton, NJ: Princeton University Press, 1984), 85.

7. Cohen, *Under Crescent and Cross*, 145.

8. Cohen's introduction examines the ideologies of political myths employed for the sake of pro- and anti-Islamic argument in Israeli-Palestinian conflicts (*Under Crescent and Cross*, 3–14). He provides a succinct overview of the research on the issue in his introductory chapter.

9. One thinks first and foremost of Shmuel ha-Levi ben Yosef ha-Nagid (שמואל הלוי בן יוסף הנגיד, 993–1056; better known in Arabic as Abu Isḥaq Isma'il bin Naġrilla), warrior, statesman, and vizier in Berber Granada.

10. Cf. Ruth von Bernuth, "Zwischen Kreuzrittern und Sarazenen," "denn es wird weder der Kampf gegen die Heiden als eines der wesentlichen narrativen Elemente herausgenommen noch einfach umbesetzt in einen Kampf der Juden gegen die Heiden" (p. 416), "for neither the conflict against the heathens is abstracted as one of the essential narrative elements, nor is it simply recast as a conflict of Jews against the heathens" [*sic*].

11. L. Fuks, ed., *Das altjiddische Epos Melokîm-Bûk*, 2 vols. (Assen: Van Gorcum, 1965); with facsimile of *editio princeps*, Augsburg 1543; *EYT* 45; Baumgarten, *Introduction*, 151–155.

12. Wulf-Otto Dreeßen and Hermann-Josef Müller, eds., *Doniel: Das altjiddische Danielbuch nach dem Basler Druck von 1557*, 2 vols., Litterae 59 (Göppingen: Kümmerle, 1978); with facsimile of *editio princeps*, Basel, 1557; *EYT* 57.

13. Felix Falk, ed., *Das Schmuelbuch des Mosche Esrim Wearba: Ein biblisches Epos aus dem 15. Jahrhundert* (Assen: Van Gorcum, 1961); with facsimile of *editio princeps*, Augsburg 1544; *EYT* 47; Baumgarten, *Introduction*, 143–152.

14. *EYT* 60; Baumgarten, *Introduction*, 137, 302.

15. Leo Landau, ed., "A Hebrew-German (Judeo-German) Paraphrase of the Book Esther of the Fifteenth Century," *Journal of English and Germanic Philology* 18 (1919): 497–555; Baumgarten, *Introduction*, 331–341, 366–385.

16. While the Yiddish term is not as ubiquitous as its Middle High German reflex, it does appear in early Yiddish literature even beyond the genre of epic: : שרייאן ווערט איר אלי גלייך איר טערקין אונ' אך היידן. "all of you alike will shout, you Turks and heathens," from Jacob ben Benjamin Tousk (Taussig) of Prague, איין שוין נייא ליד פון משיח *A Fine, New Poem on the Messiah* (Amsterdam 1666), st. 21,1 (*EYT* 108). The late twentieth-century editors of the Middle Yiddish *Book of Daniel* apparently viewed the term as so very integrated into early Yiddish epic literature that they insert it in their Roman-alphabet transcription of the text even when the Hebrew-alphabet original shows no trace of the word: די מיט דען כלים טריבן ויל שפוט אונ' שנד *di* haidėn *mit den celim tribėn vil spöt uṅ schȧnd* (st. 273,4); while the editors offer no justification for their insertion, one might hope that it was based only on their conception of metrics.

17. On the medieval Christian (and modern scholarly) use of the term *heid*, "heathen," see my *Vernacular and Latin Literary Discourses*, 37–40.

18. This metaphorical use of the term is, however, not exclusively employed to designate the Philistines; it also is used for the young Israelites in the desert (Joshua 5:7).

19. There is a variant reading: בייהם, which is most likely a scribal error for ביצים.

20. The appearance of the term in early Yiddish quasi-secular epic is also often quite unrelated to Muslims; cf. דער טויבֿל בֿירטש הין אז בֿוייער שוועביל "the Devil draws them as a match does fire" (*Pariz and Viene* st. 303,7); גלייך ווי אין דער טויבֿיל יאגט "just as if the Devil were chasing him" (*Bovo d'Antona* st. 595,2); דער טייבֿל אויש אים גליטא "the devil glowed out of him" (*Her Ditraykh* st. 174,8; edition: *Dietrich von Bern (1597)*, facsimile ed. John A. Howard [Würzburg: Königshausen und Neuman, 1986]).

21. Oxford, Bodleian Library, Opp. 19, ed. Landau, "A Hebrew-German (Judeo-German) Paraphrase."

22. On this tradition, see esp. Jacob Lassner, *Demonizing the Queen of Sheba: Boundaries of Gender and Culture in Postbiblical Judaism and Medieval Islam* (Chicago: University of Chicago Press, 1993).

23. Lagarde, *Hagiographa Chaldaice*, 232. See also Moritz, *Targum Scheni*; and Munk, *Targum Scheni*.

24. Cf. Lassner, *Demonizing*, 20, where it is also noted that Pseudo–Ben Sira suggests that biblical Israelite women shaved their pubic hair, since it was dangerous to men, as evidenced in the post-biblical legend (BT *Sanh* 21a) that during his rape of his sister Tamar (whose mother was a concubine, *not* an Israelite woman), Amnon's genitals were mutilated by becoming entangled in her unshaven pubic hair.

25. According to Lassner, *Demonizing*, 84.

26. Qurʾān 27:15–44; Ṭabarsī, *Majmaʿ* 19:229; Balkhī, *Badʾ* 3:108. Arabic and Hebrew share the word for arsenic (Hebrew זַרְנִיךְ and Arabic زرنيخ). Lassner suggests a Persian origin for the

term, which was then also borrowed into Talmudic Aramaic (זרניך BT *Hullin* 88b; Lassner, *Demonizing*, 130), which suggests a common origin for both the post-biblical Hebrew and post-Qur'ānic Arabic usage, but without evidence of which of these two might be the origin of the other. Aḥmad ben Muḥammad ben Ibrāhīm ath-Tha'labī (eleventh century), in his *'Arā'is al-majālis* includes a lengthy tale of Sulaymān and Bilqīs (the traditional name in Arabic texts for the character of the Queen of Sheba); here Bilqīs, whose mother was a jinn, has not only hairy ankles but in one passage also hooves like a mule, although in a subsequent passage her feet and ankles are said to be beautiful, although still hairy; the text claims that this was the first use of a depilatory (Lassner, *Demonizing*, 199–200). Cf. also the Middle Yiddish biblical paraphrase with commentary, the *Tsene-rene* (Hanau 1622; *EYT* 98).

27. The sense of קארזיף *karzayf/karzif* is not straightforward. If construed phonetically as in the first suggested transcription, it might designate some type of soap or cleansing product, perhaps a Yiddish reflex of German *Kurseife*, "medicinal/treatment soap" or German *Kernseife*, "curd soap / Marseille soap," a very strong soap made by traditional methods from vegetable oil, lye, and soda ash, here with the addition of chalk, which would function as a depilatory abrasive, although it would whiten the skin only if not washed off. A second possibility, which fits the context better, but which has a phonological obstacle (צ/ז), would be the word קרצף, which in its Talmudic context means "scrape/scratch" (Mishnah, *Beyzah* 2.8), which is precisely the sense of abrasion necessary for depilation.

28. The current connotation of כושי in Israeli Hebrew as an insulting racial slur against Blacks does not reflect the more neutral and strictly geographical usage of ancient Hebrew.

29. Dreeßen and Müller, eds., *Doniel*, st. 122,1. Interestingly, in an editorial addition to the text, mentioned above (st. 273,4), Dreeßen and Müller seem to mirror this usage in their addition of the word *haidėn*, albeit without any textual justification. Two lines earlier in that same stanza, however, the word גוים *goyim*, "non-Jews," actually appears in the text as a designation of the Babylonian nobles whom Belshazzar allowed to drink from the sacred vessels that had been looted in the previous generation from the Temple in Jerusalem; thus when the editors insert the word *haidėn* two lines later to designate the same people, they recapitulate the ethnically opaque terminological dichotomy found in st. 122.

30. Ed. Leviant, *King Artus*. See also Manfred Kern, "Verwilderte Heldenepik in hebräischen Lettern. Literarischer Horizont und kultureller Austausch im *Dukus Horant*," *Mittelalterliche Heldendichtung außerhalb des Nibelungen- und Dietrichkreises (Kudrun, Ortnit, Waltharius, Wolfdietriche), 7. Pöchlarner Heldenliedgespräch*, ed. Klaus Zatloukal, Philologica Germanica 25 (Vienna: Fassbaender, 2003), 109–134; Tamar S. Drukker, "A Thirteenth-Century Arthurian Tale in Hebrew: A Unique Literary Exchange," *Medieval Encounters* 15 (2009): 114–129; Martin Przybilski, "Ein anti-arthurischer Artusroman: Invektiven gegen die höfische Literatur zwischen den Zeilen des מלך ארטוש (Melech Artus)," *Zeitschrift für deutsches Altertum und deutsche Literatur* 131 (2002): S. 409–435.

31. Kazis deals with issues of sources in great detail in the introduction to his edition. For the Latin text, see Alfons Hilka, ed., *Historia Alexandri Magni (Historia de preliis): Rezension J1* (Meisenheim am Glan: A. Hain, 1979).

32. As Edith Hall so brilliantly theorizes and documents the process in her study *Inventing the Barbarian: Greek Self-Definition through Tragedy* (Oxford: Clarendon, 1989).

33. *Alexander*, 131 and 133.

34. E.g., *ungetriuwe*, "perfidy" (lines 3673, 3679, 3683, 3710, etc.); *deheine triuwe*, "no loyalty" (lines 3691); *valschlîche*, "perfidiously" (line 3682); *valsche*, "perfidious" (line 3702).

35. E.g., lines 3652, 3667, 7480, 7509, 7586, 8277, 8523, 8574, 8601, 8621, 8918, 9158, among *many* other instances.

36. Cambridge, Trinity College, F.12.44, fol. 67r, lines 3418–3419; cf. Landau, *Arthurian Legends*, 97–97a.

37. Robert G. Warnock incidentally notes the elimination of the anti-Muslim motifs; see "The Arthurian Tradition in Hebrew and Yiddish," in *King Arthur through the Ages*, ed. Valerie M. Lagorio and Mildred Leake Day, vol. 1 (New York: Garland, 1990), 193.

38. Judah ben Isaac ibn Shabbetai, 'מנחת יהודה', 'עזרה הנשים', ו'עין משפט' - מהדורות מדעיות בלווית מבוא, חילופי גירסאות, מקורות ופירושים, ed. Matti Huss, 2 vols. (diss. Jerusalem 1991) ["Minhat Yehudah," "Ezrat ha-nashim" ve-"En mishpat"], 2:25, lines 584–586; translation from Judah Ibn Shabbetai, "The Misogynist," ed. and trans. Raymond Scheindlin, 269–294, in *Rabbinic Fantasies: Imaginative Narratives from Classical Hebrew Literature*, ed. David Stern and Mark J. Mirsky (New Haven: Yale University Press, 1990), 285. Talya Fishman attempts to reverse some aspects of the conventional interpretation of Judah's text as a misogynistic diatribe: "A Medieval Parody of Misogyny: Judah ibn Shabbetai's 'Minḥat Yehudah sone hanashim,'" *Prooftexts* 8 (1988): 89–111.

39. Jefim Schirmann, "Der Neger und die Negerin: zur Bildersprache und Stoffwahl der spanisch-hebräischen Dichtung," *Monatschrift für Geschichte und Wissenschaft des Judentums* 83 (1939): 481–92.

40. Scheindlin, "Misogynist," 292–293 n. 49.

41. Hamburg, Staats und Universitätsbibliothek, Cod, hebr. 289, fol. 60v; Landau 105. On independent women identified as she-devils, such as Brünhild and Kriemhild in the *Nibelungenlied*, see my *Brides and Doom*, chap. 5: "Teuton as Amazon: The Devil's Bride and the She-Devil," 137–169.

42. Cited here is a plausible, perhaps even the likely Tuscan text on the basis of which the Yiddish poet reconceived and rewrote the epic: *Paris and Viena. Inamoramento de li nobeli amanti Paris & Viena: historiato: & nouamente corretto* (Venice: Melchior Sessa, 1528). Treating it as a "source," however, as many scholars have earlier suggested, is quite troubled, since the two texts are very different in so many ways.

43. John Block Friedman notes that Muslims are often portrayed as dogs, both in image and word by medieval Christians; in *The Monstrous Races in Medieval Art and Thought* (Cambridge, MA: Harvard University Press, 1981), 67.

44. Interesting in relation to this passage is the assumption by Armin Schulz (whose focus is actually on the narrator's apparent reversal of position) that the Soldan's imprisonment of the spy is an "Ausdruck besonderer heidnischer Perfidie," "expression of especial heathen perfidy"; Schulz, *Die Zeichen des Körpers*, 28. Schulz's complex and generally perceptive study is one of the few forays of theoretically informed literary criticism into the field of early Yiddish studies. It is quite unclear how he might construe the Soldan's actions in this way, since *Perfidie* presupposes a betrayal of trust, and the imprisonment of a hitherto unknown enemy spy hardly qualifies as betrayal (one might indeed attribute perfidy to the act of the spy who pretends to be someone he is not). Schulz's assumption seems grounded in an unacknowledged acceptance of the Christian caricature of Muslim character. Erika Timm likewise seems to project a prejudicial sensibility onto the text: "Verglichen mit dieser Hierarchie auf christlicher Seite wird diejenige auf mohammedanischer Seite etwas kursorischer gezeichnet. Der Sultan ist ein Mensch des Augenblicks," "Compared with this hierarchy on the Christian side, the one on the Mohammedan [*sic*!] side is somewhat more cursory. The sultan is a man of the moment"; she claims that the sultan is "zornig," "wrathful," and "leichtgläubig[] gegenüber Paris," "gullible vis-á-vis Paris"; the Mameluk prison guards are said to be frightening in themselves, "potentiell sehr brutal . . . disziplinlos . . . dümmlich-lärmend . . . volltrunken[] . . . abstoßend," "potentially very brutal . . . without discipline . . . inanely raucous . . . completely drunk . . . repugnant"; Timm, *Paris un*

Wiene, cv. Since she never acknowledges the ideological context in which such characterizations are constructed and participate, and since the text offers little actual evidence for her dichotomy of Christian versus Muslim character valuation, one might well be tempted to see that valuation arising less from the text's cultural assumptions than the scholar's.

45. Facsimile ed. in John A. Howard, *Fortunatus* (Würzburg: Königshausen und Neumann, 1991).

46. On the specific function of Prester John in proto-Eurocentric discourse, see my *Vernacular and Latin Literary Discourses*, 90 and 193. Interestingly, this motif appears in the Tuscan *Paris e Viena*, when Paris travels to India where "Prete Ianni" lives (Hv.r); this motif is quite absent from the Yiddish *Pariz and Viene.*

47. Padua was the most important Ashkenazi community, with the highest Ashkenazi population in Italy at the turn of the sixteenth century; see Weil, *Élie Lévita*, 31, 175.

48. As in the previous chapter, reference will also be made here to the sixteenth-century manuscripts of *Bovo* when relevant while generally citing the author's own edition (1541). This narrative has excited interest in other iterations of the tradition, as well; on the treatment of the Muslim question in the medieval Welsh version of the Anglo-Norman *Boeve de Haumtone*, see Matthieu Boyd, "Celts Seen as Muslims and Muslims Seen by Celts in Medieval Literature," in *Contextualizing the Muslim Other in Medieval Christian Discourse*, ed. Jerold C. Frakes (New York: Palgrave, 2011), 25–30.

49. Robert Black offers an extensive bibliography of Humanistic texts concerning the Turks, in his *Benedetto Accolti and the Florentine Renaissance* (Cambridge: Cambridge University Press, 1985), chap. 9, 224–285. See also Margaret Meserve, *Empires of Islam in Renaissance Historical Thought*, Harvard Historical Studies 158 (Cambridge, MA: Harvard University Press, 2008).

50. John Patrick Donnelly, "The Moslem Enemy in Renaissance Epic: Ariosto, Tasso and Camoëns," *Yale Italian Studies* 1 (1977): 163–164.

51. Antonio Franceschetti, "On the Saracens in Early Italian Chivalric Literature," in *Romance Epic: Essays on a Medieval Literary Genre*, ed. Hans-Erich Keller, Studies in Medieval Culture 24 (Kalamazoo: Medieval Institute Publications/Western Michigan University, 1987), 207.

52. Gloria Allaire, "Noble Saracen or Muslim Enemy? The Changing Image of the Saracen in Late Medieval Italian Literature," in *Western Views of Islam in Medieval and Early Modern Europe: Perception of Other*, ed. David R. Blanks and Michael Frassetto (New York: St. Martin's Press, 1999), 181.

53. Allaire, "Noble Saracen," 181.

54. Nancy Bisaha "'New Barbarian' or Worthy Adversary? Humanist Constructs of the Ottoman Turks in Fifteenth-Century Italy," in *Western Views of Islam*, 186.

55. Bisaha, "New Barbarian," 188.

56. Bisaha, "New Barbarian," 194–195.

57. Daniel J. Vitkus, "Early Modern Orientalism: Representations of Islam in Sixteenth- and Seventeenth-Century Europe," in *Western Views of Islam*, 207–208.

58. I hope to treat this vexed issue of Levita's Tuscan "source" in adequate detail elsewhere. Judah A. Joffe was the first to opine that Levita's source was the "1497 Toscana edition" (i.e., Guidone Palladino, *Buouo di Antona di Guidone Palladino. Regunto et reuisto* [Bologna: Caligula di Bazalieri, 1497; extant: London, British Library IA 28994]); see Judah A. Joffe, ed., *Elye Bokher, poetishe shafungen in yidish, ershter band: Bovo d'Antona* (New York: Judah A. Joffe, 1949), 7 (English), 25 (Yiddish). Erika Timm has followed Joffe (Timm, "Wie Elia Levita," 61–81). Careful analysis of *Bovo* and Palladino's *Buouo* make abundantly clear, however, that the latter

cannot serve as the source of the former in any normal sense of the term "translation." Under such circumstances, I cite two distinct versions of the Tuscan romance here for the sake of illustration: Palladino's *Buovo* (the unpaginated and unfoliated text is cited by gathering) and the anonymous *Buovo d'Antona: cantari in ottava rima (1480)*, ed. Daniela Delcorno Branca (Roma: Carocci, 2008); hereinafter designated: "1480."

59. St. 151, 152, 157, 173, 176, 178, 183, 184 (2x), 195, 197, 199, 203, 235, 258, 263, 272, 277, 595, 598, 602, 603, 604, 605.

60. On the problematic interpretation of the medieval and early modern European geographical designators "Babylon" and "Babylonia" (in their various cognate forms)—Cairo or Mesopotamian Babylon?—see my *Early Yiddish Epic*, xlvii–xlix.

61. Levita's 1541 edition reads דראקון, while the manuscript, National Library of Israel, Ms. Heb. (2)8° 7565, 15v, provides an alternate reading: בראקין (cf. MHG *bracke*, "hunting dog"). Rosenzweig strangely claims that Joffe "emended this word to *drakun*" (*A Yiddish Romance*, 274, n. 316). But since Joffe's edition is a facsimile edition, it is unclear how Rosenzweig imagines he could have "emended" any reading.

62. In Palladino's text, Ormino similarly, albeit more briefly, responds to Luchaferro's declaration of love: "Tu mi pare el diauol da linferno," "You seem to me the Devil from Hell" (Palladino, *Buouo*, b2ra).

63. In the 1480 Tuscan version, after the battle between the forces of the Soldan and King Erminio begins, Buovo is informed by a local boy on the streets that his king has been attacked "da quelli malvasi cani," "by these wicked/cursed dogs" (canto V, st. 47, line 1, 79). In *Bovo* the same phrase is employed to describe the attack by Bovo and his allies on Makabrun's presumably Christian vassals from Mainz (st. 581,1); later, the presumably Muslim Pashamont addresses the presumably Christian Teyrets with the same term (st. 600,3).

64. The stanza is lacking Jerusalem Heb. (2)8° 7565, fol. 17r.

65. Rana Kabbani, *Imperial Fictions: Europe's Myths of Orient* (Macmillan 1986; repr., London: Pandora 1994), 15–16.

66. Kabbani, *Imperial Fictions*, 16, citing Dorothee Metlitzky, *The Matter of Araby in Medieval England* (New Haven, CT: Yale University Press, 1977), 175.

67. In designating themselves as "pagans," the Muslim characters are terminologically involved by the poet in their own Otherization.

68. Jerusalem, Ms. Heb. (2)8° 7565, fol. 18r, employs a synonym: שמיש בול "shit abundantly." Bovo continues to reject conversion, even as he is offered his freedom and the Suldan's daughter as bride in exchange (243, 245, 251). On Bovo's refusal to convert, see especially Chone Shmeruk, *Prokim*, 150–151.

69. This episode is missing in the British Library exemplar of Palladino's *Buouo*, due to pages lost from the text, but it is clear that the complete text included that episode, since Buouo later washes off the blackface in order to reveal himself to Drusiana (c2rb).

70. Lynn Tarte Ramey points out an interesting parallel in the *Sieve de Barbastre*: Christians successfully pass through Muslim lines by blackening their skin first with ointment but then have to clean off the disguise with vinegar before the French king will acknowledge them as Christian (*Christian, Saracen and Genre in Medieval French Literature* [New York: Routledge 2001], 46). She also notes an interesting twist on blackface disguise: Nicolette, a Muslim, flees her homeland when her father tries to marry her to a noble Muslim; she engages in both race and class disguise by blacking up to disguise herself as a minstrel and cross-dressing as male (86).

71. Earlier in the text, he uses the blackface compound to disguise himself *not* as a Muslim but as a beggar-pilgrim and גינג הריין אז איין שפנייולן "entered [looking] like a Spaniard," i.e., presumably like a Christian on pilgrimage to Santiago de Compostela in Galicia.

72. As the case of Gahmuret and Belakane in Wolfram's *Parzival*, among others, had demonstrated several centuries earlier. It is in such texts likewise impossible to conceive of the non-Muslim converting to Islam in order to marry a Muslim bride. See my *Vernacular and Latin Literary Discourses*, chap. 4, "Mandatory Muslim Metamorphosis," 59–95. Von Bernuth's assumption that Margarete converts from Islam to Judaism depends on her prior assumption that Bovo is Jewish; she offers no compelling evidence for either assumption ("Zwischen Kreuzrittern und Sarazenen," 427).

73. Cf. the similar usage in the formula employed in David's marriage proposal to Abigail (conveyed by his messenger) in the Yiddish *Book of Samuel*: ווילשטו דָוִד נעמן ער וויל דיך גערן הון "if you will take David, he will eagerly have you" (st. 651,4). Cf. also the similar formula used by Margarete in response to the proposal by Bovo of Terets as her "substitute" mate, after he is reunited with Druzeyne: וואלט ער נורט מיך · וויא גר גערן וועלט איך נעמן "if only he wanted me, how very eagerly I would take him" (st. 637,3–4).

74. מרגריטה מוש מירש וואל דר לאבן דש איך דיך נים אונ' זי ור טרייב "Margarete will just have to let me take you [Druzeyne] and drive her away" (st. 634; lacking in Jerusalem, Ms. Heb. (2)8° 7565, where the text breaks off at the bottom of fol. 62v with st. 633).

75. On Venetian-Ottoman relations, especially on luxury trade and pilgrim and diplomatic exchanges, see Deborah Howard, "Cultural Transfer between Venice and the Ottomans in the Fifteenth and Sixteenth Centuries," in *Cultural Exchange in Early Modern Europe*, vol. 4, *Forging European Identities, 1400–1700*, ed. Herman Roodenburg (Cambridge: Cambridge University Press, 2007), 138–177.

76. Since the city was never captured until Napoleon's anticlimactic arrival and never bombarded, looted, or burned, Venetian archives are full and, but for the ravages of humidity, comprehensive.

77. See Weil 101. On Egidio, see Francis X. Martin, "The Problem of Giles of Viterbo: A Historiographic Survey," *Augustiniana* 9 (1959): 357–379; 10 (1960): 43–60; Martin, "The Registers of Giles of Viterbo," *Augustiniana* 12 (1962): 142–160; Martin, "Giles of Viterbo and the Monastery of Lecceto: The Making of a Reformer," *Analecta Augustiniana* 25 (1962): 225–253; Martin, *Friar, Reformer, and Renaissance Scholar: Life and Work of Giles of Viterbo, 1469–1532* (Villanova, PA: Augustinian Press, 1992); Charles Astruc and Jacques Monfrin, "Livres latins et hébreux de cardinal Gilles de Viterbe," *Bibliothèque d'Humanisme et Renaissance* 23 (1961): 551–554; Francois Secret, *Les Kabbalistes chrétiens de la Renaissance* (Paris: Dunod, 1964), 106–126; John W. O'Malley, "Giles of Viterbo: A Sixteenth Century Text on Doctrinal Development," *Traditio* 22 (1966): 445–450.

78. Thomas E. Burman, *Reading the Qur'ān in Latin Christendom, 1140–1560* (Philadelphia: University of Pennsylvania Press, 2007), 9. The text was bilingual, with parallel columns of the original Arabic text, a Latin translation, exegetical notes, and a Roman transcription of the Arabic text (Burman, 149).

79. Burman comments specifically on this issue: "Though I have come across no explicit connection between Egidio da Viterbo's Qur'ān edition and his intense—and very learned—interest in Kabbalah, there is certainly a relationship between these two initiatives at some level, both growing out of his broader and abiding interest in Semitic languages" (Burman, *Reading*, 195).

80. Burman, *Reading*, 160.

81. Burman, *Reading*, 20; Robert Bonfil, *Jewish Life*, 173.

82. Burman, *Reading*, 163.

83. Burman, *Reading*, 176–177.

84. Although interestingly Weil seems to deny any and all political involvement on Levita's part: "Mis à part les malheurs qui ont interrompu ses travaux, il ne semble avoir été affecté par

aucun événement politique ou social," "Aside from the calamities that interrupted his work, he seems not to have been affected by any political or social event" (*Élie Lévita*, xx).

85. One must also keep in mind that only a single literary genre is here examined. Beyond the confines of epic, there is sometimes significant attention to issues of relations with Muslims. For a rather different context, see, e.g., Martin Jacobs *Islamische Geschichte in jüdischen Chroniken: Hebräische Historiographie des 16. und 17. Jahrhunderts* (Tübingen: Mohr Siebeck, 2004). While Jakob Katz's subject is Jewish-Christian relations in northern France and Germany, his analysis is nonetheless of methodological relevance to the present case: Jakob Katz, *Exclusiveness and Tolerance: Studies in Jewish-Gentile Relations in Medieval and Modern Times* (New York: Schocken, 1961), esp. chap. 15, "The Political Application of Tolerance," 182–196. As an afterthought to the analysis of this chapter, one should acknowledge an intriguing complication that at several points in the narrative Levita suggests that Druzeyne is Jewish, *not* Christian, which identity, if "true," would obviously complicate any reading of *Bovo*. Von Bernuth's assumption of Bovo's Jewish identity, noted earlier, adduces no compelling evidence nor does it exhaust the interpretive possibilities.

Chapter Nine

Conclusion

In the course of the chapters, the reader has been taken on a roller-coaster ride of contemporary modes of critical analysis as they were deployed to come to terms with the broad range of cultural issues presented by the texts adduced. At this point, it might be possible to step back from the material and gain some perspective on the individual analyses in the context of the larger thesis of the volume, that is, that a translation of culture took place across a range of literary genres of early Yiddish literature via discursive negotiation, for after all it is a matter of analytical selection and adaptation that makes early Yiddish literature possible. As the reader will have noticed rather quickly, the analytical trajectories of the book are in significant ways somewhat disconcerting: its protean thesis evolves as the series of case studies unrolls. But in none of the cases does the conventional scholarly mode of argumentative discourse quite suffice. Often it seems that evidence leads in the direction of one of perhaps many possible conclusions, only in the end to remain tantalizingly elusive. Perhaps a brief final pass through the issues will clarify some salient issues.

The earliest extant love song in Yiddish—those few brief, faded, inappropriately (one might posit) sited Yiddish lines that were textually recorded (and likely sung) by Ashkenazic Jews at least along the margins of, if not indeed within, the cultural and scholarly realms of Italian Humanism—is subjected to a kind of "archeological" historicism that seeks its conditions of production and circumstances of reception (origin, authorship, date of composition, scribal history, and provenance): an example of erotic poetry that draws its imagery, poetic style, and sensibility from a melding of the aesthetic traditions of both traditional Jewish literature and the surrounding Gentile culture of Humanist northern Italy, while remaining very strictly and centripetally Jewish and even more restrictively Ashkenazic, since composed not in the Jewish language of high culture, Hebrew, which was also known to non-Ashkenazic Jews, as well as some Christian representatives of Humanism, but in Yiddish, which all but sealed it to Gentile access and even to non-Ashkenazic Jewish access. And even in terms of its internal, Jewish *Sitz im Leben*, the poem is remarkable, since its unique textual inscription is as an intrusive supplement added to the protective parchment covering of a book, that is, that scribal space conventionally "available" for impertinent scribblings by scribes, students, book owners, and peddlers (and, later, librarians). In this case, the impertinent vernacular scribbling was on a core text of the sacred textual tradition. The erotic impulse crosses the cultural boundary between Gentile and Jew and the vernacular and quasi-secular text crosses the material boundary *onto*, although not *into*, the Hebrew book. There could hardly be a more pointed and concrete realization of the metaphor of cultural translation, especially insofar as it manifests an essential liminality. Nor could there be a better illustration of the provisional, *essai*-like mode of the analysis offered by the present volume, for the specific details that would nail down the mode of cultural translation that enabled such a conventional, almost caricatured, example of late and thus, one might imagine, strictly literary courtly love poetry to appear in Yiddish elude us and thus block a conclusive, evidence-based philological argument. Ultimately, however, the trail leading to the author, scribe, and mechanics of the inscription and (community?) reception of the love song cannot be followed to the end point at which such issues might be resolved, which leaves us hanging—intrigued, tantalized, and unsatisfied, except by the insights gleaned along that trail itself.

The cultural milieu of the Roman tradition of pasquinades and the alleged Venetian Jewish tradition of satirical broadsheets, posted at specific sites in the two cities, is precisely that in which Levita's "Ha-Mavdil" is to be conceived and comprehended. Here one must keep in mind that it is not a matter of seeking a tangible source for Levita's poem or style or mode of composition, but rather of a fertile cross-cultural impulse that arose in the confluence of traditional Hebrew satire and incipient Humanist/Roman/Venetian pasquinade. For once again, however, the facts of the case do not provide a complete enough picture of the Gentile-Ashkenazi connection to enable that larger contextualization through a conclusive argument, since those facts undo precisely the connections necessary: the chronology of the author's life and place of residence, the date of the poem's composition, and the inception of the two Italian traditions of pasquinade are incompatible. Again, one seems so close to establishing a direct connection that then disappears into vapor, leaving behind in its trace, however, a still richer, since not philologically delimited interpretive field.

With respect to the Purim plays, the issue of cultural translation must be addressed on at least two levels. First, the genre of drama is itself imported whole cloth from the majority surrounding culture, but that literary form, in large part stripped of its Gentile content, is then immediately and exclusively filled with an intensely inward-focused Jewish para-liturgical tradition. One should keep in mind that the importation of the dramatic form included not simply the "mechanics" of drama as multi-part publicly enacted narrative, but obviously of performance, of staging, of the incorporation of music as an element of a larger conception as entertainment, and of conventional conceptions of character types, such as the rascally comic role of Pickelherring/Mordecai, of those of *commedia del arte*, of Baroque *Staatsaktionen*, of the eighteenth-century operatic tradition. Thus, while the dramatic content (the biblically narrated, but midrashically conceived, averted genocide of Jews during the reign of Ahasuerus) was strictly Jewish, it was more than merely the basic structure of drama that was adopted from Gentile dramatic culture. Secondly, the quasi-historical setting of the Purim play in southwestern Asian antiquity opened some possibilities for the "safe" politicization of themes of Jew versus Gentile, of ruling elite versus subject or even servant populace, and intriguingly of gender conflict in the "long ago and far away." That "safety" of that distant setting was then frequently (but irregularly enough that it remained safe) undone by identification of characters and situations with those of contemporary sixteenth-, seventeenth-, and eighteenth-century Europe, such that the now strictly Jewish drama gestured beyond the boundaries of contemporary Jewish culture while still maintaining a focus on Jewish life. These issues are expressed in the plays and were here analyzed especially through attention to individual characters: in Vashti's anti-usurper/anti-nouveau elitism that—due to her particular and peculiar personal situation at court—inevitably also becomes a gender-defined insurrection; in Mordecai, whose character is constructed as a very human participant in a very structured and politicized semiotic game of moves and counter-moves that can doom or save an entire people.

The focal issues of the chapters on early Yiddish epic throw the problems of cultural translation into sharper relief, since the Yiddish texts participate in a broad literary tradition consisting of a cluster of sub-genres, well known and in some cases presenting one or more possible "source" texts from which the Yiddish poet-adapters might have worked. In the early Yiddish treatment of the issues of wiving and the Muslim Other in Gentile epic, two distinct strategies of cultural translation are found: in the former case the strategy chosen leads to a revision of the conventional wiving motif by means of the selective exclusion of the majority of potentially but not actually adaptable texts, which leads to the subtle but inescapable genre-bending of the wiving epic; and in the latter case, a second strategy enables a radical reconception of the underlying motivation for the portrayal of the hero's primary antagonists and thus ultimately a radical reconception of the plots and narratives themselves. In each case, then, Old and Middle Yiddish quasi-secular epic, even when adapted from known and extant Christian epics, become collectively, if not always individually, quite distinct from those Christian texts and sub-genres.

From a purely empiricist perspective, one might almost posit that the book documents its failure, chapter-by-chapter, insofar as it seeks to approximate an evidentiary case by means of a series of triangulating, tactical interventions in the "field" of early Yiddish literature. The chapters, as the book, jump up and down, as it were, and point at issues that are reasonably well defined but defy conclusive proof in the conventional empirical sense. The chapters adumbrate arguments that—almost in a Borgesian sense—*could* be made, if only that one final piece of compelling evidence were adducible, if only that one key piece of the puzzle could be identified and inserted in place, which would suddenly make sense of the array of hitherto amorphous evidence around it, enabling an immediate fitting of multiple other pieces. But we all know that precisely *that* piece of evidence rarely exists in humanistic discursive analysis, since every piece of evidence simply complicates rather than solves the puzzle. And that complexity, that stimulus to further attempts at understanding, to further *essais*, is after all the ultimate point of such analysis. It is certainly the point of this book. Yet even if a quasi-failure in a strictly empirical sense, such a cluster of *essais* still might aspire to some mode of discursive analytical accomplishment.

It is in any case indeed a messy book, as I warned the reader in the opening pages, for it again and again offers suggestive conclusions, as it crosses cultural and linguistic boundaries—Jew and Gentile, poet and scholar, ecclesiastic and rabbi, speakers and authors of Yiddish, Aramaic, Tuscan, Hebrew, and German—as it teases out trails of evidence, weaving a web of suggestions, a series of *essais* or *Versuche* that insinuate rather than compellingly argue toward conventional empirical conclusions. As I hope the web of suggestions has nonetheless effectively proposed, such *essais*, such *Versuche*, such tentative and experimental trials, such probing efforts themselves may constitute a productive contribution toward redefining a scholarly understanding of early Ashkenazic cultural history and may perhaps even indicate a productive practice if not a method for further para- if not post-philological studies of the still under-studied word-hoard that is early Yiddish literature.

Appendix: Elia Levita's Short Poems[1]

Elijah ben Asher ha-Levi Ashkenazi (Elia Levita / Elye Bokher)
די שריפה בון ווענדיג "The Great Fire of Venice" (1514)

The two manuscript witnesses of the poem differ radically in their length: the Cambridge manuscript (Trinity College Library, F.12.45 [*olim* MS Addl. 136], fos. 2r–3v, sixteenth century) has thirteen stanzas, while the Oxford manuscript (Bodleian Library, MS Can. Or. 12, fos. 258r–261v, copied 1553) has twenty-five; it seems clear that stanzas are lost from both the middle and the end of the poem. The translation is from the edition of the manuscripts in *EYT* 34, where the Oxford manuscript functions as the base text and only substantive variants from the Cambridge manuscript are noted; stanzas in C that differ radically from O are added in the notes.[2] As the song's headnote indicates, it is to be sung to the tune of the Sabbath *zemer* צור משלו אכלנו "The Lord, our Rock, whose food we have eaten, let us bless Him," which is traditionally sung during the Sabbath meal; the final line of each stanza of the hymn ends with the tetragrammaton יהוה, which since the name of God was early tabu-ized, was pronounced as *adonay* "LORD"[3]); the final line of each stanza of the Yiddish poem concludes, however, with 'אבוניי' *abonay*, a further step in the tabu-ization even of the substitute pronunciation.

Elye Bokher composed this song about the Great Fire of Venice.
A song to the tune of *Tsur mishelo akhalnu*.

Now I would also like to sing a bit,
With my poor voice,
Of things that have happened recently,

Which everyone ought to know:
Of the plague and pestilence,
That have happened here this time
In the great fire in Venice,
Which the LORD has consumed with fire.[4]

There was a great lamentation—
That the Rialto burned here—
By merchants and by gentlemen,
And by Jews, both young and old.
Jews call Jews,
So that they come right away
And quickly load up wares.[5]
For the sake of the LORD!

People were madly loading things up
And taking them far away.
Some were causing damage;
They were going off to the side.
They thought they would become rich
In a very short time.
They were glad to see the disaster
And gave thanks to the LORD.

Some ran to smother with sacks[6]:
They would have liked to take it all.
One came upon a pile of basins;
He loaded them on his shoulders
And fell down the steps with them—
So that the Rialto resounded with his fall.
He ran off and left them lying there,
And cried: "Alas, LORD!"

Thereafter he continued his toil 5
And loaded himself with sacks.
Once he wanted to stash
An installment in a hiding place.
A Gentile saw him skulking away
And spoke and snatched the basins;
He was whacking him in the head,
So that he ached for the LORD.

Thereafter he ran into an alley
And sought to and fro,
Whether he might snatch anything:

Then he found a tailor's shears.
He lost them again;
He did not carry them very far.
And the one is born into poverty—
That is bestowed on him by the Lord.

They say that vessels were snatched[7]
Indeed with malicious deceit,
By Mordkhe Itsik Tsutlayn.
He had them in a chest.
But it was said that it belonged to his sister
Inside there was nothing else
Than, truly, the genuine dishonor and blasphemy
Of those who do not believe in the Lord.

Goods were brought in there
That had been Mikhl Furt's
That had been taken from him
The house was quite poverty-stricken.
But a ban[8] had been imposed.
Then he went to see Mordkhe
And said: "Give it back, on your life,
Which is as dear to you as is the Lord."[9]

The ban is not to be annulled,[10]
And Reb Khaye[11] told the pious parson,
Who said he would pass it on
That one should have nothing to do with Gentiles.
Thus had they also promised him
And they shook his hand on the pact.
But they nonetheless broke it
And the oath to the Lord.

They believed the calumny 10
And what had been brought to their ears
That will yet make them leprous;
As our books say:
And those who have spread slander,
They will be stricken in their bodies.
Thus is it found written
In the Torah of the Lord.

They suspected even honest people:
How might the son of the honored Rabbi Anshil[12]
Have kept silent for the ban

And then turned informer?
But if they wanted to tell the truth,
They ought to pardon him,
For he is an upstanding Jew,
And one who fears the LORD.

But thus Michal Zimt/Limt[13] was zealous,[14]
Who is an honorable man,
No one saw him.
He attended to the poor,
For that has always been his handiwork,
Wherever he was able to do so.
For which reason good fortune and prosperity
Are granted him by the LORD.

But his uncle, Mendin Vitsn,
He is not so honest[15]:
He could in all fairness sit
Beside a loathsome youth.
He left me lying in prison,
Contrary to justice and the will of God
That will I carry with me even unto death,
Which I must still render to the LORD.

He also wanted to aggravate Petakhia,
Who refused to hide it for him.[16]
He told him quite dryly/indifferently
About Yoysef Kastil Frank.[17]
He sang to him of robbery,
Of many a wild escapade.
Whether it is actually to be believed,
That is known only to the LORD.

And Esther Furt, his in-law—[18] 15
He dressed her up indeed—
How she parades in as Lady Venus
Decked out quite prettily.
He made them scratch behind their ears.[19]
He showed off with[20] her.
He swore the truth of everything
A thousand times by the LORD.

And the goods of Isaac Kulpi
They were also charged to him:
A gown lined with fox-fur—

He has also lost, among the other things,
The very honorable pauper
Sought it everywhere.
Indeed whoever took it,
He is sought by the LORD.

And it did not profit him
That I was named [in the denunciation].
Hillel—one might well charge him—
He divided up the sack of spoils.
That that is what happened—
He confessed it himself.
But he never saw the coat—
So he swears by the LORD.

But the sack of new razors/shearing blades—
That he most certainly took.
He carried it away like a Caesar.
There is good evidence of that.
It is indeed no lie:
He went ashly pale—
As it could be brought to pass
By our dear LORD.

What could he do about his great misfortune,
That the pursuit began immediately?
He stashed it
Under a board in his chamber.
He wrapped it in some trousers
And said: "These goods
Were sent to me by Elye Bokher's wife,"
And so, may the LORD help him.

I will let this scurrility pass 20
And will let it be as it may.
I would have more to write,
If I dared to say more.
But I would like to stifle fabrications.
At present, I would like to let it go.
I fear that I might be thrashed.
May the LORD protect me.

Nothing enrages me more
Than when a pauper does something
So that he is in one way or another lost:

Everyone enjoys drinking his blood.
Whatever the wealthy do,
That is quite alright with everyone.
One lets it all slide.
May the Lord have mercy.

A pauper does it secretly,
And necessity drives him to it.
And generally the wealthy,
They do it openly.
And if I were to say everything
That they will yet steal,[21]
The days of my life would not suffice,
Of the days granted by the Lord.

And throughout all Italy
The matter has an evil form:
No sin is dishonorable.
Everyone does as pleases him.
A pious/honorable man is seldom found,
Among the [young or] old.
The Jewish faith proceeds [unsteadily, as if] on stilts:
No one recognizes the Lord.

Cursed be war,
And the one who invented it.
The life of many a one
Has been snuffed out by war.
And it is still not satisfied—
It has only just awakened.
That I would have to tell a lie—
May the Lord excuse me from that.

Now I would like to tell you 25
Who thought up this here concoction:
You really ought to know him.
He is well known for his handicraft:
He is one of the young men[22]
Who is constantly fighting/drinking[23] with them.
And therewith a good and blessed Purim
May the Lord grant you.

Elijah ben Asher ha-Levi Ashkenazi (Elia Levita / Elye Bokher)
הַמַבְדִיל בֵין קוֹדֶשׁ לְחוֹל "Ha-Mavdil Song" (1514)

There are two manuscript witnesses of the poem: the Oxford manuscript (Bodleian, MS Can. Or. 12, fos. 203r–207r, copied 1553) comprises fifty-five stanzas, while the Cambridge manuscript (Trinity College Library, F.12.45 [*olim* MS Addl. 136], fos. 4r–9v, sixteenth century) has sixty-eight and a half stanzas; one folio is missing at its end. It seems likely that the Cambridge manuscript presents a text closer to the original composition: more stanzas are transmitted and more correctly transmitted in the poem's established poetic form (without defective stanzas and verses). Working backward from the poem's claim that it consists of seventy-five stanzas, Nokhm Shtif eliminated as not original parts of the composition: stanza 3 from the Oxford manuscript and stanzas 4, 36, and 37 from the Cambridge manuscript.[24] He then constructed a probable structure of the original form of the poem, based on the extant stanzas in both manuscripts, but transmitted in neither of them:

1	OC1
2	O2
3	C2
4	C3
5	OC5
6	O4/C6
7–25	C7–25
26–35	O6–15/C26–35
36–66	O16–46/C38–68
67–75	O47–55

While Shtif's reconstruction of the seventy-five-stanza version on the basis of the two surviving manuscripts of the poem is compelling, all extant stanzas are here included; those eliminated from Shtif's count are here bracketed but retained in the order in which they occur in the manuscripts. The poem is translated from the manuscripts (as edited in *EYT* 35, with the revisions of that edition indicated in the notes here). The *piyyut* (liturgical poem) from which the form of the Yiddish poem is derived is widely available, for example, http://www.zemirotdatabase.org/view_song.php?id=75.

Elye Bokḥer, may his memory be for a blessing, made this.

OC1
The distinction between the holy and the profane[25]
Between me and Hillel, the despicable clod,

Who has as many defects
As there are stars in the night.

O2
Hillel, you have thrown down the gauntlet with me
And trained your obsession on me.
It will be your end,
Before the conclusion of the night.

C2
He has once again composed a poem about me,
But few people have found it funny.
For he managed to think up nothing but lies.
Thus in truth he ought not to live out the night.

C3
In my first poem indeed one could read,
How he behaved during the great fire:
How he was honored/loaded[26] down
Was there well seen by night.

[**O3**
Ah, you contemptible clod,
You are full of all scurrility.
You are well known everywhere,
Where you have been but a single night.

C4
For he must have a great deal of money and property.
He wastes it all in gluttony:
His mouth does not rest an entire day
And into the still watches of the night.[27]]

O5/C5
For he is indeed a great glutton, 5
Through which he is quite bankrupted.
He has a brother who is a priest.
Sooner or later he will take refuge there some night.

O4/C6
His poor soul might well lament
That he is as nearly a Gentile as he can be.
In the morning he never prays as far as *Blessed is the One who spoke*,[28]
Nor the afternoon prayer, nor the evening prayer by night.

C7
And he is undisturbed by going to the synagogue,
Except when he finds a small sign in the book of Sabbath Torah readings[29]—
A distinction that even a child comprehends—
On which he ponders an entire night,

C8
And enters the synagogue with a great shout,
And says, "It is thus and so, by G-d,"
And speaks of all and sundry,
As if he were speaking in a dream by night.[30]

C9
And he imagines himself knowledgeable in Hebrew grammar,
But he does not even know the basic verbal conjugation.[31]
If you are a grammarian, then tell me:
What is the function of the letter *he* at the end of the word לַיְלָה "night"?

C10
The word לַיְלָה "night" is after all a masculine noun:
Look at בַּלַּיְלָה הַהוּא "on this night,"[32] you great depraved one.
Just as you *earn* your fees from your students,
So may you prosper through the night.

C11
Oh, that the falling sickness would take hold of you,
For you know absolutely nothing.[33]
I taught you after all for many an hour,
By God's will, many a night.

C12
It is certainly true, what I tell you.
When he was living in Moyshe Verbe's house in a filthy place,
Lice feasted on him by day,
And ice by night.

C13
People who wish to be entertained,
They eavesdrop on his lessons with his students:
He bellows at them like an ox,
So that one might well be afraid by night.

C14
He teaches chaotically, mixing the important with the trivial:
One [student] is learning to translate [into Yiddish]; another is sleeping.

One is learning the Song of Songs; the other the Passover Haggadah.
One says "day"; the other says "night."

C15
They learn from him many evil habits 15
Moreover, he does not earn a lot of dough,
And teaches some twenty-five hours
In a single day, and in a single night.

C16
He gathers them all together, whatever he can and may.
His clients[34] have a great complaint:
He gets up three hours after sunrise
And goes to bed at the onset of the night.

C17
All the clients whom he has had—
He has treated them scurrilously.
He has earned his money by skullduggery:
Thievery by day, and thievery by night.

C18
At the onset of night he began to shout that he wanted
to run off to his darling:
She had come—all decked out—from Marghera;
She lay down with him: there was shoving aplenty between them.
And the one did not draw near to the other the entire night.[35]

C19
For he supports himself with his crafts:
Sometimes he runs a shell game, sometimes cards,[36]
For he has Gentiles who lie in wait for him,
Until late in the night.

C20
For he is being pursued by the Cavi di Sestiere,[37] 20
The Avogaria[38] and Corte Forestieri,[39]
The Pivighe[40] and Cataveri.[41]
And by the watch of the night.[42]

C21
He makes denunciations so that they stick to a person like glue.
Everyone knows of his dealings with Matis,
And the denunciation that he made against Kalmen Terviz,[43]
So that he had many a horrible night.

C22
He wanted to get them away from house and home;
He thought that he would get off scot-free,
If they were made silent as a mouse.
Sometime they will nab him in the night

C23
And will pay him his proper wages.
But if someone had already arranged things for him,[44]
Then he would not need to walk about in armor:
He might lie in his bed every night.

C24
And if someone needs a false witness,
Then he is prepared to be a paid witness.
Avrom Vitsn is also credible,
And Cosilio, who serves him day and night.[45]

C25
How he made an assignation with a Greek man,
So that in truth he was to give it a try in bed.
They were seen sneaking away together.
And they were quiet all night.[46]

O6/C26
Now, because I wish to entertain you well,
Then I will sing to you of his three wives:
How none of them wanted to stay with him.
They came to a full acquaintance with him in the very first night.

O7/C27
He had the first one for a good while,
But never went even a single mile with her.
He always claimed that he had no time,
Neither by day, nor by night.

O8/C28
Later, of course, he had to grant her a divorce.
Then there was a swarm competing for her:
What she long missed out on while she was with him,
She made up for in a single night.

O9/C29
Thereafter he took another,
A pious maiden, quite a pure one.

Yet she had from him but little delight:
Never a good day, and never a good night.

O10/C30
When he was to take her maidenhood,
The oaf did not have enough vigor.
He bought a nice carp,
Which he kept in the chamber overnight.

C31
And he got up a full hour before dawn,
And gave the fish a great wound,
And squeezed out a full pound of blood,
And smeared the bed-sheet with it, all day and night.

O12/C32
He thought to deceive the women:
They found the fish scales lying on the bed-sheet.
In all of Mestre it was not kept secret:
Everyone knew before it was night.

O13/C33
The poor fool naturally screamed bloody murder.
Her heart was rarely glad.
She said: "Let the day perish on which I was born,[47]
And the angel whose name is 'night.'

O14/C34
"O what a 'proper'[48] husband I have!
He does not even touch me the whole night long.
If I move over close to him, he then moves farther away."
And the one did not draw near to the other the entire night.[49]

O15/C35
Thereafter he left her and went to Cividale del Friuli,[50]
And the oaf took all her property.
Because of him, they[51] had to go around begging.
She went to bed hungry many a night.

[C36
Thereafter she moved to live with her mother in Udine,
Although she suffered great distress.
The poor soul, she was in great need.
She had no money to move to Portogruara.[52]

C37
Thereafter she moved again, and her wagon got stuck in the mire,
And her backside was exposed,
As if one had been poking into it
The entire night.]

O16/C38
Thereafter she moved to live with her father in Ferrara,
Although the change was difficult there.
The poor fool did not get off scot-free:
She passed away one night.

O17/C39
He never sat the seven days of mourning[53] for her,
Even though it was still within the thirty-day period after burial.[54]
He forgot to make the ritual tear in his garment.[55]
He lit no candle on any night.

O18/C40
And he was impatient to find another.
He went so far as to travel around inland.
He chased after all the marriage brokers.
He took no rest, neither by day nor by night.

O19/C41
Thereafter he found one there in Mantua—
A place where he was unknown.
But there they gave him neither money nor surety,
Nor clothing for the day, nor clothing for the night.

O20/C42
Immediately after the wedding, he drove her out.
He hired her out to another household,
From great anxiety and from great dread
That he would have to be with her the entire night.

O21/C43
And when they were led away to sleep together,
He did not do what is proper for a man:
He carried on a wild activity with her.
She wept and screamed the entire night.

O22/C44
He engaged with her in strange things.
He wanted to earn the fish with his finger.[56]

Cuzi Montagnana[57] and Shmuel Zinger—
One would like to listen to for an entire night,

O23/C45
Just as they had earlier sung so many a fine tale:
How he had bought a magpie,[58]
Which he slaughtered and made bleed.
And that was in the middle of the night.[59]

O24/C46
Then he pulled out the magpie,
And said: "Look, Esther, my dear Esther.
Smear the bed-sheet with this, as long and firmly as possible.
Maintain my honor this night.

O25/C47
"Tell everyone how I was a man,
Then I will serve you however I can.
Whatever you desire, just give me the order[60]:
Let me but come untainted through this night."

O26/C48
The poor fool promised him what he wanted:
Just so that he would never claw her again.
But she thought: "If I get away from you this time,
You will never again catch me any night."

O27/C49
Thus she did not often lie beside him.
She led him to believe that she was constantly having her period.
Great strife arose between them:
Evening and morning, day and night.

O28/C50
She no longer wanted to be where he was.
She well recognized that he was a wicked fool.
Thereafter she ran away from him outright.
And she arose while it was still night.[61]

O29/C51
She took Anshl Tsitsayl[62] with her.
He followed after her in great haste.
His ship sped away like an arrow.
And he separated himself from them by night.[63]

O30/C52
He [Hillel] caught up with her not far away
And went aboard the ship on which she was
And said: "Why do you want to run away from me?
How is this night different?"[64]

O31/C53
He preached her a long sermon
That she should come back to Venice.
She could not get rid of him.
And he stayed there for the night.[65]

O32/C54
She said: "All your babble will not help you.
You are never again to claw me with your finger.
If you cannot lay the eggs, then you should not cackle.
You are no watchman, [calling out] what is left of the night?[66]

O33/C55
"I do not want to put up with it, that you befoul me,
And slobber on me and pollute me
And waggle with your finger inside me
Vigorously the entire night.[67]

O34/C56
"And that you befoul me with the stench of your farts!"
They struck each other—I want to cut this short—
He struck her in the head, so that she collapsed.
And she wept bitterly in the night.[68]

O35/C57
He had with him three or four Gentiles—
All of the lads an evil crew.[69]
He had to pay them; thus did they fulfill the terms of their contract—
Ever a hireling of the day and a hireling of the night.

O36/C58
And he returned to Venice shamefaced,
And complained to the community authorities and the rabbis
And was constantly concerned with these matters
In thoughts from the visions of the night.[70]

O37/C59
Thereafter it was of course interjected
That he ought to grant her a divorce.
She was glad to give him all that she had:
Not a penny did she retain overnight.

O38/C60
But he then wanted yet another.
But he found no ship that would make delivery to him.
No one wanted to burden[71] themselves with him,
For terror of the night.[72]

O39/C61
For he does not do as the other old men,
Who by day make their wives cheerful.
But he does no wife any favors by day;
She has it still worse by night.

O40/C62
And he has not changed his evil behavior:
He screws cats and dogs.
In Cividale he violated a female dog:
He kept it in bed every night.

O41/C63
All Jews [=everyone] know this tale well:
Just ask Moyshe Shivdetln[73] or Refoel.
They are both still alive, praise be to God.
They would also tell of what chances by night.[74]

O41/C64
And when he has his way with[75] a maiden of four or five years of age,
He fondles her, front and back,
A pious Jewish woman swore to me
By the Creator of the day and the night,

O43/C65
How she was once on his trail;
Then she saw him leading her little girl away with him
Into a run-down chamber outside the city-gate.
And the darkness he called night.[76]

O44/C66
For the sake of her honor I do not wish to identify her by name,
But he certainly deserves to be burned.
In Padua he had mutilated hens
That he screwed day and night.

O45/C67
On the Volta dei Negri[77] a wretched thing took place:
I wish that Moyshe Yentilomer[78] were still alive.
The words flow forth day by day,
And night by night.[79]

O46/C68
And with that I will leave it,
Although I could continue it even longer.
But if I were to have it written down, it would not suffice
Forty days and forty nights.[80]

O47/C69
Hillel, I have repaid you for what you have done.
It would have been better for you to stay at home.
Take this: it is indeed written for you.[81]
Let that stick in your craw all night.[82]

O48
If you knew how your poem befits you,
You would be ashamed even to write a poem.
If you want to compete with me in poetry,
It will be like the difference between day and night.

O49
O ignoramus! O villain!
Now see this page upon the wall!
I made it with my own hand;
You make such a one this very night![83]

O50
I promise you: before a month passes, 70
I will write one about you in Hebrew,
Composed in the poetic form of the "Shekel ha-kodesh."[84]
And you will meditate on it day and night.[85]

O51
And be on guard:[86] I will go to Pesaro.[87]
Through the printing shop, the poems ought still to reach
As far as bats [fly][88]
In the night.

O52
And in the end I will leave you the poem,
On which you can sharpen your teeth.
The poem has as many stanzas
As, according to *gematria*, does the word "night."

O53
There are seventy-five of them altogether,
And "Hillel" and "Cohen" also have the same total.
Each is seventy-five in number,
And "Hillel" [הילל] has the same letters as "night" [לילה].

O54
And the year that we are now entering,
That will also be seventy-five.
May God deliver us from our affliction,
And from our exile, which is like the night.

O55
For He has always been one who drives away our suffering,
May He deliver us, male and female.
That is what Elye ha-Levi, the author, prays and requests of
The One who gives songs in the night.[89]

Notes

1. While the introductory remarks and notes here contextualize some aspects of the poems, a fuller explication is to be found in chapter 3. My translations are by no means to be imagined as poetic translation (they are divided into lines only for the sake of the readers' convenience in consulting the original texts); indeed I have deliberately sacrificed literary style for semantic precision. The recent translations, both Italian and English, by Claudia Rosenzweig are quite unreliable, with frequent wholesale misinterpretations of vocabulary and even more frequent misunderstandings of Old Yiddish grammar and syntax; consequently in the following pages few references are made to her work. The Italian translation is Claudia Rosenzweig and Anna Linda Callow, trans., *Elye Bokher, due canti yiddish: rime di un poeta ashkenazita nella Venezia del cinquecento*, Quaderni di Traduzione 4 (Siena: Bibliotheca Aretina, 2010). English translations of several stanzas are included in Claudia Rosenzweig, "Rhymes to Sing and Rhymes to Hang Up: Some Remarks on a Lampoon in Yiddish by Elye Bokher (Venice 1514)," *The Italia Judaica Jubilee Conference*, ed. Shlomo Simonsohn and Joseph Schatzmiller (Leiden: Brill, 2013), 143–165.

2. I now find my hesitation in *EYT* to connect the poem with the Rialto fire of 1514 and thus to date the poem to that year quite baffling. See also the edition: חנא שמרוק, "השיר על השריפה בוונציה לאליהו בחור", קבץ על יד [סדרה חדשה], 6 [16], חלק ב [1966], 343–368.

3. Here, as in general in the Anglophone tradition, this multi-layered sign will be represented by the word LORD in small caps.

4. Lev 10:6.

5. One should keep in mind that such an unspecified action could as easily be intended to save merchandise from the fire as to steal it for oneself.

6. Or: "load up into sacks"; cf. Grimm, *DWB*, vol. 12, col. 1179: *löschen*, "verb. ausdruck der seefahrer, nach einer gethanen reise die güter und waaren aus einem schiff ausladen," "verbal expression of seafarers: at the end of voyage to unload goods and wares from a ship."

7. The line is troubled, perhaps meaning more abstractly "the command/authority has been exceeded"; but the context seems to demand something more concrete.

8. A ban on Jews informing on other Jews to the Venetian authorities.

9. Or, less likely: "if the LORD is dear to you."

10. In the Cambridge manuscript, stanzas 10–11 are in reverse order and differ substantially:

> When that same morning the ban was imposed,
> Then R' Khaye told the pious priest;

He said: You need have no concern,
One will have nothing to do with Gentiles,
They gave him their handshake.
But they broke it
And the pact of the LORD.

They believed the calumny
That had been brought to their ears.
That makes the people leprous,
As our books say:
He will be stricken in his body.
Thus one finds it in the Gemara [in the Talmud, the rabbinical commentary on the Mishnah]
And in the Torah of the LORD.

11. Perhaps Rabbi Ḥiyyah Meir ben David, who worked for Daniel Bomberg as a proofreader on the publication of the Talmud; cf. Cecil Roth, *History of the Jews in Venice* (Philadelphia: Jewish Publication Society, 1939), 252.

12. Shmeruk suggests an identification with Anselmo (Asher) del Banco, a powerful Ashkenazi banker in Venice ("Al sreyfe," 346 n. 5); on Anselmo, see also David Jacoby, "New Evidence on Jewish Bankers in Venice and the Terraferma (c. 1450–1550)," *Ha-Yehudim veha-Yam ha-Tikhon: kesafim banḳaʾut u-misḥar benleʾumi ba-meʾot 16–18 / The Mediterranean and the Jews, Banking, Finance, and International Trade*, ed. Ariel Toaff and Shimon Shwartzfuchs (Ramat Gan: Bar-Ilan University Press, 1989), 162–170.

13. In this word it is not possible to distinguish between initial צ and ל in the script of the manuscript; Shmeruk reads צימט.

14. Among the senses of the verb ווייבלן is an agitated and purposeful busyness, as of a court summoner; cf. German *weibeln*, Grimm, *DWB*, vol. 28, col. 379.

15. In Old Yiddish, the word *shlekht* often persisted in the older sense of "straight, proper, honest"; cf. the entry for פשט "simple" in Levita's *Ha-Tishbi*, which includes the gloss בל"א שלעכט ובלעז דישטישו "in Yiddish *slekht* and in Romance [Italian] *disteso*"; in: תשבי: *Lexicon hebraicvm vtilissimvm* (Basel: Paulus Fagius, 1558), 185; likewise cf. early New High German *schlecht*, "common, smooth, right, upright, proper"; see esp. Grimm, *DWB*, vol. 15, col. 527, #8.f.11.

16. Grimm, *DWB*, vol. 1, col. 1107, *unter die bank stoszen*, "neglect, forget."

17. Perhaps Yoysef Castelfranco (=Castelfranco Veneto in Treviso province); see Y. Boksenboim, ed., *Iggerot yehude Italya. Mivhar mehameʾa hashesh-esre* (Jerusalem: Ben-Zvi Institute, 1994), 45 n. 3, 311.

18. Stanza fifteen differs in the Cambridge ms.:

And Esther Furt, his in-law
He also dressed up:
As she comes parading in as Verziz
Decked out in a yellow veil.
He made them scratch behind their ears.
What he saw and delighted in
He swore to the truth of it all
A thousand times by the LORD.

19. In early New High German, the idiom indicated confusion, embarrassment, or a recognition of having lost a game; cf. Grimm, *DWB*, vol. 11, col. 2077, #II,1,e.

20. The Oxford ms. has גשטוצט; cf. Grimm, *DWB*, vol. 20, col. 765, *stutzen*, D3, "prunken/protzen."

21. Lexer, *ânen* "*berauben*," "steal" (vol. 1, col. 68). There is no need for the emendation by Erik and Shmeruk to טונן "do."

22. Yiddish בחורים *bokherim*, underlined in the manuscript, indicating its supplementary sense, here suggesting Levita, i.e., Elye *Bokher* as author.

23. Cambridge ms. ועכט "fights"; Oxford ms. צעכט "drinks."

24. Nokhm Shtif, "Elye ha-Levi's lid 'ha-mavdil,'" *Tsaytshrift* 1 (1926): 150–158.

25. The first line of the *piyyut*: הַמַּבְדִּיל בֵּין קֹדֶשׁ לְחוֹל.

26. The Hebrew נכבד connotes both senses; here "honored" would obviously be ironic.

27. Cf. Ps 90:4, וְאַשְׁמוּרָה בַלָּיְלָה, and the *piyyut*, line 6.

28. I.e., ברוך שאמר, the *beginning* of the morning prayer.

29. The סִידְרָה/סדרה.

30. The phrase בַּחֲלוֹם הַלָּיְלָה appears in Gen 20:3 and 31:24 and 1 Kings 3:5.

31. That is, בנין (ה)קל.

32. Despite ending with the letter *he*, which often marks a grammatically feminine noun in Hebrew, the noun לילה "night" is masculine, as indicated in this phrase by the accompanying masculine demonstrative adjective/pronoun that agrees grammatically with it.

33. Literally: "you know neither פּי *pi* nor פֶּע *pe*," i.e., cannot distinguish the one from the other.

34. I.e., the parents of his pupils.

35. Cf. Ex 14:20, וְלֹא-קָרַב זֶה אֶל-זֶה, כָּל-הַלָּיְלָה.

36. Still the most useful study of early Ashkenazic gaming is Yitskhok [Isaac] Rivkind, *Der kamf kegn azart shpiln bay yidn. A shtudye in finf hundert yor yidishe poezye un kultur-geshikhte* (New York: YIVO, 1946).

37. Venetian *Cavi di sestiere* (Ital. *capi sestiere*): the Venetian state authorities of the six districts (*sestiere*) of the city.

38. The Venetian *Avogaria di Comun*: the Venetian state judiciary.

39. The Venetian court that dealt with issues and conflicts between Venetians and non-Venetians or among non-Venetians resident in Venice.

40. Venetian *piovego* (pl. *pioveghi*): the Venetian state office that dealt with usury, among other issues; Giuseppe Boerio, *Dizionario del dialetto Veneziano* (Venice: Giovanni Cecchini, 1856), 512.

41. Venetian *catavèr* (pl. *cataveri*): a judicial office charged with the collection of taxes and mercantile fees, in addition to issues having to do with resident Jews (Boerio, *Dizionario*, 148–149).

42. Referring to the office of the *Signori/nobili de notte*, in charge of public order during the night.

43. Terviz = Treviso, a city in the Veneto northwest of Venice.

44. The line is difficult, especially since it mediates the previous lines, in which those whom Hillel has denounced pursue him, and the following lines in which he seems secure and without fear of them. This line seems on the surface to mean "If someone had already put him to death," but at this period the word הין ריכֿטן retains as one of its primary denotations the sense "arrange" or "make arrangement for" (Grimm, *DWB*, vol. 10, col. 1465, "hinrichten," #1).

45. Avrom Vitsn and Cosilio are unknown, apparently associates of Hillel.

46. Cf. Judges 16:2, וַיִּתְחָרְשׁוּ כָל-הַלַּיְלָה, as the Gazites conspire to murder Samson.

47. Cf. Job 3:3, יֹאבַד יוֹם, אִוָּלֶד בּוֹ.

48. Again the word שלעכֿט, here certainly either ironic "proper," or perhaps one of the term's other connotations: "common" or already "horrible."

49. Cf. st. 18,4, above; cf. also Ex 14:20.

50. The Yiddish representation of the place name Shivdeteln derives from the Friulian dialect form of the place name Cividât.

51. Ms. מוישטן זיא "they had to . . .": perhaps a copy error for the singular verb = "she had to. . . ."

52. A town in the eastern Veneto.

53. שִׁבְעָה *shive*, a seven-day period after the death of father, mother, son, daughter, brother, sister, or spouse, is the first period of אֲבֵלוּת *avelut*, "mourning."

54. שְׁלֹשִׁים *shloshim*, the thirty-day period of mourning after burial, which enjoins particular practices on the bereaved, is the second period of *avelut*. If this period has elapsed before one obligated to sit *shive* becomes aware of the death, then that obligation is reduced.

55. A ritual tearing of the outer garment worn (on the right side for a spouse)—קְרִיעָה *keriah*—before the funeral or immediately after.

56. The common Jewish tradition of fish as a symbol for fertility begins indirectly in Gen 1:22: פְּרוּ וּרְבוּ, וּמִלְאוּ אֶת-הַמַּיִם בַּיַּמִּים "be fruitful and multiply and fill the waters in the seas." BT *Ket* 5a directly associates fish with the virginity of the bride. The fish, which becomes associated especially with human sexuality as a representation sometimes of the female, sometimes of the male genitalia, is given an explicitly sexual sense in BT *Yoma* 75a, where דאגה *daga*, "fish," is identified as Israel's illicit sexual desires; Rashi (ad BT Yoma 75a) comments that דאגה is a direct euphemism for sexual intercourse. This usage illuminates the behavior attributed to Hillel in Levita's poem. The "earning" of the fish requires further explication, however. According to the minor tractate שְׂמָחוֹת *Semaḥot* (chaps. 8 and 14), generally appended to the Babylonian Talmud, the סעדת דגים "fish meal" was a traditional part of the marriage ceremonial (see Isidor Scheftelowitz, "Das Fisch-Symbol im Judentum und Christentum," *Archiv für Religionsgeschichte* 14 (1911): 376 [1–53, 321–392]). In sixteenth-century Poland (as indicated in Moses Isserles's commentary on *Shulchan Aruch, Yore deʾa*, 391), this meal symbolizing the "earning of the fish" was termed the פִּיש־מאָל "fish repast," a meal of fish supplied by the groom to relatives, in-laws, and guests on the day after the wedding in celebration of the satisfactory consummation of the marriage, including, especially, the confirmation of the bride's virginity (cf. Jousep Schammes, *Minhagim di-ḳ.ḳ. Vermaiśa le-Rabi Yuzpa Shamash*, ed. Binyamin Shelomoh Hamburger and Yitsḥaḳ [Eric] Zimmer, 2 vols. (Jerusalem: Mifʿal torat ḥakhme Ashkenaz, Mekhon Yerushalayim, 1988–1992), 2:49. The phrase is thus used metaphorically in the same narrative situation (bride and groom during the wedding night) in the *Seyder noshim* in Cambridge University Library Or. Add. 547, 80b (copied in Mestre in the first half of the sixteenth century): פאר דינט נון דער חתן די פיש "if the bridegroom now earns the fish . . ."; the manuscript has been transcribed and translated in *Many Pious Women*, ed. and trans. Harry Fox and Justin Jaron Lewis (New York: Walter de Gruyter, 2011), 235 (see also the accompanying note). In Levita's poem the significance of the phrase is interestingly turned on its head *not* to relate to the bride's suitability, but rather to signify the *groom's* satisfactorily proving himself via the consummation of the marriage, and signifies simply successful completion of coitus and thus a euphemism for the sex act. A related, but different, Sephardic custom is described by Annette B. Fromm, also having to do with the post-consummation purchase of a fish by the groom for the bride and throwing it at her feet to frighten her such that she would always fear the husband! (cf. "Among the Jews of Ioannina: Symbolic Enactments," *Jewish Folklore and Ethnology Review* 15, no. 2 (1993): 104–106).

57. A familiar Ashkenazi surname in fifteenth-century Italy; a Cusi (Meshullam) Montagnana operated a Hebrew printing house in Piove di Sacco in 1475; see Aron Freimann, "Haben jüdische Flüchtlinge aus Mainz im XV. Jahrhundert den Buchdruck nach Italien gebracht?" *Journal of Jewish Bibliography* 1 (October 1938–July 1939), 9–11.

58. Shtif, "Elye ha-Levi's lid," 153 n. 23/4, construes the word פוטה as "turkey," glossing: "italyenish *putto*, daytsh *pute*, a [*sic*] italyenishe hun, *truthuhn*," "Italian *putto*, German *pute*, an Italian hen = turkey" (the first letter of *putto* is printed as *d*, upside down, apparently a printer's error). Following Shtif, Rosenzweig also translates as *tacchino*, "turkey" (*Due canti yiddish*,

104). If, however, one identifies פוטה as "turkey," then one must somehow account for the apparent change of species into אגלשטָר, which normally means "magpie" in the first line of the next stanza, which Shtif manages to do by identifying that word as a translation equivalent of Hebrew רחם "womb/uterus" in early Yiddish biblical translation (Shtif, "Elye ha-Levi's lid," 153–154 n. XXIV/2), thus imagining that Hillel instructed his wife to extract that organ from the slaughtered turkey and smear the sheets with it instead of doing so with the entire bird. Rosenzweig silently retains Shtif's posited species change. Problems abound: first, the turkey could not have appeared in Europe until Columbus's return from his first voyage in 1493 and was perhaps not taken to Europe for several decades thereafter. In any case, its spread across Europe was slow and often proceeded via importation first to the Ottoman Empire and then back to various regions of southern and central Europe. It is a thorny question as to when the animal was known in Venice, but in any case seems unlikely by the time of Levita's poem in 1514. Secondly, there is no evidence of the use of the word *put(t)a* as "turkey" in any language contemporary with the poem: the later Low German dialect term *Puter/Pute* eventually became standard German (probably the source of Shtif's conception of the word) but did not appear until near the end of the eighteenth-century (Friedrich Kluge, *Etymologisches Wörterbuch der deutschen Sprache*, 20th ed., ed. Walther Mitzka [Berlin: Walter de Gruyter, 1967], entry: *Truthahn*, p. 795). The problems are nonetheless easily solved and without resorting to speculative solutions: *putta* was in fact already established in Tuscan by the late fifteenth century in the sense *gazza*, "magpie" (Salvatore Battaglia, *Grande Dizionario della lingua italiana* [Turin: Unione tipografico-editrice torinesei, 1988], vol. 14, definition 2, p. 1066). In this line of the Yiddish text, it is then the Romance-component Yiddish word for magpie that appears, while in the next stanza, it is the Germanic-component Yiddish word that is used. No turkey or uterus need be conjured.

59. Cf. Ex 12:29: וַיְהִי בַּחֲצִי הַלַּיְלָה "And it came to pass at midnight."

60. Or perhaps: "just promise me."

61. Cf. Prov 31:15: וַתָּקָם, בְּעוֹד לַיְלָה; I have adjusted the verb tense in the translation to fit the context.

62. Rosenzweig suggests: Tsitsayl < Sacile in Friulia (*Due canti yiddish*, 105 n. 44).

63. Cf. Gen 14:15: וַיֵּחָלֵק עֲלֵיהֶם לַיְלָה.

64. Echoing the phrase from the Passover Haggadah.

65. Cf. Gen 32:14: וַיָּלֶן שָׁם, בַּלַּיְלָה.

66. Cf. Isaiah 21:11: שֹׁמֵר מַה-מִּלַּיְלָה; also in the Haggadah.

67. Cf. Ex 14:21: עַזָּה כָּל-הַלַּיְלָה.

68. Cf. Lam 1:2: בָּכוֹ תִבְכֶּה בַּלַּיְלָה.

69. According to Shtif, "Elye ha-Levi's lid," 155, קָנְפָּאִים < Ital. *convoio/convoglio*; cf. also Venetian *convogiár/convoiare*, in Boerio, *Dizionario*, 194.

70. Cf. Job 4:13: בִּשְׂעִפִּים, מֵחֶזְיֹנוֹת לָיְלָה.

71. Yiddish *leveran* < Venetian *levár* / Ital. *levare*, "raise, lift, take on," and Yiddish *impazirn* < Venetian *impazzár* / Ital. *impacciare*, "hinder"; cf. Boerio, *Dizionario*, 327, 368. Rosenzweig's attempt to derive the latter word from *infacere*, "impregnare, impregnarsi," puts a fine point on a potential bride-to-be's reluctance to marry Cohen, but seems here perhaps less probable in terms of the metaphorical context (*Due canti yiddish*, 107 n. 55).

72. Cf. Ps 91:5: מִפַּחַד לָיְלָה; and Song of Songs 3:8: מִפַּחַד בַּלֵּילוֹת.

73. Shivdetln < Cividale.

74. That is, nocturnal pollution; cf. Dt 23:11: מִקְּרֵה-לָיְלָה.

75. Shtif, "Elye ha-Levi's lid," 156, suggests the Hebrew idiom הבא על הנערה as the source for the sexual connotation of קומט אויבר איין מיידלן, but the sense seems already to have been present in the German component of Yiddish (as witnessed in modern dialect usage).

76. Cf. Gen 1:5: וְלַחֹשֶׁךְ קָרָא לָיְלָה.

77. A district in Padua.

78. Cf. Ital. *gentiluomo,* "gentleman, patrician."

79. Cf. Ps 19:3: יוֹם לְיוֹם, יַבִּיעַ אֹמֶר; וְלַיְלָה לְּלַיְלָה, incorporated into the *piyyut*, line 18.

80. Cf. Gen 7:12, etc.: אַרְבָּעִים יוֹם, וְאַרְבָּעִים לָיְלָה.

81. The final two lines of this stanza are difficult. For the third line, Shtif suggests emending די to דיר "for you" and construing גריבן > רייבן "rub"; or perhaps an omitted ש and thus גשריבן "written," and thus: "Herewith you have what I have smeared on you / written for you" ("Elye ha-Levi's lid," 157). Rosenzweig's *cicciolo* (*Due canti yiddish*, 120) apparently for גריבן > mod. Yid. גריווון "crackling" has the advantage of simplicity but the disadvantage of making no sense.

82. If one reads the fourth word as ליג "lie" (often the manuscript distinction between ג and ב is difficult to discern), then, on the basis of Grimm, *DWB*, vol. 11, col. 2398, *kropf* 3g: "*einen auf dem kropfe lassen*, von einem gefoppten, den man triumphierend seinem irrthum oder ärger überläßt," "of one who has been cheated/hoaxed, whom one triumphantly leaves to stew in his own error or vexation"; thus the line might be rendered: "lie down for the night with this belly-full."

83. Or: "I will make another like it this very night." The sentence lacks a grammatical subject and begins with the verb מך, which could be imperative ("[you] make") or first-person singular indicative with the subject pronoun deleted ("I make"); following the previous sentence where the same verb was used in the perfect tense (הון איך גמכט "I have made"), the present/future מך without the subject pronoun is perfectly idiomatic. But it seems that the poem's speaker is challenging Hillel to demonstrate his poetic prowess (that is, his lack thereof).

84. The reference may be to the twelfth-century collection by the Iberian rabbi and biblical commentator, Joseph Kimḥi, *Shekel hakodesh* (*The Holy Shekel*): *The Metrical Work of Joseph Kimḥi*, ed. Hermann Gollancz (Oxford: Oxford University Press, 1919).

85. Cf. Joshua 1:8: וְהָגִיתָ בּוֹ יוֹמָם וָלַיְלָה.

86. Accepting Shtif's emendation of הון to הוט; "Tsugab un oysbeserungen," *Tsaytshrift* 2–3 (1928): col. 897.

87. Gershon Soncino's printing shop was in Pesaro, which had already printed several of the scholarly works by Levita (beginning in 1507); see Weil, *Élie Lévita*, 43–47.

88. Shtif's brilliant emendation, adding the rhyme word װליהן "fly" to what is otherwise an incomplete stanza.

89. Cf. Job 35:10: נֹתֵן זְמִרוֹת בַּלָּיְלָה; and the *piyyut* "Ha-Mavdil," line 16.

Bibliography

Adelman, Howard. "Finding Women's Voices in Italian Jewish Literature." In *Women of the Word: Jewish Women and Jewish Writing*, edited by Judith R. Baskin, 50–69. Detroit: Wayne State University Press, 1994.

———. "Italian Jewish Women." In *Jewish Women in Historical Perspective*, edited by Judith R. Baskin, 2nd ed., 150–168. Detroit: Wayne State University Press, 1998.

Albright, W. F. "The Lachish Cosmetic Burner and Esther 2.12." In *A Light unto My Path: Old Testament Studies in Honor of Jacob M. Myers*, edited by H. N. Bream, R. D. Heim, and C. A. Moore, 25–32. Philadelphia: Temple University Press, 1974.

Allaire, Gloria. "Noble Saracen or Muslim Enemy? The Changing Image of the Saracen in Late Medieval Italian Literature." In *Western Views of Islam in Medieval and Early Modern Europe: Perception of Other*, edited by David R. Blanks and Michael Frassetto, 173–185. New York: St. Martin's Press, 1999.

Amram, David Werner. *The Makers of Hebrew Books in Italy: Being Chapters in the History of the Hebrew Printing Press*. London: Holland Press, 1963.

Appaduraia, Arjun. "Theory in Anthropology: Center and Periphery." *Comparative Studies in Society and History* 28 (1986): 356–374.

Appiah, Anthony. "Strictures on Structures: The Prospects for a Structuralist Poetics of African Fiction." In *Black Literature and Literary Theory*, edited by H. L. Gates, Jr., 127–150. New York: Methuen, 1984.

Aptroot, Marion, and Roland Gruschka, eds. *Isaak Euchel: Reb Hennoch, oder: Woß tut me damit. Eine jüdische Komödie der Aufklärungszeit*. Hamburg: Buske, 2004.

Aranoff, Deena. "Elijah Levita: A Jewish Hebraist." *Jewish History* 23 (2009): 17–40.

Aretino, Pietro. *Pasquinate di Pietro Aretino ed anonime per il conclave e l'elezione di Adriano VI*. Edited by Vittorio Rossi. Palermo/Torino: Carlo Claussen, 1891.

———. *The Works of Aretino: Dialogues*. Translated by Samuel Putnam. New York: Covici-Friede, 1933.

———. *The Works of Aretino: Letters and Sonnets*. Translated by Samuel Putnam. New York: Covici-Friede, 1933.

———. *Scritti scelti*. Edited by Giuseppe Guido Ferrero. Turin: UTET, 1970.

———. *Sonetti lussuriosi e pasquinate*. Edited by M. B. Sirolesi. Rome: Newton Compton, 1980.

———. *Edizione nazionale delle opere di Pietro Aretino*. Edited by Giovanni Aquilecchia and Angelo Romano. Rome: Salerno editrice, 1992–.
———. *Le carte parlanti*. Edited by Giovanni Casalegno and Gabriella Giaccone. Palermo: Sellerio, 1992.
Ariosto, Ludovico. *The Satires of Ludovico Ariosto*. Translated by Peter Desa Wiggins. Athens: Ohio State University Press, 1976.
Asholt, Wolfgang. "Karnevaleske Welt und ihre Aufhebung in der französischen Literatur zu Ende des 16. Jahrhunderts." In *Zwischen Renaissance und Aufklärung*, edited by Klaus Garber and Wilfried Kürschner, 25–47. Amsterdam: Rodopi, 1988.
Astruc, Charles, and Jacques Monfrin. "Livres latins et hébreux de cardinal Gilles de Viterbe." *Bibliothèque d'Humanisme et Renaissance* 23 (1961): 551–554.
Babbi, Anna Maria. "In margine alla fortuna del Paris e Vienna." *Quaderni di Lingue e Letterature* (Verona) 11 (1986): 393–397.
———, ed. *Paris e Vienna: romanzo cavalleresco*. Venice: Marsilio, 1991.
Baca, Murtha. "Aretino in Venice, 1527–37, and 'La Professione del Far' Lettere." Diss., UCLA, 1978.
Bach, Alice. *Women, Seduction, and Betrayal in Biblical Narrative*. Cambridge: Cambridge University Press, 1997.
Bacher, Wilhelm. "Elija Levitas wissenschaftliche Leistungen." *Zeitschrift der deutschen morgenländischen Gesellschaft* 43 (1889): 206–272.
———. "Zur Biographie Elija Levitas." *Monatsschrift für Geschichte und Wissenschaft des Judentums* 37 (1892–1893): 398–404.
———."Die hebräische Sprachwissenschaft vom 10ten bis zum 16ten Jahrhundert." In *Die Geschichte der rabbinischen Litteratur während des Mittelalters und ihre Nachblüte in der neueren Zeit*, edited by J. Winter-A.Wünsche, 133–235. Trier: Siegmund Meyer, 1894.
Bal, Mieke. *Lethal Love: Feminist Literary Readings of Biblical Love Stories*. Indiana Studies in Biblical Literature. Bloomington: Indiana University Press, 1987.
Barkan, Leonard. *Unearthing the Past: Archaeology and Aesthetics in the Making of Renaissance Culture*. New Haven, CT: Yale University Press, 1999.
Baron, Salo Wittmayer. *A Social and Religious History of the Jews*. 18 vols. 2nd ed. New York: Columbia University Press, 1993.
Bartsch, Karl, ed. *Kudrun*. 5th ed. Wiesbaden: Brockhaus, 1980.
Baruchson, Shifrah. *Sefarim ye-ḳorʾim: tarbut ha-ḳeriʾah shel yehude iṭalyah be-shilhe ha-renesans*. Ramat Gan: Bar-Ilan University Press, 1993.
Basin, M. *Antologye finf hundert yor yidishe poezye*. 2 vols. New York: Literarisher farlag, 1917.
Baskin, Judith R., ed. *Jewish Women in Historical Perspective*. Detroit: Wayne State University Press, 1991.
———. "Jewish Women in the Middle Ages." In *Jewish Women in Historical Perspective*, edited by Judith R. Baskin, 94–114. Detroit: Wayne State University Press, 1991.
———. "Some Parallels in the Education of Medieval Jewish and Christian Women." *Jewish History* 5 (1991): 41–51.
———. "From Separation to Displacement: The Problem of Women in *Sefer Hasidim*." *Association for Jewish Studies Review* 19 (1994): 1–10.

———. "Women of the Word: An Introduction." In *Women of the Word: Jewish Women and Jewish Writing,* 17–34. Detroit: Wayne State University Press, 1994.

Baskins, Cristelle K. "Typology, Sexuality, and the Renaissance Esther." In *Sexuality and Gender in Early Modern Europe: Institutions, Texts, Images,* edited by James Grantham Turner, 31–54. Cambridge: Cambridge University Press, 1993.

Battaglia, Salvatore. *Grande Dizionario della lingua italiana.* Vol. 14. Turin: Unione tipografico-editrice torinesei, 1988.

Baum, Jutta. "Queen Esther." In *History of Yiddish Studies: Papers from the Third Annual Oxford Winter Symposium in Yiddish Language and Literature, 13–15 December 1987,* edited by Dov-Ber Kerler, 71–79. Winter Studies in Yiddish 3. Chur: Harwwood, 1991.

———. *Studien zu den westjiddischen Estherdichtungen.* Hamburg: Buske, 1996.

Baumgarten, Jean. "Le Ghetto assiégé, l'insurrection de 1616 contre les Juifs de Francfort d'après un poème en yiddish ancien, la *Megilat vintz.*" *Pardès* 5 (1987): 141–158.

———. *Le Yiddish.* Paris: Presses Universitaires de France, 1990.

———. *Introduction à la littérature yiddish ancienne.* Paris: Cerf, 1993. Edited and translated by Jerold C. Frakes as *Introduction to Old Yiddish Literature.* Oxford: Oxford University Press, 2005.

Bäuml, Franz H., ed. *Kudrun: Die Handschrift.* Berlin: Walter de Gruyter, 1969.

Beal, Timothy K. "Tracing Esther's Beginnings." In *A Feminist Companion to Esther, Judith and Susanna,* edited by Athalya Brenner, 87–110. The Feminist Companion to the Bible 7. Sheffield: Sheffield Academic Press, 1995.

———. *The Book of Hiding: Gender, Ethnicity, Annihilation, and Esther.* London: Routledge, 1997.

Bechstein, Reinhold, and Peter Ganz, eds. *Gottfried von Straßburg, Tristan.* Wiesbaden: Brockhaus, 1978.

Beck, Adolf. "Die Rache als Motiv und Problem in der 'Kudrun.' Interpretation und sagengeschichtlicher Ausblick." In *Nibelungenlied und Kudrun,* edited by Heinz Rupp, 454–501. Wege der Forschung 54. Darmstadt: Wissenschaftliche Buchgesellschaft, 1976.

Belkin, Ahuva. "'Habit de Fou' in Purim Spiel?" *Assaph: Studies in the Theatre* 2/c (1985): 40–55.

———. "*Zmires purim*—The Third Phase of Jewish Carnivalistic Folk-Literature." In *The Politics of Yiddish: Studies in Language, Literature and Society,* edited by Dov-Ber Kerler, 149–156. Winter Studies in Yiddish 4. London: Alta Mira, 1998.

———. *Ha-Purim thpil: ʿiyunim ba-teatron ha-Yehudi ha-ʿamami.* Jerusalem: Mossad Bialik, 2002.

———. "Low Culture in the Purim Play." In *Yiddish Theatre: New Approaches,* edited by Joel Berkowitz, 29–43. Littman Library of Jewish Civilization. Oxford: Littman Library, 2003.

Bell, Dean Phillip. *Jews in the Early Modern World.* Lanham: Rowman and Littlefield, 2008.

Berger, Shlomo. "Functioning within a Diasporic Third Space: The Case of Early Modern Yiddish." *Jewish Studies Quarterly* 15 (2008): 68–86.

———. "Jiddisch und die Formierung der aschkenasischen Diaspora." Translated by Gregor Pelger. *Aschkenas* 18–19 (2008–2009): 509–527.

Berkowitz, Adena K., and Rivka Haut, eds. *Sha'arei simḥa.* Jersey City, NJ: KTAV, 2007.

Berkowitz, Joel, and Barbara Henry, ed. *Inventing the Modern Yiddish Stage: Essays in Drama, Performance, and Show Business.* Detroit: Wayne State University Press, 2012.

Berliner, Abraham. *Ein Gang durch die Bibliotheken Italiens, Vortrag.* Berlin: Julius Benzian, 1877. Reprinted in Abraham Berliner, *Gesammelte Schriften,* 3–29. Frankfurt am Main: J. Kaufmann, 1913.

Bernheimer, Carolus. *Fontes Ambrosiani in lucem editi cura et studio Bybliothecae Ambrosianae, V: Codices Hebraici Bybliothecae Ambrosianae.* Milan: Biblioteca Ambrosiana, 1933.

Bernuth, Ruth von. "Zwischen Kreuzrittern und Sarazenen: Der jüdische Held in Elia Levitas *Bovo d'Antona.*" In *Das Potenzial des Epos: die altfranzösische Chanson de geste im europäischen Kontext,* edited by Susanne Friede and Dorothea Kullmann, 411–431. Heidelberg: Winter, 2012.

Bhabha, Homi K. "Frontlines/ Borderposts." In *Displacements: Cultural Identities in Questions,* edited by Angelika Bammer, 269–272. Bloomington: University of Indiana Press, 1994.

———. *The Location of Culture.* London: Routledge, 1994.

Bikard, Arnaud. "Elia Levita's Yiddish Works: Echoes of the Italian Renaissance in the Poetical Creation of a Jewish Humanist." In *Jewish Migration: Voices of the Diaspora,* edited by Raniero Speelman, Monica Jansen, and Silvia Gaiga, 32–39. Italianistica Ultraiectina 7. Utrecht: Igitur Publishing, 2012.

Bilik, Dorothy. "Tsene-rene: A Yiddish Literary Success." *Jewish Book Annual* 51 (1993–1994): 96–111.

Bisaha, Nancy. "'New Barbarian' or Worthy Adversary? Humanist Constructs of the Ottoman Turks in Fifteenth-Century Italy." In *Western Views of Islam in Medieval and Early Modern Europe: Perception of Other,* edited by David R. Blanks and Michael Frassetto, 185–205. New York: St. Martin's Press, 1999.

———. *Creating East and West: Renaissance Humanists and the Ottoman Turks.* Philadelphia: University of Pennsylvania Press, 2004.

Black, Robert. *Benedetto Accolti and the Florentine Renaissance.* Cambridge: Cambridge University Press, 1985.

Blakeslee, Merritt R. *Love's Masks: Identity, Intertextuality and Meaning in the Old French Tristan Poems.* Woodbridge: Boydell and Brewer, 1989.

Blumstein, Andrée Kahn. *Misogyny and Idealization in the Courtly Romance.* Studien zur Germanistik, Anglistik und Komparatistik 41. Bonn: Bouvier, 1977.

Boerio, Giuseppe. *Dizionario del dialetto Veneziano.* Venice: Giovanni Cecchini, 1856.

Bonatti, Bruno. *Ariosto Pensoso: Lettura delle Satire.* Florence: Nuova Toscana editrice, 1984.

Bonfil, Robert. "Bittuyim le-yihud 'am Israel be-Italia be-tekufat ha-renesans." *Sinai* 76 (1975): 36–46.

———. "The Historian's Perception of the Jews in the Italian Renaissance: Toward a Reappraisal." *Revue des Etudes Juives* 143 (1984): 59–82.

———. "How Golden Was the Age of the Renaissance in Jewish Historiography?" *History and Theory: Studies in the Philosophy of History; Essays in Jewish Histori-*

ography, edited by Ada Rapoport-Albert, *Beiheft* 27 (1988): 78–102. Reprinted in *Essential Papers on Jewish Culture in Renaissance and Baroque Italy*, edited by David B. Ruderman, 219–251. New York: New York University Press, 1992.

———. *Gli Ebrei Italia nell'epoca del Rinascimento*. Florence: Sansoni, 1991. Translated by Anthony Oldcorn as *Jewish Life in Renaissance Italy*. Berkeley: University of California Press, 1994.

———. *Rabbis and Jewish Communities in Renaissance Italy*. Littman Library of Jewish Civilization. Oxford: Oxford University Press, 1999.

Boor, Helmut de, ed. *Das Nibelungenlied*. 21st ed. Revised by Roswitha Wisniewski. Wiesbaden: Brockhaus, 1979.

Bornholdt, Claudia. *Engaging Moments: The Origins of Medieval Bridal-quest Narrative*. Reallexikon Der Germanischen Altertumskunde—Ergänzungsband. New York: Walter de Gruyter, 2005.

Borochov, Ber. "Di geshikhte fun der yidisher literatur, 4) Venetsyaner geshefts- un libshaft-briv." In *Shprakh-forshung un literatur-geshikhte*, edited by Nakhman Meizl, 192–194. Tel Aviv: Peretz, 1966.

Bosworth, Joseph, and T. Northcote Toller. *An Anglo-Saxon Dictionary*. Oxford: Oxford University Press, 1898; reprint, 1980.

Bowden, Betsy. "The Art of Courtly Copulation." *Medievalia et Humanistica*, n.s., 9 (1979): 67–86.

Bowden, Sarah. *Bridal-Quest Epics in Medieval Germany: A Revisionary Approach*. London: Modern Humanities Research Association, 2012.

Boyarin, Daniel, ed. *Purim and the Cultural Poetics of Judaism—Theorizing Diaspora*. Special issue, *Poetics Today* 15 (1994).

Boyd, Matthieu. "Celts Seen as Muslims and Muslims Seen by Celts in Medieval Literature." In *Contextualizing the Muslim Other in Medieval Christian Discourse*, edited by Jerold C. Frakes, 21–38. New York: Palgrave, 2011.

Braden, Gordon. "Applied Petrarchism: The Loves of Pietro Bembo." *Modern Language Quarterly* 57, no. 3 (1996): 397–423.

Bradford, Sarah. *Lucrezia Borgia: Life, Love and Death in Renaissance Italy*. London: Viking, 2004.

Branca, Daniela Delcorno, ed. *Buovo d'Antona: cantari in ottava rima (1480)*. Roma: Carocci, 2008.

Brand, C. P. *Ludovico Ariosto: A Preface to the "Orlando Furioso."* Edinburgh: Edinburgh University Press, 1974.

Brandt, Robert, et al., eds. *Der Fettmilch-Aufstand. Bürgerunruhen und Judenfeindschaft in Frankfurt am Main 1612–1616*. Frankfurt am Main: Historisches Museum Frankfurt, 1996.

Bremond, Claude. *Logique du récit*. Paris: Seuil, 1973.

Brenner, Athalya, ed. *A Feminist Companion to Esther, Judith and Susanna*. The Feminist Companion to the Bible 7. Sheffield: Sheffield Academic Press, 1995.

Bronner, Leila Leah. "Esther Revisited: An Aggadic Approach." In *A Feminist Companion to Esther, Judith and Susanna*, edited by Athalya Brenner, 176–197. The Feminist Companion to the Bible 7. Sheffield: Sheffield Academic Press, 1995.

Brooke, Christopher N. L. *The Medieval Idea of Marriage*. Oxford: Oxford University Press, 1989.

Brown, Patricia Fortini. *Venice and Antiquity: The Venetian Sense of the Past.* New Haven, CT: Yale University Press, 1996.

———. *Private Lives in Renaissance Venice: Art, Architecture, and the Family.* New Haven, CT: Yale University Press, 2004.

Buber, Salomon. *Leben und Schriften des Elias Bachur, genannt Levita.* Leipzig: Fritsche, 1856; repint, Tel Aviv: Ẓion, 1972.

Bumke, Joachim. "Liebe und Ehebruch in der höfischen Gesellschaft." In *Liebe als Literatur: Aufsätze zur erotischen Dichtung in Deutschland,* edited by Rüdiger Krohn, 25–45. Munich: Beck, 1983.

Burckhardt, Jacob. *Die Kultur der Renaissance in Italien: Ein Versuch.* 10th ed. Stuttgart: Alfred Kröner, 1976.

Burman, Thomas E. *Reading the Qur'ān in Latin Christendom, 1140–1560.* Philadelphia: University of Pennsylvania Press, 2007

Butzer, Evi. *Die Anfänge der jiddischen* purim shpiln *in ihrem literarischen und kulturgeschichtlichen Kontext.* Jidische schtudies 10. Hamburg: Helmut Buske, 2003.

Byock, Jesse. *Feud in the Icelandic Saga.* Berkeley: University of California Press, 1982.

Cabrera, Sarandy, ed. and trans. *Sonetos lujuriosos & pasquines del Aretino: seguidos de otros sonetos lujuriosos, dudas amorosas y otras dudas amorosas de autores anónimos de tradición aretinesca y de un soneto de Giorgio Baffo.* Montevideo: Vintén Editor, 1991.

Cairns, Christopher. *Pietro Aretino and the Republic of Venice: Researches on Aretino and His Circle in Venice, 1527–1556.* Biblioteca dell' "Archivum Romanicum," 1st ser., 194. Florence: L. S. Olschki, 1985.

Calabi, Donatella, Ugo Camerino, and Ennio Concina. *La Città degli ebrei.* Venice: Albrizzi, 1991.

Calabi, Donatella, and Paolo Morachiello. *Rialto: le fabbriche e il Ponte. 1514–1591.* Turin: Einaudi, 1987.

Calimani, Riccardo. *The Ghetto of Venice.* Translated by Katherine Silberblatt Wolfthal. New York: M. Evans, 1987.

Cancionero general: que contiene muchas obras de diuersos autores antiguos. Anvers: M. Nucio, 1557.

Caplan, Marc. *How Strange the Change: Language, Temporality, and Narrative Form in Peripheral Modernisms.* Stanford, CA: Stanford University Press, 2011.

Cargill, Oscar. *Drama and Liturgy.* New York: Columbia University Press, 1930.

Carmi, T., ed. *The Penguin Book of Hebrew Verse.* Harmondsworth: Penguin, 1981.

Chiodo, Carmine. "La satira del Seicento nella storia della critica." *Critica Letteraria* 11, no. 4 (1983): 773–802.

Chojnacki, Stanley. "The Power of Love: Wives and Husbands in Late Medieval Venice." In *Women and Power in the Middle Ages,* edited by Mary Erler and Maryanne Kowaleski, 126–48. Athens: University of Georgia Press, 1988.

Chotzner, Jospeh. *Hebrew Satire.* London: K. Paul, Trench, Trübner, 1911.

Chubb, Thomas Caldecot. *Aretino: Scourge of Princes.* New York: Reynal and Hitchcock, 1940.

Cleugh, James. *The Divine Aretino.* New York: Stein and Day, 1966.

Clough, Cecil H. "Pietro Bembo's Library Represented in the British Museum." *British Museum Quarterly* 30 (1965): 3–17.

Codde, Philippe. "Polysystem Revisted: A New Comparative Introduction." *Poetics Today* 24 (2003): 91–126.

Cohen, Mark R. *Under Crescent and Cross: The Jews in the Middle Ages*. Princeton, NJ: Princeton University Press, 1994.

Cohn, Albert. *Shakespeare in Germany in the Sixteenth and Seventeenth Centuries*. London: Asher, 1865.

Colditz, Siegfried. "Die jiddische Fragment vom Herzog Horand in seinem Verhältnis zum Gudrunepos und dem König Rother." *Mitteilungen aus dem Arbeitskreis für Jiddistik* 2 (1960): 17–24.

———. "Das hebräisch-mittelhochdeutsche Fragment vom 'Dukus Horant.'" *Forschungen und Fortschritte* 40 (1966): 302–306.

Concina, Ennio. "Parva Jerusalem." In *La città degli ebrei: il ghetto di Venezia: architettura e urbanistica*, by Ennio Concina, Ugo Camerino, and Donatella Calabi, 11–24. Venice: Albrizzi, 1991.

Cooperman, Bernard Dov. *Jewish Thought in the Sixteenth Century*. Cambridge, MA: Harvard University Press, 1983.

Cozzi, Gaetano, ed. *Gli ebrei e Venezia*. Milan: Edizioni Comunità, 1987.

Craig, Kenneth M., Jr. *Reading Esther: A Case for the Literary Carnivalesque*. Louisville, KY: Westminster John Knox Press, 1995.

Croce, Elena. *Periplo italiano: Note sui narratori italiani dei primi secoli*. Milan: Mondadori, 1977.

Cuccaro, Vincent. *The Humanism of Ludovico Ariosto: From the Satire to the Furioso*. Ravenna: Longo, 1980.

Curschmann, Michael. *Der Münchener Oswald und die deutsche Spielmännische Epik*. Munich: Beck, 1964.

———. *Spielmannsepik: Wege und Ergebnisse der Forschung von 1907–1965, mit Ergänzungen und Nachträgen bis 1967*. Stuttgart: Metzler, 1968.

Dauber, Jeremy. *In the Demon's Bedroom: Yiddish Literature and the Early Modern*. New Haven, CT: Yale University Press, 2010.

Däumer, Matthias. "Das Lachen des verbitterten Idealisten. Parodie und Satire im *Widuwilt*." In *Ironie, Polemik und Provokation*, edited by Coral Dietl, Christoph Schanze, and Friedrich Wolfzettel, 259–285. Schriften der internationalen Artusgesellschaft 10. Berlin: Walter de Gruyter, 2014.

Davidson, Herbert. "Medieval Jewish Philosophy in the Sixteenth Century." In *Jewish Thought in the Sixteenth Century*, edited by Bernard Dov Cooperman, 138–139. Cambridge, MA: Harvard University Press, 1983.

Davidson, Israel. *Parody in Jewish Literature*. New York: Columbia University Press, 1907.

Davis, Robert C., and Benjamin Ravid, eds. *The Jews of Early Modern Venice*. Baltimore: Johns Hopkins University Press, 2001.

Debenedetti, Santorre, and Cesare Segre, eds. *Ludovico Ariosto, Orlando Furioso*. Bologna: Commissione per i testi di Lingua, 1960.

Deleuze, Gilles, and Félix Guattari. *Kafka: Pour une littérature mineure*. Paris: Éditions de Minuit, 1975.

Dionisotti, Carlo, ed. *Carteggio d'amore, 1500–1501: Maria Savorgnan—Pietro Bembo*. Florence: Felice le Monnier, 1950.

Dishon, Judith. "Images of Women in Medieval Hebrew Literature." In *Women of the Word: Jewish Women and Jewish Writing*, edited by Judith R. Baskin, 35–49. Detroit: Wayne State University Press, 1994.

Donahue, Charles, Jr. "The Canon Law on the Formation of Marriage and Social Practice in the Later Middle Ages." *Journal of Family History* 8 (1983): 144–158.

Donnelly, John Patrick. "The Moslem Enemy in Renaissance Epic: Ariosto, Tasso and Camoëns." *Yale Italian Studies* 1 (1977): 162–170.

Dreeßen, Wulf-Otto. "Zur Rezeption deutscher epischer Literatur im Altjiddischen—Das Beispiel 'Wigalois'—'Artushof.'" In *Deutsche Literatur des späten Mittelalters: Hamburger Colloquium 1973*, edited by Wolfgang Harms und L. Peter Johnson, 116–128. Berlin: Schmidt, 1973.

———. "Die altjiddischen Estherdichtungen: Überlegungen zur Rekonstruktion der Geschichte der älteren jiddischen Literatur." *Daphnis* 6 (1977): 27–39.

———. "Midraschepik und Bibelepik: Biblische Stoffe in der volkssprachlichen Literatur der Juden und Christen des Mittelalters im deutschen Sprachgebiet." *Zeitschrift für deutsche Philologie* 100 [Sonderheft] (1981): 78–97.

———. "Wigalois—Widuwilt: Wandlungen des Artusromans im Jiddischen." in *Westjiddisch: Mündlichkeit und Schriftlichkeit/Le Yiddish occidental: Actes du Colloque de Mulhouse*, edited by Astrid Starck, 84–98. Aarau: Sauerländer, 1994.

———. "Horant als *Schadchen*?" *Jiddistik-Mitteilungen*, no. 23 (April 2000): 1–9.

Dreeßen, Wulf-Otto and Hermann-Josef Müller, eds. *Doniel: Das altjiddische Danielbuch nach dem Basler Druck von 1557*. 2 vols. Litterae 59. Göppingen: Kümmerle, 1978.

Drukker, Tamar S. "A Thirteenth-Century Arthurian Tale in Hebrew: A Unique Literary Exchange." *Medieval Encounters* 15 (2009): 114–129.

Duby, Georges. "Le mariage dans la société du haut moyen âge." In *Il matrimonio nella società altomedievale*, 15–39. Settimane di studio del centro italiano de studi sull'alto medioevo 24. Spoleto: Presso la sede del centro, 1977.

———. *Le chevalier, la femme et le prêtre*. Paris: Hachette, 1981.

Dufournet, Jean, ed. *Aucassin et Nicolette*. Paris: Garnier-Flammarion, 1973.

Eagleton, Terry. *Literary Theory: An Introduction*. 2nd ed. Minneapolis: University of Minnesota Press, 1996.

Ego, Beate, ed. *Targum Scheni zu Ester: Übersetzung, Kommentar und theologische Deutung*. Tübingen: Mohr, 1996.

Einbinder, Susan L. "A Proper Diet: Medicine and History in Crescas Caslari's *Esther*." *Speculum* 80 (2005): 437–463.

El-Gabalawy, Saad. "Aretino's Pornography and Renaissance Satire." *Rocky Mountain Review of Language and Literature* 30, no. 2 (Spring 1976): 87–99.

———. "Aretino's Pornography and English Renaissance Satire." *Humanities Association Review / La Revue de l'Association des Humanités* [Kingston, Canada] 28 (1977): 9–19.

Elliger, Karl, and Wilhelm Rudolph, eds. *Torah neviim u-ketuvim / Biblia Hebraica Stuttgartensia*. 2nd ed. Stuttgart: Deutsche Bibelgesellschaft, 1967.

Elyada, Aya. *A Goy Who Speaks Yiddish: Christians and the Jewish Language in Early Modern Germany*. Stanford, CA: Stanford University Press, 2012.

Erik, Max [Zalmen Merkin]. "Bletlekh tsu der geshikhte fun der elterer yidisher literatur . . . a paskvil fun Elye Bokher—dos lid vegn der sreyfe in Venetsye." *Tsaytshrift fun dem institut far vaysruslendisher kultur* 1 (1926): 173–178.

———. *Vegn altyidishn roman*. Warsaw: Der veg tsu visn, 1926.
———. "Vegn 'Mayse Briye ve-Zimre.'" In *Shriftn fun yidishn visnshaftlekhn institut* [filologishe serye] 1 (Vilnius, 1926), col. 153–162 = *Landoy-bukh: Dr. Alfred Landoy tsu zayn 75stn geboyrntog dem 25stn november 1925*. Vilnius: Kletskin, 1926.
———. *Di geshikhte fun der yidisher literatur: fun di eltste tsaytn biz der haskole-tkufe, fertsnter-akhtsnter yorhundert, mit bilder un melodyes*. Warsaw: Kultur lige, 1928; reprint, New York: Congress for Jewish Culture, 1979.
———. "Inventar fun der yidisher shpilman-dikhtung." *Tsaytshrift* 1 (1928): col. 545–588.
Ertzdorff, Xenja, and Marianne Wynn, eds. *Liebe-Ehe-Ehebruch in der Literatur des Mittelalters*. Beiträge zur deutschen Philologie 58. Gießen: Schmitz, 1984.
Even-Zohar, Itamar. "The Function of the Polysystem in the History of Literature." In *Papers in Historical Poetics*, 11–13. Tel Aviv: Porter Institute for Poetics and Semiotics, 1978.
———. "The Polysystem Hypothesis Revisited." In *Papers in Historical Poetics*, 28–35. Tel Aviv: Porter Institute for Poetics and Semiotics, 1978.
———. *Polysystem Studies*. Special issue, *Poetics Today* 11 (1990): 1–268.
Even-Zohar, Itamar, and Chone Shmeruk. "Lashon 'otentit, mesirat dibur 'otenti: ivrit ve-yidish." *Hasifrut* 30–31 (1981): 82–97.
Faini, Marco. *Pasquinate*. Part 2 of *Operette politiche e satiriche*. Vol. 6 of *Edizione nazionale delle opere di Pietro Aretino*. Roma: Salerno editrice, 2012.
Falcone, Giandomenico. "Pensiero religioso, scetticismo e satira contro il pedante nella letteratura del Cinquecento." *Rassegna della Letteratura Italiana* 88 (1984): 80–116.
Falk, Felix. *Das Schemuelbuch des Mosche Esrim Wearba: Ein biblisches Epos aus dem 15. Jahrhundert*. Einleitung und textkritischer Apparat von Felix Falk, aus dem Nachlaß herausgegeben von L. Fuks. 2 vols. Assen: Van Gorcum, 1961.
Feffer, Solomon. "Of Ladies and Converts and Tomes: An Essay in Hebrew Book Lore." *Jewish Book Annual* 19 (1961–1962): 3–16.
Ferrero, Giuseppe Guido. *Scritti Scelti di Pietro Aretino*. 2nd ed. Turin: Unione Tipograficor-Editrice Torinese, 1970.
Finlay, Robert. "The Foundation of the Ghetto: Venice, the Jews and the War of the League of Cambrai." *Proceedings of the American Philosophical Society* 126 (1982): 140–154.
Fisch, Harold. "Reading and Carnival: On the Semiotics of Purim." In *Purim and the Cultural Poetics of Judaism—Theorizing Diaspora*, edited by Daniel Boyarin, special issue, *Poetics Today* 15 (1994): 55–74.
Fish, Stanley. *John Skelton's Poetry*. New Haven, CT: Yale University Press, 1965.
Fishelov, David. "The Prophet as Satirist." *Prooftexts* 9, no. 3 (1989): 195–211.
Fortis, Umberto. *The Ghetto on the Lagoon: A Guide to the History and Art of the Venetian Ghetto (1516–1797)*. Rev. ed. Translated by Roberto Matteoda. Venice: Sorti Edizioni, 2001.
Fortis, Umberto, and Paolo Zolli. *La parlata giudeo-veneziana*. Rome: B. Carucci, 1979.
Fourquet, Jean. "Ernest-H. Lévy et le Dukus Horant" [review of Fuks, *The Oldest Known Literary Documents*]. *Études Germaniques*, 14 (1959): 50–56.
Fox, Harry, and Justin Jaron Lewis, eds. *Many Pious Women*. New York: Walter de Gruyter, 2011.
Fox, Michael V. *Character and Ideology in the Book of Esther*. Columbia: University of South Carolina Press, 1991.

Frakes, Jerold C. "Metaphysical Structure as Narrative Structure in the Medieval Romance." *Neophilologus* 69 (1985): 481–489.

———. *Brides and Doom: Gender, Property and Power in Medieval German Women's Epic*. Middle Ages Series. Philadelphia: University of Pennsylvania Press, 1994.

———. "1697: The Earliest Extant Yiddish Purimšpil Is Traced to Leipzig." in *Yale Companion to Jewish Writing and Thought in German Culture: 1096–1996*, edited by Sander L. Gilman and Jack Zipes, 55–60. New Haven, CT: Yale University Press, 1997.

———. "The Female Gaze and the Liminal Window in Medieval Epic." In *De consolatione philologiae: Studien zur älteren und neueren deutschen und skandinavischen Literatur und Sprache. Festgabe für Evelyn Firchow*, edited by Anna Grotans et al., 85–100. Göppingen: Kümmerle, 2000.

———, ed. *Early Yiddish Texts, 1100–1750, with Introduction and Commentary*. Oxford: Oxford University Press, 2004; rev. ed., 2008.

———, ed. *The Cultural Study of Yiddish in Early Modern Europe*. New York: Palgrave, 2007.

———. *Vernacular and Latin Literary Discourses of the Muslim Other in Medieval Germany*. The New Middle Ages Series. New York: Palgrave, 2011.

———, trans. *Early Yiddish Epic*. Syracuse, NY: Syracuse University Press, 2014.

———. "Outliers of Yiddish Literature: Early and Late, Italy and Poland, Rhetorical and Peripheral." *Jewish Quarterly Review* 104 (2014): 289–306.

Fram, Edward, ed. *My Dear Daughter: Rabbi Benjamin Slonik and the Education of Jewish Women in Sixteenth-Century Poland*. Cincinnati: Hebrew Union College Press, 2007.

Franceschetti, Antonio. "On the Saracens in Early Italian Chivalric Literature." In *Romance Epic: Essays on a Medieval Literary Genre*, edited by Hans-Erich Keller, 203–211. Studies in Medieval Culture 24. Kalamazoo: Medieval Institute Publication / Western Michigan University, 1987.

Freimann, Aron. "Haben jüdische Flüchtlinge aus Mainz im XV. Jahrhundert den Buchdruck nach Italien gebracht?" *Journal of Jewish Bibliography* 1 (Oct 1938–July 1939): 9–11.

Friedman, John Block. *The Monstrous Races in Medieval Art and Thought*. Cambridge, MA: Harvard University Press, 1981.

———. *Orpheus in the Middle Ages*. Cambridge: Harvard University Press, 1970; reprint, Syracuse: Syracuse University Press, 2000.

Fromm, Annette B. "Among the Jews of Ioannina: Symbolic Enactments." *Jewish Folklore and Ethnology Review* 15, no. 2 (1993): 104–106.

Froning, Richard, ed. *Das Drama des Mittelalters*. Deutsche National-Literatur 14. Stuttgart: Union Deutsche Verlagsgesellschaft, 1891–1892.

———, ed. *Das Drama der Reformationszeit*. Deutsche National-Litteratur 22. Stuttgart: Union Deutsche Verlagsgesellschaft, 1895.

Fuks, Leo [Laib], ed. *The Oldest Known Literary Documents of Yiddish Literature (c. 1382)*. 2 vols. Leiden: Brill, 1957.

———, ed. *Das altjiddische Epos Melok̂îm-Bûk̂*. 2 vols. Assen: Van Gorcum, 1965.

Fuks-Mansfeld, Renate. "West- und Ostjiddisch auf Amsterdamer Bühnen gegen Ende des achtzehnten Jahrhunderts." In *Westjiddisch: Mündlichkeit und Schriftlichkeit/*

Le Yiddish occidental: Actes du Colloque de Mulhouse, edited by Astrid Starck, 112–118. Aarau: Sauerländer, 1994.

Ganz, Peter F. "*Dukus Horant*: An Early Yiddish Poem from the Cairo Genizah." *Journal of Jewish Studies* 9 (1958): 47–62.

———, ed. *Gottfried von Straßburg, Tristan*. 2 vols. Wiesbaden: Brockhaus, 1978.

Ganz, Peter F., Frederick Norman, and Werner Schwarz. "Zu dem Cambridger Joseph." *Zeitschrift für deutsche Philologie*, 82 (1963): 86–90.

———, eds. *Dukus Horant*. Altdeutsche Texbibliothek, Ergänzungungsreihe 2. Tübingen: Niemeyer, 1964.

Gardiner, Harold Charles. *Mysteries End: An Investigation of the Last Days of the Medieval Religious Stage*. New Haven, CT: Yale University Press, 1946.

Geiger, Ludwig. *Das Studium der hebräischen Sprache in Deutschland vom Ende des XVten bis zur Mitte des XVIten Jahrhunderts*. Breslau: Schletter, 1870.

Geißler, Friedmar. *Brautwerbung in der Weltliteratur*. Halle: Niemeyer, 1955.

———. "Brautwerbung." In *Reallexikon der germanischen Altertumskunde*. 2nd ed. Vol. 3, 421–425. New York: Walter de Gruyter, 1978.

———. "Brautwerbungssage." In *Reallexikon der germanischen Altertumskunde*. 2nd ed. Vol. 3, 425–428. New York: Walter de Gruyter, 1978.

Gellinek, Christian. "Marriage by Consent in Literary Sources of Medieval Germany." *Studia Gratiana* 12 (1967): 555–579.

———. *König Rother: Studie zur literarischen Deutung*. Bern: Francke, 1968.

Gennep, Arnold van. *The Rites of Passage*. Translated by Monika B. Vizedon and Gabrielle L. Caffee. Chicago: University of Chicago Press, 1960.

Gill, R. B. "The Structures of Self-Assertion in Sixteenth-Century Flytings." *Renaissance Papers* (1983): 31–41.

Ginsburg, Christian David. *The Massoreth ha-Massoreth of Elias Levita*. London: Longmans, Green, Reader and Dyer, 1867.

Giustiniani, Vita R. "Homo, Humanus, and the Meaning of Humanism." *Journal of the History of Ideas* 46 (1935): 167–196.

Gollancz, Hermann, ed. *Joseph Kimḥi, Shekel hakodesh (The Holy Shekel): The Metrical Work of Joseph Kimḥi*. Oxford: Oxford University Press, 1919.

Goodman, Philip. *The Purim Anthology*. Philadelphia: Jewish Publication Society, 1949.

Gordon, Milton. *Assimilation in American Life: The Role of Race, Religion, and National Origins*. New York: Oxford University Press, 1964.

Gorin, Bernard. *Di geshikhte fun yidishn teater*. New York: Literarisher Ferlag, 1918.

Gouhier, Henri Gaston. "Note sur l'Anti-Humanisme à propos de Bérulle." *Dieu vivant* 23 (Paris 1953): 145–150.

Goy, Richard J. *Building Renaissance Venice: Patrons, Architects and Builders, c. 1430–1500*. New Haven, CT: Yale University Press, 2006.

Gravdal, Kathryn. "Chrétien de Troyes, Gratian, and the Medieval Romance of Sexual Violence." *Signs: Journal of Women in Culture and Society* 17 (1992): 558–585.

Greenblatt, Rachel L. "David Oppenheim." In *The YIVO Encyclopedia of Jews in Eastern Europe*, edited by Gershon David Hundert, 2:1287–1288. New Haven, CT: Yale University Press, 2008.

Grendler, Paul F. "The Rejection of Learning in Mid-Cinquecento Italy." *Studies in the Renaissance* 13 (1966): 230–249.

Grenzler, Thomas. *Erotisierte Politik—Politisierte Erotik: Die politisch-ständische Begründung der Ehe-Minne in Wolframs "Willehalm," im "Nibelungenlied" und in der "Kudrun."* Göppingen: Kümmerle, 1992.

Grimm, Jacob, and Wilhelm, eds. *Deutsches Wörterbuch.* 2nd ed. Leipzig: Hirzel, 1854–1971; reprint, Hildesheim: Olms, 2003–. http://germazope.uni-trier.de/Projects/DWB.

Grino, Raimundo. "Importancia del Meturgeman de Elias Levita y del ms. Angelica 6-6 para el estudio del mismo sefarad." *Revista del Instituto Arias Montano de Estudios Hebraicos, Sefardies u de Oriente Proximo* 31 (Madrid 1971): 353–361.

Gross, Heinrich. *Die Satire in der jüdischen Literatur.* Augsburg: Adolf Alkalay und Sohn, 1908 = *Monatsschrift für Geschichte und Wissenschaft des Judentums* 52.

Grossfeld, Bernard, ed. *The First Targum to Esther: According to the MS Paris Hebrew 110 of the Bibliothèque Nationale.* New York: Sepher-Hermon, 1983.

———, ed. *The Two Targums of Esther, Translated with Apparatus and Notes.* The Aramaic Bible 18. Edinburgh: T. and T. Clark, 1991.

Grünbaum, Max. *Jüdischdeutsche Chrestomathie.* Leipzig: Brockhaus, 1882.

Gudemann, Moritz. *Geschichte des Erziehungswesens und der Cultur der Juden in Italien, Deutschland und Frankreich während des Mittelalters.* 3 Bde. Vienna: A. Hölder, 1880–1888; reprint, Amsterdam: Philo, 1966.

Haines, J. L. *The Phonology of the "Bovobukh": Contribution to the History of East Franconian Yiddish.* Diss., Columbia University, 1979.

Hall, Edith. *Inventing the Barbarian: Greek Self-Definition through Tragedy.* Oxford: Clarendon, 1989.

Halm, Karl, ed. *Cornelius Tacitus, Libri qui svpersvnt*, vol. 2, part 2, *Germania, Agricola, Dialogus de Orationibus.* Leipzig: Teubner, 1964.

Hamburger, Binyamin Shelomoh, and Yitsḥak [Eric] Zimmer, eds. *Jousep Schammes, Minhagim di-ḳ.ḳ. Vermaiśa le-Rabi Yuzpa Shamash.* 2 vols. Jerusalem: Mif'al torat ḥakhme Ashkenaz, Mekhon Yerushalayim, 1988–1992.

Haraszti-Takács, Marianne. "Fifteenth-Century Painted Furniture with Scenes from the Esther Story." *Jewish Art* 15 (1989): 14–25.

Harshav (Hrushovski), Benjamin. "The Discovery of Accentual Iambs in European Poetry and Their First Employment in a Yiddish Romance in Italy (1508–1509)." In *For Max Weinreich on His Seventieth Birthday*, edited by Lucy Davidowicz et al., 108–146. The Hague: Mouton, 1964.

———. *The Meaning of Yiddish.* Berkeley: University of California Press, 1990.

Hartsock, Nancy. "Rethinking Modernism: Minority vs. Majority Theories." *Cultural Critique* 7 (Autumn 1987): 187–206.

Hecker, Kristine. "The Concept of Theatre Production in Leone de' Sommi's *Quattro dialoghi* in the Context of His Time." In *Leone de Sommi and the Performing Arts*, edited by Ahuva Belkin, 189–208. Tel Aviv: Assaph, 1997.

Hellerstein, Kathryn. "Songs of Herself: A Lineage of Women Yiddish Poets." *Studies in American Jewish Literature* 9 (1990): 138–150.

———. "Canon and Gender: Women Poets in Two Modern Yiddish Anthologies." *Shofar: An Interdisciplinary Journal of Jewish Studies* 9 (1991): 9–23. Reprinted in *Women of the Word: Jewish Women and Jewish Writing*, edited by Judith R. Baskin, 136–152. Detroit: Wayne State University Press, 1994.

Helm, Rudolfus, ed. *Apulei Platonici Ladaurensis Metamorphoseon Libri XI*. Leipzig: Teubner, 1907.

Hilka, Alfons, ed. *Historia Alexandri Magni (Historia de preliis): Rezension J1*. Meisenheim am Glan: A. Hain, 1979.

Hoecke, Willy van, and Andries Welkenhuysen, eds. *Love and Marriage in the Twelfth Century*. Leuven: Leuven University Press, 1981.

Hooks, Bell. *Ain't I a Woman: Black Women and Feminism*. Boston: South End Press, 1982.

Horowitz, Elliott. "The Rite to Be Reckless: On the Perpetration and Interpretation of Purim Violence." In *Purim and the Cultural Poetics of Judaism—Theorizing Diaspora*, edited by Daniel Boyarin, special issue, *Poetics Today* 15 (1994): 9–54.

———. *Reckless Rites: Purim and the Legacy of Jewish Violence*. Princeton, NJ: Princeton University Press, 2006.

Hösle, Johannes. *Pietro Aretinos Werk*. Berlin: Walter de Gruyter, 1969.

Howard, Deborah. "Cultural Transfer between Venice and the Ottomans in the Fifteenth and Sixteenth Centuries." In *Cultural Exchange in Early Modern Europe*, vol. 4, *Forging European Identities, 1400–1700*, edited by Herman Roodenburg, 138–77. Cambridge: Cambridge University Press, 2007.

Howard, John A. *Dietrich von Bern (1597)*. Würzburg: Königshausen und Neuman, 1986.

———. *Fortunatus*. Würzburg: Königshausen und Neumann, 1991.

Huss, Matti, ed. "Judah ben Isaac Ibn Shabbetai, 'Minhat Yehudah,' 'Ezrat ha-nashim' ve-'En mishpat.'" 2 vols. Diss., Jerusalem, 1991.

Iannucci, Amilcare A. "Ariosto's Satire-Epistle to Bembo: Meditations on Humanism and the Value of a Humanistic Education." *Humanities Association Review / La Revue de l'Association des Humanites* [Kingston, Canada] 30 (1979): 147–160.

Jackson, W. T. H. *The Hero and the King: An Epic Theme*. New York: Columbia University Press, 1982.

Jacobs, Martin. *Islamische Geschichte in jüdischen Chroniken: Hebräische Historiographie des 16. und 17. Jahrhunderts*. Tübingen: Mohr Siebeck, 2004.

Jacobs, Neil G. *Yiddish: A Linguistic Introduction*. Cambridge: Cambridge University Press, 2005.

Jacoby, David. "Les juifs à Venise du XIVe au milieu du XVIe siècle." In *Venezia centro di mediazione tra Oriente e Occidente (secoli XV-XVI); aspetti e problemi*, edited by Hans-Georg Beck et al. (Florence: Olschki, 1977), 1:163–216.

———. "New Evidence on Jewish Bankers in Venice and the Terraferma (c. 1450–1550)." In *Ha-Yehudim veha-Yam ha-Tikhon: kesafim banḳa'ut u-misḥar benle'umi ba-me'ot 16–18 / The Mediterranean and the Jews, Banking, Finance, and International Trade*, edited by Ariel Toaff and Shimon Shwartzfuchs, 151–178. Ramat Gan: Bar-Ilan University Press, 1989.

Jaeger, Achim. *Ein jüdischer Artusritter: Studien zum jüdisch-deutschen "Widuwilt" ("Artushof") und zum "Wigalois" des Wirnt von Gravenberc*. Tübingen: Niemeyer, 2000.

JanMohamed, Abdul R., and David Lloyd, eds. *The Nature and Context of Minority Discourse*. Oxford: Oxford University Press, 1990.

Jensen, Ejner J. "The Wit of Renaissance Satire." *Philological Quarterly* 51 (1972): 394–409.

Jones-Davies, M. T., ed. *La Satire au temps de la Renaissance*. Paris: Touzot, 1986.
Jónsson, Finnur, ed. *Edda Snorra Sturlusonar*. Copenhagen: Gyldendal, 1931.
Julian, John. *A Dictionary of Hymnology*. London: Murray, 1915.
Kabbani, Rana. *Imperial Fictions: Europe's Myths of Orient*. London: Macmillan, 1986; reprint, London: Pandora, 1994.
Kalmar, Ivan Davidson, and Derek J. Penslar. *Orientalism and the Jews*. Waltham, MA: Brandeis University Press, 2005.
Kapteyn, J. M. N., ed. *Wirnt von Grafenberg, Wigalois*. Translated by Sabine Seelbach and Ulrich Seelbach. Berlin: Walter de Gruyter, 2005
Karpeles, Gustav. *Jewish Literature and Other Essays*. Philadelphia: Jewish Publication Society, 1895.
Katz, Dovid. "Hebrew, Aramaic and the Rise of Yiddish." In *Readings in the Sociology of Jewish Languages*, edited by Joshua Fishman, 85–103. Leiden: Brill, 1985.
Katz, Eli. "Six Germano-Judaic Poems from the Cairo Genizah." Diss., UCLA, 1963.
Katz, Jakob. *Exclusiveness and Tolerance: Studies in Jewish-Gentile Relations in Medieval and Modern Times*. New York: Schocken, 1961.
Kayserling, Meyer. *Die jüdischen Frauen in der Geschichte, Literatur und Kunst*. Leipzig: Brockhaus, 1879.
Kazis, Israel J., ed. *Sefer Toldot Alesandrus ha-Makdoni*. Cambridge, MA: Mediaeval Academy of America, 1962.
Kendrick, Laura. "Medieval Satire." In *European Writers: The Middle Ages and the Renaissance, I: Prudentius to Medieval Drama; II: Petrarch to Renaissance Short Fiction*, edited by William T. H. Jackson, 1:337–375. New York: Scribner's, 1983.
Kerler, Dov-Ber, "East Meets West: The Dialectal Climate of Two Early Eastern European Yiddish Prints." In *Dialects of the Yiddish Language*, edited by Dovid Katz, 69–84. Winter Studies in Yiddish 2. Oxford: Pergamon Press, 1988.
———. *The Origins of Modern Literary Yiddish*. Oxford: Oxford University Press, 1999.
Kern, Manfred. "Verwilderte Heldenepik in hebräischen Lettern. Literarischer Horizont und kultureller Austausch im *Dukus Horant*." In *Mittelalterliche Heldendichtung außerhalb des Nibelungen- und Dietrichkreises (Kudrun, Ortnit, Waltharius, Wolfdietriche), 7. Pöchlarner Heldenliedgespräch*, edited by Klaus Zatloukal, 109–134. Philologica Germanica 25. Vienna: Fassbaender, 2003.
Kerth, Thomas. *King Rother and His Bride: Quest and Counter-Quests*. Rochester, NY: Camden House, 2010.
Kidwell, Carol. *Pietro Bembo: Lover, Linguist, Cardinal*. Montreal: McGill-Queen's University Press, 2004.
Kimball, Roger. "Lessons from Juvenal." *New Criterion* 21, no. 8 (2003). http://www.newcriterion.com/articles.cfm/Lessons-from-Juvenal-1755
Kinoshita, Sharon. *Medieval Boundaries: Rethinking Difference in Old French Literature*. Philadelphia: University of Pennsylvania Press, 2006.
Kluge, Friedrich. *Etymologisches Wörterbuch der deutschen Sprache*. 25th ed. Berlin: Walter de Gruyter, 2012.
Knaeble, Susanne. "Ironische Distanzierung im Fokus intellektuellen Erzählens. Der westjiddische *Widuwilt* als Rezeptionsgegenstand." In *Ironie, Polemik und Provokation*, edited by Coral Dietl, Christoph Schanze, and Friedrich Wolfzettel,

85–108. Schriften der internationalen Artusgesellschaft 10. Berlin: Walter de Gruyter, 2014.

Koehler, Ludwig, and Walter Baumgartner. *Hebräisches und Aramäisches Lexikon zum alten Testament*. 3rd ed. Edited by Johann Jakob Stamm. Leiden: E. J. Brill, 1990.

Koishwitz, Otto. *Der Theaterherold im deutschen Schauspiel des Mittelalters und der Reformationszeit: ein Beitrag zur deutschen Theatergeschichte*. Berlin: E. Ebering, 1926.

Kölbing, Eugen, ed. *The Romance of Sir Beues of Hamtoun*. EETSES 46, 48, 65. London: K. Paul, Trench, Trübner and Co., 1885, 1886, 1894; reprinted as one vol., 1973.

Könecker, Barbara. "Zum literarischen Charakter und der literatrischen Intention des altjiddischen Schmuelbuchs." In *Kontroversen, alte und neue: Auseinandersetzung um jiddische Sprache und Literatur, Jüdische Komponenten in der deutschen Literatur—die Assimilationskontroverse*, edited by Walter Röll und Hans-Peter Bayersdörfer, 3–12. Tübingen: Max Niemeyer, 1986.

Krapp, George Philip, and Elliott van Kirk Dobbie, eds. *The Exeter Book*. Vol. 3 of *The Anglo-Saxon Poetic Records*. New York: Columbia University Press, 1936.

Kristeller, Paul Oskar. *Iter italicum: A Finding List of Uncatalogued or Incompletely Catalogued Humanistic Manuscripts of the Renaissance in Italian and Other Libraries*. Vol. 2, *Italy: Orvieto to Volterra, Vatican City*. 3rd ed. Leiden: E. J. Brill, 1977.

Krugman, Paul. *The Self-Organizing Economy*. Oxford: Blackwell, 1996.

Kuhn, Hans. "Kriemhilds Hort und Rache." In *Festschrift Paul Kluckhohn und Hermann Schneider gewidmet zu ihrem 60. Geburtstag*, 84–100. Tübingen: Mohr/Siebeck, 1948. Reprinted in Hans Kuhn, *Kleine Schriften*, 2:65–79. Berlin: Walter de Gruyter, 1971.

Labov, William. "Rules for Ritual Insults." In *Language in the Inner City: Studies in the Black English Vernacular*, edited by William Labov, 297–353. Philadelphia: University of Pennsylvania Press, 1973.

Lachmann, Karl, ed. *Wolfram von Eschenbach, Parzival, Willehalm* and *Titurel*. 6th ed. Berlin: Walter de Gruyter, 1926.

Lagarde, Paulus de, ed. *Hagiographa Chaldaice*. Leipzig: Teubner, 1873; reprint, Osnabrück: Otto Zeller, 1967.

Landau, Leo. *Arthurian Legends, or the Hebrew-German Rhymed Version of the Legend of King Arthur*. Part 1 of *Hebrew-German Romances and Tales and Their Relation to the Romantic Literature of the Middle Ages*. Teutonia 21. Leipzig: Avenarius, 1912.

———, ed. "A Hebrew-German (Judeo-German) Paraphrase of the Book Esther of the Fifteenth Century." *Journal of English and Germanic Philology* 18 (1919): 497–555.

Larivaille, Paul. *Pietro Aretino*. Rome: Salerno editrice, 1997.

Larner, John. *Marco Polo and the Discovery of the World*. New Haven: Yale University Press, 1999.

Lassner, Jacob. *Demonizing the Queen of Sheba: Boundaries of Gender and Culture in Postbiblical Judaism and Medieval Islam*. Chicago: University of Chicago Press, 1993.

Laurenson, Ian. "A Pasquinade for John Owen." *Notes and Queries* 26 (1979): 403–405.

Leclanche, Jean-Luc, ed. *Le Conte de Floire et Blancheflor*. Paris: H. Champion, 1983.

Lembke, Astrid. "Ritter außer Gefecht. Konzepte passiver Bewährung im *Wigalois* und im *Widuwilt*." *Aschkenas* 25 (2015): 63–82.

Lesley, Arthur M. "Hebrew Humanism in Italy: The Case of Biography." *Prooftexts* 2 (1982): 163–177.

———. "Jewish Adaptations of Humanist Concepts in Fifteenth- and Sixteenth-Century Italy." In *Essential Papers on Jewish Culture in Renaissance and Baroque Italy*, edited by David B. Ruderman, 45–62. New York: New York University Press, 1992.

Leviant, Curt, ed. and trans. *King Artus: A Hebrew Arthurian Romance of 1279*. Studia Semitica Neerlandica 11. Assen: Van Gorcum, 1969.

Levita, Elias [Elye Bokher]. *Sefer ha-Tishbi*. Isny: Fagius, 1541.

———. *Elye Bokher: poetishe shafungen in yidish*. Edited by Judah A. Joffe. New York: Judah A. Joffe Publication Committee, 1949.

Levi, J. *Elia Levita und seine Leistungen als Grammatiker*. Breslau: Schottlaender, 1888.

Lewis, Bernard. *The Jews of Islam*. Princeton, NJ: Princeton University Press, 1984.

Lexer, Matthias. *Mittelhochdeutsches Handwörterbuch*. 3 vols. Leipzig: Hirzel, 1872–1878; reprint, Stuttgart: Hirzel, 1979.

Licht, Jacob. "Calendar." In *Encyclopaedia Judaica*, 2nd ed., edited by Michael Berenbaum and Fred Skolnik, 5:43–53. Detroit: Macmillan Reference USA, 2007.

Linder, Amnon, ed. *The Jews in Roman Imperial Legislation*. Detroit: Wayne State University Press, 1987.

———, ed. *The Jews in the Legal Sources of the Early Middle Ages*. Jerusalem: Israel Academy of Sciences and Humanities, 1997.

Linn, Irving, ed. "Widwilt, Son of Gawein." Diss., New York University, 1942.

Loerzer, Eckart. *Eheschließung und Werbung in der "Kudrun."* Munich: Beck, 1971.

Luciani, Gérard. "La Dérision politique à Venise." *Filigrana* 5 (1998–1999): 183–205.

Lustiger, Arno. "Der Fettmilchaufstand in Frankfurt und die Juden." In *Scheidewege. Rudolf Pfisterer zum 70. Geburtstag*, 23–31. Düsseldorf: Der kleine Verlag, 1985.

Luzio, Alessandro. *Pietro Aretino nei Primi Suoi Anni a Venezia e la Corte dei Gonzaga*. Turin: Ermanno Loeschr, 1888.

———. "Pietro Aretino e Pasquino." *Nuova antologia di scienze, lettere ed arte*, 3rd ser., 28 (1890): 679–708.

Mack, Charles R. *Thermal Spas of Renaissance Italy*. Columbia: University of South Carolina, 2003.

Malter, Henry. "Purim Plays." In *The Jewish Encyclopedia*, edited by Isidore Singer, 10:279–280. New York: Funk and Wagnalls, 1945.

Marchetti, Valerio, Jean Baumgarten, and Antonella Salomoni, eds. *Elia Bahur Levita, Paris un Viene, Francesco Dalle Donne, Verona 1594*. Bologna: Università degli studi di Bologna, Dipartimento di discipline storiche; Arnaldo Forni Editore, 1988.

Marcus, Ivan G. *The Jewish Life Cycle: Rites of Passage from Biblical to Modern Times*. Seattle: University of Washington Press, 2004.

Martin, Francis X. "The Problem of Giles of Viterbo: A Historiographic Survey." *Augustiniana* 9 (1959): 357–379; 10 (1960): 43–60.

———. "Giles of Viterbo and the Monastery of Lecceto: The Making of a Reformer." *Analecta Augustiniana* 25 (1962): 225–253.

———. "The Registers of Giles of Viterbo." *Augustiniana* 12 (1962): 142–160.

———. *Friar, Reformer, and Renaissance Scholar: Life and Work of Giles of Viterbo, 1469–1532*. Villanova, PA: Augustinian Press, 1992.

Marucci, Valerio, ed. *Pasquinate del Cinque e Seicento*. Roma: Salerno editrice, n.d. [1988].
———. "L'Aretino e Pasquino." In *Pietro Aretino nel cinquecentenario della nascita*, 1:67–86. Rome: Salerno editrice, 1995.
Marucci, Valerio, Antonio Marzo, and Angelo Romano, eds. *Pasquinate romane dei Cinqucento*. 2 vols. Testi e documenti di letteratura e di lingua 7. Rome: Salerno editrice, n.d. [1983].
Marzo, Antonio, ed. *Pasquino e dintorno*. Rome: Salerno editrice, 1990.
Massumi, Brian. *A User's Guide to Capitalism and Schizophrenia: Deviations from Deleuze and Guattari*. Cambridge, MA: MIT Press, 1992.
Marek, P. S. "Narodniĭ variant odnoï dramy." *Perezhitoye* 2 (1910): 226–235.
Matut, Diana. *Dichtung und Musik im frühneuzeitlichen Ashkenas* (Leiden: E. J. Brill, 2014).
Mauss, Marcel. "Essai sur le don: Forme et raison de l'exchange dans les sociétés achaïques." *L'Année Sociologique*, 2nd ser., 1 (1923–1924). Reprinted in Marcel Mauss, *Sociologie et anthropologie*, 143–279. Paris: Quadrige / Presses Universitaires de France, 1950; 5th ed., 1993.
McRae, Andrew. "Renaissance Satire and the Popular Voice." In *Imperfect Apprehensions: Essays in English Literature in Honour of G. A. Wilkes*, edited by Geoffrey Little, 5–17. Sydney: Challis, 1996.
Medan, Meir. "Elijah Levita." In *Encyclopaedia Judaica*, 2nd ed., edited by Michael Berenbaum and Fred Skolnik, 12:730–732. Detroit: Macmillan Reference USA, 2007.
Medine, Peter E. "Praise and Blame in Renaissance Verse Satire." *Pacific Coast Philology* 7 (April 1972): 49–53.
Metlitzky, Dorothee. *The Matter of Araby in Medieval England*. New Haven, CT: Yale University Press, 1977.
Meneghetti, Gildo. *La vita avventurosa di Pietro Bembo: Umanista, poeta, cortigiano*. Venice: Tipografia Commerciale, 1961.
Meserve, Margaret. *Empires of Islam in Renaissance Historical Thought*. Harvard Historical Studies 158. Cambridge, MA: Harvard University Press, 2008.
Meyer, Heinz. "Bartholomäus Anglicus, 'de proprietatibus rerum'. Selbstverständnis und Rezeption." *Zeitschrift für deutsches Altertum* 99 (1988): 237–274.
Migne, Jacques-Paul, ed., Peter Comestor, "Historia libri Esther," col. 1489–1506. In *Adami Scoti . . . Magistri Petris Comestoris*. Vol. 198 of *Patrologiae cursus completus* [*Patrologia Latina*]. Paris: Migne, 1855.
———, ed., Hrabanus Maurus, "Expositio in librum Esther," vol. 3, col. 635–670. In *B. Rabani Mauri opera omnia*. Vol. 109 of *Patrologiae cursus completus* [*Patrologia Latina*]. Paris: Migne, 1864.
Miller, David Neal. "Transgressing the Bounds: On the Origins of Yiddish Literature." In *Origins of the Yiddish Language*, edited by Dovid Katz, 95–103. Winter Studies in Yiddish 1. Oxford: Pergamon, 1987.
Millet, Victor. *Germanische Heldendichtung im Mittelalter: Eine Einführung*. Berlin: Walter de Gruyter, 2008.
Mills, C. Wright. "Situated Actions and Vocabularies of Motive." *American Sociological Review* 5 (1940): 904–913.
Minkoff, N. B. *Elye Bokher: un zayn Bovo-bukh*. New York: M. Vakser, 1950.
Mone, Franz Josef, ed. *Schauspiele des Mittelalter*. Karlsruhe: C. Macklot, 1846.

Monfrin, Jacques. *Abélard. Historia Calamitatum.* Paris: J. Vrin, 1962.

Monro, David B., and Thomas W. Allen, eds. *Homeri Opera.* Vol. 1, *Iliadis libros I–XII continens.* 3rd ed. Oxford: Clarendon, 1920.

Moritz, David, ed. *Das Targum Scheni zum Buche Esther: nach Handschriften herausgegeben.* Crakow: Fischer, 1898.

Moschetti, Andrea. *Il Gobbo di Rialto e le sue relazioni con Pasquino.* Venice: Frateli Visentini, 1893.

———. *Ancora il Gobbo di Rialto.* Venice: Fratelli Visentini, 1896.

Muir, Edward. *Mad Blood Stirring: Vendetta and Factions in Friuli during the Renaissance.* Baltimore: Johns Hopkins University Press, 1993.

Munk, Leo. *Targum Scheni zum Buch Esther: nebst variae Lectiones* (Berlin: J. Benzian, 1876).

Myers, David N., ed. *Acculturation and Its Discontents: The Italian Jewish Experience between Exclusion and Inclusion.* Toronto: University of Toronto Press, 2008.

Neugröschel, Joachim. *The Dybbuk and the Yiddish Imagination: A Haunted Reader.* Syracuse: Syracuse University Press, 2000.

Newman, Zelda Kahan. "Elye Levita: A Man and His Book on the Cusp of Modernity." *Shofar* 24 (2006): 90–109.

Niditch, Susan. "Esther: Folklore, Wisdom, Feminism and Authority." In *Underdogs and Tricksters: A Prelude to Folklore,* 126–145, 168–170. San Francisco: Harper and Row, 1987. Reprinted in *A Feminist Companion to Esther, Judith and Susanna,* edited by Athalya Brenner, 26–46, The Feminist Companion to the Bible 7. Sheffield: Sheffield Academic Press, 1995.

Niger, Shmuel. "Shtudyes tsu der geshikhte fun der yudisher literatur, 1) di yudishe literatur un di lezern." In *Der Pinkes,* 138–185. Vilnius: Kletskin, 1912. Abridged translation by Sheva Zucker as "Yiddish Literature and the Female Reader," 70–90, in *Women of the Word: Jewish Women and Jewish Writing,* edited by Judith R. Baskin (Detroit: Wayne State University Press, 1994).

Nylén, Erik, and Jan Peder Lamm. *Bildsteine auf Gotland.* Neumünster: Wachholtz, 1981; 2nd ed., 1991.

Olrik, Jørgen, and Hans Henning Ræder, eds. *Saxonis Gesta Danorum.* 2 vols. Copenhagen: Levin og Munksgaard, 1931, 1935.

O'Malley, John W. "Giles of Viterbo: A Sixteenth Century Text on Doctrinal Development." *Traditio* 22 (1966): 445–450.

Ortmann, Christa, and Hedda Ragotzky. "Brautwerbungsschema, Reichsherrschaft und Staufische Politik: Zur politischen Bezeichnungsfähigkeit literarischer Strukturmuster am Beispiel des 'König Rother.'" *Zeitschrift für deutsche Philologie* 112 (1993): 321–343.

Ortner, Sherry B. "Theory in Anthropology Since the Sixties." *Comparative Studies in Society and History* 26 (1984): 126–166.

Papio, Michael. *Keen and Violent Remedies: Social Satire and the Grotesque in Masuccio Salernitano's Novellino.* New York: Peter Lang, 2000.

Paucker, Arnold. "Yiddish Versions of Early German Prose Novels." *Journal of Jewish Studies* 10 (1959): 151–167.

Peleg, Yaron. *Orientalism and the Hebrew Imagination.* Ithaca, NY: Cornell University Press, 2005.

Penkower, Yitzhak. "Iyyun meḥuddash be-sefer massoret ha-massoret le-Eliyyahu Baḥur: iḥur ha-niqqud u-biqqoret sefer ha-Zohar." *Italia* 8 (1989): 36–50.
Podriachik, Leyzer. "Bovo D'Antona." *Sovetish heymland / Sovetskaia rodina* (Moscow) 10, no. 1 (1970): 145–146.
Posner, Arthur. "Literature for Jewish Women in Medieval and Later Times." In *Women*, vol. 3 of *The Jewish Library*, edited by Leo Jung, 63–83. London: Soncino, 1970.
Prescott, Anne Lake. "Humour and Satire in the Renaissance." In *The Cambridge History of Literary Criticism*, vol. 3, *The Renaissance*, edited by Glyn Norton, 284–291. Cambridge: Cambridge University Press, 1999.
Price, David. *Johannes Reuchlin and the Campaign to Destroy Jewish Books*. Oxford: Oxford University Press, 2010.
Prilutski, Noyakh [Noah Prylucki]. "Purim-shpilen fun Noyakh Prilutski's zamlungen." *Zamlbikher far yidishn folklor filologye un kulturgeshikhte* 1 (1912): 125–188; (1917): 143–157.
Prinz, Joachim. "A Rabbi under the Hitler Regime." In *Gegenwart in Rückblick*, edited by H. A. Strauss and K. R. Grossmann, 231–238. Heidelberg: Lothar Stiehm, 1970.
Przybilski, Martin. "Ein anti-arthurischer Artusroman: Invektiven gegen die höfische Literatur zwischen den Zeilen des מלך ארטויש (Melech Artus)." *Zeitschrift für deutsches Altertum und deutsche Literatur* 131 (2002): 409–435.
Quaglio, Antonio Enzo. "Intorno a Maria Savorgnan I: Per una riedizione delle lettere." *Quaderni Utinensi* 5–6 (1985): 103–118.
———. "Intorno a Maria Savorgnan II: Un 'sidio' d'amore." *Quaderni Utinensi* 7–8 (1986): 77–118.
Rabello, Alfredo Mordechai. "Domenico Gerosolimitano." In *Encyclopaedia Judaica*, 2nd ed., edited by Michael Berenbaum and Fred Skolnik, 5:739. Detroit: Macmillan Reference USA, 2007.
Raboni, Giulia, ed. *Pietro Bembo e Lucrezia Borgia. La grande fiamma. Lettere 1503–1517*. Milan: Rosellina Archinto, 1989.
Ramey, Lynn Tarte. *Christian, Saracen and Genre in Medieval French Literature*. New York: Routledge 2001.
Ravid, Benjamin. "The Legal Status of the Jews of Venice to 1509." *Proceedings of the American Academy for Jewish Research* 54 (1987): 169–202.
———. "The Religious, Economic, and Social Background and Context of the Establishment of the Ghetti of Venice" In *Gli ebrei e Venezi, secoli XIV-XVIII*, edited by Gaetano Cozzi, 211–259. Milan: Edizioni Comunità, 1987.
———. *Studies on the Jews of Venice, 1382–1797*. Aldershot: Ashgate, 2003.
———. "How 'Other' Really Was the Jewish Other? The Evidence from Venice." In *Acculturation and Its Discontents: The Italian Jewish Experience between Exclusion and Inclusion*, edited by David N. Myers, 19–55. Toronto: University of Toronto Press, 2008.
Reidt, Heinrich. *Das geistliche Schauspiel des Mittelalters in Deutschland*. Frankfurt am Main: C. Winter, 1868.
Reynolds, Anne. "Cardinal Oliviero Carafa and the Early Cinquecento Tradition of the Feast of Pasquino." *Humanistica Lovaniensia: Journal of Neo-Latin Studies* 34A (1985): 178–208.

———. "The Classical Continuum in Roman Humanism: The Festival of Pasquino, the *Robigalia*, and Satire." *Bibliotheque d'Humanisme et Renaissance* 49, no. 2 (1987): 289–307.
———. "La satira a Roma e la prima festa 'ufficiale' di Pasquino nel 1509." *Esperienze Letterarie: Rivista Trimestrale di Critica e Cultura* 13, no. 3 (1988): 15–26.
Rivkind, Yitskhok [Isaac]. *Der kamf kegn azart shpiln bay yidn. A shtudye in finf hundert yor yidishe poezye un kultur-geshikhte*. New York: YIVO, 1946.
Robinson, Lillian S. *Monstrous Regiment: The Lady Knight in Sixteenth-Century Epic*. New York: Garland, 1985.
Rosenberg, Felix. "Über eine Sammlung deutscher Volks- und Gesellschaftslieder in hebräischen Lettern." *Zeitschrift für die Geschichte der Juden in Deutschland* 2, no. 3 (1888): 232–296; 3, no. 1 (1889): 14–28.
———. "Der Estherstoff in der germanischen und romanischen Literatur." In *Festschrift, Adolf Tobler zum siebzigsten Geburtstage dargereicht von der Berliner Gesellschaft für das Studium der neueren Sprachen*, 333–354. Braunschweig: G. Westerman, 1905.
Rosenzweig, Claudia. "Parody, Infamy and History in a Yiddish Manuscript of the Italian Renaissance." In *Report of the Oxford Centre for Hebrew and Jewish Studies, Academic Year 2011–2012*, 105–113. Oxford: Oxford Centre for Hebrew and Jewish Studies, n.d.
———. "La letteratura yiddish in Italia: L'esempio del *Bovo de-Antona* di Elye Bocher." *Acme: Annali della Facoltà di Lettere e Filosofia dell'Università degli Studi di Milano* 50, no. 3 (September–December 1997): 159–189.
———. "Il poema yiddish in versi *Bovo d'Antona* in una versione manoscritta del xvi secolo." *Medioevo Romanzo* 26 (2002): 49–68.
———. "Rhymes to Sing and Rhymes to Hang Up: Some Remarks on a Lampoon in Yiddish by Elye Bokher (Venice 1514)." In *The Italia Judaica Jubilee Conference*, edited by Shlomo Simonsohn and Joseph Schatzmiller, 143–165. Leiden: Brill, 2013.
———, ed. *Bovo d'Antona by Elye Bokher: A Yiddish Romance*. Leiden: Brill, 2015.
Rosenzweig, Claudia, and Anna Linda Callow, trans. *Elye Bokher, due canti yiddish: rime di un poeta ashkenazita nella Venezia del cinquecento*. Quaderni di Traduzione 4. Siena: Bibliotheca Aretina, 2010.
Roskies, David G. "Yiddish Popular Literature and the Female Reader." *Journal of Popular Culture* 10 (1977): 852–858.
Rossi, Giovanni Bernardo de. *Historisches Wörterbuch der jüdischen Schriftsteller und ihrer Werke*. 2nd ed. Bautzen: F. A. Reichl, 1838; reprint, Amsterdam: Philo, 1967.
Rossi, Vittorio, ed. *Pasquinate di Pietro Aretino ed anonime per il conclave e l'elezione di Adriano VI*. Palermo/Turin: Carlo Claussen, 1891.
Roth, Cecil. *A History of the Jews in Italy*. Philadelphia: Jewish Publication Society, 1916.
———. *History of the Jews in Venice*. Philadelphia: Jewish Publication Society, 1930; New York: Schocken, 1975.
———. *The Jews in the Renaissance*. Philadelphia: Jewish Publication Society, 1959.
Ruderman, David B. *The World of a Renaissance Jew: The Life and Thought of Abraham ben Mordecai Farissol*. Cincinnati: Hebrew Union College Press, 1981.
———. "The Italian Renaissance and Jewish Thought." In *Renaissance Humanism: Foundations, Forms, and Legacy*, edited by Albert Rabil Jr., 1:382–433. Philadelphia: University of Pennsylvania Press, 1988.

———. *Kabbalah, Magic and Science: The Cultural Universe of a Sixteenth-Century Jewish Physician*. Cambridge, MA: Harvard University Press, 1988.

———, ed. *Essential Papers on Jewish Culture in Renaissance and Baroque Italy*. New York: New York University Press, 1992.

———. *Early Modern Jewry: A New Cultural History*. Princeton, NJ: Princeton University Press, 2010.

Ruderman, David B., and Giuseppe Veltri, eds. *Cultural Intermediaries: Jewish Intellectuals in Early Modern Italy*. Philadelphia: University of Pennsylvania Press, 2004.

Rudwin, Maximillian Josef. *A Historical and Bibliographical Survey of German Religious Drama*. Pittsburgh: University of Pittsburgh Press, 1924.

Rusi, Michela. "Abusi 'gaddiani' nella Venezia del Settecento (Antonio Bianchi)." *Quaderni Veneti* 34 (2001): 129–144.

Ryding, William. *Structure in Medieval Narrative*. The Hague: Mouton, 1971.

Said, Edward. *Orientalism*. New York: Random House, 1978.

Sanders, Christopher, ed. *Bevers Saga, with the text of the Anglo-Norman* Boeve de Haumtone. Stofnun Árna Magnússonar á Íslandi, Rit 51. Reykjavík: Stofnun Árna Magnússonar á Íslandi, 2001.

Sanuto, Marino. *I Diarii*. Edited by Federico Stefani et al. Venice: A spese degli editori, vol. 17, 1886; vol. 23, 1888.

Scaglione, Aldo, ed. *Matteo Maria Boiardo, Orlando Innamorato*. Berkeley: University of California Press, 1989.

Scheftelowitz, Isidor. "Das Fisch-Symbol im Judentum und Christentum." *Archiv für Religionsgeschichte* 14 (1911): 1–53, 321–392.

Scheindlin, Raymond. *Wine, Women, and Death: Medieval Hebrew Poems on the Good Life*. Philadelphia: Jewish Publication Society, 1986; reprint, Oxford: Oxford University Press, 1999.

Scherman, Nosson, ed. *Siddur: Sabbath and Festival*. Brooklyn: Mesorah, 1998.

Scherman, Nosson, and Meir Zlotowitz, eds. *Midrash Rabbah: The Five Megillos; Ruth/Esther*, ArtScroll Series. Brooklyn: Mesorah Publications, 2011.

Schirmann, Jefim. "Drama, hebräisches." In *Encyclopaedia Judaica*, edited by Jakob Klatzkin and Ismar Elbogen, 6:17–26. Berlin: Eshkol, 1930.

———. "Der Neger und die Negerin: zur Bildersprache und Stoffwahl der spanisch-hebräischen Dichtung." *Monatschrift für Geschichte und Wissenschaft des Judentums* 83 (1939): 481–492.

Schmid-Cadalbert, Christian. *Der Ortnit AW als Brautwerbungsdichtung: Ein Beitrag zum Verständnis mittelhochdeutscher Schemaliteratur*. Bibliotheca Germanica 18. Bern: Francke, 1985.

Schmidt-Wiegand, Ruth. "Kriemhilds Rache. Zu Funktion und Wertung des Rechts im Nibelungenlied." In *Tradition als historische Kraft: Interdisziplinäre Forschungen zur Geschichte des früheren Mittelalters*, edited by Norbert Kamp und Joachim Wollasch, with collaboration of M. Balzer, K. H. Krüger und L. von Padberg, 372–387. Berlin: Walter de Gruyter, 1982.

Schröbler, Ingeborg. *Wikingische und spielmännische Elemente im zweiten Teil des Gudrunliedes*. Halle: Niemeyer, 1934.

Schüler, Meier [Meïr]. "Das Bovo-Buch." *Zeitschrift für hebræische Bibliographie* 20 (1917): 83–94.

Schulz, Armin. *Die Zeichen des Körpers und der Liebe: "Paris und Vienna" in der jiddischen Fassung des Elia Levita*. Hamburg: Kovač, 2000.

Schwartz, Rudolf. *Esther im deutschen und neulateinischen Drama des Reformationszeitalters*. Oldenburg: A. Schwartz, 1894.

Schwarzfuchs, Simon. *A Concise History of the Rabbinate*. Oxford: Blackwell, 1993.

———. "Rabbi, Rabbinate." In *Encyclopaedia Judaica*, 2nd ed., edited by Michael Berenbaum and Fred Skolnik, 17:1–19. Detroit: Macmillan Reference USA, 2007.

Secret, Francois. *Les Kabbalistes chrétiens de la Renaissance*. Paris, Dunod, 1964

Segal, Agnes Romer. "Yiddish Works on Women's Commandments in the Sixteenth Century." In *Studies in Yiddish Literature and Folklore*, 37–59. Research Projects of the Institute of Jewish Studies. Monograph Series 7. Jerusalem: Hebrew University, 1986.

Sennett, Richard. *Flesh and Stone: The Body and the City in Western Civilization*. New York: Norton, 1994.

Shahan, Thomas J. "Baths and Bathing in the Middle Ages." In *The Middle Ages: Sketches and Fragments*, 286–296. New York: Benzinger Brothers, 1904.

Shandler, Jeffrey. *Adventures in Yiddishland: Postvernacular Language and Culture*. Berkeley: University of California Press, 2006.

Shatski, Yankev [Shatzky, Jacob]. "Pariz un Viene." *Filologishe shriftn* 1 (1926): col. 187–196.

———. "Geshikhte fun yidishn teater." In *Algemeyne entsiklopedie. Yidn b*, col. 389–414. Paris: Dubnov-Fond, 1940; reprint, New York: Central Yiddish Culture Organization, 1948.

———. "Der kamf kegn purim-shpil in praysn in 18tn y[or]h[undert]." *Yivo-bleter* 15 (1940): 28–38.

Shatski, Yankev, et al. "Purim-shpiler." In *Leksikon fun yidishn teater*, edited by Zalmen Zilbertsveig, vol. 3, col. 1653–1756. New York: n.p., 1959.

Shiper, Yitskhok [Ignacz Schipper]. *Geshikhte fun yidišn teater-kunst un drama fun di eltste tsaytn biz 1750*. 3 vols. Warsaw: Kultur-lige, 1923–1928.

———. "A yidishe libe-roman fun mitl-elter: tsushtayer tsu der geshikhte vegn dem ufkum fun mayse briye ve-zimre." *Yivo-bleter* 13 (1938): 232–245.

Shmeruk, Chone. "Di 'Moyshe rabeynu bashraybung'—an umbakante drame fun 18tn yorhundert." *Di goldene keyt* 50 (1964): 296–320.

———, ed. "Ha-shir al ha-sreifah be-venetsyah le-Eliyahu Baḥur," *Kobez al yad*, n.s., 6 (1966): 343–368.

———. *Sifrut yidish: perakim le-toldoteah*. Tel Aviv: Porter Institute for Poetics and Semiotics, 1978. Revised Yiddish translation: *Prokim fun der yidisher literatur-geshikhte*. Tel Aviv: I. L. Peretz, 1988.

———, ed. *Meḥazot mikrayim be-yidish (1697–1750)*. Jerusalem: Israel Academy of Sciences and Humanities, 1979.

———. "Tsi ken der kembridzsher manuskript shtitsn di shpilman-teorye in der yidisher literatur?" *Di goldene keyt* 100 (1979): 251–271. English translation: "Can the Cambridge Manuscript Support the *Spielmann* Theory in Yiddish Literature?" *Studies in Yiddish Literature and Folklore*. Research Projects of the Institute of Jewish Studies, Monograph Series 7. Jerusalem: Hebrew University, 1986, 1–36; 1988, 97–120.

———, ed. *Pariz un vyenah: mahadura biqqortit be-ẓeruf mavo, he'arot ve-nispaḥim.* Jerusalem: Israel Academy of Sciences and Humanities, 1996.

———. "Yiddish Printing in Italy." In *Yiddish in Italia: Yiddish Manuscripts and Printed Books from the 15th to the 17th Century / Manoscritt e libri a stampa in yiddish dei secoli XV-XVII*, edited by Chava Turniansky and Erika Timm, 171–180. Milan: Associazione Italiana Amici dell'Università di Gerusalemme, 2003.

Shtif, Nokhm [Bal-Dimyen]. *Humanizm in der elterer yidisher literatur. A kapitl literatur geshikhte.* Kiev: Kultur Lige, 1919.

———. "Elye ha-Levi's lid 'ha-mavdil.'" *Tsaytshrift* 1 (Minsk 1926): 150–158.

———. "Naye materyaln tsu Elye ha-Levi's ha-mavdil lid." *Shriftn* 1 (Kiev 1928): 148–179.

Shulman, Eliezer. *Sfas Yehudis-Ashkenozis ve-Sifruso.* Riga: E. Levin, 1913.

Shulvass, Moses Avigdor. "The Knowledge of Antiquity among the Italian Jews of the Renaissance." *Proceedings of the American Academy for Jewish Research* 18 (1948–1949): 291–299.

———. "Ashkenazic Jewry in Italy." *Yivo Annual of Jewish Social Sciences* 7 (1952): 110–131.

———. *Ḥaye ha-yehudim be-italyah bi-teḳufat ha-renesans.* New York: Ogen, 1955. Translated by Elvin I. Kose as *The Jews in the World of the Renaissance.* Leiden: Brill, 1973.

Silberstein, Sandra. "Ideology as Process: Gender Ideology in Courtship Narratives." In *Gender and Discourse: The Power of Talk*, edited by Alexandra Dundas Todd and Sue Fisher, 125–149. Advances in Discourse Processes 30. Norwood, NJ: Ablex, 1988.

Smith, Jerry C. "Elia Levita's Bovobuck: A Yiddish Romance of the Early 16th Century." Diss., Cornell University, 1968. Published as *Elia Levita Bachur's Bovo-Buch* (Tucson: Fenestra Books, 2003).

Spivak, Gayatri Chakravorty. Translator's preface to *Of Grammatology*, by Jacques Derrida. Baltimore: Johns Hopkins University Press, 1967.

———. "Can the Subaltern Speak?" In *Marxism and the Interpretation of Culture*, edited by Cary Nelson and Lawrence Grossberg, 271–313. Urbana: University of Illinois Press, 1988.

Staerk, Willy. "Die Purim-Komödie *Mekhires Yoysef.*" *Monatsschrift für Geschichte und Wissenschaft des Judentums*, n.s., 30 (1922): 294–299.

Stallybrass, Peter, and Allon White. *The Politics and Poetics of Transgression.* Ithaca, NY: Cornell University Press, 1986.

Steadman, John M. "'Teeth Will Be Provided': Satire and Religious or Ecclesiastical Humor." *Thalia: Studies in Literary Humor* 6, no. 1 (Spring–Summer 1983): 23–31.

Steinschneider, Moritz. "Die jüdischen Frauen und die jüdische Literatur." *Hebräische Bibliographie* 1 (1858): 66–68; 2 (1859): 33–35; 19 (1879): 9–11, 33–35, 81–83.

———. "Hebraistinnen." *Hebräische Bibliographie* 20 (1880): 65–69.

———. "Purim und Parodie." *Monatsschrift für Geschichte und Wissenschaft des Judenthums* 46 (1902): 176–187, 275–280, 372–376, 473–478, 567–582; 47 (1903): 84–89, 169–180, 279–286, 360–370, 468–474; 48 (1904): 242–247, 504–509.

Stern, David, and Mark J. Mirsky, eds. *Rabbinic Fantasies: Imaginative Narratives from Classical Hebrew Literature.* New Haven, CT: Yale University Press, 1990.

Stern, Elsie. "Esther and the Politics of Diaspora." *Jewish Quarterly Review* 100 (2010): 24–53.

Stern, Moritz, ed. *Lieder des venezianischen Lehrers Gumprecht von Szczebrszyn* [*sic*] *(um 1555). Ivri-taytesh shprakh-denkmeler* / Deutsche Sprachdenkmäler in hebräischen Schriftcharakteren 1. Berlin: Hausfreund, 1922.

Stokes, Francis Griffin, ed. and trans. *Epistolae obscurorum virorum*. London: Chatto and Windus, 1925.

Strauch, Gabrielle. *Dukus Horant: Wanderer zwischen zwei Welten*. Amsterdam: Rodopi, 1990.

Thelen, Lynn. "The Internal Source and Function of King Gunther's Bridal Quest." *Monatshefte* 76 (1984): 143–155.

Timm, Erika. "Beria und Simra: Eine jiddische Erzählung des 16. Jahrhunderts." *Literaturwissenschaftliches Jahrbuch*, n.s., 14 (1973): 1–94. Reprinted in Erika Timm, *Graphische und phonische Struktur des Westjiddischen unter besonderer Berücksichtigung der Zeit um 1600*, appendix 4, 521–553. Tübingen: Niemeyer, 1987.

———. "Zwischen Orient und Okzident: Zur Vorgeschichte von 'Beria und Simra.'" *Literaturwissenschaftliches Jahrbuch*, n.s., 27 (1986): 297–307.

———. "Wie Elia Levita sein Bovobuch für den Druck überarbeitete. Ein Kapitel aus der italo-jiddischen Literatur der Renaissancezeit." *Germanisch-Romanische Monatsschrift*, n.s., 41 [72] (1991): 61–81.

———. *Historische jiddische Semantik*. Tübingen: Niemeyer, 2005.

Timm, Erika, and Gustav Adolf Beckmann. *Paris un Wiene: Ein jiddischer Stanzenroman des 16. Jahrhunderts von oder aus dem Umkreis von) Elia Levita*. Tübingen: Niemeyer, 1996.

Tirosh-Rothschild, Hava. "In Defense of Jewish Humanism." *Jewish History* 3, no. 2 (1988): 32–57.

———. "Jewish Culture in Renaissance Italy: A Metholodological Survey." *Italia, Studi e ricerche sulla storia, la cultura e la letteratura degli ebrei d'Italia* 9 (1990): 63–96.

———. *Between Worlds: The Life and Thought of Rabbi David ben Judah Messer Leon*. Albany: State University of New York Press, 1991.

Todorov, Tzvetan. *Introduction à la littérature fantastique*. Paris: Seuil, 1970.

Tolkien, J. R. R. "*Beowulf*: The Monsters and the Critics." *Proceedings of the British Academy* 22 (1936): 245–95. Reprinted in *An Anthology of Beowulf Criticism*, edited by Lewis E. Nicholson, 51–103. Notre Dame: University of Notre Dame Press, 1963.

Tomalin, Margaret. *The Fortunes of the Warrior Heroine in Italian Literature: An Index of Emancipation*. Ravenna: Longo Editore, 1982.

Toscan, Jean. "Du côté de Pasquin: Le Poète Francesco Berni et le pape Adrien VI." In *Commentaires, parodies, variations dans la littérature italienne de la Renaissance*. Paris: Université de la Sorbonne Nouvelle, 1987.

Troyer, Kristin De. "An Oriental Beauty Parlour: An Analysis of Esther 2.8–18 in the Hebrew, The Septuagint and the Second Greek Text." In *A Feminist Companion to Esther, Judith and Susanna*, edited by Athalya Brenner, 47–70. The Feminist Companion to the Bible 7. Sheffield: Sheffield Academic Press, 1995.

Tsinberg, Yisroel [Israel Zinberg]. "Oys der alt-yidisher literatur." In *Shriftn fun yidishn visnshaftlekhn institut* [filologishe serye], vol. 3, col. 173–184. Vilnius: Kletskin, 1929.

———. *Altyidishe literatur fun di eltste tsaytn biz der haskole-tkufe*. Vilnius: Tomor, 1935; vol. 6 of *Di geshikhte fun der literatur bay yidn*, 9 vols. Vilnius: Tomor, 1929–1937;

repr., Buenos Aires: Alveltlekher yidisher kultur-kongres, 1964–1970. Translated by Bernard Martin as *Old Yiddish Literature from Its Origins to the Haskalah Period*, vol. 7 of *A History of Jewish Literature*. Cincinnati: Hebrew Union College Press, 1975.

Turner, Victor. *The Ritual Process: Structure and Anti-structure*. Chicago: Aldine, 1969.

———. *Dramas, Fields, and Metaphors: Symbolic Action in Human Society*. Ithaca, NY: Cornell University Press, 1974.

———. *Image and Pilgrimage in Christian Culture: Anthropological Perspectives*. New York: Columbia University Press, 1978.

———. *Celebration: Studies in Festivity and Ritual*. Washington, DC: Smithsonian Institution Press, 1982.

———. *From Ritual to Theatre: The Human Seriousness of Play*. New York: Performing Arts Journal Publications, 1982.

———. *On the Edge of the Bush: Anthropology as Experience*. Tucson: University of Arizona Press, 1985.

———. *The Anthropology of Experience*. Urbana: University of Illinois Press, 1986.

———. *Blazing the Trail: Way Marks in the Exploration of Symbols*. Tucson: University of Arizona Press, 1992.

Turniansky, Chava. "Pariz un Viene—mi-sifrut yidish be-italyah shel ha-meah ha-16." *Chulyot* 4 (1997): 29–37.

Turniansky, Chava, and Erika Timm, eds. *Yiddish in Italia: Manoscritti e libri a stampa dei secoli XV–XVII / Manuscripts and Printed Books from the 15th to the 17th Century / Yiddish in italye*. Milan: Associazione Italiana Amici dell'Università di Gerusalemme, 2003.

Vogt-Spira, Gregor. "Ansätze zu einer italisch-römischen Frühgeschichte der Satire in der Philologie der Spätrenaissance." In *Über Texte: Festschrift für Karl-Ludwig Selig*, edited by Peter-Eckhard Knabe and Johannes Thiele, 263–272. Tübingen: Stauffenburg, 1997.

Vos, H. D. *Elia Levita's* Bovo d'Antona. *Commentary*. Typescript 2012.

Vries, Jan de, ed. *Rother*. Heidelberg: Winter, 1922.

Waddington, Raymond B. "Meretrix est stampifacata: Gendering the Printing Press." In *Habent sua fata libelli: Books Have Their Own Destiny: Essays in Honour of Robert Schnucker*, edited by Robin B. Barnes et al., 131–141. Sixteenth-Century Essays and Studies 50. Kirksville, MO: Thomas Jefferson University Press, 1998.

———. *Aretino's Satyr: Sexuality, Satire, and Self-Projection in Sixteenth-Century Literature and Art*. Toronto: University of Toronto Press, 2004.

Wagenseil, Johannes Christoph. *Belehrung der Jüdisch-Teutschen Red- und Schreibart*. Königsberg: Paul Friedrich Rhode, 1699.

Walfish, Barry Dov. *Esther in Medieval Garb: Jewish Interpretation of the Book of Esther in the Middle Ages*. Albany: State University of New York Press, 1993.

———. "Kosher Adultery? The Mordecai-Esther-Ahasuerus Triangle." *Prooftexts* 22 (2002): 305–333.

Wallace, Nathaniel. "The Darkened Vision of Renaissance Satire." *Pennsylvania English* 14, no. 2 (Spring–Summer 1990): 36–53.

Warnock, Robert G. "Wirkungsabsicht und Bearbeitungstechnik im altjiddischen 'Artushof.'" *Zeitschrift für deutsche Philologie* [Sonderheft *Jiddisch*] 100 (1981): 98–109.

———. "Frühneuzeitliche Fassungen des altjiddischen 'Artushofs.'" In *Kontroversen, alte und neue: Akten des VII. Internationalen Germanisten-Kongresses Göttingen 1985*, edited by Albrecht Schöne. *Auseinandersetzungen um jiddische Sprache und Literatur, Jüdische Komponenten in der deutschen Literatur—die Assimilationskontroverse*, edited by Walter Röll and Hans-Peter Bayerdorfer, 13–19. Tübingen: Niemeyer, 1986.

———. "The Arthurian Tradition in Hebrew and Yiddish." In *King Arthur through the Ages*, edited by Valerie M. Lagorio and Mildred Leake Day, 1:189–208. New York: Garland, 1990.

———. "Widwilt." In *The New Arthurian Encyclopedia*, edited by Norris J. Lacy et al., 512–513. Chicago/London: St. James Press, 1991.

Weil, Gérard E. *Élie Lévita: Humaniste et Masorète (1469–1549)*. Studia Post-Biblica 7. Leiden: E. J. Brill, 1963.

Weinhold, Karl, ed. *Weihnacht-Spiele und Lieder aus Süddeutschland und Schlesien*. Vienna: Braumüller, 1875.

Weinreich, Max. *Shtaplen: fir etyudn tsu der yidisher shprakh-visnshaft un literatur-geshikhte*. Berlin: Vostok, 1923.

———. *Bilder fun der yidisher literatur-geshikhte*. Vilnius: Tomor, 1928.

———. "Tsu der geshikhte fun der elterer Akhashveyresh-shpil." *Filologishe shriftn (fun Yivo)* 2 (1928): col. 425–452.

Weissler, Chava. "The Traditional Piety of Ashkenazic Women." In *Jewish Spirituality from the Sixteenth-Century Revival to the Present*, edited by Arthur Green, 245–275. New York: Crossroad Press, 1987.

———. "For Women and for Men Who Are Like Women: The Construction of Gender in Yiddish Devotional Literature." *Journal of Feminist Studies in Religion* 5 (1989): 7–24.

———. "Woman as High Priest: A Kabbalistic Prayer in Yiddish for Lighting Sabbath Candles." *Jewish History* 5 (1991): 9–26. Reprinted in *Essential Papers on Kabbalah*, edited by Lawrence Fine, 525–546. New York: New York University Press, 1995.

Wenzel, Edith. "*Bovo d'Antona (Bovo-bukh)* und *Paris un Wiene*. Ein Beitrag zur jiddischen Literaturgeschichte des 16. Jahrhunderts." In *Integration und Ausgrenzung. Studien zur deutsch-jüdischen Literatur- und Kulturgeschichte von der frühen Neuzeit bis zur Gegenwart*, edited by Mark H. Gelber, Jakob Hessing and Robert Jütte, 19–34. Tübingen: Niemeyer, 2009.

Wienbeck, Erich, Wilhelm Hartnacke, and Paul Rasch, eds. *Willehalm: Aliscans: kritischer Text*. Halle: Niemeyer, 1903; reprint, Geneva: Slatkine Reprints, 1974.

Wilken, Ernst Heinrich. *Geshichte der geistlichen Spiele in Deutschland*. Göttingen: Vandenhoeck und Ruprecht, 1872.

Zacharias, Rainer. "Die Blutrache im deutschen Mittelalter." *Zeitschrift für deutsches Altertum* 91 (1961/1962): 167–201.

Zaeske, Susan. "Unveiling Esther as a Paradigmatic Radical Rhetoric." *Philosophy and Rhetoric* 33 (2000): 193–220.

Zallinger, Otto. *Die Eheschließung im Nibelungenlied und in der Gudrun*. Vienna: Hölder-Pichler-Tempsky, 1923.

———. "Heirat ohne 'Trauung' im Nibelungenlied und in der Gudrun." *Veröffentlichungen des Museum Ferdinandeum in Innsbruck* 8 (1928): 337–359.

Zancan, Marina. "L'intellettualità femminile nel primo cinquecento: Maria Savorgnan e Gaspara Stampa." *Annali d'Italianistica* 7 (1989): 42–65.

Zanrè, Domenico. *Cultural Non-Conformity in Early Modern Florence*. Aldershot: Ashgate, 2004.

Zedner, Joseph, ed. *Vayosef Avraham: hu perush ha-Raba' al Ester*. London: D. Nutt, 1850.

Zfatman, Sarah. *Ha-siporet be-yidish me-reshitah ad "shivḥei ha-besht" (1504–1814)*. 2 vols. Diss., Hebrew University. Jerusalem: Hebrew University, 1983.

Zhirmunskiĭ, Viktor M. *Narodniĭ geroicheskiĭ epos*. Moscow/Leningrad: Akademia Nauk, 1962.

———. "The Theme of Heroic Courtship." In *The Study of Russian Folklore*, edited by Felix J. Oinas, 39–48. The Hague: Mouton, 1975.

Zoller, Israel. "Theater und Tanz in den italienischen Ghettis." *Mitteilungen zur jüdischen Volkskunde* 29 (1926): 596–598.

Index

JEROLD C. FRAKES

received a Ph.D. in medieval Germanic studies at the University of Minnesota after study in Austria and Germany. He taught in the Departments of Comparative Literature and German Literature at the University of Southern California for many years and in 2006 moved to the University at Buffalo. He is the recipient of multiple research fellowships, among others, from the Alexander von Humboldt Foundation, the John Simon Guggenheim Foundation, the Radcliffe Institute for Advance Study, and the National Endowment for the Humanities.

www.ingramcontent.com/pod-product-compliance
Lightning Source LLC
LaVergne TN
LVHW050149080826
844660LV00002B/132

* 9 7 8 0 2 5 3 0 2 5 5 1 7 *